T0295414

THE TRANSFORMATION OF
AMERICAN HEALTH INSURANCE

THE
TRANSFORMATION
OF AMERICAN
HEALTH INSURANCE

On the Path to Medicare for All

TROYEN A. BRENNAN

JOHNS HOPKINS UNIVERSITY PRESS | *Baltimore*

© 2024 Johns Hopkins University Press
All rights reserved. Published 2024
Printed in the United States of America on acid-free paper

2 4 6 8 9 7 5 3 1

Johns Hopkins University Press
2715 North Charles Street
Baltimore, Maryland 21218
www.press.jhu.edu

Library of Congress Cataloging-in-Publication Data

Names: Brennan, Troyen A., author.
Title: The transformation of American health insurance : on the path to
Medicare for all / Troyen A. Brennan.
Description: Baltimore : Johns Hopkins University Press, 2024. | Includes
bibliographical references and index.
Identifiers: LCCN 2023041984 | ISBN 9781421449098 (hardcover ; alk. paper) |
ISBN 9781421449104 (ebook)
Subjects: MESH: United States. Patient Protection and Affordable Care Act. |
Insurance, Health—history | Health Care Reform—history | National Health
Insurance, United States | Medicare | History, 20th Century | United States
Classification: LCC HG9396 | NLM W 275 AA1 | DDC 368.38/200973—
dc23/eng/20240209
LC record available at https://lccn.loc.gov/2023041984

A catalog record for this book is available from the British Library.

Special discounts are available for bulk purchases of this book.
For more information, please contact Special Sales at specialsales@jh.edu.

CONTENTS

PREFACE

This book examines the historical evolution of health care insurance in the United States and, based on that winding path, offers a set of predictions about where we are headed. Today, and for much of the past sixty years, our health insurance has primarily consisted of four types of coverage: (1) commercial insurance provided to employees by their employers, (2) the federal government's Medicare program for those over age 65 and for the disabled, (3) the state/federal Medicaid insurance program for low-income people, and (4) a variety of solutions for people who buy insurance as individuals. By far the largest number of beneficiaries are covered by employer-sponsored insurance provided by commercial insurers. Many would see employer-sponsored insurance as the bedrock of our health care system.

My view is contrarian. I see the lifespan of employer-sponsored insurance as being limited to another decade or two. Instead, Medicare will become the form of insurance for all Americans, a program known as Medicare for All. But in this prediction, I add one small wrinkle. Most advocates for Medicare for All envision a single governmental payer and the elimination of private insurance companies. That may be the outcome of the evolutionary forces that are driving employer-sponsored insurance toward extinction. But just as likely, in many ways, is a Medicare for All program that includes private insurance companies, delivering a set of insurance benefits that are dictated by the federal government and relying on a payment structure set forth by the government. This might best be termed "Medicare Advantage for All," taking the title of the privatized Medicare program that today serves nearly half of all Medicare beneficiaries.

This prediction—that we are on a path to government-sponsored health insurance for everyone—is based on my reading not only of the current state of American health care, but also by how we have gotten here (in particular, how health insurance has evolved) and by the financial and demographic forces we face in going forward. The path to how we arrived at where we are today, however, is often overlooked. Most health policy analyses jump into our current situation with perhaps only a cursory look back. Such an ahistorical approach misses the long-term forces at work and fails to consider the forward momentum inherent in the health care system, particularly in health insurance.

The evaluations of America's peculiar health care system have been growing grimmer. To be succinct, health care in the United States costs too much and provides too little value. Our country's health care statistics on nearly every front are worse than those of similar industrialized nations. A report by the highly respected Commonwealth Fund notes that the United States spends more on health care as a share of its economy than the twelve other richest Organization for Economic Co-operation and Development (OECD) countries (paying out nearly twice as much as the average OECD nation) but has the lowest life expectancy for its citizens. We also have the greatest number of hospitalizations from preventable causes and the highest rate of avoidable deaths.[1] Moreover, our maternal mortality is humiliatingly high.

While many leaders in American health care have long lamented our overall public health statistics, most thought that the United States was the best place to be when acute care was needed. In terms of health care performance rankings, even that is no longer the case. As a Commonwealth Foundation report notes, "The U.S. is an outlier: its performance falls well below the average of the other [ten] countries and far below the two countries ranked directly above it."[2]

The causes of our American health care system's failures have been carefully dissected over the years by health policy experts, economists, physicians, and journalists. There are plenty of targets: our fractured primary care program, our overutilization of hospitals and procedures, our drug pricing, our rapacious insurers, and—especially—our failure to provide decent care for all of our citizens, no matter what their race, ethnicity, or income. Comprehensive reform programs tackle many of these problems, usually by emphasizing the need to change how we pay for health care, close gaps in coverage, and improve health equity. These impulses have given rise to spasms of reform, the most recent being the Affordable Care Act, also known as Obamacare.

Perhaps our most glaring deficiency—the failure to provide universal coverage—is the prominent theme for reformers (usually progressive Democrats). By and large, they campaign for the creation of a single-payer system for health care, often described as Medicare for All. An excellent rendition of the advocacy for access is Jonathan Cohn's *The Ten Year War: Obamacare and the Unfinished Crusade for Universal Coverage*.[3] Cohn details not only the politics surrounding Obamacare, but also the efforts to save it from Republican-led legislative modifications, as well as from a series of harrowing legal challenges. The martial references in the title ("War" and "Crusade") fully represent the mindset of the advocates for health reform in the United States. They have a goal—the provision of health insurance for all, supported by the government—and a commitment to change.

The opponents of health care reform that would improve access through a government-controlled system often refer to the reformers' goal as "socialized medicine." The term is pejorative and was first used by the American Medical Association to attack health care reforms backed by the Truman administration. Then, as now, socialism was viewed dimly by a large part of the American political spectrum. To them it suggested overwhelming governmental interventions that reduced individual liberty and replaced private industry innovations with torpid governmental agencies. The term has stuck, and it is found in every political argument opposed to efforts to improve access to and reduce costs for health care services that require new governmental interventions.

But today, and for much of the last two decades, the focus on the government's role has not been on governmental ownership of both the financing and the delivery of health care. That duality is a more exact definition of socialized medicine, seen in the US Department of Veterans Affairs (VA) health system. The VA owns its hospitals and clinics, employs its providers, and finances its patients' care. It is unique in American health care—and not necessarily held out as a model.

Instead, the main alternative to the health care system we have today is the move to a single governmental payer, replacing private health insurance. This might best be known as *socialized health insurance*. Under the single-payer format, private hospitals, providers, and most other health care institutions would remain in the same corporate structure in which they reside today, but they would all be paid directly by the government. According to many current modeling exercises, this approach is seen as increasing equity, lowering administrative costs, and improving health outcomes. But socialized health insurance, while indeed a tremendous policy step, is an incremental one, compared with socialized medicine.

An even more incremental way to get to socialized health insurance is to leave private payers in place as facilitators of the program. The key goals for health reform advocates who endorse single-payer socialized health insurance are (1) universal access, so anyone can get health insurance and health care when they need it; and (2) governmental control over the health insurance system, to ensure that it emphasizes patient welfare. That control entails setting the rates of payment to private doctors and hospitals. But it does not mean that private insurance must be eliminated. Today, Medicare Advantage private insurance plans operate under governmental control and use rates of payment set by the government. Medicare for All could then mean either a single traditional Medicare payer or multiple private payers, all participating in the Medicare Advantage program. The main differences between Medicare for All and Medicare Advantage for All are that (1) the former eliminates for-profit insurance entities from the game, and (2) the former costs less, because of administrative efficiency.

The thesis of this book is that those are our choices. Counter to most views on the political left and right, I believe that socialized health insurance is inevitable over the next two decades. The part of health care that is not directly controlled by the federal government— employer-sponsored insurance bought from commercial insurers—is mortally wounded. As long-term trends continue to unspool, it is only a matter of time before employers either give in and willingly purchase federal health insurance (what might be called Medicare Advantage–based socialized health insurance) or face a government willing to institute the complete replacement of the current multiple-payer system with a single-payer one (traditional Medicare socialized health insurance). As this occurs, the other major governmental insurers—Medicaid and the Affordable Care Act–inspired exchanges—will be homogenized into Medicare-based programs.

This thesis is controversial, on at least two major points. The first is my view of employer-sponsored insurance. Its success is usually seen as a bulwark against further governmental intervention in health care financing. But employer-sponsored insurance is slowly unspooling, becoming too costly and inducing poorer quality care. As the government's programs have grown and evolved, they are slowly making private insurance both unaffordable and irrelevant. That evolution will progress over the course of the 2030s and into the 2040s.

Second, I argue that the goals of socialized health insurance can be met without eliminating private insurance companies. The government can—and, today, does—exert the control it needs to ensure patient welfare by regulating private insurers. The privatized parts of Medicare (Medicare Advantage and the Medicare Part D drug benefit), as well as the Medicaid program and the exchange insurance markets set up by the Affordable Care Act, all demonstrate successful governmental control today. Socialized health insurance can tolerate private administration, and indeed thrive with it.

But the survival of private insurers is not a given. The key catalytic event—the failure of employer-sponsored insurance—will leave the country with two choices. One is that there will be an evolution in which private employers could cover their employees through a Medicare Advantage–type product. The other is a much more rapid set of reforms, based on a single traditional Medicare–type payer. That choice depends in part on how insurers behave over the next two decades, as well as on political responses to that behavior, which I cannot predict. It also depends on private programs matching the efficiency of a single-payer one. So there is some uncertainty going forward, as we should expect.

But there should be none around the key point of this book: that a sufficient number of long-term trends will align, such that I can predict the end of employer-sponsored insurance. I can also predict the growth of coverage through the exchange markets and Medicaid, as well as the continued evolution of Medicare, which will ensure the eventual ascension of socialized health insurance. Indeed, our country has been moving down that path for years.

I believe this is not a typical view of health care reform. Today's health care debate does not really dwell on the employer-sponsored insurance sector. I do. I will argue that employers were almost unintentionally thrust into the job of being health care purveyors and were and remain ill equipped for the role. Moreover, I believe that changes in the relationship between employer-sponsored and government-sponsored insurance, as well as the ever-increasing costs of health care, are almost assuredly causing lethal strains in the employer-sponsored sector. Based on a nearly seventy-year review—from just after the end of World War II, when employer responsibilities emerged, to the present—one must come away with the view that over the next decade, or perhaps the next two decades, employers will attempt to shed their side job of health care oversight and return it to the government. This is not a widely shared perspective, but I believe evolutionary changes in our country, our finances, and the shape of our health care system itself make this projected pathway compelling.

Only very rarely in the past have health policy experts suggested that employer-sponsored insurance is coming to an end. The best exception was set forth by Ezekiel Emanuel in his 2014 book about the Affordable Care Act (ACA).[4] He predicted the end of employer-sponsored insurance occurring sometime before 2020, as the exchange insurance markets started by the ACA matured. But he was wrong. The ACA exchanges waivered before they strengthened and steadied. Moreover, the advance of Medicare Advantage is much clearer today than it was ten years ago, and employer-sponsored insurance is almost as prominent now as it was before the Obamacare reforms. More importantly, the strains in the employer-sponsored sector have become clearer with time.

The other controversial part of the argument is about the government's role in health care today: Medicare, Medicaid, and the exchange markets created by Obamacare. Again, my view is somewhat contrarian. I see these programs as becoming ever stronger in terms of the health care they support. They slowly but surely are closing the coverage gap and improving the quality of care. I am one of very few people with an extensive background in private health insurance who would state that the government's programs are better in terms of equity, patient welfare, and efficiency than commercial insurance programs.

My views are based on experience and an examination of the historical record. The evolutionary development of Medicare, from its start in 1965 to the present, is usually not part of the health care reform storyline, at least in the kind of detail required to understand how much Medicare has progressed. In a view counter to the usual reform story, I see the public/private collaborations in Medicare, known as Medicare Advantage, and Medicare Part D's coverage of medications as programs that offer an alternative version of socialized health insurance.

The health care exchanges set up by the Affordable Care Act for those less able to afford commercial health insurance are a close cousin to privatized Medicare, adding new ideas and wrinkles to how health care can thrive. The same is true of Medicaid, the insurance for low-income people that was created at the same time as Medicare. Medicaid's administration is largely in private hands, but its coverage and policies are dictated by the government. The genius of the Affordable Care Act is that it creates a pincer effect between Medicaid and the exchanges, which eventually could lead to universal coverage for all citizens. My view, then, is that the government's programs are becoming sturdier with time and are not weakened by relying on carefully overseen private companies—in particular, insurers. So, unlike the typical advocate for socialized health insurance, I see a potential place for private insurers administering government-sponsored plans.

The deterioration of the employer-sponsored sector and the growing strength of federal programs are linked, and the growth of the government's role inexorably undermines employers' benefits programs. This disruption of employer-sponsored insurance was not intended, and was accidental. The path I refer to—the nature of health care's evolution—is not a straight one. It drifts through the slow, sometimes halting lurch of progress at the heart of our health care system.

The meandering evolution of health insurance is driven by governmental programs and regulation, in particular by how and how much they pay providers and drug companies. To understand this relationship between government- and employer-sponsored insurance requires not only a close examination of their respective histories and development, but also an understanding of the broader economic, social, and demographic forces that are shaping health care in the twenty-first century. What becomes clear, I believe, is that we are indeed on a path to a government-controlled insurance system, setting prices and ensuring patient welfare, while also achieving universal access—the goals of socialized health insurance.

Most of this book, then, is a careful description and analysis of our recent health care history, making these points about the evolution of federal programs and employer-sponsored insurance. Its goal will be to anticipate what happens over the next two decades, building on the long-term trends I have observed.

Four phenomena, persistently present over the last sixty years of health care administration in our country, shadow the discussion, and I should make them explicit here. The first is that health care reform has always been incremental; there has never been a big bang. Every major Medicare, Medicaid, and ACA-based policy change has taken only a few steps forward; has been based on a series of reform ideas that have been resident for years; and has left adjacent policies untouched, to be taken up again over the next few years.

In this regard, I think Americans concur with Charles Lindblom's classic description of political change: our political system is incapable of putting in place "comprehensively rational" solutions, so we muddle through, taking those halting steps.[5] That is why this story requires close attention to the history of health care reform, so I can trace its evolution, anticipating where our health policy muddling is headed. And it is why any prediction about change should entail a staged, or gated, approach. This insight on incrementalism casts doubts on the viability of a sudden turn to a single-payer system, but that is not entirely out of the question.

Second, the overwhelming problem with American health care is its deep dependence on a fee-for-service financial system. Doctors, hospitals, and other providers traditionally produce a service and then sell it to insurers. The patient is a rather passive participant.

Providers make money when they do more and charge more. An insurer's main job is to police these prices and resist new, costly interventions, particularly those without merit. To do so, insurers can and do require an evidence-based demonstration of value for the patient. That sets insurers up as the adversaries of providers. An insurer's attempt to reduce costs is a difficult, rearguard action, and it only partially blunts the providers' efforts to do more. The beneficiary (the patient) will usually be aligned with the provider's recommendation and resist the insurer's efforts.

An important corollary to fee-for-service arrangements is that all the key players a patient encounters—doctors, nurses, hospitals, medical device manufacturers, pharmaceutical manufacturers, pharmacies and pharmacists, employers' health benefit staff, and insurers—are profit seekers, driving toward a profit margin. In fee-for-service plans, that margin is the battle around providers doing more and insurers trying to get them to do less, or at least less of what has no value for patients.

Any reform toward a better future should replace fee-for-service care with managed care—that is, those who provide health care for patients are operating under a fixed budget—in order to redesign that care and ensure the health of the population. I believe the path to socialized health insurance is a boon for patient welfare, but to be successful it must be a path that entails managed care and strives to eliminate fee-for-service payments. Employer-sponsored insurance has made little (if any) progress on this front, and that is what ultimately dooms it. The fee-for-service engine will eventually make employer-sponsored insurance unaffordable.

Third, primary care must be considered the crucial part of the health care system and treated as such. Any set of reforms will be successful only insofar as each individual, especially each sick person, has a primary care team directing that care, helping to make wise decisions on behalf of the patient, and emphasizing prevention as much as treatment. The evidence for this could not be clearer. Primary care is essential to good health care management—that is, the combination of a focus on patient welfare and a sustainable system for financing that care.

Fourth, while we, as Americans, realize that we live in a country that seems at times to be irreducibly polarized, we should recognize that the consensus about access to health care has changed. While as little as thirty years ago it was widely accepted that a private health insurer could simply refuse to provide coverage for a person with a preexisting condition, that is no longer the case. Today, Americans increasingly presume that some degree of health care access is just and fair. To cite another example of our changing health care ideology, a ballot initiative in a red state to require Medicaid expansion would not have been conceivable in 1990. While authors like Cohn wax pessimistic, and even distraught, about the slow approach of universal access, taking a slightly longer view allows one to see the progress we have made toward shared assumptions about the humanity of access to health care. This changing set of assumptions is another factor impelling us along the socialized health insurance pathway.

Make no mistake, though, this book is not based on morality. I do, however, believe that there is a moral responsibility to ensure that all have access to decent health care. But in this book I am consciously attempting to eschew advocacy. My goal is not to argue for what *should be*, but rather to trace the evolution of our health care system and predict what *will be*. Perhaps I am overly optimistic, but I believe that where we are headed will be a much more just and fair health care system.

My approach is nonetheless businesslike. I will posit that the best way to understand any issue in health care is to discover who profits, and how they do so. The whole system is totally comprehensible from that viewpoint. The outcomes that the system produces may be substandard, but in every niche, some players are taking appropriate steps to make money. Following this profit seeking, in the context of the history of our health care system's development, enables both comprehension and prediction. It also provides insights into why understanding governmental oversight is necessary. The targets of regulation are those pinch points where profit conflicts with patient welfare.

I do not believe the profit motive can be eliminated from a health care system. I also believe profit brings innovation, and innovation is desperately needed. But, in some places, profit motives can be so corroding to the goals of an efficient and equitable health care system that they must be regulated. Moreover, I contend that the government has shown itself capable of appropriately regulating for-profit entities. My orientation will be that the market, so long as it is properly reined in, can not only exist with, but also help bring about a more fair, just, and efficient health care system.

Others do not agree. Donald Berwick has specifically called on physicians, nurses, and nonprofit hospitals to eliminate other for-profit entities in health care, including pharmaceutical firms and insurers.[6] I do not think this is possible politically. More importantly, it overlooks that all of the producers, including the providers, are motivated by profit seeking. This view is supported by almost all of the economic analyses of health care, and certainly by my personal experience. I cannot say that the people I knew (and know) who are running hospitals or physician groups see things much differently from managers of insurance companies.

There is a message here, though, for all the profit seekers, whether insurers or groups of doctors or chains of hospitals. If they only have a narrow focus and push for greater profit, even when it means crossing the line regarding patient welfare, they risk creating a political context for a more thoroughly *public* administration of health care, in particular a single-payer system, or even a movement toward fully socialized medicine. Profit is often blinding. But if that blinding, or even shortsightedness, happens unacceptably frequently, the public's impulse will be shifted in the direction of a single-payer format.

My concerns about the profit motive, and the control of it through regulation, are informed by over forty years of study on health care administration. Over that period, I have worked in hospitals and with integrated delivery systems, physician organizations, insurance companies, pharmacy benefit managers, and retail pharmacies. For half that time, I also took care of patients. Being at one point or another on almost all sides of critical questions in health policy and administration, I think I have developed a balanced view of the benefits and foibles of the business of health care. In my view, there are no villains, nor any heroes—just people going about their business.

That conclusion may sound a bit callous or abstract. As a result, I should note that over those forty years, I have also been very impressed with my fellow employees' commitment to patient welfare, most palpably on the provider side, but also found throughout the entire structure of health care. While profits explain things, nearly everyone in the health care business is trying to do the right thing, especially for the patients/beneficiaries. I am critical of aspects of how we care for and finance the care of sick people, but those complaints are structural. They are not intended to blame hardworking people who are trying to do the right thing.

A corollary to this business-oriented approach is that it does not allow a discussion of the most humane and pleasing aspects of health care: human commitment to the well-being of the patient. Doctors, nurses, and other health care providers generally will be treated as profit seekers in this book, but that is only part of what they do. Sadly, this will not be a book that goes into the details of the grace, loyalty, and altruism that are so important to patient care.

Although I draw on my own experience in health care administration, none of what transpires here is inside information. It is all on full view, easily accessed on internet search engines. That is not to say that our health care system is transparent—anything but. Health care, particularly in terms of employer-based and government-sponsored insurance, is complicated and poorly understood. Even people long immersed in the system cannot always explain the underlying rationales for why things happen. So I do spend a good part of the book explaining, in some detail, health insurance and financing. That is the only way to identify their faults and suggest the nature of their evolution.

Finally, in terms of full disclosure, I did work in and around private health insurance for sixteen years and still have stock holdings in the company for which I worked. Some might see that as influencing my views and forming the basis for my outlining a program of socialized health insurance that spares private insurers from extinction. Readers will have to decide if my argument is persuasive, fully warned about my potential conflict of interest.

In the end, this effort complements another that I wrote thirty years ago. That book was about justice, political morality, and health care.[7] It focused on what should be. This one is about the business of health care: how it has evolved and where it will head. But both volumes end up at the same place, at least in part. What I have seen over the last six decades is an evolution toward a more just health care system, with, going forward, the promise of much better organization and outcomes. It is a path, albeit a slow and winding one, to socialized health insurance, which will be palpably better for patients and citizens than our current system. I hope that optimistic case stands up to careful study.

ACKNOWLEDGMENTS

Two old friends and mentors read an early draft of this book. Jack Rowe, now a professor at Columbia University but previously CEO at Aetna and Mt. Sinai Medical Center in New York, shares my experience of being both in health care delivery and health insurance. Jerry Kassirer, long a professor at Tufts Medical School, was the editor of the *New England Journal of Medicine*. Jerry actually suffered through two drafts. My wife, Wendy Warring, read portions of the book and was always ready to debate issues, clarifying my views even when we disagreed, which was often.

CHAPTER ONE

Why Health Insurance Is Tied
to Employment

THE PATH TO SOCIALIZED health insurance does not necessarily entail
eliminating the role of private insurers. The Medicare Advantage program, which I will discuss in detail, shows how government-sponsored
insurance can be administered by private parties. In addition, socialized health insurance does not necessarily require payment for care
through general tax revenues. In a socialized system, the government
can require employers to pay for this insurance, as it does today, through
an employer mandate. This is very much the way that socialized health
insurance works in countries like Germany.

But what is eliminated within socialized health insurance is the role
of employers as purchaser and their control over the health insurance
policy itself. Today, the health insurance policy for millions of Americans is largely defined by the human resources staff where you work,
although, in the last decade, the federal government has begun to put
limits on the employers' prerogatives. Through 2010, however, the
breadth and depth of much of American health insurance was a matter
that was decided by employers.

The path I believe we are on—toward socialized health insurance—
entails the government's definition of the health insurance policy, its
oversight of the quality of care, and its control over payments for

providers. That is coming. The thesis of this book is that, given the growth of governmental health care programs and their inherent superiority over employer-sponsored insurance, employers will either be interested in voluntarily giving up their ownership of insurance or will have it wrested from them by new legislation, which they may not really oppose. The government's policies will be more comprehensive and less expensive than private health care coverage provided through employers.

This prediction will be surprising to many. It should be. The basic facts in today's health care system suggest a sturdy employer sector. In 2020, the Census Bureau reported that as of 2019, 183 million people had health insurance through their place of employment. Altogether, over half of Americans, about 57 percent, access health care through their employer or their spouse's or parents' employer.[1] Most people presume that their employer will pay for their health insurance. Employer-sponsored health benefits are an enduring foundation for American health care—and for American society.

The rest of the health insurance landscape, that not paid for by employers, relies on the government. People over age 65, many of whom have retired from work, qualify for Medicare, the government-run program. People who are not working can get their insurance through Medicaid, a governmental program that is intended as a safety net for low-income individuals. Today, the government also organizes insurance through quasi-public markets, known as *exchanges*, which were part of the reforms in the 2010 Affordable Care Act, also referred to as Obamacare. The exchanges make subsidized plans available for those without other coverage whose income is generally too high to qualify for Medicaid. The public perception is that these governmental programs are supplements, at least in the big picture, to the insurance policies available through their employers.

That presumption is flatly wrong today. The employer-sponsored health insurance sector is not nearly as large as the overall number of beneficiaries would suggest. In 2020, the government actually paid for more than half of all health care in the United States.[2] Private businesses contributed only 17 percent of the nation's total health expenditures. The rest was paid for by individuals, or by employees paying their share of their employer-sponsored insurance. Thus, contrary to public perception, employers do not play the dominant role in financing health care.

Perhaps more importantly, employers do not have a plan or an agenda for the insurance they offer. Our historical review will show how employers entered the health care arena nearly accidentally, or at least passively. They were ill placed to be the overseers of health care then, and even more so now. They have not driven improvements or developed a strategy for a better health care system. They have remained on the periphery of the system's overall financial structure, which is driven by providers and insurers. Employers have just paid the bills. The result is that today, as employers begin to appreciate the stresses and pressures of their responsibility for health insurance, the overwhelming majority are looking to the government for answers.[3] This is no surprise, given the history of the employers' role in health insurance.

The Birth and Growing Pains of American Health Insurance

The story starts at the beginning of the twentieth century. Influenced by nascent social welfare in Europe, some employers, and more unions, began to develop mutual aid programs and sickness benefits.[4] The first medical services for workers were created by the International Garment Workers Union in 1913. This was the beginning of the relationship between union membership and health insurance, a marriage that persists today. For all the obvious reasons, unions advocated for welfare measures like health insurance that were otherwise not available to workers.

Physicians opposed these early efforts to tie health care benefits to union membership or employment, preferring a direct financial relationship between doctor and patient.[5] The reasons for organized medicine's opposition to any financial intermediary depend on one's perspective. Some might argue that this was based on the morality inherent in medical ethics, where only a doctor could be committed to the welfare of a patient.

Others might see it as being derived from less lofty inclinations. Doctors could increase their income by taking advantage of the power relationship inherent in their command of medical knowledge, power that could only be diminished by the insertion of an intermediary (unions, employers, or insurers). Either way, from the point of view of the organized medical profession, the best thing for patients was to have only their doctor involved in medical decision making—not insurers, or employers, or unions.

There is consensus on this point. Almost all historians and medical sociologists agree that physicians resisted any external financial mediation of a doctor-patient relationship. This professional insistence on isolation also applied to early progressive efforts to consider a strong governmental role in paying for health care. Physicians wanted to be free to assess patients, make diagnoses, and outline treatment plans. Patients would pay discrete fees for each step of the process—hence the term fee-for-service health care.

Physician support for cash payment on a fee-for-service basis was encapsulated in the fight against the recommendations of the Committee on the Costs of Medical Care (CCMC). This late 1920s initiative, led by eight prominent foundations, attempted to find a rational basis for organizing health care and its financing. The majority report of the CCMC endorsed either public or private insurance for health care.

The minority report, by organized medicine, took a dim view of intervention by third parties (the doctor being party one, and the patient party two). The medical profession would countenance such third-party intervention only if it was organized and remained controlled by them. The American Medical Association (AMA) promoted local and state medical societies as the intermediaries for organizing doctor negotiations with any sources of health care financing. Thus the American medical establishment strongly preferred payment mechanisms that were isolated from the real business of health care.

While doctors remained suspicious of insurers, hospitals could see the benefit, in particular through prompter payment resulting from not having to bill the beneficiary directly. It was much better for a hospital to get direct payment for services rendered from an insurer than to collect that debt from someone who had recently suffered a bout of illness. If insurers were passive and did not meddle with medical care, then why not let them pay the bills?

By the late 1920s and early 1930s, the first Blue Cross programs had been formed, emerging out of benevolent organizations aimed at helping poor people pay for their care. The "Blues" initially provided third-party insurance for hospitalizations, parented to some extent by the American Hospital Association, which (as noted above) did not share the AMA's antipathy to insurance. The Blues were state based, with a loose national organization, so they posed little risk for effectuating any change at the federal level. For the first fifteen years of their operation, Blue Cross plans only offered hospital insurance.

Individuals or employers could buy a Blue Cross plan to insure against the costs of hospitalization. Insurers came to prefer employers as customers since the key to their business was predictable risk. Every health insurance policy is based on a set of calculations that determines whether the amount in premiums paid by a group will more than cover the estimated cost of their illnesses. Employees in a large firm typically represent a broad set of relatively healthy individuals, making the risk calculation more accurate. Such an employer would, in actuarial terms, bring an average pool of morbidity to a contract, enabling the insurer to predict the risk of illness and develop a reasonable set of contract terms.

Policies sold to individuals do not allow for such actuarial confidence, even when disparate individuals are gathered into a group, such as in an individual policy marketed in a particular geographic area. In this circumstance, an insurer can be less sure that it is going to get a representative sample of the overall population. So employers as clients were attractive to insurers. The door was open for those who wanted to provide hospital insurance for their employees.

Slowly, grudgingly, doctor insurance evolved along the same lines as hospital insurance. It made sense to many that Blue Cross hospital insurance could be paired with a similar arrangement for physician care. The California Physicians' Service, which opened for business in 1939, was the first Blue Shield plan. Blue Shield for doctors was the sister of Blue Cross for hospitals. Membership in Blue Shield plans (organized, like Blue Cross ones, on a state basis) grew rapidly to 41 million people by 1958. Eventually, many of the Blue Cross and Blue Shield plans merged in their respective states, giving rise to the familiar structure we know today.

One other concurrent historical development deserves mention. When the Blue Cross plans were birthed, prepaid group plans also emerged, modeled on the program developed by Sidney Garfield for Kaiser construction workers at dam, aqueduct, and canal projects in the western United States, especially California. These programs provided coverage for all Kaiser employees for one set fee. Physician services, hospital services, and insurance were combined in a single package, with prepayment by the employer on the workers' behalf. The hospital workers and doctors were Kaiser employees. Rather than fees being paid for individual services, doctors were salaried.

This approach became known as a staff model health maintenance organization, or HMO. It was called a *health maintenance organization* to emphasize that the incentive in a prepaid plan was to keep everyone healthy, avoiding illness and its attendant costs. The *staff model* part indicated that the organization employed all of the medical staff, including doctors and nurses.

The organizational structure of an HMO was decisively different from the passive Blue Cross Blue Shield insurer, working with private practice, fee-for-service doctors. In a staff model HMO, the insurer essentially employed the doctors and operated the hospitals and clinics. The entire organization was committed to dealing with the risk of illness, not just the insurer part of the function. Providers were aware of the need to avoid unnecessary medical interventions. This was the beginning of *managed care*—that is, a program where insurance risk and medical judgment are annealed, ensuring that health care is value based.

Working within an overall budget in a managed care organization, as opposed to getting paid for each service provided, changed the financial dynamic for doctors. This global budget was intended to cover the costs of care for a population of individual patients. Insofar as a doctor managed to avoid unnecessary care that normally might occur in a fee-for-service setting, the entire budget would not be spent. By managing care, a doctor in a prepaid setting, working on a set budget to provide services for a population of patients, would make more money and avoid wasteful care. So prepaid managed care was the antithesis of fee-for-service care. Under a fee-for-service program, providers earned more by doing more. Under managed care, the structure of medical practices had to be modified to anticipate illness and prevent it.

Any kind of managed care program, where the doctors were working for an organization that was taking the entire financial risk for the costs of care, required a complicated corporate structure. In nearly every state, medical societies had successfully lobbied for bans on the *corporate practice of medicine laws*. These essentially prohibited doctors from being employed by companies, particularly managed care companies.[6] For example, California's Knox-Keene Health Care Service Plan Act of 1975 forced the Kaiser program into maintaining a separate hospital corporation, insurance company, and medical group, with the latter called Kaiser Permanente.[7] These laws, championed by medical societies, did not shut down early HMOs, but they did hamper their development.[8]

To some extent, one might have thought that a managed care plan would make more sense for an employer providing health benefits for its employees. Certainly, one motivation for providing health insurance was to keep the workforce productive and healthy. Managed care's incentives were in alignment with that precept, but not so much in fee-for-service care. Yet businesses did not seek out or promote managed care. Instead, they remained largely impartial. They accepted insurance company–mediated fee-for-service payments and did not confront the medical profession's hostility toward managed care.

Although waging battles with managed care, the organized medical profession, over the course of the 1950s and 1960s, became more comfortable with Blue Cross Blue Shield programs and other commercial insurers, so long as that insurance was based on fee-for-service care. Physicians even began to accept direct payment from the insurer, slowly abandoning traditional indemnity arrangements (the insurer pays the patient, who then pays the doctor). Insurer payments did not interfere with medical practice and relieved doctors of worries about debt collections, just as they had relieved hospitals of these same worries.

By the early 1940s, some key foundational elements of employer-sponsored insurance were in place. Employers, and their insurers, would be passive regarding the organization of health care. They accepted the fee-for-service gospel of doctors (and hospitals) and did not promote managed care. They were not going to interfere with the development of health policy.

Health Insurers, Employers, and Providers

Medical insurance grew, and much of this insurance continued to be provided by employers. Employee groups gave insurers the actuarially steady population they needed to accurately quote costs. World War II prompted changes in employment laws that were geared toward productivity and control of inflation, which, in turn—largely inadvertently—accelerated the growth of employer-sponsored insurance. The key policy step was President Franklin Roosevelt's decision to freeze wages, except for pension and health benefits. Though employers couldn't offer higher wages, they could attract scarce workers by offering the best benefits. Soon thereafter, Congress passed a 90 percent tax rate on profits greater than what was earned by a corporation the previous year, creating another incentive to spend money on employee benefits.[9]

Health coverage by employers increased massively. Before the war, about 10 percent of employees had insurance through their work; after the war, that number rose to 30 percent.[10] Moreover, health insurance began to seem like a profitable line of insurance. CIGNA and Aetna were the first multiproduct-line (casualty, property, and life) for-profit insurers that entered the health care market in 1951. Unions had controlled their own health plans before the war, but the Taft-Hartley Act of 1947 banned this practice. Instead, unions negotiated with employers about the shape and scope of their insurance offerings. This change put employers in control of health insurance benefits. Now employers could use not only the Blues, but also national insurers as potential suppliers.

More importantly, in 1954, the Internal Revenue Service clarified the double effect of the tax treatment on health care benefits. Health benefits were not to represent taxable income for employees. The costs associated with them could be treated as a business expense and deducted by a corporation before calculating its tax liability. This tax break is extraordinary, and today is quite costly to the government. I will return to this topic when discussing potential future reforms, but for now I see it as having been another major impetus for employers to provide health benefits. Health insurance could be regarded as a tax-free benefit for employees.

The United States was not alone in linking health insurance and employment. Since Otto von Bismarck's reforms in Germany in the late nineteenth century, much of the Western industrialized world had accepted, if not celebrated, tying social welfare benefits to employment. Improving an employee's health made particularly good sense, especially if that employee stayed with the firm for a lengthy period. The two interrelated rationales were that keeping an employee healthy would, in the long term, be beneficial to the company; and the company's health programs could effectuate better health. Thus health care was tied to the promotion of employee wellness.

In the 1950s this reasoning was sound, since an employee's tenure was long enough to justify that investment. Bureau of Labor Statistics data show that in 1933, the average tenure for employees aged 51–60 was 13 years, but this decreased to 9 years by 1963, and today is down to 7.5 years. For those aged 41–50, their average tenure dropped from 10 years in 1933 to 5 years by 1973. Today, the median tenure is 4.1 years overall, and in the private sector it is 3.7 years. For those 25–34 years old, 2.8 years is the median.[11]

So today, given that in many industries an employee is only going to stay with the firm for four years or less, it is hard to justify an investment that would promote health and wellness. For example, if I, as an employer, held on to my employees for twenty years, I might earn a return from a program that screened for hepatitis C and treated those who were infected. But, at four years' tenure, I would just be shipping healthy workers off to new employers. Thus the long-term investment thesis of tying health insurance to a firm's workers does not really obtain. Yet, remarkably, that thesis has justified employer-sponsored insurance for many years.

Nonetheless, with these multiple financial incentives from the federal government, particularly the tax treatment of health benefits, employer-sponsored insurance grew rapidly through the 1950s. By 1960, 70 percent of workers were insured by their employer. There were three major sources of health insurance: Blue Cross plans; small, usually state-based nonprofit plans; and large national insurers. The latter, known as *commercial insurers*, such as Aetna and CIGNA, were generally multiline insurers who migrated into health care after World War II. Over time, almost all of them gave up their other lines of insurance and focused on health care.

These commercial insurers co-evolved with the Blue Cross plans, but with a sharper business focus than the nonprofit Blues. Furthermore, they had not "grown up" with organized medicine's oversight, so they were more immune to the concerns of doctors. They brought a stronger set of risk management tools to health insurance than had previously been the case. An insurance company's management of risk is different from their management of health care. Ultimately, though, both approaches have the same intent: to eliminate unnecessary care and reduce costs.

Three insurance tools, developed in the 1950s and 1960s, deserve mention. First, commercial insurers rated an individual person's risk, whereas Blue Cross plans typically used a community rating. A *community rating* assumes that a person within a given population has average health risks, while an individual risk assessment tailors the plan and costs to a single beneficiary. Individual risk assessments had huge implications for human beings. Those with a history of poor health would pay higher premiums or could even be uninsurable. As recently as the 1970s, nearly every state allowed individual risk assessment and accepted its implications.

Second, to combat moral hazard, commercial insurers imported (from other lines of insurance) out-of-pocket payments from the beneficiary, known as *cost sharing*. *Moral hazard* is a lack of incentive to take precautions when one is protected from poor outcomes—in this case, by insurance. For example, if I do not have to pay anything, I might decide that I want an expensive magnetic resonance imaging (MRI) test for my sore knee. The use of *co-payments* (fees paid at the time of service), *deductibles* (certain initial amounts of coverage paid by the beneficiary), and *co-insurance* (payment of a percentage of any cost) indicates to the beneficiary that treatment is not "free" and so should help control utilization. If I must pay some of the cost of an MRI out of pocket, I probably would think twice about having it done.

Third, commercial insurers were more likely to engage in utilization management. Expensive, and perhaps unnecessary, procedures or hospitalizations could be avoided by requiring prior authorization (permission from the insurer before the intervention was undertaken) or by reviewing the event after it had occurred and refusing payment. Utilization management borders on clinical oversight, and so has chronically created health provider dissatisfaction.

But dissatisfaction with these techniques was not so sharp that doctors and their representatives were prepared to boycott the insurers that employed them. The utility of insurance, so long as it was relatively distant from clinical encounters, still outweighed some of the frustrating aspects for the AMA and medical societies. As a result, the insurance industry was allowed to evolve. A focus on the elimination of unnecessary costs was important to employers, and they welcomed and grew to expect more oversight of health care by insurers.

We should be clear that health insurance was not purely market based. It was regulated rather carefully by state insurance commissioners, especially in requiring sufficient financial reserves. Commercial insurers had to operate a designated subsidiary in each state (licensed by that state) that complied with the state's laws. The same rules applied to Blue Cross Blue Shield plans (and were even more stringent in some cases, such as requiring a community rating).

These were standard insurance regulations. But the state insurance commissioner accepted an insurer's business practices, including the exclusion of bad risks—whether it was for property and casualty insurance, or health insurance. Nonetheless, there was at least some oversight, as well as a regulatory structure at the state level that could later evolve.

It is also important to note that standard insurance tools were not the only way to adjust risk. Rates of payments to providers were as important (if not more so) to offering a competitive premium to a customer. The Blue Cross Blue Shield plans usually had a dominant market position in terms of the percentage of the population enrolled in them. In many states, their market share could be greater than 50 percent, so physicians and hospitals could not afford to walk away from the rates being offered by the Blue Cross Blue Shield plans. As a result, the Blues' plans contracted with hospitals and doctors for lower rates of payment, which were favorable for these plans and, presumably, their beneficiaries.

For commercial insurers, on the other hand, their respective memberships waxed and waned. Over the years, commercial insurers merged: some grew, and others failed. But few of the national commercial insurers ever approached the market share of a local Blue Cross plan. Thus they were more reliant on risk management tools: utilization management, the exclusion of high-risk patients, and out-of-pocket programs.

The evolution of the relationships among employers, insurers, and providers proceeded along these lines from the end of World War II until the mid-1960s. Three often overlooked developments in the 1970s and 1980s, however, helped to mature employer-sponsored insurance into what we know it as today.

Framing of Modern Health Insurance in the 1970s
The Health Maintenance Organization Act

The story of health insurance recounted to this point, bringing us up to the early 1970s, is widely accepted and frequently told. This standard history, however, leaves out a few key details from the 1970s that help explain the evolution of health insurance currently provided by employers.

But before turning to them, I should note that part of this standard history is the Nixon administration's reform efforts. To make health insurance more affordable and more readily available to all Americans, President Richard Nixon based a new proposal around the *employer mandate*.[12] This entailed requiring employers to provide health insurance for their workers.

Requiring employers to pay for health insurance did not involve raising taxes, so the conservative Republican administration could embrace it. To complement the employer mandate, the Nixon team developed a subsidized program for low-income people that would be more extensive than Medicaid, the state/federal program that provided health insurance for some of this population since 1965. The Nixon proposal was, as Stuart Altman and David Schactman note with some pride (Altman was an advisor to the Nixon, Clinton, and Obama administrations' reform efforts), comprehensive in scope, but it never got a hearing, as the Democrats (led by unions and Senator Ted Kennedy) went in another direction, while conservative senators (led by Senator Russell Long) pursued still a third. Notably, private insurers most likely would have been eliminated by Nixon's "Partners Program."

In his second term, Nixon continued to advocate for an employer mandate but kept private insurance in place. Democrats were worried that the Nixon proposals did not go far enough to improve access and suggested a single government-payer program to address those concerns. But Senator Kennedy could not get sufficient support for eliminating insurance companies, so he teamed with Representative Wilbur Mills on a new plan, where the Social Security Administration would collect the employers' payments and then negotiate with the insurers. The insurers, in turn, could vary the cost-sharing terms, specifically deductibles and co-insurance, and they would be the *intermediaries* paying the claims.

In many ways, one can see the entire range of health insurance–reform options between Nixon's second-term proposal and the Kennedy-Mills plan: an employer mandate, a single-payer format, and a government/private payer hybrid. Ultimately, no plan was able to move forward, as both Kennedy and Nixon failed to compromise, and the prospect of reform faded with Nixon's political star after Watergate. Comprehensive efforts wouldn't be made again for another fifteen to twenty years, but the parameters of debate for American health care reform were set.[13] Specifically, "health care reform" came to stand for very occasional spasms of political activity that promised a substantially different, government-based program going forward: one emphasizing broader access. As Presidents Harry Truman (in 1949), Richard Nixon, and, eventually, Bill Clinton proved, these spasms often led to nothing.

This is where the standard history of American health care jumps to the Clinton administration's proposed reforms. In between the spasms of reform, however, the private health insurance system continued to evolve. That evolution was modified and encouraged by much less prominent legislation and court decisions, the effects of which are nonetheless profound. In the 1970s, two such statutes provided great examples of unsung (perhaps better described as "accidental") health care reform. They are the Health Maintenance Organization Act and the Employee Retirement Income Security Act. Together, and unexpectedly, they helped define the health care system we inherited today. The third critical, but again somewhat unrecognized, defining change in the structure of health care in the United States came from the Supreme Court's decision in 1982 in the case of *Arizona v. Maricopa County Medical Society*. (I will discuss each of them in turn.) These kinds of largely unplanned changes in the characteristics of the health care system are what give one a sense of a meandering progression down a somewhat uncertain path. Health care reform is halting and sometimes involves half steps and stumbles, but its general direction is constant.

The Health Maintenance Organization Act was what was left of the Nixon administration's much larger effort to control inflation in health care. The brainchild of Paul Ellwood (he came up with the name "Health Maintenance Organization"), the act was surgical in its promotion of managed care through HMOs. First, it displaced the states' corporate practice of medicine laws (which had long been prized and protected by medical societies and organized medicine) that had frustrated the group practice of medicine. Second, it provided federal grants to help new HMOs get started. Third, and most importantly, the HMO Act created a requirement for employers with more than twenty-five employees to offer an HMO plan, presuming that the employer's geographic area had such a plan. The penalty for not doing so was to lose the preferential tax treatment of health care benefits. This put the HMO/managed care brand and concept in the market for good. The AMA's historical effort to suffocate managed care finally had failed.

The importance of the HMO Act cannot be overstated. It not only slapped down physician-placed obstacles to managed care, but also used the tax benefit to create a market for managed care organizations. Before this, the market was based simply on the perceived benefits of a health care plan, and something different, such as managing care, could not get traction broadly.

Now the door was opened, at least theoretically, for using prepayment and provider-based risk to get doctors to think through exactly what care was necessary and to profit by doing less rather than more. Insurers slowly accommodated themselves to provider risk and developed a new series of options for employers. Managed care was no longer a fringe issue, as conventional insurers offered new tools that could be incorporated into a plan for their employer clients, making such plans much more flexible. Over the late 1970s and 1980s, managed care moved toward the mainstream of employer-based health insurance.

The HMO Act resuscitated managed care. Today, and over the last thirty years, as we will see, the dynamic between managed care and fee-for-service care, with the latter usually dominating, has been a critical factor in the evolution of health insurance.

We should also, at this point, draw a connection between *value-based care* and *managed care*. The latter is the older term, while the former is more recent. Today, we exhort providers to undertake care that provides value and really improves a person's health in a cost-effective manner. Managed care refers to a financial architecture and subsequent redesign of services that promote value-based care. You can only profit in managed care if you eliminate medical waste, or non-value-based care. Presumably, with some set of incentives, you can also promote value-based care in fee-for-service plans, but the profit motive in fee-for-service is indifferent to value. As we move forward, I will be careful about the subtle differences between managed care and value-based care.

The Employee Retirement Income Security Act and the Rise of Self-Insurance

The Employee Retirement Income Security Act (ERISA) was more profoundly influential in the evolution of employer-based insurance than was the HMO Act. At the time it was passed, however, its effect on the structure of health care insurance was entirely unanticipated. ERISA was designed to protect participants in employers' benefit plans, particularly pension plans. It was born after a series of well-publicized pension program failures left many employees without any safety net. Those pensions had been regulated mainly by the states. To solve lax state oversight, ERISA relied on a broad *preemption doctrine*, meaning that federal law supplants all state laws. ERISA essentially swept away any state laws dealing with employee benefits and created a huge role for the Department of Labor in the future oversight of benefits. Employers, especially multistate employers, welcomed ERISA as providing a single playing field, rather than fifty.[14]

ERISA was focused largely on financial integrity issues and on pension funds. But it was broadly worded, and federal court cases, including some that went to the Supreme Court, soon began to make it clear that ERISA also applied to health insurance benefits. Moreover, it had the unanticipated effect of making it possible for an employer's health insurance program to be immune from state oversight of its health benefits. The manner in which this occurred is based on the arcane operation of the law. Simply put, so long as an employer *self-insures* for the risk of employee illnesses and uses the insurer as a third-party administrator to operate the program, it qualifies for ERISA preemption and gains the benefits of immunity from state regulation. In effect, ERISA changed employers from plan purchasers to plan designers.

The following example illustrates the advantages of self-insurance. Suppose a state requires an insurer to cover a certain benefit: treatment for infertility. States regulate insurance, so they can mandate coverage for this benefit. Every insurance policy sold in that state would have to include coverage for fertility treatment services, which adds cost. But an employer who self-insures under ERISA would not have to provide this coverage, since that employer is not considered to be an insurer. Escaping the rules set forth by states, especially through state mandates, can make an insurance policy 5–7 percent less costly than one that must comply, which is more than worth the small trouble of setting up a self-insurance structure.

The health benefits consultants who advised employers soon recognized the new opportunity opened up by ERISA. Instead of buying insurance programs from the few options that were provided by the insurers themselves, companies made their human resources departments responsible for designing an insurance program tailored to their firm. The insurer still calculates the risk, does the contracting with providers, pays all of the bills, and does all the utilization management, but the employer holds the risk. Employees rarely notice this change, as most still think they have Blue Cross or Aetna for their insurer. In reality, their employer is their insurer.

It is amazing that after nearly forty years of the self-insurance mechanism's prevalent use, it is still largely invisible to the general public, even to informed health policy people. By the early 1990s, over two-thirds of large corporations had moved to self-insurance. Today, ERISA-qualified self-insurance continues to grow, being offered to ever-smaller employers by consultants.

The price differential for self-insured employers derives largely from escaping regulatory oversight. An employer defines the benefits that make up its health insurance plan, unfettered by external regulation. This degree of independence was modified somewhat by the Affordable Care Act, as we will see, but it persists today.

ERISA solidified the relationship between health insurance and employment. An employer was no longer just buying a health insurance plan on behalf of its employees, but actually was responsible for designing that plan. In addition, since self-insurance required more sophisticated purchasing, employers began to look for advice beyond health insurers, turning to independent benefits consultants. Risk now sat with the corporation, particularly the human resources team, who controlled the benefits budget. The benefits management team within an HR department could not afford to be wrong.

Unfortunately, control over benefits did not spawn a great deal of innovation on the part of human resources teams. There are at least four major explanations for this relative lethargy. The first is their budget. One might expect that the executive team would put pressure on the human resources team to reduce costs. But health care, at least to my eye, is treated as special in executive suites, in that there is a general presumption of inflation, today somewhere in the 5–8 percent range. Nor do many companies have success stories about interventions that have reduced these costs. So the HR team, to some extent at least, gets a pass in that health care cost inflation is a given.

Second, most employers have a uniform health care benefit, where executive teams have the same set of benefits as other employees. A small number of senior executives may have access to all sorts of employment perks, such as company jets and limousine services, but their health insurance policy is the same as that of the average worker. This tends to eliminate from consideration ideas that would substantially limit benefits.

Third, human resources departments dislike "noise." Employee complaints to their supervisors about benefits eventually make their way to the HR team. These complaints are seen as being the fault of the human resources department. Even when there might be real cost savings, overall employee satisfaction, or a lack thereof, can cancel the possibility of significant innovation.

Finally, there are relatively subtle ways to reduce costs when you control the benefits. In particular, employers have key levers in terms of setting the premium for the portion that employees will pay and in determining the cost share, or the out-of-pocket payments made by individual employees. These provisions can be manipulated rather quietly to reduce costs for employers—and increase them for employees. Concerns about costs can be addressed by a subtle thinning of the company's insurance policy.

All four factors lead to a certain passivity, or at least reticence, about substantial changes in benefits design that go beyond premium sharing and out-of-pocket provisions. Rocking the boat is not a good thing.

There is another symptom of this passivity, however, that is quite striking. The employer is the insurer, but the HR team is very insistent that insurance companies continue to play the insurer role. This rule applies especially to decisions about benefits that cause dissatisfaction. For example, consider an expensive drug that is covered by the company's plan for specific health indications. An employee's doctor wants to use it as a treatment for a condition for which that treatment is not indicated. The insurer would review this and deny payment for that particular form of care, as part of its utilization management program. The patient and the doctor might appeal and follow the process set forth in the plan's documents, but the health insurer/third-party administrator is expected to resolve the issue.

The real insurer—that is, the employer—avoids these kinds of disputes, treating them as issues between the employee and the "insurer" (in reality, the third-party administrator). Health insurers understand that part of their role as third-party administrators is to take the blame for treatment denials. Employers do not want to get involved in tough decisions, so they pretend that these decisions lie elsewhere.

The entire process suggests a lack of responsibility. Employers' benefits teams do not typically rock the boat. In many cases, they even pretend that they are not piloting the boat. As a result, employer-sponsored insurance glides along without substantial innovation and exhibits great hesitancy about changes that might result in employees' ire.

In addition, at least during the first forty years of ERISA's reign, there was little governmental oversight. The federal courts were clear in averring that state law could not apply. But at the same time, the Department of Labor did not develop substantial rules for employer-sponsored health insurance. Employers have owned the health benefits they offer to their employees, but it has been very difficult to identify much strategy or leadership on the part of employers, and there has been no plan set forth by the federal government.

The peculiar result is a displaced sense of ownership. ERISA's impact was to freeze into place the assumption of employers' control over the benefits they provide, including insurance. Employers supposedly controlled health insurance, but they did not act like they did. They generally were not willing to be creative, for fear of creating employee dissatisfaction. In some ways, the term *plan sponsor*, rather than plan owner, captures this passivity. ERISA also removes much of the positive benefits of regulation from commercial insurance. Liran Einav, Amy Finkelstein, and Ray Fisman are correct when, in their 2022 book *Risky Business: Why Insurance Markets Fail and What to Do About It*, they state that "'letting the market take care of itself' is usually the wrong response if insurance markets are going to realize their full potential to provide protection and security in an uncertain world."[15]

Doctors and Antitrust Laws

The third foundational change in health law during the 1970s and early 1980s was the decision of the Supreme Court in *Arizona v. Maricopa County Medical Society* in 1982. It might seem odd that an antitrust decision would have such a large role in health care policy, but the ruling decisively changed the relationship of doctors to insurers. Understanding how requires some background in antitrust law.

Legal commentators had long seen not just the AMA, but also state medical societies, as engaging in anti-competitive activity. The Justice Department had successfully sued the AMA, as have private complainants, all alleging the use of market power to reduce patient demand for alternative providers, such as chiropractors.[16] But these cases just involved professional organizations.

Individual professionals, including individual doctors, had been immune from antitrust enforcement until 1975, when the Supreme Court, in the case of *Goldfarb v. Virginia State Bar*, decided that lawyers were also "in commerce."[17] Before that, federal enforcers could address anti-competitive activity by professional associations, such as the AMA, but not by individual doctors. The Justice Department and various states had nonetheless long seen the processes that medical societies used to negotiate on behalf of independent doctors as price fixing. *Goldfarb* allowed litigation to ensue in the late 1970s regarding such arrangements.

The most prevalent negotiating strategy used by medical societies had been to create nonprofit corporations (foundations) composed of doctors. Such foundations were ostensibly intended to promote fee-for-service medicine, but what they really did was aggregate individual physicians to create market power vis-à-vis insurers. Individual doctors did not have much leverage to negotiate with insurers, but, aggregated into a "foundation," they did. The AMA supported these sorts of arrangements, as they leveled the playing field for doctor/insurer bargaining.

The Maricopa Medical Society operated just this kind of foundation. The foundation would negotiate rates on behalf of doctors and then bill for them. In other words, the insurer did business with the foundation, not the member doctors. The foundation justified its activity by asserting that it was merely setting maximum fees that doctors could charge and was thereby pro-competitive. But the federal government argued that the foundation was also setting a floor, and this floor would probably be more than individual doctors could negotiate for themselves. In short, the government saw price fixing between doctors, who should, under the antitrust law, be competing with one another.

The Supreme Court agreed that this arrangement violated the Sherman Antitrust Act.[18] The foundation, and many similar arrangements like it, had to be disbanded, and individual providers were left to negotiate with insurers on their own. The ruling essentially eviscerated the role of a medical society as a joint contractor on behalf of practicing physicians.

This was a disaster for solo practitioners or a small group practice, as such entities had little ability to resist the fees offered by insurers, which were often set at or near the Medicare payment rates. As we shall see, contracting is a critical tool used by insurers to reduce costs. After *Maricopa County*, only large hospital systems (relatively few existed then) could negotiate with insurers on anything approaching a meeting of equals. Without the aggregation of doctors that a medical society could bring together, individual practitioners and small group practices simply had to take what insurers were offering.

From an insurer's point of view, the main effect of the application of antitrust laws to doctors was to create uniformity and predictability. So long as doctors stayed disaggregated as individual producers of medical care, they could not develop the kind of market power necessary to increase their rates of reimbursement. With hospitals generally disaggregated as well in the 1970s and 1980s, the costs of a network of providers for insurers were predictable. From the insurers' side of the bargaining table (representing employers), the situation was steady, and the providers had fewer levers to reset the status quo.

To increase their income, providers had to rely on greater volumes of care, rather than price negotiations. This was limited by the amount of additional time physicians had to see more patients or perform new procedures. Fortunately (for physicians' incomes), a great deal of new technology in terms of procedures and diagnostics, particularly radiology, was introduced over the course of the 1970s and 1980s. Technologies such as cardiac catheterizations and computed tomography (CT) scans increased incomes for specialists and hospitals.

But for small provider groups and generalists, antitrust litigation closed off the most straightforward way to boost their incomes—payment rate increases. The implications for primary care doctors were substantial. They could not really integrate new technology into their practice. Most of what they did was captured by *evaluation and management* (E&M) codes. These were reimbursed poorly, and there was only so much time in the day. Thus began the relative impoverishment of primary care, at least compared with other specialties.

Maricopa County put in motion a long-term trend of doctors leaving small private practices and joining hospitals or large groups, in order to be able to negotiate higher fees. For those unable or unwilling to join up with hospitals, their only choice was to attempt to do more—in particular, more procedures. As a result, fee-for-service providers now focused on new procedures and new technologies.

None of this is to say that health care inflation flattened during the 1980s. According to the Kaiser Family Foundation, national health expenditures increased (in 2021 dollars) from $711 billion in 1980 to $1,314.2 billion in 1990, close to doubling.[19] But insurers no longer faced the threat of aggregated physician bargaining, unless those doctors became employed by larger entities, particularly hospitals. In addition, small-practice primary care was left with few options for reimbursement optimization and began to fall behind other specialties.

More importantly, after *Maricopa County*, health care costs for employers that were generated by physicians were limited to additional labor by doctors and new technologies. These could be predicted by actuaries. Insurers could count on reasonably steady inflation in their annual accounting of at least this subset of benefit costs. This relative calm allowed the self-insured employer basis for health benefits to set down roots and become the default approach through much of the 1980s, as well as the dominant model right up to the present. As we will see, *Maricopa County* also created an incentive for the consolidation of health providers through large group employment, eventually drawing hospitals and doctors closer together.

Employers, Insurers, and (Largely) Accidental Health Policy Development

In summary, I believe these three key legal determinations played a large role in shaping the evolution of health insurance and, by the early 1990s, establishing its base in employment. The HMO Act introduced notions of managed care into health care efforts, in order to reduce costs. The dynamic of competition between fee-for-service care and managed care was permanently put on the table for our health care system.

ERISA made the human resources staff at corporations and their insurance consultants, the main decision makers in private coverage. But somehow it did not put employers in the driver's seat. Instead, they became passive passengers, not attempting to steer the health care system at all.

Maricopa County prohibited physician aggregation and put the insurers in a strong position in terms of negotiations with physicians over rates—at least until physicians and hospitals found new ways to develop market power. Moreover, it began the relative starving of primary care.

All three of these key factors, as well as the other foundational issue—the tax treatment of health benefits—are rarely discussed in traditional descriptions of American health care policy. That is because they are part of the winding path aspect of health care change, unlike the president-led bursts in 1970, 1992, and 2009. But, as we will see, these reforms along the evolutionary pathway play a crucial role in explaining the development of our health care system over the thirty years from 1990 to 2020.

If this evolution of health policy seems haphazard, it should. When these legal interventions took place, no one foresaw the impact they would have. There was no comprehensive rationality applied to the problems of American health care. Instead, as a country, we muddled into a situation where employers were autonomous, following the guidance of the market. Moreover, employers ended up tied to a passive relationship with a fee-for-service-driven health care system, albeit one with some ingredients of managed care because of the HMO Act.

Employers were relatively inadvertent participants, but by 1980 they had accepted a central role for many Americans since, at that point, 71 percent of those under 65 had health insurance through their workplace.[20] Employers exercised responsibility but rarely acted as if they had the prerogative to initiate change. Physicians still were largely independent, based in a fee-for-service mode, but not capable of bargaining effectively with insurers. Hospitals were on track to become much more sophisticated large businesses. Insurers honed their self-insurance products and focused on the employer market. From this point, I will continue to follow these key players and their interactions with the Clinton and Obama campaigns to improve access to health care.

CHAPTER TWO

What Do Health Insurers Do?

───────────

SINCE THIS BOOK is about the evolution of health insurance in the United States, it is important to describe in more detail exactly what it is insurers do. It should be somewhat surprising that a description is necessary, given the ubiquity of health insurance. But the insurers' functions are quite obscure, partially because they are complicated, and partially because much of the health benefits industry prefers to remain in the shadows. I know this well. Years ago, when I left academic hospital administration to go to work for an insurer, most of my friends lamented that I was "going to the dark side."

What motivates this predilection toward secrecy? At its core, health insurers estimate the amount of care a specified population will need and then attempt to reduce demand sufficiently to meet that estimate. For their business purposes, less care is better. So long as the avoided care is unnecessary, there is no moral qualm in pursuing this goal, but that caveat requires a good deal of explanation. Most in the industry choose to avoid transparency and tolerate (some might say cause) a great deal of ignorance on the part of beneficiaries. The incentives in fee-for-service care point directly against insurers. More care, whether value-based or not, is profitable for providers.

To trace where health insurance is headed, though, a clear-eyed state-ment of the insurer's function is critical. I will have to be frank and describe those functions from the point of view of the insurer, which will center on profit. As I discuss health insurance and relate that to the path toward socialized health insurance, it is also important to keep in mind that there are three key players involved: private health insur-ers, private employers, and the government. Private employers and insurers collaborate in what is known as commercial insurance, the majority of which involves self-insurance by employers, as described in chapter 1. The government can provide health insurance directly, the traditional Medicare program being the best example. Private in-surers can contract with the government to administer government-sponsored programs, such as Medicare Advantage. It will be impor-tant, as I start to set up the ultimate dance between these three players, to begin to highlight the nuances among insurance functions, depending on who is sponsoring and who is administering them.

One other point should be made at the outset. The major role of in-surers of all stripes is to reduce the costs of care, coping with the infla-tion engine that is fee-for-service health care. Their push to identify ways to reduce costs for clients is relentless.

Others, including many in the insurance industry, might argue that improving the quality of care is *a*, if not *the*, key function of insurers. There are specific measures of the quality performance by insurance companies, and these are evaluated by payers (employers, the govern-ment, and even individuals) in the selection of an insurer. The most prominent example is the Star ratings in the Medicare Advantage pro-gram, which carry substantial bonuses if certain criteria are met. These are based on quality-of-care measures, known as HEDIS (Healthcare Ef-fectiveness Data and Information Set) measures, developed by the Na-tional Committee for Quality Assurance.[1] (I will return to these when discussing the government's programs.) These kinds of measures cer-tainly matter to insurers.

But, in my experience, in the selection of insurers by employers, or in the discussions about the value of insurers by shareholders or boards of trustees, quality performance overwhelmingly takes a back seat to cost issues. I would argue that no one with experience in the industry can possibly dispute that the cost of care is the key driver of insurance, as will be seen when reviewing the insurers' function.

One component of overall quality—the beneficiaries' experience— is important to insurers and payers. Excellent phone service and the successful resolution of beneficiary questions are prominent goals for benefits operation teams. These measures of the quality of business operations are very carefully monitored by health insurance executives, but that is not to say that they are successful in terms of pleasing the consumer. Rather, they are notoriously bad. A recent study by Statista showed that health insurance ranked twenty-first out of twenty-three industries in net promoter score.[2] Some of this dissatisfaction occurs because many people only interact with their insurer when it has done something to reduce costs, usually by denying a benefit.

One exception to the rule of cost over clinical quality does exist: governmental sanctions. When an insurer is administering a government-sponsored program and cuts corners on quality that can be measured, the insurer can be removed from the program. This is a disaster for that company. As we will see, private insurers therefore spend a greater amount of time and effort on health benefits in governmental programs than they do in commercial programs. Few in the health insurance industry would dispute this assertion. But even with this important caveat, my description of health insurance centers on cost containment. As was discussed in the previous chapter, four functions dominate cost containment: assessing and avoiding risk, coping with moral hazard, negotiating with providers, and employing utilization management, which I will now discuss in more detail.

Assess Risk (and Avoid It)

Insurers' business focuses on risk, which, for health insurers, is the risk of illness. Actuarial science is the study of risk. The work of actuaries was historically based on an aggregation of data over long periods, and it now is increasingly complemented by statistical methods. The health-insurer actuary's role has been to assess how much illness a group of people may expect to incur in the coming year and how much that amount of illness will cost. These estimates then determine the quoted price of coverage. Prediction is critical, and random events, which are rampant in health care and disease, can make those forecasts difficult.

To avoid unpleasant surprises, actuaries prefer large numbers—the bigger the group, the less likely it is for random events to disturb the overall predicted disease load / cost estimate. In addition, an actuary prefers a stable insured group, without a lot of flux in and out. That is why insurers like large employers as clients and get nervous about smaller groups. The smaller the group, the more costly any random event will be. In a group of 500 employees, a person needing a bone marrow transplant due to acute leukemia is a catastrophe, since that one person could absorb most of the premiums paid by more than a hundred people for the year.

For most large employers, the insurer is not taking the risk—the employer is. But prediction is still critical for an insurer acting as a third-party administrator, since an employer, as the client, will not like surprises in the costs for provided benefits. A human resources department, when considering which insurer to hire, will be looking for guarantees around the overall inflation of health care costs. If an insurer misses its estimates, it can be forced to pay penalties. So an insurer needs accurate information on the previous few years' utilization by the employee group, in order to make predictions about the next year's costs. The actuaries also account for changes in medical practices that might increase costs, such as expensive new procedures to treat common illnesses.

When the government is the insurer in a public health benefits program like traditional Medicare, the assessment of risk is somewhat less critical—the costs always must be covered. But prediction still plays a role, as identifying trends helps the government understand how to pull available levers on cost control. In a government-sponsored program like Medicare Advantage, risk calculation is very important for private contractors (insurers), as they will receive a finite amount of money from the government to cover the costs of illness. Poor predictions mean no profits.

In private individual and employer markets, it is important to note that insurers not only estimate risk, but also employ techniques to avoid bad risks before writing a policy. Insurers do not like to discuss these tools, as they are designed to keep sick people from getting insurance. And what is allowed today is much less harsh than what was legal and acceptable in 1990. But it is important to be frank. Private health insurance has traditionally sanctioned efforts to keep sick people out of the group that is offered a health care policy.

The term that is often used to describe such techniques is *regressive*, which can mean returning to a former, less advanced state; or, in terms of taxes, taking proportionately more from those with lower incomes. In health insurance, regressive behavior consists of not including poor risks in the eventual pool. It is a neutral term for a rather inhumane set of practices.

Risk-avoidance techniques are clearly outside the moral presumptions of health care, which hold that medical professionals should be committed to caring for all people. Medical ethics entails a total commitment to the good of the patient. Thus health insurance—and, in particular, unregulated private health insurance—is not really part of the moral sphere of health care. Hence the lack of transparency. This is a subject that insurers do not usually discuss.

If insurers were honest, they would admit that risk avoidance is a correct business practice, in that it is sensible from a financial point of view. In 1990, the accepted and legally permissible techniques for risk avoidance were quite broad. It was only later that regulation by the Affordable Care Act would narrow them. This is an important point. The regulation of health insurance, especially in federal Medicare and Medicaid plans, pulls insurance closer to the norms set out by medical ethics—norms that put patient welfare in the priority position. In traditional Medicare, no risks could be avoided, an approach the government re-created in Medicare Advantage. In both programs, all citizens must be offered health insurance.

This is a major reason why regulations are so important. When insurance companies are guided only by best business practices, they are motivated to reduce risk by refusing to cover the most expensive cases.

Such behavior is regressive, as health services research has made it very clear that the availability of health insurance will save lives.[3] This insight is not only the basis of any argument for universal coverage,[4] but also for insurer oversight.

The issue of risk avoidance has long been salient in the part of health insurance I have not discussed much: the market for private insurance for those who do not have employer coverage, the *individual market*. In the individual market historically, preexisting conditions could mean higher premiums or, in many states, no available health insurance for someone seeking it. By the 1990s, some states had begun to require insurers to offer such coverage if they were going to be allowed to market individual policies, but most states did not. Insurers, as businesses, were free to determine whom to cover.

In 1990, preexisting-condition limits on coverage were, as they are today, less applicable in the fully insured (but not self-insured) group market, where employers are the main clients. While an insurer might refuse to quote a price for health insurance for an employer with a few very sick people, that practice would not be widespread. But where employees have a choice, often because their spouse has other insurance available, an insurer will attempt to avoid risk by making the policy less attractive to the sick. This is known as *avoiding adverse selection*, and the techniques are used throughout the insurance industry.

Once sick people were in an insured group, in 1990 they could still face discrimination, based on a different set of risk-dampening business techniques. The most prominent of these was a monetary limit on benefits. Either in a fully insured situation, or in the benefits definition for a self-insured employer, policies could entail a threshold figure ($250,000, $500,000, or $1,000,000 would have been typical) over which the policy would no longer pay during a given year (annual limit). Or an insurer could choose to put a lifetime limit into place, where, after hitting a certain monetary threshold, the policy is exhausted. The benefits of such limits on the costs of the policy for the ultimate payer were direct and clear. They also allowed an insurer to make much more careful predictions about ultimate costs.

Treating such strategies as acceptable business practices sounds jarring today. Any patient advocate—indeed, any informed citizen—would most likely object to adverse selection strategies or limits on a policy. But through the first sixty to seventy years of health insurance in the United States, these were widely accepted features of health insurance policies.

As a society, our presumptions about fairness and justice in the distribution of health care resources have fundamentally evolved over the last thirty years, bringing us closer to a system that treats people according to their needs, rather than their potential profitability. Nonetheless, insurance markets require substantial regulation if they are going to approach the norms of a just health care system. Government-sponsored programs do a much better job than commercial ones.

Address Moral Hazard through Cost Sharing

Moral hazard (in health insurance) describes a lack of incentive to avoid health risks or costly health care procedures once one is insured—since insured benefits are free to the beneficiary. Moral hazard plays a huge role in our health care system in that fee-for-service care thrives through moral hazard. Physicians are free to order any tests or procedures they deem appropriate for an insured person. Much of what an insurer does to control costs, as we will see, is to police providers, trying to enforce the thin line between necessary and unnecessary.

But moral hazard can also be addressed at the beneficiary level by making benefits not quite free, thus forcing a beneficiary to make choices. This is called *cost sharing*. In health insurance, three techniques are used for cost sharing (not including the annual or lifetime limits noted above): deductibles, co-payments, and co-insurance. A deductible is the amount one must pay out of pocket before the insurance kicks in. *Deductibles* are precise and allow actuaries to have some control vis-à-vis the overall cost of the policy. In 1990, deductibles were generally rather small, ranging between $200 and $500 per year. Deductibles have become much higher across the board in the twenty-first century.

Co-payments are specific amounts that must be paid every time a benefit is used. They are generally attached to higher-cost treatments that have no discernible benefit over lower-cost ones. They usually involve much smaller amounts than deductibles, primarily ranging from $20 to $200. They rely on the beneficiary, as a consumer, to make decisions that will ultimately reduce the costs of the overall policy. Co-payments are especially prominent in pharmacy benefits, intended, for example, to drive people to use generic medications rather than more expensive brands.

Finally, there is *co-insurance*, which requires the insured beneficiary to pay a percentage of the costs of any treatment, often above a certain threshold. For a sick person, these costs can be quite high. Some policies add an *out-of-pocket limit*: after a beneficiary hits the out-of-pocket maximum, that person no longer incurs further payments.

The general point of cost sharing is to ensure that beneficiaries have some skin in the game and do not make bad (unnecessarily costly) decisions simply because they have insurance—that is, the moral hazard problem. All three of these techniques can predictably lower costs for the payer. Many employers will offer several different plans to employees, with variations in the co-payments, deductibles, and co-insurance. During *open enrollment*, an employee chooses from an array of plans (often as many as twenty), all developed in concert by the third-party administrator (insurer), the company's human resources team, and the benefits consultants. If a beneficiary selects a plan with high out-of-pocket features (higher cost sharing), then generally the premium contribution by the employee is lower. In employer-sponsored insurance, and in most government-sponsored plans, beneficiaries' two expenses are what they pay in terms of their premium contribution and what they pay out of pocket.

No matter if a beneficiary chooses *thicker* (less cost sharing) or *thinner* (more cost sharing) insurance, there will be some out-of-pocket payments. Such payments will either reduce demand (in the case of deductibles) or shift that demand to lower-cost alternatives (in the case of co-payments). Co-insurance will tend to decrease a demand for ongoing therapies unless there is an ongoing benefit for the patient. All three choices bring consumer decision making to the fore and reduce moral hazard. For the payer, not only are there behavioral changes that reduce the use of costly treatments, but also cost savings, as part of the therapy is paid out of pocket by the consumer.

I should make three further points about consumerism and cost sharing. The first is the consumers' choice at the time of their benefits selection. It has long served the interest of everyone in the insurance industry to presume that beneficiaries are rational shoppers who would make the right decision when they enroll in a benefits program. Consumers could decide which permutation of out-of-pocket spending and premium contribution made sense for them. The metaphor of rational shoppers reinforced the metaphor of optimally working markets, which, in turn, would justify resistance to governmental oversight.

George Loewenstein and colleagues have recently demonstrated just how distant these metaphors are from the truth.[5] The company they examined had, like many companies, developed a whole panel of options for employees, offering different risk-sharing arrangements. The HR team and their consultants presumed that this would be a good thing for their employees, treating them as reasonable consumers. In addition, the firm was a health care company, so at least it theoretically had beneficiaries who were even better educated than the standard set of health insurance consumers.

The economists evaluated the spending by that company's employees after they made their health insurance selections and found that the majority of employees chose plans that would end up costing them more than simpler plans would have. The authors' summary of their research is worth quoting at some length: "Testing alternative explanations with a series of hypothetical choice experiments, we find that the popularity of [less favorable] plans was not primarily driven by the size and complexity of the plan menu, nor informed preferences for avoiding high deductibles, but by employees' lack of understanding of health insurance. Our findings . . . raise doubts about the welfare benefits of health reforms that expand consumer choice." A lot of cost sharing is wrapped up in verbiage about "consumer choice," but the above research revealed that view as rhetorical, since most consumers are poorly equipped to understand their choices among various health insurance benefits.

The second point I should make about cost sharing concerns another aspect of its goals and intents. The assumption of rationality dictates that while under the influence of cost sharing, beneficiaries will avoid unnecessary health care, but not care that they really need. Health economists and health services researchers have evaluated these assumptions for years, and the consensus has changed over time. It is now quite clear that cost sharing often causes beneficiaries to defer the care that they need.[6] So I cannot presume consumer rationality in this setting, either.

This is part of the reason why the poor health effects of cost sharing are a matter of greater discussion today, since the whole enterprise of cost sharing has become more prominent. An important part of the story of twenty-first-century American health insurance is the growth of cost sharing, both in terms of the number of beneficiaries who face it, and the average cost of out-of-pocket payments. Part of this growth is a greater belief in the rhetoric of consumerism.

The third important point about cost sharing to reduce moral hazard, and thus overutilization, is that it is much more a creation of private, employer-sponsored health insurance than it is of government-sponsored programs. Medicare certainly has cost sharing, and (as we will see in chapter 6), the government-sponsored drug program, Medicare Part D, does use co-payments. But, generally speaking, emphasizing consumerism to combat moral hazard is not a big part of Medicare, and almost no part of Medicaid, where the low incomes of the beneficiaries do not allow them to have even a theoretical choice.

What government- and employer-sponsored insurance have in common, however, is that any cost sharing lowers the overall cost for the payer. When a patient pays a deductible, a co-payment, or a co-insurance fee, that money eventually either makes its way back to the payer or displaces charges the employer would otherwise face, thus reducing the costs of providing health insurance. Out-of-pocket payments have grown, making the health insurance bill more affordable for those supplying the policies, especially for an employer. It is much less clear that cost sharing is prompting wiser choices by employees/patients. Increasingly, cost sharing appears to simply add greater obstacles to necessary care. (I will discuss this much more in later chapters.)

Contract with a Provider Network
Paying Hospitals

The other three approaches to cost control by insurers are much less morally (if not emotionally) freighted than risk avoidance and cost sharing. They consist of paying hospitals, paying doctors, and employing utilization management.

Let us start with negotiating the network, which is the part of an insurer's function that providers know best. In a private commercial setting, an insurer, acting as the third-party administrator for an employer (or acting on its own behalf, when a client is fully insured by a health plan), must contract with health care providers and pay for any care an individual beneficiary receives. The major categories of providers are doctors and other health care practitioners, hospitals, long-term care facilities, and pharmacies. (For a variety of reasons, a pharmacy is a different animal, which will be discussed in chapter 5.)

Physician and hospital negotiations get most of the attention from insurers. In terms of paying providers, government-sponsored programs are much different from the programs developed by private insurers on behalf of employers. The government names the price, while private insurers must negotiate. Realizing this is key to understanding how our health care system will develop over the next two decades.

The best place to start regarding the government's advantage is Medicare payments to hospitals. Hospital accounting has never been a very exact science. One might reasonably presume that, as hospitals began to bill insurers in the 1930s and 1940s, there was some formal or structured approach to their billing, but that is not the case. Historically, there were efforts to develop a standard structure for hospital bills, but these never came to much. As a result, hospital billing systems, and their relationship to the costs of providing care, remained (and remain) murky.

By the time the Medicare and Medicaid Act was passed in 1965, the definition of *reasonable payment* for hospital services wasn't clear enough to be included in the new federal program. Just after the act's passage, the newly minted Medicare authorities had to negotiate with the American Hospital Association and the Blue Cross Association about the mechanics of reimbursement in order to get the program started. These negotiations were held entirely in private. Only very general principles were published by the Department of Health, Education, and Welfare, or DHEW (the predecessor to the Department of Health and Human Services) in 1966. The concept of *usual and customary payments* dominated these principles, but this meant little more than paying what had always been paid by private insurers, with an annual inflation kicker.

Both the Democratic side of the Senate and DHEW warned that this lack of clarity could have severe cost implications for Medicare. But the precedent was set: Medicare would pay what hospitals had typically or usually charged commercial insurers. That aspect was built on an amorphous mixture of market power, precedent, and the simplest cost accounting.

Through the 1970s and into the mid-1980s, commercial and Medicare prices for hospital services tracked very closely.[7] Medicare, like commercial insurers, paid regular fees for services—such as the per-day price for a hospital stay or the costs of an emergency department visit—without much negotiation. These fees, the usual and customary charges, would be summarized in an annual cost report—basically, an itemized receipt that a hospital prepared independently. The government would pay some interim fees for services provided, but the final settling up could occur more than a year after the close of the calendar year. This was known as a *retrospective payment system*.[8]

The problem with this system was that it created steady inflation, and thus was unsustainable. As a result, Congress passed the Social Security Amendments of 1983, which mandated a new prospective payment structure. It was called "prospective," as the payment was set by a medical diagnosis, no matter how long the hospital stay, rather than a retrospective per diem payment. In so doing, Congress followed the lead of a few successful experiments in states, particularly New Jersey, that incorporated the use of a new tool in health care cost accounting: the diagnosis-related group (DRG).

Developed by John Thompson and Robert Fetter, the DRGs were not initially intended as payments for hospital care. Rather, they were a risk stratification tool. They functioned under the assumption that each patient within a specific DRG would get much the same care as any other patient in that DRG. So, for example, DRG 193 was for a hospital admission for simple pneumonia, whereas DRG 177 was for a hospitalization for complex pneumonia. In other words, hospitals charged according to the specific illnesses they were treating. The DRG system accommodated the complexity that is inherent in medical care. Some hospitalizations would have several DRGs assigned to them. And the DRGs themselves could be modified to indicate greater severity, such as endotracheal intubation for complex pneumonia.

Although the DRGs were designed to help insurers assess risk, the Health Care Financing Administration (HCFA), which operated Medicare (the predecessor to today's Centers for Medicare & Medicaid Services, or CMS), rushed them into service as billing codes. Each hospitalization would be assigned a specific DRG (or set of DRGs), and that DRG would be paid for by a predetermined fee.

Under the DRG program, hospitals were incentivized to discharge patients as quickly as possible. If a hospital was paid the same amount whether the patient was there for five days or seven days, it was better to discharge them in five days. The resulting reduction in the length of stays for people on Medicare—nearly 20 percent—was a great lesson in how financial incentives can radically change health care. The hospital cost report never went away, but instead of hospitals setting their own rates, the HCFA (and later the CMS) controlled the price at which the DRGs were reimbursed.

Commercial insurers could not dictate prices the way the government could, so they had to continue to negotiate with hospitals. Nonetheless, the DRG system gave insurers insight into what hospitals were charging Medicare and provided a point of reference for where their own price negotiations could begin. Some insurers chose to parallel the DRG methodology, but many opted to stay in a per diem payment structure, usually because their payment systems had been based on a per diem approach for a long time.

For private health insurers, leverage was the most important negotiating card. An insurer's ability to obtain better (lower) payment rates was largely a matter of the threat that the insurer would not contract with a hospital if that hospital did not lower its rates. The threat was credible, insofar as the insurer had a high percentage of the overall insured population and the hospital had a relatively small share of the hospital beds in a particular metropolitan area. The reverse could also be true, since it still involved one form of market power versus another form. Blue Cross plans, with the largest market share, typically got the best rates. But no private insurer, not even Blue Cross, could compete with the government in terms of leverage, as the government sets the reimbursement amounts.

Over the course of the 1980s, hospitals developed contracting teams (very small at the start) that would negotiate aggressively with insurers for better rates. Hospitals and providers generally disdained the insurers' network teams, and those feelings were largely reciprocated. The interests of these teams were diametrically opposed: providers chronically believed they needed more revenue, and the network teams were directed to minimize payments to hospitals, making their overall insurance product less expensive and, therefore, more competitive.

In the two decades after the introduction of the DRGs, the hospital/insurer trench warfare settled into a matter of "costs" and "charges," shadowed by Medicare rates. Hospitals traditionally had no thorough cost-accounting mechanisms that helped them understand the true costs of the services they provided. In their dealings with insurers, hospitals relied on their usual and customary charges. Negotiations would drive discounts to these charges, but, nonetheless, the result was rates that were based on an insurer's leverage and negotiating talent, rather than on the true cost of care, which remained murky. As long as the true costs of providing care were less than the discounted charges, a hospital could prosper—it was not an exact science. (I should note that cost accounting in health care is not impossible—any review of a German health care bill will indicate that. But it has suited everyone in the United States to avoid precision.)

As the 1980s progressed, hospitals were charging commercial insurers increasingly inflated rates, while Medicare rates, set by the HCFA, tended to remain fairly steady. Payment from some private insurers was so much higher that it could *cross-subsidize* other, more miserly payers, including Medicare. As a result, it made sense for hospitals to inflate their charges annually at rates greater than background inflation. Thus these charges were much higher than the discounted rate that many insurers paid. From a hospital's perspective, its overall revenue was a *market basket*, based on a range of payment rates from various payers.

It is important to note that hospitals like the idea of cross-subsidization. It implies that they seek higher payments from private insurers because they are underpaid by government programs. Many economists would argue instead that hospitals would seek larger payments even in the absence of lower government rates, which seems likely to me. So when I use the term cross-subsidy going forward, I am not employing it as a justification. Rather, it is simply a matter of profit maximization.

An enduring theme in health care financing in the United States, particularly hospital financing, is that small or lazy insurers who do not or cannot negotiate discounts will pay much higher prices for the same services than insurers who are assiduous negotiators, have market power, or have both. Over time, some insurers could end up paying double what other insurers did. When I supervised our hospital's rate-negotiating team in the 1990s, we had even sharper disparities than that—in effect, four small national insurers were responsible for all our profit margin.

There was one other catch to this odd set of arrangements. Any patient paying out of pocket, who thus could not take advantage of insurer-negotiated rates, paid higher charges. Therefore, a person without insurance could face astronomical bills when being admitted to a hospital. This strikes many as unjust (and it is), but it can also simply be seen as a byproduct of insurer/hospital negotiating rates. The same result could occur if a hospital, or the doctors working there, were *out of network* (not contracted with a beneficiary's insurer). Out-of-network hospitals or doctors were free to bill an individual directly, usually based on astronomical charges. These extraordinarily high bills—*surprise billing*—often astonished the unsuspecting beneficiary.

By 1990, hospital costs for commercial insurance policies were complicated, but they were comprehensible once the financial incentives and power relationships were clear. Medicare paid on a DRG basis and named the price it would pay. In many states Medicaid rates were even lower than Medicare ones, another example of the government setting the price. Commercial insurers with a large market share paid higher rates, probably a good deal higher than Medicare ones, even by the early 1990s. But small-market-share insurers paid much higher rates, closer to the advertised price for services, or *charges*. An insurer's ability to attract business, through lower costs for self-insured employers was very much dependent on the *discounts* earned through negotiation and the portrayal of such discounts on consultants' spreadsheets.

At that point, two key themes in payments to hospitals emerged. The first was that the government's payment was straightforward—for Medicare, a clear rate paid by the HCFA (which later became the CMS) was based on a DRG. Second, payment rates were beginning to splay, based on the insurer: low for government payers, medium for some large insurers, and high for insurers with less market leverage. This disparity between payers, and the cross-subsidy between them, would persist and grow more prominent during the following thirty years, and it will become unsustainable over the next two decades.

Paying Doctors

Before Medicare, doctors had followed the hospitals' lead and simply submitted their bills to insurers, who paid them. But by 1990, physician payment was quite a bit different from hospital payment. Given the greater variety of services doctors rendered, they needed a uniform coding system. The American Medical Association recognized this and decided to solve the problem by creating its own standardization, which allowed it to retain some control over physician payments. In 1966 the AMA published the first Current Procedural Terminology (CPT) code book, designed to help in the standardization and automation of payments to doctors. The CPT code book is a living document. It has been updated continuously by the CPT Editorial Panel, which consists of seventeen members (many of whom are doctors) approved by the AMA's Board of Trustees.

By the early 1980s, the federal government stepped up to limit physician costs, as it had with hospitals. Since the existing CPT codes were available to provide an infrastructure for payment, the HCFA did not have to invent the program, like it did with the DRGs. It based its Healthcare Common Procedure Coding System (HCPCS) on the CPT program and required all physicians billing Medicare to use the HCPCS's codes, which eventually would give the government control over the fee amount. The same requirement was applied to Medicaid in 1986. The CPT codes provided the language for billing but did not determine the amounts paid. Going forward, CPT/HCPCS would be the common currency for physician payments, and commercial insurers fell in line.

Through the mid-1980s, the paid reimbursement rates were based on physician charges, but the HCFA had grown dissatisfied with this, as it had with the hospital payment structure. Less than twenty years after the passage of the Medicare and Medicaid Act, the government was prepared to name its own prices, over the objections of physicians.

William Hsiao had received several grants from the federal government and other sources to develop a methodology for a rational reimbursement for physicians' services. He called his program the *resource-based relative value scale* (RBRVS). The scale was based partly on economics and partly on psychology, and it was designed to identify the value associated with specific physician interventions. It used three key factors: the physician's work, the costs to the practice in undertaking a certain intervention, and professional liability insurance. Each CPT would eventually be assigned a relative value unit (RVU), which, by adding a geographic modifier (the fourth factor in some renditions) and then a monetary conversion, produced a rate of payment.[9]

Hsiao's research was incorporated into the Omnibus Budget Reconciliation Act of 1989, and Medicare switched to the new payment schedule, starting on January 1, 1992. The RBRVS determined the appropriate payment for a huge range of services. Medicare now had control over the fee schedule for physicians as well as hospitals.

But the assignment of RVUs to the CPT code, as well as the revaluation of specific codes, was left in the hands of the Specialty Society Relative Value Scale Update Committee (RUC), operated by the American Medical Association. To be precise, the Centers for Medicare & Medicaid Services (the HCFA in the past) delegated this responsibility to the AMA's RUC, but many saw this arrangement as a capture of the regulatory process by the regulated entity. The AMA fox appeared to be guarding the cost-control henhouse, since, while the CMS determined the payment for RVUs, the RVU assignment remained in organized medicine's hands. The RUC has chronically been accused of favoring surgery and interventional subspecialties, to the detriment of the primary care codes,[10] with the latter codes being systematically undervalued.[11] Those making this charge believe the AMA historically has been dominated by procedure-based physicians, profiting on fee-for-service payments.

Nonetheless, it is reasonable to state that the bureaucratic basis for price controls for Medicare payments to physicians was fully in place by the early 1990s. Certainly the government controlled the valves of the main spigot. One point I should reiterate is that the Medicare & Medicaid Act passed in 1965, so it took twenty to twenty-five years before full price controls were in place for both doctors and hospitals. It took the government about the same amount of time to decide to set prices for pharmaceuticals (2003–2026), as we shall see.

With the federal government controlling per service reimbursement, physicians might have tried to increase their income by treating more and more patients. To counter the drive for profit through volume, the government utilized the Sustainable Growth Rate (SGR) initiative to proportionately decrease the rate of pay to physicians as their patient volume increased. Physicians could do more, but the SGR was meant to reduce payments in proportion to the increase in services.

The SGR was intended to systematically drive down the cost of care for patients whenever that cost exceeded a preset budget. But it did not work. Each year, medical interventions exceeded the targets set by the SGR, and doctors should have faced cuts. Physician lobbyists, however, were able to influence Congress to step in and stop the cuts. As the can was kicked down the road, the accumulated excess costs were known as the *SGR overhang*. Eventually, in 2015, the SGR was eliminated. Now the CMS much more straightforwardly sets out planned reimbursement rates and then modifies those proposals as lobbying occurs.

Private insurers use the CPT codes for payment, but, just as with hospital payments, the insurers need to negotiate their rates. After the *Arizona v. Maricopa County Medical Society* ruling, however, physicians didn't have much bargaining power, so the publicly available Medicare rates became the default amount. Physicians could only gain negotiating leverage by joining a larger group or becoming affiliated with hospitals.

The use of these coding systems, for both hospital care and physicians' services, gave the insurers a reference amount with which to begin their negotiations. The coding architecture also provided an additional approach to cost reduction. Providers coded their services when they submitted bills. It stood to reason, then, that they acted as profit maximizers and utilized the most advantageous set of codes, whether they were CPT codes for physicians or the DRGs for hospitals. On the Medicare side, doctors had to be careful, due to a specific set of fraud and abuse laws that had evolved to punish those who overcoded. The same should have applied in private or commercial insurance contexts, but the penalties were not equally severe. To defend against this sort of fraud, private insurers began to check the submitted codes against other documentation, to ensure that physicians and hospitals weren't overcharging.

The war over codes was primitive in the early 1990s, as it was mostly done by hand, but it evolved rapidly. Today, complex algorithms are used, and a coding review involves a good deal of administrative costs. But it is worth the effort by insurers, in order to block unnecessary or inappropriate codes. For example, policing the DRGs can save tens if not hundreds of thousands of dollars on some hospitalizations.

These kinds of disputes lead to enmity between insurers and providers, but each has a business interest to pursue. As the costs of health care have risen, each service is worth more and more. Therefore, an investment in making sure that a bill is paid, or not paid, makes good sense. The price of health care services has risen much faster than background wages, so bringing in more personnel to code and recode is cost effective. In addition, both sides now bring artificial intelligence techniques to the fight. In this vortex, the collateral administrative cost of programs cannot be overlooked. Physician and hospital negotiations, and follow-up scrutiny of submitted codes, have become a major part of insurers' cost controls, most likely the most important part today.

Reducing Risk through Utilization Management

The third major effort made by insurers to reduce costs paid to providers is known as *utilization management*. Insurers have long scrutinized treatment plans that doctors or hospitals propose for patients and have decided whether they meet the standard of care, according to the insurer's reading of the medical literature on efficacy. From an insurer's viewpoint, physicians have been driven by fee-for-service incentives to perform care that is not necessary. Utilization management counters this provider profit drive.

Health services researchers Don Berwick and Andrew Hackbarth have argued that overtreatment costs the health care system nearly $200 billion, and that fraud and abuse amounted to another $177 billion in 2012.[12] More recently, William Shrank and colleagues concluded that overtreatment and low-value care cost the health care system $75.7 to $101.2 billion per year. (With regard to the rate negotiation issues outlined above, Shrank and colleagues found $230.7 to $240.5 billion in pricing failure, and they estimated that administrative complexity costs $265.6 billion.)[13] The point is, if a health insurer could eliminate unnecessary costs, then health care and health insurance become more affordable for customers.

The overuse of medical care isn't surprising, since physicians control demand, as well as supply. They recommend therapies to patients, who are not equipped to make informed choices. In some situations, physicians recommend and provide unnecessary care, influenced somewhat by the profit motive. Again, I am not saying that all physicians provide unnecessary care, or that the profit motive is overwhelming. Rather, I see profit as a steady influence, and sometimes it does come into play. When the call is close on what therapy to provide, profit has its say.

This is especially true when there isn't a clear path forward for a certain treatment. In this regard, prescribing medications is different from providing procedure-based health care. Medications, at least since the Kefauver-Harris Drug Amendments to the 1962 Food, Drug, and Cosmetic Act, can be introduced into commerce only after two randomized control trials have proven their efficacy. Much of the rest of medical care, especially expensive procedure-based treatments, isn't required to have any demonstrable statistical value to become part of standard care. As a result, the line between appropriate and not appropriate can become quite blurry.

To be clear, this isn't how most doctors view their practice. Physicians know through experience what has really helped their patients, and their impressions are often supported by an awareness that many of their colleagues are probably doing the same thing, usually based on some promising initial evidence. Because most physicians are confident of their own expertise, they do not readily accept external oversight, especially by insurance companies. But that is the purpose of utilization management: an insurer program to deny care that lacks reasonable evidence of efficacy.

Some will take offense at this characterization of physician decision making, thinking it overlooks or belittles the ethical commitment to the patient that is at the center of medical ethics and medical practice. I believe that most doctors are totally committed to the good of their patients. But a half century of health services research shows that economic incentives do prompt the use of more treatments.[14]

I should note that a commitment to good patient care and profit motives are not the only reasons that care is provided, especially unnecessary care. Doctors often cite the fear of malpractice litigation. Patients have long brought lawsuits against doctors, alleging that these doctors failed to reach the standard of a reasonable medical practitioner and, because of that, injured the patient. Since the standard of care can be difficult to define, doctors have erred on the side of caution, which typically means ordering extra tests, and sometimes undertaking additional procedures, just to avoid litigation. The most recent estimate was that $45.6 billion were spent on services motivated by defensive medicine in 2008.[15] But even at that level, the effect of defensive medicine is a small part of the overall waste problem in American health care. In any case, utilization management was the insurers' answer to overutilization prompted by fee-for-service health care in 1990 (and still is today).

It is important to note that utilization management plays a much more prominent role in commercial insurance policies provided by employers than it does in traditional Medicare, where, as we will see, its use has been rare. Utilization management appears in Medicare Advantage, but more gingerly than in a commercial setting.

While it makes great sense to have insurers prevent unnecessary health care (care without a sufficient evidence base), the entire program of utilization management remains very controversial—largely because it blocks treatment plans a physician and patient have decided to pursue. In that light, although providers do not see it this way, insurers tread lightly when challenging a physician's decision. Three points demonstrate that caution.

First, the initial decision to deny coverage under a health insurance plan is the start of the process. That decision may be made by a nurse (or, in the case of drugs, a pharmacist). The doctor can then appeal, and the insurer will have a physician review the case. Once that clinical determination is made, a secondary appeal—an *objective review*—is almost universally available, often by a physician outside of the insurance company. All this is set forth in the contract between the insurer/third-party administrator and the employer, and much of it is required by ERISA. The outside impartial reviewer provision is meant to yield specific protection for patients from the financial incentive for the plan and the employer, which is to deny the coverage.

Second, a typical case involving utilization management is not a matter of an experimental therapy or a high-cost procedure. Much more likely, it is the need for hospitalization, for more days spent in the hospital, or for admission to a skilled nursing facility or an inpatient rehabilitation facility—mundane decisions that nonetheless involve care that is quite costly. Insurers have long had teams that track hospitalized patients and assess when patients should be ready for discharge, especially when they are paying on a per diem basis, as opposed to a DRG. Payment based on a DRG puts the risk for any extra hospitalization days on the hospital, which is why, all else being equal, DRG admissions are usually going to be shorter than admissions paid on a per diem basis. The important point here is that utilization management disappears when risk shifts from an insurer to a provider.

Third, the concerns about utilization often center on a delay in care as a doctor pursues the appeals process set forth by ERISA (for self-insured employers), by the state (for fully insured commercial clients), or by the federal government (for Medicare and Medicaid). All of these programs have very specific requirements, with substantial penalties if the review process is not completed on time. Penalties for delays are often much more expensive for the insurer than the extra utilization would be. Medicare and Medicaid are much stricter and more feared regulators of utilization management. Hence the Medicare prior authorization programs are less exuberant than in the employer-sponsored sector.

In my experience it is often not worth an insurer's effort to pursue an appeal process. In particular, the Medicare Advantage program, with its very firm rules and substantial penalties to ensure that contracting insurers provide all the necessary care, stands out from other insurance arrangements, especially self-insured plans. The Medicare Advantage approach to oversight of utilization management does indicate that a regulatory scheme can provide extra protection for beneficiaries.

One final point deserves discussion. I have heard insurance executives referring to utilization management as a "quality program." That view entails characterizing compliance with evidence-based standards as quality health care, which, in some ways, it is. But I should be clear—utilization management is meant to reduce the costs of care.

Since I am making the claim that the key purpose of health insurance is to help keep health care affordable, a reasonable person would ask, How much can these various tools save for clients, especially self-insured employers? The answer is not something that has been the subject of peer-reviewed research, and so we must rely on the industry itself. Unfortunately, like many things in health insurance, the industry prefers not to talk about these issues.

In my experience with insurers, and talking with many others over the years, the savings are significant. Regarding network rates, it matters what one compares the negotiated rates with: charges (which are astronomical), or some overall market basket of insurer rates. It is reasonable to say that an insurer with quite favorable rates in a particular geographic area could have a 7–9 percent cost advantage over its competitors. Another 5 percentage points could come from coding interventions, and the same amount from utilization management. So the stakes are not small at all.

Obviously there are costs associated with using these tools, but the return on investment for utilization management interventions is generally at a ratio of 10:1 for the insurer/third-party administrator, and even higher for coding interventions and rate negotiations. Employers and their consultants have little doubt about the value of these cost-reducing programs. That is why they have been such sturdy parts of the health insurance industry for the last thirty years.

Keeping People Healthy: Disease Management and Wellness

The final function of insurers is to improve participants' health, using wellness and disease management programs. While these programs absorb a lot of energy from insurers, and many employers buy them, there is less evidence that they accomplish much. They are also very much in the domain of the employer-sponsored sector.

Health insurers have long realized that if they can keep their members healthy, overall costs will be lower. They already knew this in 1990 and had some programs then that promoted health. This is one area of cost control, however, that really came into its own in the twenty-first century, unlike the tools I have just reviewed, which were quite mature in 1990. So I go slightly out of our historical sequence to finish the story on insurer functions.

Insurer efforts to promote health take two forms, defined by the target populations. Wellness programs are designed for the general population and focus on preventive health: eat right, lose weight, get exercise, and cease smoking. Disease management programs, on the other hand, are oriented toward those with chronic illnesses. These two programs have evolved over the last thirty years and are now the cornerstones of a growing, entrepreneur-based industry.

Today the wellness / health promotion industry is heavily digitally based, has a great deal of hype associated with it, and much capital behind it. But it is predicated on a common insight—exhorting people to take care of themselves can reduce overall health care costs. Often, but not always, wellness programs are focused on people with poor health behaviors, but who have not yet developed a chronic disease.

Disease management, on the other hand, focuses on patients with a chronic disease. Before digital techniques came on the scene, disease management was formulated on the belief that a nurse calling a patient on the telephone could help guide that patient toward better care: take medications, eat properly, identify new signs of fragility, and work with providers to react quickly to any impending deterioration.

Wellness and disease management programs have persisted because they made sense and because clients expected them. It is equally true that published evidence on them has been mixed for years. For example, some small studies have suggested a benefit,[16] but usually that benefit, when it does exist, has been rather small.[17] In addition, the programs generally varied a great deal regarding their intent, so the elements that were most efficient about them remained an open question.[18]

That being said, some of the wind behind the disease management sails was lost nearly a decade ago. The CMS's leadership was justifiably interested in what value Medicare beneficiaries would derive from disease management and care coordination. Over the course of almost ten years, Medicare conducted six demonstration projects involving nearly thirty-four disease management programs. The Congressional Budget Office coldly summarized the results in a definitive publication in January 2012: "All of the programs in those demonstrations sought to reduce hospital admission by maintaining or improving beneficiaries' health, and that reduction was the key mechanism through which they expected to reduce Medicare expenditures. On average, the 34 programs had no effect on hospital admissions or regular Medicare expenditures. . . . After accounting for the fees that Medicare paid to the program . . . Medicare spending either was unchanged or was higher in nearly all the programs."[19]

Now there are literally hundreds of articles evaluating various types of disease management for a wide variety of chronic diseases. Some have shown impressive results in reducing unnecessary utilization and costs, but many others have failed to find such results. Disease management provided by insurers still has its supporters, and many employers buy programs that feature nurses who are assigned to sick patients and maintain telephone contact with them. Benefits managers buy it because it seems sensible, and they do not really probe for evidence of its efficacy. Fifteen years ago, disease management had a lot of momentum as a cost-prevention measure. That momentum has diminished for standard insurer programs, but disease management is still a part of many insurance contracts. It is a good example of how a reasonable concept remains a part of our health care system, even though the return on investment is uncertain.

The same might be said of the generic wellness programs. These are recommended by many benefits consultants, developed by well-meaning insurers, and bought by human resources teams at corporations. The intention is to reduce health care costs by getting people to take better care of themselves. The activities in an average wellness program focus on diet, exercise, and the use of preventive testing and services. In theory, better habits will reduce health care costs. While it is a good theory, the evidence has long been lacking. Clearly, eating better, exercising, avoiding alcohol and tobacco, and reducing stress will prevent illness, and thus reduce health care costs, but the programs themselves have generally failed to bring about those behaviors.

In a series of publications, Soeren Mattke and team members revealed that more than half of the employers they surveyed had a wellness program in place, and these employers overwhelmingly believed that the programs reduced absenteeism and, therefore, health care costs.[20] But only half of the employers had tried to evaluate the programs, and only 2 percent found savings. In terms of health care costs, Mattke's team itself could not identify statistically significant differences associated with the wellness programs.

Recently, several randomized control trials of wellness programs have reinforced the Mattke team's findings. Zirui Song and Katherine Baicker randomized nearly 33,000 workers at a large retail/warehouse firm who were involved in a wellness program emphasizing nutrition, exercise, and stress reduction. While 8–13 percent reported better exercise and eating habits, there were no differences in clinical markers of their health, health care spending, or absenteeism between the group randomized to the intervention and the control group.[21] Their follow-up analysis after three years was equally grim.[22] Another similar randomized control trial reached the same conclusion.[23]

It is difficult to argue with these studies, but many employers still eagerly offer wellness programs in the hope of reducing health care costs. Maybe some do work, but hard evidence is thin. These types of programs would only be so prevalent in a world as sparing of hard evaluations as employer-sponsored insurance is. Insurers certainly continue to deliver disease management and wellness programs, and employers buy them as add-on programs to their standard benefits. But in some ways they demonstrate the inadequacy of employer-sponsored insurance, especially regarding health care promotion.

Yet there is always hope. Today that hope focuses on serving programs that promote disease management and wellness using digital interventions. They may hold some promise, as I will discuss in chapter 9. Their forebearers, however, have produced more smoke than fire.

Recapitulation

In summary, insurers are generally oriented toward reducing costs. By using cost sharing, utilization management, rate negotiation, and coding adjustments, they are able to do so. Quality assurance is much less prominent, except where there are substantial financial incentives to comply with particular measures. This is especially true in Medicare.

More importantly, government-sponsored health insurers emphasize rate setting as their most important approach to containing costs. As a result, the federal government does not need to rely as much on cost sharing, nor on utilization management, especially in traditional Medicare. As we will see, Medicare Advantage uses both, but with much more regulatory oversight, because it is a government program, not simply a form of private insurance. These are the basic insights that are the building blocks for understanding how government-sponsored and employer-sponsored insurance have evolved from 1990 to 2020 and will continue to evolve over the next twenty years.

CHAPTER THREE

Health Care in the 1990s: To Manage or Not Manage Care

The Essence of Managed Care

The previous chapter's discussion of the role of insurers (private and governmental) presumed a fee-for-service architecture. Within this architecture, health care providers earn more money by doing more. So most of the effort by insurers was and is to reduce costs by eliminating the extra, income-maximizing procedures that fee-for-service-incentivized providers do, or to hold down the rates of payment (the fees) for services rendered.

As I discussed in chapter 1, however, there is another way to control costs: managed care. *Managed care* is a matter of bringing incentives to avoid unnecessary care into the health care provider's, (usually the doctor's) economic calculus. In its simplest form, doctors are paid on a set budget to care for a group of patients and get to keep any surplus at the end of the year. Physicians must carefully weigh treatment plans to be as efficient as possible, thus changing the structure of their practice. Put another way, a health care provider must ensure that only value-based interventions are delivered. This change in their financial incentives requires a good deal of careful redesign.

For example, a patient with relatively few risk factors for cardiac disease might go to a primary care doctor because of nonexertion-related chest pain. This is unlikely to be cardiac in origin. Nonetheless, a primary care physician (PCP) is in a fee-for-service environment, making more money by seeing more patients, so the appointment has to be short. A referral to a cardiologist gets that patient out of the exam room quickly. The cardiologist, also on the fee-for-service treadmill, refers the patient for testing, including a cardiac catheterization. The costs of this scenario to the system are high—and unnecessary—but they enhance income for fee-for-service-based, profit-maximizing providers.

In a managed care regime, a PCP takes responsibility for the downstream costs. The PCP slows the process down, listens to the patient, and perhaps refers that person for a treadmill-based exercise test, which will probably be negative. No cardiologist and no invasive testing are involved. The financial incentives are turned on their head, compared with the fee-for-service scenario. A side effect, or benefit, of this approach is that the number of patients a PCP sees must be reduced, in light of the time needed to adequately manage their care. But the costs of PCPs taking extra time per patient are more than made up for by the avoidance of unnecessary care. In this health care redesign, a PCP is now anticipating problems and, most likely, working with a team of providers (nurse practitioners, care managers, pharmacists) to ensure they can keep the patient healthy.

It is important to note two other key aspects of managed care. First, a doctor's responsibility here is to consider the overall cost of treatment, specifically by providing value-based care. Some patients will require very expensive care, and others will incur very little cost. But all should be treated with an eye to the efficient use of health care resources. A good managed care doctor will scrutinize key decisions from the perspectives of expense and value and then choose wisely. Nonetheless, we should recognize that this might also create an incentive to try to avoid having costly patients in one's practice.

Second, managed care doctors get no break from providing high-quality care. Both the tenets of medical ethics and professionalism, as well as the regulatory oversight of medical practices, require these physicians to meet the standard of care expected of a reasonable medical practitioner. The same is true regarding malpractice liability. So managed care cannot mean substandard care, even if that substandard care would be less expensive. In some ways, then, managed care is more complicated than the fee-for-service alternative.

By reimagining the care process to ensure that a patient stays healthy, a practitioner in a managed care environment is really providing the type of care all of us desire. We want to stay healthy and avoid hospitals. So it is up to a managed care provider to design a means to accomplish that goal.

If insurers can organize providers into a managed care regime, it gives the former another, more comprehensive approach to reducing costs. Providers operating on a fixed budget take much of the responsibility for cost control away from an insurer. Thus the dynamic between managed care and fee-for-service care is a crucial aspect of the historical evolution of health insurance.

In this chapter, I will outline managed care in the context of 1992, a key date for health policy. The election of President Bill Clinton brought about a new wave of health care reform, which was based in many ways on managed care. Managed care has a longer and more interesting history that precedes the 1990s,[1] but for our purposes, picking up the thread in 1992 is sufficient. Another point also deserves mention. Much of the Clinton administration's reform effort focused on employer-sponsored insurance. But many of the themes eventually rubbed off on the government-sponsored programs, as we shall see.

Constructing a Health Plan for Employees Circa 1992

To understand the infiltration of managed care into health insurance more generally, it is valuable to outline the kinds of products insurance companies offer to employers. (In the previous chapter, I reviewed tactics, not products—the difference will become clear.) Taken from the point of view of an employer's human resources team, there are four key product choices to make. By 1990, the first choice an employer had to make was whether to use a self-insured format or opt for a fully insured plan, with the risk carried by the insurer. There were then—and are today—significant economic benefits associated with self-insurance. Primarily, there is freedom from state-based mandates about the provision of care. In addition, a multistate employer's plan, if it was self-insured, faced a single, not overly intrusive regulatory structure, operated through the Department of Labor, rather than fifty different plans licensed in fifty states. In a fully insured context, on the other hand, insurance/employer plans are overseen by the state, and the format for the plan itself, as well as its actuarial structure, must be approved by each state in which it is offered.

The second set of design features an employer would have to choose in 1992 was the set of incentives used to drive a reasonable choice of services for employees, often through out-of-pocket spending mechanisms: deductibles, co-payments, and co-insurance. In 1992, and up until the game-changing reforms of Obamacare (discussed in chapter 7), there were few limits on out-of-pocket payments. An employee's share of the cost of health care could be very high. In addition, an employer could place total limits on the policy's payment—for example, no coverage after $500,000 of expenditures by the insurer. The design of the plan and its generosity were very much an employer's choice.

As we have seen, beneficiaries, as consumers, have had very little understanding of these insurance/financial tools. Even by 1992, however, that did not keep risk sharing from being characterized as "consumer features" and offered to employees as "benefit choices." The language around increasing consumer choice is felicitous, but we should be clear that, just as important as creating incentives for appropriate employee behavior, including cost sharing in a benefits plan, reduced costs for employers. Any employee's out-of-pocket payment reduces the burden on the employer. So, for the human resources team, a mix of deductibles, co-payments, and co-insurance was very much a financial decision. The set of choices by an employer was largely unregulated, limited only by the ERISA requirement that the benefits meet an actuarial value of 60 percent—that is, they would cover, on average, 60 percent of the health care costs for the employee pool.[2]

The third decision for an employer was the amount of the premium paid by individual employees. Even from the beginning of employer-sponsored health insurance, employees have always paid a portion of the premium, referred to as a *premium contribution*. This was perhaps even more important to an employer as a method for reducing the costs of health insurance. Historically, premium contributions were not subject to federal oversight (although Obamacare changed that).

The final set of decisions by an employer, even as early as 1992, would be determining the role of managed care in the health insurance plan, particularly management by a primary care doctor. The choices were *indemnity* (essentially no management of care), a health maintenance organization (usually a model anchored by a primary care doctor, who oversaw a patient's care), or an intermediate format, called the *preferred provider organization*.

Some background on the developments between the Nixon-inspired efforts at reform in 1974 (including the HMO Act) and those of President Clinton after 1992, is helpful to understand the differences between these three options. By 1992, after eighteen years, the HMO Act had percolated into health insurance generally. Because employers needed to offer an HMO as a benefit if one existed in the area where their employees were located, traditional insurers needed to be ready to compete with HMOs. Although this *dual choice provision* expired in 1995, it originally played a very important role. The 1980s are seen as a growth phase for managed care, and for health maintenance organizations in particular.[3]

Traditional HMOs were the staff model type, exemplified by Kaiser Permanente, where a consolidated organization essentially owned hospitals, employed the doctors, and performed all insurance functions. These types of programs were concentrated in California. But many of the new HMOs in the 1980s were based on *independent practice associations* (IPAs), made up of independent doctors who contracted to work together with insurers. These doctors were not employed by the IPAs, but they agreed to follow treatment guidelines and accept incentives set forth by the associations. These guidelines and incentives could vary by insurance contracts. An IPA might contract for some insurance arrangements that were largely based on fee-for-service costs, with little management by the IPA. But in some cases, the IPA might take a contract that was based on an overall budget, and the expectation would be that the IPA would create strong incentives for physicians to manage patient care. An IPA taking an overall budget as payment from an insurer was essentially a virtual HMO.

Doctors participating in an IPA could still have their own independent contracts with insurers for nonmanaged insurance products. This kind of arrangement, where a doctor would have some patients in fee-for-service contracts and others in managed care contracts, created great complexity for physicians. For example, in a primary care doctor's office, some patients would be on the fee-for-service treadmill, while others require the careful decision making of managed care.

Nonetheless, an IPA contract gave both insurers and doctors flexibility about participating in managed care contracts. For doctors, additional patients would come to them through participation in the IPA managed care contract, creating new revenues, but with the caveat that care for these patients would have to be managed. For insurers, a virtual health maintenance organization could be assembled through the IPA.

The Blue Cross insurers saw the advantages of the IPA format and began to develop their own HMO products. This allowed managed care techniques to diffuse much more broadly into the American health insurance mainstream than would have been possible if managed care remained dependent on staff model HMOs, such as Kaiser's. An insurer, like a Blue Cross Blue Shield plan, could offer an HMO format for employers who sought the reduced costs produced by care management.

The key to the managed care IPA structure was the role of primary care physicians as health care managers—they would decide what care was needed for a patient, making decisions consistent with managing within a set budget. The IPA would take *capitation*, getting paid an average budget for each patient. The per-patient budget was based on a calculation of average use, so a PCP could save money by selecting the least expensive form of effective care: the value-based one. This cost-conscious choice of treatments left a greater fund balance at the end of the year, which was then distributed back to the participating doctors. In some ways, a PCP could be characterized as a *gatekeeper*, deciding who needs further care. But this term cheapens the sophisticated decision making necessary to maintain a successful practice yet ensure a high level of care.

Not every employer was ready to jump into a health maintenance organization format, even one that relied on IPAs. But they wanted some management of their employees' health care, so as not to be left at the mercy of full fee-for-service charges.

It was not long before a middle path evolved, known as *preferred provider organizations* (PPOs). This format, which first started in Denver, Colorado, was a combination of patient incentives (co-payments) and practice guidelines for health care providers. Beneficiaries would pay a smaller (or no) co-payment if they chose a doctor who was one of the preferred providers. These providers were "preferred" by the insurer if they were willing to follow certain guidelines and parameters for care, such as agreeing to admit patients to lower-cost hospitals.

This cadre of doctors might also agree to charge slightly lower fees. They did so because the PPO would funnel patients to them, creating a larger volume of patients and making up for the discount. In addition, the preferred doctors could earn bonuses by performing well on measures that indicated their patients' care was being managed. *Precertification programs* (consulting with the insurer before a procedure was completed) and *second opinion requirements* (getting another doctor to agree that a care plan made sense) could be layered on top of this structure. Given their relatively loose organizational format, IPAs were naturally attracted to PPO arrangements, as the financial requirements were less stringent than the management of capitation.

By 1990, Blue Cross Blue Shield plans, allied with independent practice associations, were using this entire set of management tools. (So, too, were national for-profit insurers.) An employer could select an indemnity, PPO, or HMO plan, with the latter featuring the primary care gatekeeper. In 1990, indemnity was still the most popular choice, but the concepts were in place to operate PPO and HMO plans. Insurers drove the patients' choices by manipulating out-of-pocket spending amounts.

The entire health insurance industry accommodated itself to managed care, and more physician/physician and physician/hospital collaborations were stimulated by the alignment of managed care and patient choice. Physicians would want to collaborate with hospitals that understood and responded to the demands of managed care. Hospitals had to be willing to allow gatekeeping primary care doctors to direct the care of their hospitalized patients, to ensure that only cost-effective interventions were undertaken. (This was long before *hospitalists*, or doctors hired by the hospital to direct the care of the hospitalized patient, came on the scene.) Oversight from primary care doctors helped keep hospital bills lower, a benefit for all entities operating on a fixed budget.

But insurers retained the upper hand in the evolution of the health care system. The IPAs had to be careful about how they negotiated contracts, because of the antitrust rules laid down by the Supreme Court in *Arizona v. Maricopa County Medical Society* (see chapter 1), so insurers had an advantage when it came to organizing plans. Insurers also had a lot of freedom to experiment on behalf of self-insured customers as a result of ERISA. Except for individual and small-employer markets, they were not hemmed in by state regulation.

The foundational parameters of employer-sponsored insurance plans that were in place by 1990 have not changed much to this day. The choice of plan type by the purchasing employer, however, has evolved dramatically. In 1988, 73 percent of plans for covered workers were still traditional indemnity ones, 16 percent were HMOs, and 11 percent were PPOs. The high-water mark for HMOs was 1996, when 31 percent of beneficiaries were enrolled in an HMO plan, along with 28 percent in PPOs. Indemnity plans had fallen to 27 percent, while 14 percent were covered by a type of health insurance that combined features from HMO and PPO plans. By 2006, indemnities had faded to 3 percent, HMOs were down to 20 percent, and PPOs dominated, at 60 percent. The remaining 17 percent were covered by other types of plans.[4] These numbers highlight a striking change in the evolution of the health insurance system. The numbers also indicate that insurers' relationships with physicians and hospitals evolved dramatically in the 1990s, setting the table for our twenty-first-century health care system. In short, the use of managed care rose and fell.

This foundational set of four product choices by an employer—self-insured versus fully insured, the amount and type of risk sharing, premium contributions, and HMOs versus PPOs—remains true today.

Managing Care and Managed Competition

Efforts to reduce costs in a fee-for-service environment require a great deal of interference by health insurers. In managed care all this interference is avoided by internalizing the costs of care within the doctor/patient relationship. If unnecessary care is ordered and rendered, those costs are borne by the managed care organization, including the doctor. Managed care obviates the need for outside insurer influences. If a managed care company cannot reduce waste in health care, then its premiums rise, and competition leads to a loss of beneficiaries. With the amount of waste in the US health care system running at 10–30 percent of the total,[5] there should be plenty of room for competition between care managers.

By 1990, expert health services researchers estimated that HMOs covered 15 percent of the American population, nowhere near what advocates had hoped for in the 1970s.[6] But there was still promise, as many believed managed care could be the solution to the inflation that had plagued American health care since the mid-1970s. From 1974 to 1982, health care prices rose an average of 14.1 percent per year, and from 1983 to 1992, by 9.9 percent per year.[7] There was general agreement that fee-for-service insurance plans would overwhelm our ability to pay, and evidence that managed care and patient-based economic incentives could help keep health care affordable.

Hence a prominent health reform theory and proposal that was built on managed care and the design of competing plans—creatively labeled *managed competition*—gained some ascendance. Stanford economist Alain Enthoven had outlined and modified the theory of managed competition in a series of books and articles, beginning in the 1970s.[8] He was convinced that rethinking insurer competition could cure many of the problems in fee-for-service health care. According to Enthoven, managed competition "is a purchasing strategy to obtain maximum value for money for employers and consumers. It uses rules for competition, derived from rational microeconomic principles, to reward health plans that do the best job of improving quality, cutting costs, and satisfying patients with more subscribers and revenue. The best job is in the judgment of both the employer, armed with data and expert advice, and informed, cost-conscious consumers."[9]

Managed competition essentially involved competition between managed care plans, primarily as staff model HMOs, for employers' business. The managed care plans would be standardized through governmental regulation. Employers would select the most efficient plans and let employees choose among them. Note the reliance in this theory on the ability of both the plan sponsor (the employer's human resources department) and cost-conscious consumers to choose the best plan. Advocacy for a system of managed competition rested on the assumption that both employers and consumers will make reasonable, informed selections regarding health plans.

I should take a moment to probe a bit deeper into the Enthoven model. The assumption that rational economic choices would prevail seemed perfectly acceptable when Enthoven was writing. Since that time, however, economists have shown that individuals do not always act in a manner defined by economists as rational. People often make decisions that are not in their real financial interest because of the difficulty they have in comprehending the outcomes of particular choices. This field of scholarship is called *behavioral economics*.[10]

In one study, reviewed in the previous chapter, the overwhelming majority of people working for one large employer chose plans that cost more and provided fewer real benefits, undermining the whole idea of employees as good consumers of health insurance choices.[11] More broadly, in health care we see people making bad choices about their health: overeating, smoking, not exercising, not taking their prescribed medications. In light of this, health care economists have come to understand that choices are not governed by economic rationality and have argued that insights from psychology are necessary to develop strategies that improve behaviors.[12] These folks argue that "nudges" (in the form of small gifts or other material incentives), rather than just exhortation, can lead to real behavioral change and improve health.[13]

Enthoven also presumed economic rationality on the part of employers' benefits plan designers. He expected the head of the benefits section to decide on the best design for that company's health care plan, based on the internal logic of health care. But a benefits manager has numerous other considerations, including overall employee satisfaction. That satisfaction may be quite tightly tied to the status quo. So any change, no matter how financially beneficial, could be disruptive. That might well keep employers' benefits managers from acting "rationally."

These insights from behavioral economics tend to undermine Enthoven's reliance on plan sponsors and employees. Health care decisions are complicated. Both benefits managers and employees are insufficiently informed, and people cannot always act as the purely rational economic decision makers that Enthoven's model entails. Nevertheless, faith in economic rationality is important as we examine health policy in 1992, because that faith inspired the structure of the health reform effort undertaken by the Clinton administration.[14] In addition, the gut instinct of managed competition—that managed care–based insurers would have incentives to lower costs—made sense. Employers should therefore be attracted to them.

The Clinton team's reliance on Enthoven was understandable. His work was very widely read and admired. Perhaps more importantly, his work was more than theoretical. He had outlined a better structure for health care and took the time to address technical problems in the insurance market. For example, Enthoven pointed out that employers with less than 10,000 employees would not be sufficiently actuarially sound to participate in the managed competition marketplace. Those employers with fewer employees would therefore have to sign up for insurance through health insurance purchasing cooperatives (HIPCs), which would be organized in each state or metropolitan area. He argued that HIPCs would best be incorporated as nonprofit membership entities and would carefully select participating health plans. He even had a model for HIPCs, the California Public Employees Retirement System (CalPERS), which did indeed contract with insurance companies on behalf of various state agencies. Managed competition, emphasizing managed care, could be a reality.[15]

Governmental oversight of the HIPCs was critical to Enthoven's model. In particular, the government was charged with risk adjustment, entailing the identification of sicker patients and a modification of the capitation payment, based on different patient populations. Risk adjustment of this sort is critical to the operation of a managed insurer market. But given the insurance claims systems that existed in 1990, this type of risk adjustment would have been quite a task.

Ultimately, the managed competition outlined by Enthoven never came to fruition. But much of its promise can be seen in what eventually evolved as the Medicare program for managed care, now called Medicare Advantage. Medicare Advantage plans compete with one another, based on federal capitation, with standard benefits structures and good risk adjustment. A strong scent of managed competition can be detected in today's Obamacare exchanges, which have a structure for enrolling individuals into public/private plans. It is useful to keep managed competition theory in mind as I follow the evolution of health care. Not so much because I have faith in consumerism or employer-sponsored insurance playing a leading role, but because of the government's critical role in organizing competition among managed care entities.

The Clinton Health Reforms

With the election of President Bill Clinton, it seemed like anything was possible. The White House and Congress were aligned, and all were ready for health care reform. There are many histories of the Clinton administration's efforts to enact health reforms, but all recount the same basic story: the Clintons and their advisors eventually offered a plan, based on the Enthoven model, that was too complicated and suggested too much governmental intervention.

Suffice it to say that the Clinton administration believed it had a mandate for reform—specifically, to bring about universal access and reduce health care waste. Veteran reformers (like Stuart Altman, a member of the original Clinton health team) believed that there were three basic options: s single-payer format, employer mandates, or tax incentive plans. The single-payer model would be similar to the situation in Canada, where the government paid the providers directly and the right to health care was assumed. The employer mandate, also known as *play or pay reform*, which was central to the Nixon administration's reforms two decades earlier, operated through employer and individual mandates, in order to force employers to get behind universal access. Tax incentive plans could help low-income populations buy insurance, but this alone would not bring about universal access, so those plans were supported primarily by Republicans. But none of these three approaches, on their own, directly addressed reduced costs.

The Clinton team needed to reduce governmental health care costs, as their core message was economic growth, tied to lower federal expenditures. Clinton himself would not repeat the mistake of his predecessor and increase taxes. In this light, it is not surprising that Clinton decided this was not the moment for a single-payer system, even though many of his advisors believed that this could be a less expensive way to finance overall health care. On the other hand, endorsing an approach based on tax incentives alone to increase coverage was not sufficiently broad.

The comparatively easiest path was the employer mandate, so-called play or pay. The government would require employers to either provide health care insurance to their employees or pay a tax on their payroll amounts to enable the government to cover the costs. Since, as we have seen, employer-sponsored health insurance is heavily marbled into our health care system, the employer mandate is a practical step toward broader reform. But if an employer did not provide health insurance benefits, it would be taxed to make up its share.

New taxes were anathema to a New Democrat like Clinton. Nonetheless, the Clinton Health Policy Group, chaired by Judith Feder and joined by Stuart Altman, chose an employer (and individual) mandate as the pathway to achieve health care reform. The proposal fell flat when it became clear that it would cost (in today's dollars) $270 billion over five years. As Altman recounts, at the meeting where the ultimate proposal was presented, Clinton put his arm around Altman and told him he was a great American. The next day, the president fired the Health Policy Group and buried the play or pay plan.[16]

The new reform team, now led by Ira Magaziner and Hillary Clinton, opted for managed competition. With a giant task force, a great deal of intellectual firepower, and a committed, newly elected president, the Clinton administration pushed forward to pass health care reform. In retrospect, the effort was short lived. The reform team, headed by the First Lady, deliberated for eight months, developing a 1,300-page legislative plan that the president unveiled to Congress in September 1993. By the midterm elections in November 1994, it was abandoned forever.

Conservatives had no problem characterizing the health reform plan as wanting too much change. The Heritage Foundation pointed out that the necessary legislation required (1) a national health board that would have complete oversight of the American health care system; (2) state-based regional health alliances that would control the availability of health plans; (3) a standard benefits package, with no consumer choice; (4) employer mandates to provide health insurance; and (5) governmental budgets having spending caps.[17] One can see the market-driven managed competition beneath this set of prescriptions, but it was a lot of change for such a substantial part of the economy.

This was especially true for the employer-sponsored insurance sector, which had traditionally been subject to weak regulatory oversight by states and now was in the process of moving to even less oversight by the Department of Labor under ERISA. Insurance decisions had been left almost entirely up to employers. The thin ERISA oversight mechanism was driving employers to self-insure, insulating them from even state oversight. As a result, employers could not and did not rally to the Clinton plan.

Many Democrats, however, argued that it took both a slick marketing campaign orchestrated by the Republicans and opposition by business interests to convince people that the proposed plan was too un-wieldy and threatened their freedom. Moreover, the Clinton team could reasonably argue that unanticipated obstacles hampered their progress. Crucially, the Congressional Budget Office (CBO) ruled that employer contributions to fund coverage in the HIPCs had to be taxed, unlike employer-sponsored benefits. Additionally, the CBO would not accept that managed care and managed competition would, by themselves, substantially lower costs.

As a result, to ensure cost control, the Clinton team had to propose an overall budget that was layered onto the managed competition su-perstructure, requiring a federal National Health Board to set the tar-gets. This type of budget generated the need for an additional, compli-cated infrastructure, and the Heritage Foundation and others seized on these new mechanisms, characterizing them as big government be-ing out of control. While the maneuvers to keep costs down while avoiding new taxes were sensible, slowly but surely the sophistication and breadth of the emerging plan ran into political hesitancy about massive changes and the growing opposition of not just insurers, but also providers and employers. Even Enthoven himself jumped ship.

There are some lessons for health reform here, and, in part, they were heeded by the authors of the Obamacare reforms fifteen years later. First, it is difficult to overcome inertia in the health industry. Health care for the commercial population was largely unregulated, and adding new regulation was difficult, given entrenched interests in the industry, particularly for insurers and hospitals. Employers and provid-ers are naturally wary of change, and they had been satisfied with fee-for-service health care for years, so it was quite understandable for providers to pass. Employers were not, nor would they be in the future, in the vanguard of health care reform.

Second, people are comfortable with decisions for patients made by doctors and worry about new overarching mandates set out by sup-posed "experts." The managed competition edifice designed by the Clinton team tried to do too much by enforcing competition locally through the Health Insurance Purchasing Cooperatives, which were easily demonized as big government. Managed competition, underlaid by managed care, was not given a chance to evolve—and it proved difficult to impose.

The political history of the Clinton administration's efforts is well told elsewhere. Here, suffice it to say that by the end of 1994, the possibility of health care reform was gone. Comprehensive reform was not seriously addressed again in the remaining six years of Clinton's presidency.

The Aftermath of Clintoncare: Managed Care in the 1990s

Clintoncare was never born. The gestational experience did, however, leave a real legacy in that it caused managed care to evolve at a somewhat faster pace in the subsequent decade. While the national political debate occurred over a relatively short two years, it set the table for the 1990s in leading many to conclude that broader management of health care was inevitable.

By the early 1990s, the concept of managed care, its ability to lower overall costs, and the development of health maintenance organization competitors had forced Blue Cross and the major commercial insurers to start their own HMO-type plans as health insurance options. The Clinton administration's focus on managed competition through managed care, and its core element—capitated payment for providers, especially primary care doctors—accelerated this development. While politics stymied the effort to impose managed care from the top, many were convinced that the future was going to involve managed care.

This movement toward managed care was particularly stressful for the hospital industry. Staff model HMOs were ready to take on capitated risk and managed care. To some extent, so were groups of physicians organized as independent practice associations. Hospital administrators worried that this might leave hospitals dependent on gatekeepers in the health care system and faced with the potential of being whipsawed for better rates by organized physicians in IPAs.

By the early 1990s, hospital leaders had come to see themselves as in control of health care's institutional development. With the growth of managed care, and then the very public debate about managed competition, most hospital executives realized that to maintain their position, they would have to evolve. The answer was relatively simple. Since primary care gatekeeping was such an important part of managing care, they would need to hire primary care doctors and train them to manage care. Alternatively, they would have to develop their own IPAs. If they chose the latter, they would need a new legal vehicle for accepting risk payments, something that became known as *physician/hospital organizations*. In any case, controlling primary care doctors (gatekeepers) would allow the hospitals to retain some control.

Moving into the mid-1990s, these new organizations—the primary care network, and the physician/hospital organization—became the key strategic themes for hospitals. Yet hospitals had little experience with managing doctors, or with managing care, so many hospitals failed when they attempted to take on a capitated payment scheme.[18]

Managed care is intended to bring the cost of care into the doctor/patient relationship. A physician must calculate what benefits a patient, without exceeding the budget for that patient's care. Theoretically, the doctor managing this care avoids unnecessary tests and procedures; chooses the lowest cost hospitals for patients; provides wellness services that prevent illness from developing; and visits previously hospitalized patients at home, rather than having them admitted to a short-term rehabilitation facility—all of which is within the normal standard of care. In short, the physician and the health care team use nothing but value-based care. Since an estimated 15–25 percent of care is unnecessary, taking waste out of the system could be quite lucrative for an at-risk primary care doctor.

But theory is not easily put into practice. Primary care providers accustomed to fee-for-service payments could not simply switch over to a managed care system. Physicians not trained in managed care felt uncomfortable considering cost-effectiveness and worried about their commitment to patients. Moreover, the administrators supporting them lacked experience in managing care. (I was definitely one of them.)

In the milieu of a long-established staff model HMO, its doctors and nurses had built these cost-containment impulses into their practices, and providers had made the extra efforts necessary to reduce costs. This mindset was also strong in some independent physician groups, especially in California. These physician groups evolved under the shadow of Kaiser Permanente and had developed a preference for managed care over a fee-for-service system.

But in the rest of the country, the new primary care networks and their allied hospitals, organized as physician/hospital organizations (PHOs), lacked that experience or wisdom. They retained fee-for-service muscle memory and did not have the templates or supports to create the necessary efficiency, so they lost money. With mounting losses, the Clinton health reform–inspired momentum began to wane. A careful review of the PHO scene in the 1990s by Lawton Burns and Ralph Muller found little improvement in the quality of care or a lowering of costs.[19]

The managed care momentum waned only slowly, however, and hospital executives continued their efforts to succeed in a managed care environment. Many hospitals became convinced that success was going to be a matter of economies of scale. A single hospital might not have a sufficient primary care base to be able to take on a large capitated population. Hospitals reasoned that they needed to acquire a more expansive primary care workforce. This would be costly and require more capital, and perhaps debt. Such an investment couldn't be shouldered by a single hospital, so administrators started looking for merger opportunities. Groups of hospitals, now called *integrated delivery systems*, would be able to provide more capital, develop a primary care base, and offer managed care plans across a metropolitan area. These groups also hoped they would be a more attractive home for primary care providers.

But with the imperfect development of managed care techniques, many of the integrated systems and large physician groups under prepaid contracts found themselves with mounting losses. They could not manage care sufficiently to squeeze a profit from their capitated payments. Ironically, though, they found they had an alternative, resulting from their increased size. Their negotiating hand had, somewhat unexpectedly, been improved through the mergers and acquisitions effectuated in the 1990s to deal with managed care. The greater the market share a hospital has, the more leverage it brings to the table. This new leverage could be used to increase the percentage of the premium in capitation—or it could be used to get better payments in a fee-for-service system. Given how difficult managing care is, the latter became the favored strategy. Hospitals and the doctors they employed headed back to negotiate better rates in fee-for-service plans, rather than managed care ones.

Consolidation essentially turned the managed care impulse on its head. The excitement and agitation over the Clinton plan had led to the rush to capitation, which, in turn, precipitated a massive uptick in the consolidation of hospitals and doctors. But that consolidation, instead of facilitating capitation, promoted fee-for-service care. Through the 1980s, hospitals had always negotiated their rates with insurers, but with a relatively small market share for any one hospital, leverage for better rates was not always available. And independent doctors were not really able to negotiate. They would generally have to accept rates similar to what Medicare would pay, leading to the ubiquitous industry measurement entitled *percent of Medicare*.

Now, however, by controlling several hospitals in a metropolitan area and employing an array of doctors, the *integrated delivery systems* could really sit at the bargaining table with insurers. Insurers could no longer use the blunt cudgel of not contracting with these systems—too many hospitals and doctors, and, therefore, too many beneficiaries would incur disruptions if there was no contract. Disrupted beneficiaries meant disrupted employees, which meant upset employers, who were the insurers' clients.

The situation in Boston provided an archetype. One new integrated system, Partners Healthcare, realized that it had a strong position in the market and decided to renegotiate its contracts, first for its hospitals, and then for its doctors. One of the first insurers it approached with this renegotiation strategy balked, and Partners' leadership threatened to not contract with them at all. As one of those leaders, and being the person responsible for getting better rates for physicians, I fully supported that strategy. Our ultimatum sat on the insurance company's chief executive officer's desk for a few days before the insurer came back to the table with a different, much more generous approach.[20] The insurer's clients were agitated because the Partners' hospitals and doctors were not going to be in the insurer's network.

The result was dramatic, in that hospitals and aggregated doctors now had much more leverage in rate negotiations and could boost commercial insurance's rates of payment. Many integrated systems saw the potential to increase commercial rates across the board. But Medicare and Medicaid did not negotiate like this. As a result, the difference between commercial and Medicare payments began to grow ever larger. The gap was approximately 10 percent from 1996 to 2001, but it began to widen dramatically thereafter, reaching 75 percent by 2012,[21] and has grown since then.

According to hospital administrators, there are many reasons why such high rates are necessary: uncompensated care, the costs of teaching, and a commitment to social problem solving lead the way. But the main reason they give today is that commercial contracts must cross-subsidize the lower payments by Medicare (and Medicaid).[22] The government does not pay enough, so big systems need to have commercial insurers pay more. Many economists might argue that hospitals would push for the highest rates possible even without these government-sponsored insurance deficits, and I tend to agree. The notion of higher rates offsetting lower ones is, in some ways, a false justification. The end result is the same, whether you accept the offset theory or not—rates from commercial insurers are being pushed ever higher.

The take-home message is worth repeating. The government controls costs when it controls reimbursement rates, so negotiators for providers will naturally shift in the direction of getting better payments from those with whom they can negotiate—that is, private insurance companies. This approach solidifies their commitment to fee-for-service health care. Doing more to earn more gains even more when you can get a rate advantage. And (arguably at least) doing more for patients with commercial insurance helps offset the poor pay from Medicare and Medicaid. The paradox of the Clinton health reform effort's emphasis on managed care is that it inadvertently led hospitals to the pathway for survival in fee-for-service plans: use leverage to increase private commercial reimbursements well above those paid by the government.

These trends have continued apace from the failure of the Clinton reform effort, as well as through the entire evolution of Obamacare. Today, the gulf between commercial insurance reimbursement and governmental reimbursement has grown dramatically.[23] In addition, the consolidation of hospitals has been unceasing, largely unhampered by the other wing of antitrust law that comes into play in health care: policing hospital monopolies in given metropolitan areas.[24]

The Clinton reform effort set the table for the foundation of the health care system that came into being by the early 2000s, which was just the opposite of what it wanted. Its emphasis on managed competition and managed care to remove waste led to provider consolidation. This, in turn, produced more sharp-edged negotiations, which led to much higher rates of payment by commercial insurers, compared with governmental payers. The integration of doctors with hospitals was put in motion and has continued up to today. Fee-for-service health care, originally threatened by managed care concepts, resoundingly triumphed. To control costs, insurers would have to turn to more risk assessment, better-negotiated contracts, and, especially, more utilization management. This describes the state of health care for the employer-sponsored insurance part of health care today, a table that was set by 2000.

This shift in strategy was impressive. The highly regarded Kaiser Family Foundation's 2022 report on employer health benefits reveals that 31 percent of plans offered to employees were HMO-based in 1996, falling to 12 percent in 2022.[25] Meanwhile, the PPOs' share more than doubled from 1996 to 2004, when it stood at 55 percent of all plans offered. And capitation as a form of payment has nearly disappeared. Samuel Zuvekas and Joel Cohen have followed this closely and have shown that by 2013, capitation payment for primary care doctors was down to about 3 percent of all physician revenues in the United States, exclusive of the West Coast, where capitation has hung on in Kaiser

Permanente and some older primary care groups.[26] Even there, though, capitation is fading. Commercial HMO enrollment (excluding Kaiser) dropped from 6.3 million in 2004 to 3.6 million in 2015.[27]

The story of the Clinton health care reforms and managed care / fee-for-service dynamics brings us to 2000. Much has changed since then, but the basic structure of health insurance, in particular the employer-sponsored part of it, was in place more than twenty years ago. What we had in 2000 is easily recognizable today. Not everyone explains the developments of the 1990s in quite this fashion, however. For example, David Dranove and Lawton Burn's *Big Med* is a formidable new discussion of the aggregation of power in hospitals and insurers.[28] But many of the same themes concerning the progress of managed care come through in it.

In any case, to understand the continued evolution of the employer-sponsored insurance sector and to see how its eventual failure could result in socialized insurance, I need to address other important parts of the health care system that developed in the first decade of the 2000s. These include the pharmacy aspects of care (to this point I have only talked about insurers, doctors, and hospitals); the role of the privatized version of Medicare, referred to as Medicare Advantage; and Obamacare, the next in the line of grand health reform efforts. But first, we must step back to understand the overall trajectory of the public's health and finances in the United States, in particular our demographic future. These long-term trends provide vital context for understanding the evolution of American health insurance and the US health care system in the twenty-first century. As we will see, they propel us down the path to Medicare for All.

CHAPTER FOUR

Twenty-First-Century Numbers

TO THIS POINT, I have been examining the twentieth-century foundation of the American health care system, in particular employers, the
government, doctors/hospitals, and insurers. Much of what we have
seen up through the end of the 1990s remains true today, providing
the context for any efforts to effect change or reform. But this book is
very much a twenty-first-century undertaking, and I particularly
want to both trace the evolution of health insurance and predict
changes that will come in the third and fourth decades of this century.

To do so, it is important to examine systemic pressure from outside
of health care: the broader social and financial trends that have influenced health policy in the first two decades of the twenty-first century.
I will avoid political prognostication; for the purposes of this book, I
will treat politics as a relatively random variable. At times the elector-
ate will move to the left, and health care reform can occur through
political intervention. At other times it swings to the right, and then
health care's evolution will be only modestly affected by politics. It appears to be a given, today, that substantial policy intervention in health
care requires a Democrat as president and firm Democrat majorities in
the House and the Senate. Republicans are more likely to leave the status quo in place. When the stars line up for the Democrats, health

reform can occur. Meanwhile, the inherent evolution of health insurance limps along, prodded by social and demographic changes, as well as by unintended influences, such as those created by ERISA.

There is no doubt that long-term social, financial, and demographic changes greatly influence the evolution of health care. I will posit five long-term trends that are so consistent and of such long duration that we can treat them as constant influences on the framework of health care throughout the first half of the twenty-first century.

First, America's population is aging, which means more and more people need to access our health care system, so I'll get into what an aging population means for financing this system. Second, we must view these demographic changes in light of the current US fund balance, in particular the limitations of deficit funding for social programs. The result of these two analyses, in conjunction with the inherent inflation of fee-for-service care, will mean that over the next decade, we, as a country, will finally come to understand that we have a health care system we cannot afford.

The other three trends are relatively unrelated to these first two (which are grounded in general demographics and finance), but they are equally compelling as vectors toward long-term health care change. The third trend is also demographically based, but it's limited to a specific group: the provider workforce, made up of nurses and doctors. This population is growing older, too, but, more importantly, it is increasingly likely to be employed. In the past doctors, as self-employed entrepreneurs, were grounded in a fee-for-service system. Doctors, as employees, participate in a much different health care system, one not as dependent on fee-for-service payments.

The fourth theme is the relative thinning of health insurance benefits for employees over the course of the first two decades of the twenty-first century. Even before the full force of demographic changes starts to drive health insurance costs up further, employers who are feeling this financial pinch have moved to reduce benefits and increase cost sharing. Thus the value of employer-sponsored insurance has shrunk, and out-of-pocket costs absorb even more of a worker's income. This phenomenon is known as *underinsurance*, and it drives employees away from the health care they need. Slowly, dissatisfaction with underinsurance will make all employees open to a different, government-sponsored program.

Theme five is that providers—hospitals and doctors—are moving into ever-larger companies and corporations. Hospitals are merging with hospitals. Physician groups are growing larger. Physicians are increasingly employed by hospitals. This process is known as *consolidation*, and it makes for bigger, stronger bargaining groups. Since there is no bargaining with the federal government, this means that consolidation is aimed at commercial insurers—specifically, at employer-sponsored insurance. Consolidated providers using leverage to get higher reimbursement rates put further pressure on employer-sponsored insurance. Consolidation eventually squeezes employers, soon intolerably so.

Putting these trends together, employer-sponsored insurance is locked in an inflationary vise that will only grow tighter throughout the twenty-first century. Demographics and deficits force the government to either slow the rate of cost increases or reduce its payments to providers. Providers turn to commercial insurance, or the employer-sponsored sector, for those dollars they cannot get from the government. Employers cut employee benefits by increasing their cost share, but eventually that maneuver runs into governmental regulations and makes government-sponsored insurance look more attractive. At some point, I predict that the government will offer to take over, and employers will assent. Let's see if this thesis is convincing.

Demographic Shifts, 2020-2040

Demographics, unlike political analyses, provide substantial certainty about what is going to happen in the future. Its measurement period is best expressed in generations. Some countries are aging more quickly than others. In 2020, the United States had 17 percent of its population over the age of 65, while in Europe that figure was 19 percent. In Japan, it was 28 percent. Perhaps even more shocking, the working-age population in Japan will decrease by 28.5 percent from 2020 to 2050.[1] It is no wonder, then, that the Japanese are thinking hard about how to adapt to a society of much older people, with fewer workers and more elderly individuals needing support. They are up against a demographic hard fact.

The story in the United States is hardly rosy—far from it. Our elderly population is currently growing at a higher rate than that of any other developed country, with the exception of Canada: expanding at a clip of 2.9 percent per year from 2010 to 2030.[2] This is the baby boomer generation, born during a period of historically high fertility rates from 1946 to approximately 1964. While our population continues to increase overall, the number of workers per elderly person has declined. There were 3.4 workers per Social Security beneficiary in 2000. That number has dropped to 2.6 in 2022 and will decrease to 2.2 by 2030.

The rapid aging of the US population has not been disruptive or costly so far. Until 2018, Americans continued to live longer and be healthier at the age of 65 than was the case in the past. This means that the health care costs associated with aging boomers have been blunted to some degree. Eventually, though, everyone gets sick.

Thus the health care cost of the baby boom generation will be back weighted, and we will begin to feel its effects more severely as we move through the 2020s and into the 2030s. A key data point, noted by the Census Bureau in 2019, is that in 2034, adults over the age of 65 will outnumber children and adolescents for the first time, with 77 million seniors and 76.5 million children under 18.

The social impact of this aging population will be modified by a series of other factors. The number of people still in the workforce is critical to a country's ability to carry a burden of elderly citizens. There will be fewer workers, confirmed by looking at worker-per-Social-Security-beneficiary statistics. The Medicare Payment Advisory Commission (MedPAC) has recently estimated that from 1980 to 2000, the number of workers per Medicare beneficiary was around 4. It had dropped to slightly less than 3 today and is expected to continue to decrease to 2.5 by 2031.[3] So each working person has more older people to support, particularly in terms of the costs of their health care.

There are other nuances we should not overlook, many of which were reviewed in an excellent report by the National Research Council (NRC) in 2012.[4] It is important to examine retirement rates, since later retirement would mean more workers, even as the country ages. Here the NRC found little relief on a macro basis—the ratio of retired years to working years in 1962 was 0.35, would rise to 0.41 by 2020, and is predicted to be 0.52 by 2050.[5] While people may not be retiring quite as often when in their early 60s, their longevity cancels out any benefits from a longer work life. The same conclusions arose from examining the old age dependency ratio (OADR)—defined as the population over age 64 divided by the population aged 20–64—and the retiree to worker ratio (RWR). Between 2010 and 2050, there will be an 81 percent increase in the OADR and a 71 percent increase in the RWR.

If productivity increased at the same pace as the workforce shrunk, then, all else being equal, resources would be available to support the elderly. The NRC noted that productivity grew at a rate of 1.56 percent from 1960 to 2010 and used this factor to estimate the aging burden. But other, perhaps more prominent voices, posit dramatically lower increases in productivity.[6] Given the available data, it would not be prudent to rely on a sudden increase in productivity to address the problem of an aging population.

The other important factor is immigration. The US population has grown more than that in many European countries, and certainly more than in Japan, because of immigration policies, and, to some extent, undocumented noncitizens. Immigrants tend to be younger and often come from countries with higher fertility rates (although fertility rates have decreased in countries like Mexico). Still, immigrants age, too, so the overall contribution of immigration as a solution to an aging US population is somewhat unclear. Reviewing this question in 2012, the National Research Council estimated that a 10 percent reduction in the OADR by 2050 would require as many as 1 million net immigrants to the United States per year, which seemed unlikely, and appears even more so today, given current attitudes in the United States toward immigration.[7]

Not only will the US population age, but its racial composition is also going to change. The proportion of the white population will decrease to 55.8 percent by 2030, down from 59.7 percent in 2020. Meanwhile, the Hispanic, Black, and Asian American populations will increase.[8] The portion of the aged population that is white, however, will only decrease to 72 percent by 2030.[9] These dynamics will no doubt raise questions of racial equity, as an increasingly nonwhite worker population is asked to carry the heavy burden of a white aging population.

As I begin to specifically examine how these demographic changes influence the organization of health care, I should note a couple of substantial changes in the disease burden. The strong public health effort to drive the rate of smoking down to less than 15 percent of American adults correlates with longer life expectancy.[10] But this effect appears to be more than offset by the obesity epidemic, and especially by the epidemic of opioid use disorders. These two health care crises create quite different demographic vectors. The obesity/diabetes burden will be quite heavy in the population over age 65 and drive health care costs up, which must be shouldered by the working population. The opioid epidemic, on the other hand, is disproportionately killing younger people, dragging down the average lifespan and reducing the working population.

Both epidemics, as well as the COVID pandemic of 2020 to at least 2023, remind us that some huge public health problems remain unpredictable. No one, or perhaps just a very few, saw the opioid and obesity surges in 1990; only Bill Gates predicted COVID. But the impact of these new disasters on the overall demographic problem in the United States will be the same: not enough workers to create a funds surplus to use in caring for the elderly.

Four stark conclusions follow from these statistics. First, if we want to avoid experiencing an impoverished old age hampered by poor health care, workers must save more to prepare for their retirement. Second, workers must pay higher taxes, in order to finance health care benefits for the elderly. Third, existing benefits for the elderly must be reduced, in order to be in line with current savings rates and taxes. Fourth, people must work longer and retire later. None of these imperatives seem likely to occur. We clearly have a severe set of problems looming with the aging of our population.

Here I will concentrate on the health care problems. The tsunami of elderly people will naturally create more pressure on Medicare, our governmental system for providing care to the disabled and elderly, and I will get into the history of Medicare later on. For now, I want to point out that Medicare will have to adapt to the cost pressure created by the aging of the US population. So long as fee-for-service health care dominates, that means lower reimbursements for providers. This will put more pressure on employer-sponsored insurance to cross-subsidize the Medicare deficits providers will face. Severe pressure on Medicare will create equal pressure on employer-sponsored insurance.

The Medicare beneficiary population will increase from 47.4 million in 2010 to 76.9 million in 2030. That is the steep part of the curve, although the decade of the 2030s will add another 7 million beneficiaries and reap most of the aging crop of baby boomers.[11] The peak of the baby boom hit age 65 in 2022, but the onset of costly health problems is now delayed until around age 70, so the back half of the 2020s should be when these costs start to rise disproportionately. That second half of the 2020s is also when the severe decrease in the number of workers per Medicare recipient will reach its nadir.

The immediate question is, Can Medicare afford it? To answer this, let's first establish an understanding of how Medicare works. Medicare is divided into four parts, helpfully identified as A, B, C, and D. Medicare Part A covers hospital care, skilled nursing facility care (to an extent), home visits, and home care. Part B supports physician services, laboratory services, durable medical equipment, and outpatient hospital services. Part D is the Medicare drug benefit, which I will review in chapter 5, while Part C is now known universally as Medicare Advantage, the privatized Medicare program operated by for-profit and nonprofit companies, which is the subject of chapter 6. For now, I will focus on Parts A and B.

Part B is financed by the Supplementary Medical Insurance (SMI) Trust Fund (as is Part D). This trust fund, in turn, is supported by annual beneficiary premiums and general tax revenues. As a result, it cannot become bankrupt—premiums can go up and new general revenues can be applied. That is true, however, only so long as beneficiaries are willing to pay higher premiums and elected representatives are willing to deficit spend ever-higher amounts. Part B costs are rising, and that is likely to continue. But the SMI Trust Fund cannot become insolvent.

On the other hand, the Hospital Insurance (HI) Trust Fund, which finances Part A, can go bankrupt. It is based on a payroll tax contribution of 2.9 percent, rising to 3.8 percent for couples earning more than $250,000. It is supplemented somewhat by accumulated interest.[12] The HI Trust Fund has always had a surplus, but it is watched carefully by health care policy experts, as its funding is limited by the payroll tax base. That is an ongoing problem as the number of workers continues to drop over the next decade.

Health policy experts and federal actuaries are highly concerned about the number of years when there will be a surplus remaining in the HI Trust Fund. The chronic cost pressures coming from fee-for-service entrepreneurialism mean that no single fix can be sufficient for long. By 2009, the estimate of the fund's remaining solvency was down to eight years. Then the Affordable Care Act (ACA) entered the picture. While known, appropriately, for its efforts to increase access, the ACA also put new payroll taxes in place (the kicker for the wealthy, as noted above), which brought in more revenue. But this was insufficient, and in 2011, new legislation cut Medicare payments to hospitals by 2 percent. This created some stability, and in the 2013–2017 period, the number of years until bankruptcy varied between twelve and sixteen years. The HI Trust Fund itself ran an annual deficit from 2008 to 2015, and then, after small surpluses, shifted to a deficit again in 2018 and 2019. The threat of insolvency seems more real than ever before, and this is just starting, as demographic changes are now coming to bear. In 2023, the current estimate is solvency until 2031, with a reprieve of three years attributed to rising payrolls and, hence, payroll tax revenues.[13] The HI Trust Fund has not yet been insolvent, and the Social Security Act has no provisions for such an event. But since there are no legislative provisions to use general revenues for this fund, Congress would have to act, or the fund would only be able to offer partial payments to hospitals.[14]

Most sources agree that the costs of Medicare are inflating much less quickly than those for private insurance plans. From 2009 to 2019, the various sources of inflation had driven an average annual growth in private health insurance costs of 3.6 percent, while the increase in Medicare spending per enrollee averaged 1.9 percent. The latter is very similar to background inflation over the same period.[15] It is some comfort, as we look at these numbers, to realize that Medicare costs, at least today, are not rising as quickly because of an aging population.[16] Health economists have been relatively surprised, and in many ways heartened, by the fact that Medicare costs are well below projections from a decade ago. The Congressional Budget Office, in a recent letter to Senator Sheldon Whitehouse, chairman of the Committee on the Budget, cited three reasons academics have given for this favorable shortfall: (1) reduced rates of payment to providers, (2) cost reductions for cardiovascular disease care, and (3) a relative shift in the use of technology to address highly expensive medical problems.[17]

There is another aspect, however. The Medicare Payment Advisory Commission is funded by Congress, and its mission is to report to Congress and the Centers for Medicare & Medicaid Services, making recommendations about the funding for and operation of Medicare. Its work is widely read and greatly respected. MedPAC has argued that while it appears that Medicare has prices under control, the number of beneficiaries and the intensity of illnesses (and hence costs) per beneficiary are increasing. The commission begins the argument with simple numbers about growth: health care spending as a percentage of our nation's gross domestic product (GDP) has increased from 7.9 percent in 1975 to 18.3 percent in 2020; private health insurance increased from 1.8 percent of GDP to 5.2 percent; and Medicare from 1 percent of GDP to 3.9 percent. That growth, they predict, will continue.[18]

Simply put, demographics are slowly driving the country toward Medicare insolvency, especially in light of the diminishing base of working individuals. The only likely answer is rate cuts. That will mean private payers—specifically, employers—paying more.

Federal Spending and Deficits in the 2020s

The other alternative for the government is to fund Medicare as necessary from general revenues, which contributes to long-term deficits. This alternative leads us to the second long-term trend to examine: the ability of the government to spend as deficits continue to grow. Congress could decide to spend more without increasing revenues, alleviating the pressure on Medicare, or it could raise taxes to do the same, without incurring more deficits. Experts estimate that increasing the payroll tax to 4 percent would bring in $490 billion to the HI Trust Fund over ten years.[19] While that seems like a simple solution, the federal government's policy toward tax increases and deficit spending in recent decades indicates that this is unlikely to happen.

A good deal of information on the US budget deficits has recently been compiled by the Congressional Budget Office in its 2023 *Long-Term Budget Outlook*.[20] (The data in the face of the pandemic are harrowing from a deficit point of view, but numbers from 2020 to 2021 represent atypical years, given the one-time impact of COVID.) The average deficit for the last fifty years has been 3.7 percent of GDP, and it is increasing. The CBO estimates that the deficit will reach 6 percent of GDP by 2033, and 10 percent by 2053. More alarming, the cumulative debt—that is, the total amount owed by the government—will rise from 98 percent of GDP to something like 181 percent by 2053.

These estimates are extraordinary, but future indebtedness is driven by the cost of borrowing—that is, the interest rate on the debt. According to the CBO report, interest rates are predicted to rise from 2.5 percent in 2023 to 6.7 percent by 2053. The CBO also assumes that "rising interest rates and persistently large primary deficits [will] cause interest costs to almost triple in relation to GDP between 2023 and 2053. Spending on the major health care programs and Social Security—driven by the aging of the population and growing health care costs—also boosts federal outlays significantly over the next 30 years." Major health care spending, mainly for Medicare and Medicaid, is expected to grow from 5.8 percent of the GDP in 2023 to 8.6 percent by 2053. These predictions are based on the twin assumptions of growth in the intensity of services and the aging of the US population. Meanwhile, GDP growth itself is anticipated to slow from 2.4 percent per year (from 1993 to 2022) to 1.5 percent in 2053. Again, demographics play a role, but so does global warming, bringing down GDP growth by 0.6 percent by 2053.

It is worth comparing the CBO's projected outlook for spending on the major social programs in just a bit more detail. The portion of noninterest federal spending attributed to Social Security should only increase from 24 percent in 2023 to 28 percent in 2053. The number of beneficiaries should also increase over that time period, from 67 million to 97 million. Like Medicare hospital insurance, Social Security has a trust fund for Old Age and Survivors Insurance as well as Disability Insurance. These funds are expected to be exhausted in 2032 and 2052 respectively, but the CBO presumes that the government will continue to meet its obligations.

Health care programs, mainly Medicare and Medicaid, are a different story. They are projected to grow from 27 percent of noninterest spending in 2023 to 38 percent in 2053. As a result of this pressure from health care, discretionary spending would decrease from 30 percent to 24 percent. Social Security, and particularly Medicare and Medicaid, would crowd out spending on all other governmental programs. In 2023, health programs cost the equivalent of 5.8 percent of GDP, and discretionary spending, 6.5 percent. By 2053, health costs are expected to rise to 8.6 percent of a much larger GDP, and discretionary spending is anticipated to be down to 5.4 percent. The crowding out of other social services caused by expanding health care costs will become even more prominent over the next two decades.

Health care is driven not only by the aging of the population, but also by the health care costs per person. The CBO predicts that more old people alone accounts for only one-third of the projected increase. But the aging of the population also drives up costs per person, which are anticipated to increase by 1 percent per year faster over the next thirty years for Medicare, compared with the previous thirty years. Medicaid growth is even faster, at 1.1 percent.

Given this and the overall budget picture, it is clear that pressure will remain on the Centers for Medicare & Medicaid Services to reduce costs per beneficiary. At least for hospital and physician services (and, very recently, drugs), the government has the critical, powerful lever of naming the prices. Slowing the rate of increase or lowering reimbursements seems to be the only option.

If you are operating a business and buying health insurance, these numbers cannot be reassuring. Your costs for health care will increase as the relative governmental rate of payment for providers decreases if providers are not going to accept reduced overall reimbursements. Looked at together, demographic aging and the growth of governmental deficits create the certainty of rising stress on the health care system—specifically employers' rising costs of providing insurance.

The Congressional Budget Office is not optimistic about the future these numbers portend, and in many ways the CBO is consistently attempting to awaken legislators and create some resolution around the issue of fiscal integrity. The CBO notes that rising debt increases private and public borrowing costs, which slows economic production. There is some good news in that the Trump tax cuts of 2017 for individuals will sunset in the mid-2020s. But by 2033, tax revenues will not rise sufficiently to keep up with increasing outlays, particularly for interest rates and health care.

Predicting interest rates is no easy business. No one was anticipating a decade of very low interest rates from 2010 to 2020. Moreover, no one really saw the tremendous increase in these rates pursued by the Federal Reserve Bank through 2023, to combat an unanticipated bout of inflation. In 2017, net interest costs for the federal government were 1.4 percent of the gross domestic product, but in 2023 they were on track to reach 2.5 percent of GDP.[21] So, over time, the CBO predictions look quite reasonable

The debt load also increases the likelihood of higher rates of inflation and erosion in global confidence in the dollar as the key international reserve currency. Given the events of the great recession, the CBO also fears an expanding risk for a fiscal crisis. If investors become worried about the US debt load, the value of Treasury securities decreases and interest rates then rise, which leads to a vicious cycle. From a business perspective, all of these considerations are realistic. We are seeing some of this come true in 2022–2023 as unanticipated rapid increases in inflation are leading to rapid increases in interest rates, which should eventually exacerbate the deficit problems.

Skepticism about this ugly prospect comes from two corners. One holds that the situation can be addressed through greater taxation. (The Biden administration has recently tested that thesis.) The other corner states that deficits simply do not matter. I will take these arguments up, if somewhat briefly.

The "increase taxes" camp is fueled by economic research over the last fifteen years, which shows that tax rates on the wealthy have dropped, and that wealth has moved from the middle class to the very rich in a way that is neither fair nor efficient.[22] (This literature was briefly reviewed in chapter 1.) The top 1 percent increased their share of wealth from 11 percent in 1978 to 20 percent today—a shocking number. This is possible because American tax rates are fairly flat across income deciles: from the tenth percentile to the ninety-ninth percentile, the tax rate is never more than a few percentage points off of 28 percent—except at the very top end, or the top 400 earners, where the tax rate actually dips to just over 20 percent.

To economists who have advised several Democratic office seekers, most prominently Elizabeth Warren, these stark statistics make the case for higher taxes on wealth. A key part of the argument is that at one time, when wealth was more evenly distributed in the 1960s and 1970s, top marginal tax rates were nearly 90 percent, and the estate tax was greater than 70 percent, with very few deductibles. Today those rates cluster around 40 percent. The progressive tax rates of the 1950s and 1960s, these economists argue, were no more or no less associated with economic growth than the incredibly regressive rates we have today.

This diagnosis leads to a relatively straightforward therapy: raise taxes. Emmanuel Saez and Gabriel Zucman call for careful policing of multinational corporation profits and aggressive taxation of *evasion*, or the practice of storing profits in countries where capital gains are taxed at much lower rates. In addition, they argue that tax rates for the very rich should move back to the levels we had in the 1950s.[23] Given the concentration of wealth in the very highest income groups, aggressive taxation here can lead to substantial revenue.

For our purposes, more equitable taxation on corporations and the rich could bring relief to the deficits that are predicted. Unfortunately, however, that relief seems unlikely. With a razor-thin majority in the House and Senate, the Biden administration cannot seriously consider anything close to these kinds of tax increases. That will have to wait for an election of landslide proportions for the Democrats—not unthinkable, but having a low probability. While tax increases are something to consider, depending on the way voters move, I think we can put aside greater taxation as a way to solve our health insurance cost issue.

There is a second way to subvert the CBO's anxieties about deficits. An increasing number of policymakers, including economists, question whether deficits really matter that much, or at all. The followers of what is known as *modern monetary theory* (MMT) make these points most assiduously. But before I evaluate these arguments, I should lightly review economists' accepted wisdom on deficits.

A widely cited National Bureau of Economic Research paper published in 1995 by Laurence Ball and N. Gregory Mankiw, provides an even-handed analysis of mainstream economists' view of deficits.[24] These authors noted that there was controversy about how important deficits were, but they generally accepted the standard arguments that the CBO follows today. Deficits reduce national savings, which, in turn, reduce investment and, eventually, exports. Moreover, assets flow abroad. These processes affect interest and exchange rates, with a natural tendency for interest rates to rise. This results in less innovation, lower productivity, and decreased purchases of domestically produced goods. Their theory seems sound.

Ball and Mankiw admitted that the empirical data on these points was spotty—and mostly consisted of lessons drawn from broad macroeconomic events (mostly disasters). More importantly, they allowed that as long as the GDP increased at a faster rate than existing interest rates, and debt grew more slowly than the GDP, then a country could outrun deficits.

Ball and Mankiw warned, however, that rolling over debt is a gamble. Such a strategy would lay many potential problems off into the future—that is, all the benefits of deficit spending would accrue to the current population, with the crunch of rising interest rates borne by a future one. Then there is the fear of a hard landing. Economists like to think that the economy operates according to certain laws and, therefore, is amenable to mathematical analysis. But crashes, like the one in 2009, do occur and are usually not predicted by the math. Hence the mainstream economists' analysis views growing deficits dimly but admits to uncertainty and to their arguments being built on an abundance of caution.

History has proven the wisdom of not asserting certainty. The United States has racked up huge deficits in the twenty-first century, but the mainstream economic prediction of doom attending these deficits has not come to pass. Most middle-of-the-road economists now admit to more uncertainty, but that does not mean that they are endorsing modern monetary theory.

MMT relies on the control that sovereign nations have over their currency. Advocates for this theory see a deficit on the government's side as a private sector surplus. They also believe that any inflation risk can be controlled by increasing taxation, and thus propose that governments should be willing to print more money and ignore deficits.[25] (The economics underlying this is well beyond what we need for our discussion here.)[26] But MMT economists do have the ear of the Democratic Party's left wing, for all the obvious reasons.

There are some (perhaps more mainstream) economists who do not subscribe to MMT but who nonetheless caution that we should be a bit less focused on deficits as we think through policy issues, including health policy. Olivier Blanchard explores the limits of deficit spending in his recent book, *Fiscal Policy Under Low Interest Rates*.[27] His point essentially is that so long as actual growth rates are greater than real, safe interest rates, then large amounts of debt might be appropriate. In this regard, he suggests that Japan's experience with high amounts of debt might be instructive. Blanchard shows how the opinion of academic economists has shifted over the last thirty years, in order to accommodate large budget deficits. David Cutler has recently applied these points, and Blanchard's conclusions, to health care, warning against making big cuts in Medicare and Medicaid to reduce the budget deficit.[28]

Be this as it may, from a business perspective, the problem with deficits looks real and is intimately tied to demographics. Some might argue that higher taxation on the wealthy will save the day. Others might believe that economists, and the world, will come to accept that deficits do not matter. Business leaders, many politicians, and most citizens will probably put little stock in either of those positions. Going forward, they need to be prepared for stringent budgets for Medicare (and all federal programs), which will put increased downward pressure on provider reimbursements, a move that has clear implications for employer-sponsored health insurance.

A Shift in Physician Workforce Demographics

The two developments discussed above, the aging of the US population and growing budget deficits, are probably the most important long-term drivers of health policy, but three other durable trends will also influence health care's evolution. The first of these three additional trends—the composition of the physician workforce—is more sociological than economic or financial.

The historical archetype for a physician's practice was either as a solo practitioner or a member of a two-to-three-person group, organized as a professional corporation. (These practices were assertively for profit and were treated as such by the law.) The doctors billed fee-for-service charges and served as members of a voluntary medical staff at a non-profit hospital. The latter might entail being on a hospital's quality of care committees or governing medical staff, but the hospital did not employ them. Fee-for-service rates and small independent physicians' practices went hand in hand.

The American Medical Association and local state medical societies discouraged physicians from being employed by hospitals or large medical groups. Organized medicine feared that such employment might influence doctors' decision making, deflecting their commitment to individual patients. This isolation also served another purpose, in that a medical society or the AMA would be the only organizing structure for the medical profession.

Through the middle of the twentieth century, in most states the AMA was successful in getting *corporate practice of medicine laws* passed, prohibiting corporations from practicing medicine or employing a physician to provide professional medical services.[29] The rationale for such laws was threefold: (1) allowing corporations to employ doctors would lead to the commercialization of medicine; (2) corporations' commitments to shareholders might not align with doctors' commitments to patients; and (3) corporate employment might interfere with independent medical judgment.

Be this as it may, the corporate practice of medicine does hold some benefits for health care systems, so there are countless exceptions to these laws today. From a historical viewpoint, the corporate practice of medicine laws has long demonstrated medical societies' historical commitment to an independent, small-practice foundation for health care and opposition to managed care. Physicians were slow to move into a more corporate employment structure.

But that has changed, happening slowly during much of the latter part of the twentieth century, and now accelerating. In 2021, the AMA noted that for the first time, less than half of all physicians worked in private practice.[30] The pace of change has been even more rapid in the last five years, including through the pandemic.[31] The most recent data suggest that the percentage of physicians employed by hospitals or corporations increased from 62.2 percent in January 2019 to 73.9 percent in January 2022.[32] One estimate later in 2022 was that hospitals employed 52 percent of physicians, and private equity or other corporations employed another 22 percent.[33] This suggests a tremendous shift through the pandemic period.

Further change will be even more rapid, given the vector of physician workforce demographics. Women now make up more than 50 percent of medical school graduates.[34] Among female doctors, only 35.7 percent are practice owners, and 31.7 percent of those under age

45 are in private practice. Over the next decade, the norm will increasingly be that doctors will be employed by hospitals and corporations who will develop their health care strategies and use doctors to provide the care.[35] This is a complete paradigm shift, compared with American medicine through the twentieth century.

The ascendance of physician employment has important implications for the financial structure of the US health care system. Private practices and small group practices were not (and generally could not) be organized to take financial risks, but they fit very well into a fee-for-service environment. The AMA's worldview was cohesive: promote small practices, oppose any alternatives to fee-for-service structures, keep corporations out of health care, and avoid any overall business rationalizations that diminished the profession's influence. But physician demographics are changing that stance, with health care poised to become more corporately structured—and a corporate structure can accommodate managed care. Large practices, supported by appropriate care management programs, can make a profit on capitation payments. Employed doctors are better team members, and care management is definitely a team sport.

The shift in the structure of physician practices, as well as the demographics underlying that shift, promote the possibility of a more widespread use of managed care. That factor will grow in importance through the 2020s.

Growth of Underinsurance in the Employer Sector

The fourth major trend in American health care is the thinning of health insurance for the average employee. I have discussed how the majority of employees today get their insurance directly from their employer, who self-insures for the health care costs of employees. They are aided in this by health insurance companies, who, in this regard, take on the role of third-party administrators. An insurer provides a variety of insurance services but does not take on risk. That risk resides with the employer, who makes the ultimate decision about the available benefits.

I have also talked about the structure of out-of-pocket health insurance payments. As with any type of insurance, the insurer (employer) pays for certain services but not others, being driven principally by the triad of deductibles, co-payments, and co-insurance. These devices help define the *risk-sharing costs* for an employee and the overall actuarial value of that health insurance policy. The *actuarial value* is the portion of a benefit that an insurance plan covers—for example, if risk sharing adds up to 20 percent of the total costs, the actuarial value is 80 percent.

The other key part of any health insurance plan, including the self-insured variety, is the degree to which the providers are expected to manage care, captured in the now familiar health maintenance organization and preferred provider organization formats. PPOs are not expected to manage care much, whereas in HMO plans, the beneficiary typically has to choose a primary care doctor, and that doctor has at least some responsibility to keep an eye on the costs and intensity of that person's care. Finally, most employers require their employees to pay a portion of the premium for their insurance, a *premium contribution* (distinguished from out-of-pocket costs, or cost sharing). Cost sharing, premium contributions, and plan types outline the structure of an insurance plan offered to an employee, and employees are often allowed to choose between certain permutations.

At the beginning of the twentieth century, employers had a great deal of flexibility in the design of their plans. Obamacare changed some of that, since the Affordable Care Act modified ERISA requirements (see chapter 7). I will foreshadow that discussion by noting here that the ACA required ERISA-sponsored plans to restrict cost sharing by maintaining at least a 60 percent actuarial value, meaning that the plan had to cover at least 60 percent of the costs of ill health for an individual employee.[36] To put these rules in perspective, the Kaiser Family Foundation has estimated that for the average family plan in 2008, out-of-pocket spending / cost sharing was 12 percent of the total costs of coverage; the family's premium contribution was just over 19 percent; and the employer's contribution was 68 percent. By 2018, that average employer contribution had dropped to 66 percent.[37]

The distinction between cost sharing and premium contributions is important. Premium contributions are the other cost of health insurance borne by workers, in addition to their out-of-pocket costs. Before the ACA, premium contributions were largely unregulated by ERISA. The ACA changed that, making sure employer-sponsored insurance would be affordable for employees and creating a ceiling for their premium contribution: 9.83 percent of an employee's household income.

The ACA therefore regulates both actuarial value / out of pocket costs (60 percent actuarial value) and employee contributions (a percentage of household income). These issues are often conflated. To be clear, an employer has two ways to reduce the costs of health insurance for a worker: out-of-pocket payments and premium contributions. Both are now regulated—to some degree. The subsidiary point is that whenever one examines the contribution of employers to the overall costs of health insurance, it is important to realize that they cover only about two-thirds of the cost for their employees.

Unfortunately, the ACA regulations do not ensure as much affordability as one might expect. In 1999, the annual premium for family coverage was $5,791. In 2022, it was $22,463, a real testament to the runaway inflation in American health care.[38] This increase in premium costs easily outstrips overall inflation and increases in workers' earnings, especially in the first decade of the twenty-first century. The increased cost of premiums has not led employers to abandon health insurance, and 99 percent of firms with more than 200 workers offer health insurance. Smaller workplaces, however, are definitely showing signs of stress. The percentage of all firms offering health insurance has fallen from a high of 68 percent at the beginning of the century to 51 percent in 2022.[39]

Responding to the twenty-first-century inflation in premium cost, the key development in the structure of health plans offered by employers in this century is the *high deductible health plan* (HDHP). The concept underlying this type of plan is that an increase in the deductible (the amount an individual pays before the insurance kicks in) forces the beneficiary to act as a consumer and carefully weigh the need for care. It can be supported with a *tax-advantaged health savings account* or *health reimbursement arrangements* that the employer can make available for employees to help with out-of-pocket costs. Note that this language of consumerism has retained legitimacy, even in the face of insights generated by behavioral economics that suggest otherwise.

The high deductible plans were basically nonexistent at the beginning of the century, but they rapidly replaced standard HMO and PPO plans. Over the last decade, about 30 percent of employers have come to offer HDHPs, with the percentage offering such a plan now being closer to two-thirds of employers with more than 1,000 workers. Approximately one-third of the workers in large firms are now enrolled in HDHPs.[40] It is worth noting how amazingly American the high deductible plan is, as it is basically unheard of in other developed countries' health care systems.

Driven by the HDHP phenomenon, but also bleeding into the typical PPO plan, most employees face relatively high deductibles today. In 2007, 58 percent of the beneficiaries in firms offering health care plans had a general annual deductible in the $1–$499 range, and only 4 percent were more than $3,000. By 2022, only 8 percent were in the $1–$499 range and 16 percent were more than $3,000.[41] These high deductibles allow employers to push more of the costs of health insurance onto their employees, reducing the costs of benefits for the employer.

High deductible plans themselves have never been shown to produce more appropriate uses of health services: they cut out both necessary and unnecessary care.[42] When individuals facing high deductibles decide to forego necessary care, and potentially have worse outcomes, they are *underinsured*. A health care insurance policy exists in order to ensure that a patient can afford care. High deductibles can lead to underinsurance—and very poor health outcomes.

Premium contributions, on the other hand, have remained relatively constant over much of the twenty-first century. The Kaiser Family Foundation has found that the percentage of premiums paid for by employees has generally averaged just over 28 percent during the last twenty years. While a constant should be good, the problem for beneficiaries is that over the same time period, the costs of health care premiums have consistently grown faster than income. By 2022, the average *monthly* premium contribution had reached $508 for family coverage.[43] To put this in perspective, consider that the median wage in 2019 was $19.33 per hour, translating into an annual wage of about $40,000 for a full-time worker.[44] Premium shares, on average, would then be about 15 percent of before-tax wages for an insured individual. So the ACA's limit on premium contributions of 9.83 percent of average wages comes into play for many employers.

When one adds together both premium contributions and cost shares, at this point an employer is usually covering about two-thirds of the health insurance costs, and the remainder is provided by the employee. Employers have been squeezed by cross-subsidy costs as the government attempts to put the brakes on Medicare spending. This cross-subsidy pressure has grown, and so have employer costs. Thus the easiest way to reduce costs was to put more of an onus on employees, through cost sharing.

Obamacare has created ceilings and floors to restrict this strategy. But the point that employer-sponsored insurance has thinned has not been lost on employees, who must deal with ever-higher premium contributions and out-of-pocket costs. In many cases, people simply cannot afford their health care. Bankruptcies spawned by medical bills remain unfortunately (and, in many cases, tragically) common.[45] Recent polling indicates that 24 percent of Americans report that they have medical or dental bills that are past due, and which they cannot afford to pay.[46]

Employers typically are not aware of the social costs of increasing premium shares and out-of-pocket spending. When done in small percentage changes over years, increasing employee contributions can be seen as a way to address annual budget challenges. Each incremental step, on an annual basis, can be acceptable; it is the accumulation that is leading to increasingly frequent situations in which people defer health care or face medical bankruptcies. Perhaps more important for businesses, though, are the federal limits, which mean that this strategy will reach its endpoint as a way to enhance employer affordability.

Provider (and Insurer) Consolidation

The fifth and final important trend over the course of the first two decades of the twenty-first century is provider consolidation. In chapter 3, I recounted that a hospital and its integrated delivery system had two choices about how to maximize income: (1) manage care to reduce waste and make a profit margin on that waste reduction; or (2) bulk up and use the market power of a multiple hospital system, along with its affiliated physicians, to bargain better and get higher rates of payment for fee-for-service care from commercial insurers. That surplus on the commercial side could be used to cross-subsidize the lower amounts paid by the government. (Note that I use cross-subsidy language as a shorthand for lower governmental rates and higher employer-sponsored rates, and not as a justification. I fully accept the argument by many economists that providers would maximize reimbursements, even without lower governmental rates.) Bulking up is easier in many ways than managing care, which is why we have seen more consolidation in the twenty-first century.[47] Insurers pursue the same strategy, to good effect.[48]

The government will worry, however, if markets become too concentrated—that is, some competitors get so much market share that they will be able to act like a monopoly and reduce competition. Here, antitrust laws will come into play, enforced by the Federal Trade Commission and the Department of Justice. These authorities have certain tests they use to decide if the threat of a monopoly is too high— that is if the market is too concentrated. For health care purposes, first, they define the market in which the competition occurs, usually a metropolitan area. Second, they use a rather simple mathematical formula to define how concentrated the market is. This is called the *Herfindahl-Hirschman Index* (HHI). The HHI is calculated by summing the squares of the market share of all competitors. Thus a perfect monopoly has a Herfindahl-Hirschman index of 10,000 (100×100). The HHI for two competitors, each with a 50 percent share, is 5,000 ([50×50] + [50×50]). Ten competitors, each with a 10 percent share, have an HHI score of 1,000. The Department of Justice considers markets with an HHI score of less than 1,500 as not concentrated; from 1,500 to 2,500 as moderately concentrated; and above 2,500 as highly concentrated. Most hospital markets are highly concentrated today.

Medicare policy is not driving consolidation, since the government sets its own prices, so stronger negotiating power isn't relevant.[49] All consolidation is aimed at commercial insurers. (I leave aside the definition of markets, which, in many ways, is just as important. The Elzinga-Hogarty market test and its lasting impact are well elucidated in Dranove and Burns's book, *Big Med*.)[50]

The effort to squeeze higher profit margins from commercial insurers has worked. MedPAC notes that from 1989 to 1998, the average margin for hospitals receiving Medicare payments was 3.8 percent, while it was 4.8 percent for payments from all payers. From 1999 to 2008, however, Medicare margins declined and commercial margins increased. And from 2009 to 2018, Medicare margins fell to −8.5 percent, while those from all payers was 6.4 percent.[51] (These data fit neatly with the information on hospital strategy presented in chapter 3.)

It should come as no surprise that these data are disputed, especially by the hospital industry, which does not want consolidation characterized as merely a way to increase costs in the system. Admitting that most likely would increase some regulatory pressure against future mergers. The hospital industry claims that after mergers, costs are not affected and quality improves, but there is little proof of that. For example, the Congressional Budget Office recently reviewed all the available material on quality and mergers, finding no relationship.[52] A recent, very thorough analysis of insurance claims reached the same conclusion.[53] At this point, most independent observers see hospital mergers solely as a revenue ploy aimed at commercial insurance rates.[54]

Consolidation is not just a matter of hospital mergers, however. Hospitals' employment of physicians can also lead to better reimbursements from Medicare. Medicare pays more for a service rendered in a hospital's outpatient department than it does if delivered in a physician's office. Moving services into a hospital improves physicians' payments by Medicare. (The CMS is not asleep at the wheel, as it is currently involved in litigation with hospital associations to make payments be site neutral.)

Physicians are willing to give up their independence to get higher payment rates. The Kaiser Family Foundation, for instance, cites one study showing that an increase in the proportion of physicians' practices owned by hospitals led to a 12 percent increase in premiums for private health insurance plans, as well as another study, using private insurance data, indicating that hospital/physician integration led to a 14 percent increase in prices for the same service.[55]

Some physicians remain wary of hospital employment. Their alternative path is to form large physician groups and get market power from that approach. It works. The Kaiser Family Foundation, reviewing the literature on physicians' horizontal consolidation, found that doctors in the most concentrated markets charged fees that were 14–30 percent higher than those in the least concentrated markets. The foundation also cited another example, where the merger of orthopedic groups in Pennsylvania led to increases of 15–25 percent across commercial payers.[56]

This phenomenon of horizontal physician consolidation is growing, engendered by venture capital firms that see an opportunity for much higher profit margins. These firms install professional management in the consolidated groups, and they understand the importance of leverage. (More on this development in chapter 8.) For now, consolidation remains a very viable margin improvement tool for providers. It has been occurring for the last thirty years, and it will persist. It is a very potent mechanism for increasing payments from commercial insurers and, thereby, increasing employer costs.

The Effects of Five Key Trends

In summary, the above numbers reveal trends that will shape health care through the 2020s and probably toward 2050. The aging US population creates many more people who expect the government to provide health care, and fewer workers are and will be available to support the aged. The government increasingly must use deficit spending to finance these costs, but most legislators will not convert to modern monetary theory. Instead, they will look for ways to cut costs. Since the federal government can name its prices, at least regarding hospital and physician reimbursements, that offers a solution for governmental payers. The Congressional Budget Office has recently reaffirmed that price controls are by far the most effective way to reduce health care costs.[57] But as that occurs, organized providers will negotiate with commercial insurers and work hard to get better payment rates to make up for their losses from the governmental programs—the cross-subsidy ploy.

The cross-subsidy pressure that provider consolidation creates will lead some employers to place more of the costs of health insurance on their workers through deductibles and co-payments, leaving at least some portion of their insured workers unable to afford care. But further movement on that front is hemmed in by the ACA's controls. Meanwhile, on the provider side, the negotiators will not be just hospitals and small independent physicians' practices, but will also include large corporations made up of many hospitals and doctors, as well as large multispecialty physician groups. Physicians are increasingly open to working in such arrangements, and that will become the norm as we move into the next decade.

None of this is new information. By 2000, it was clear that we were moving toward deficit spending, the baby boomer avalanche was going to occur, and provider consolidation was a real phenomenon. The changes I have discussed in the physician workforce have been slowly accelerating. While the use of bigger deductibles to reduce employers' health insurance costs had started by 2005, it gathered steam after 2010. Throughout the 2010s, each of these trends gained momentum.

The average benefits manager at a large corporation does not necessarily notice the dynamics created by these five trends. Prices increase each year, but inflation is accepted as more or less a given. Another year passes. Experts lament the steady increase in costs, and prominent chief executive officers start their own new initiatives to find a better way to finance health care. But there appears to be little perception that this set of very sturdy trends are simultaneously undermining the logic of an employer-sponsored insurance program. Providers will be starved by the governmental payers and will turn more strongly toward charging higher rates to employers, following a fee-for-service logic. Consolidation will help them leverage higher rates from insurers acting on behalf of employers. Costs must rise, and other employer methods to reduce costs, such as pushing them off on employees, are being closed off. Employers will face a real affordability crisis as we move into the 2020s.

This is the environment for employer-sponsored insurance that has evolved over the last twenty years. But it is only half the story. The other half is the development of government-sponsored insurance. To understand how this type of insurance fits into the picture, it is important to understand the history of the government's involvement with health insurance. In the next chapters, I'll discuss pharmacy and drug costs and provide a more detailed description of Medicare—in particular, its privatized form, Medicare Advantage. I will also review the huge new foundation for health insurance that is the byproduct of the policy reform known as Obamacare—the Affordable Care Act. With these pieces in place, I can then examine the potential replacement of commercial insurance with government-sponsored insurance, and the coagulation of the governmental programs (Medicare, Medicaid, and the ACA exchanges) as employers leave the field. This evolutionary path toward socialized health insurance becomes possible as businesses realize that governmental programs can control costs, while commercial insurance cannot.

CHAPTER FIVE

The Strange World of
Pharmacy Commerce

TO THIS POINT, I have described the health care system mostly by discussing the work that doctors and hospitals do. These services are two
of the three key products in health care—the third is pharmaceuticals.
(I am mostly leaving long-term care to the side in my discussion.) The
pharmacy part of the health care bill is not small. Somewhere between
15 and 25 percent of employers' health care budgets go toward
medications.

Aspects of payments for pharmaceuticals will reinforce the insights
developed in reviewing the other sectors—that is, governmental reimbursement is more rational and ultimately is likely to replace the commercial sector. This is an important corroboration in the evolutionary
path toward socialized health insurance. The entire architecture of the
development and sale of medications is different from medical treatments in hospitals or other health care services. If pharmaceuticals are
heading into the same troubled waters I have projected for the rest of
the health care system, this provides further support for my prediction
of a future with socialized health insurance.

It's also worth noting that regulatory oversight is distinctly different for medicines, compared with physician/hospital services. The Food
and Drug Administration (FDA) plays a central role in approving the

introduction of medications into commerce, focusing on both efficacy and safety. There is nothing similar in the physician/hospital sector of the health care economy. On the other hand, until 2022, there was no governmental control over the pricing of medications, unlike the rest of health care. Instead, almost all of the cost-control functions were done by private firms, called *pharmacy benefit managers*, which had grown up as pharmacies began to play a more important part in the health care economy.

The federal government's role has a historical explanation. The FDA was a Progressive-era institution that responded to food and drug disasters. It was built on a presumption of regulation to protect public safety. On the other hand, the federal government did not begin to pay for most Medicare medications until quite late, with the passage of Medicare Part D in 2003. It took the government over twenty years after the start of paying doctors and hospitals for Medicare beneficiaries' care to begin to dictate reimbursements for medications.

The point is, medications are different. If, however, the same themes emerge in pharmacy commerce that I have noted in the context of hospitals and doctors, that will add validity to my overall thesis regarding the ascendance of government-sponsored programs and the retreat of those that are employer sponsored. To presage this conclusion, I will discuss how private players have largely failed and how employers have allowed this to happen. The result is that the federal government is stepping in to regulate prices on behalf of its health care beneficiaries. The long-term effect of this will be new cost pressures on employers, which they have not previously faced.

Pharmaceutical Manufacturers and Manufacturing

Any discussion of pharmacy commerce must begin with the pharmaceutical manufacturers, who undertake drug discovery, testing, patent development, and marketing. It is a large industry, dominated by huge firms like Pfizer, Novartis, and Merck. The history of pharmaceuticals, going back to the nineteenth century, when many of today's current firms took shape, was about painkillers—in particular, morphine and other opiates. That changed when researchers at the University of Toronto discovered insulin's role in treating diabetes. Within a few years, Eli Lilly, an Indianapolis firm, was granted an exclusive right to purify insulin derived from cows and pigs, with a patent on the collection process. That marked the beginning of the era of pharmaceutical therapy for diseases, as opposed to treatments of pain symptoms. The current drug industry, distributed into many branches of treatment, did not really take shape until the end of World War II, with the development of antimicrobials, particularly penicillin.

Because several researchers discovered and began to produce penicillin somewhat independently, from the point of view of pharmacy commerce, the critical business issue was, Who owned the discovery? Most researchers working in the first half of the twentieth century agreed that a patent on a life-saving medication would be tantamount to unseemly commercialization. Jonas Salk, when asked who owned the patent to the polio vaccine, replied, "Well, the people, I would say. There is no patent. Could you patent the sun?"[1]

This view was shared by the US Patent Office and the United States' courts, which believed that "products of nature" should remain in the public domain. But over the course of the late 1940s, the views of both the Patent Office and the courts evolved. The critical moment came when Lederle Labs was granted a patent—and, hence, exclusive monopoly—for aureomycin (another new antibiotic) after a five-year regulatory process. Eventually, patents were also distributed for penicillin. The modern pharmaceutical firm business model was born.

Going forward, I will use the term *Pharma* to refer to the manufacturers of drugs. This will include mainline pharmaceutical manufacturers, such as Merck and Lilly, as well as those firms that produce mostly biologically based products, as opposed to chemically based ones. The latter group refers to themselves as the *Biotech industry*, and they prefer to be segregated from Pharma. But, as we will see, their business interests are very similar.

The scenario of discovering, testing, and patenting new medications defines the financial game plan of today's pharmaceutical firms. Uwe Reinhardt, a long-time health economist at Princeton, outlined the key parameters for success for Pharma over twenty years ago.[2] Reinhardt begins with a rendition of the central conundrum associated with Pharma, at least in the public's view. On the one hand—and especially today, as vaccines have helped us address the COVID pandemic—we are deeply grateful for the work that pharmaceutical company scientists and administrators do to bring us new discoveries, as well as the hope they provide for huge numbers of sick people. At the same time, the industry is seen as rapacious, with profits that are far too high, and drug costs that outstrip the ability of people—and their insurers—to pay.

Reinhardt lays this ambivalence at the foot of the government, noting that it sanctions huge profits by granting a temporary monopoly, in the form of a patent. That monopoly period dominates the strategy of pharmaceutical firms. These firms have high fixed costs related to discovery and testing, and much lower variable costs of production. Thus their large expenditures are for research and development; administrative costs associated with getting a drug approved; and then marketing costs during the monopoly period. The actual costs of production are minuscule, compared with potential profits. Research and development are fraught with uncertainty and failure, but, on the other hand, once a drug is approved, patent monopoly and heavy marketing create a wonderful financial outcome for a pharmaceutical firm.

There has been a good deal of debate over the last thirty years about whether that profit is unacceptably high.[3] I am avoiding broader moral arguments, but what I can say is that pharmaceutical firms are playing according to the rules of commerce. They are simply doing what their shareholders expect in terms of driving as much demand for, and profit from, a product as possible while it has monopoly status. Moreover, they are a highly regulated industry.

To understand the pharmaceutical industry's drive for profit in more depth, I will take a deeper look at those regulations, especially as they apply to drug discovery, patents, and marketing. I will then examine private forces, primarily pharmacy benefit managers (PBMs), who are meant to control the costs of medications (and, presumably, the profits of pharmaceutical manufacturers).

Oversight of Pharmaceutical Manufacturers:
The Food and Drug Administration

The regulation of prescription drugs in the United States is extraordinary, as is the history of that regulation. It is a nearly 100-year narrative of public health disasters, moving Congress to slowly grant more power to the Food and Drug Administration over the steady opposition of Pharma. The Pure Food and Drug Act of 1906 provided the first curbs on the adulteration and misbranding of drugs—in particular, false and misleading labeling. The FDA has put great faith in labeling ever since.[4]

Yet the 1906 legislation gave the FDA little real power over the pharmaceutical industry and could not protect the public from either the medications themselves or additives to the medications. This was made evident in 1937–1938 when the S. E. Massengill Company was found to be producing a drug that contained ethylene glycol as a solvent. Ethylene glycol, which is commonly used as antifreeze for cars' coolant systems, causes kidney damage, and over 100 people, mostly children, died before Massingill's product was recalled.

The result was the Food, Drug, and Cosmetic Act of 1938, which, for the first time, required manufacturers to submit comprehensive information on the ingredients in any new drug. This took the form of a new drug application (NDA) to the FDA. Once such information was produced for the agency, the onus was on the FDA to act within sixty days. If not, the drug could be introduced into commerce without FDA approval. For the first time, safety thresholds had been set, though there was no requirement for a drug to be proven effective. The 1938 act also paved the way for two tracks of drugs: over-the-counter and prescription medications. During the next twenty years, it would become the rule that some drugs would only be available with a doctor's prescription, while over-the-counter ones could be purchased directly by the consumer.

After thalidomide-induced birth defects affected hundreds of newborns in Europe, the Kefauver-Harris Drug Amendment of 1962 set up the final pieces of the regulatory structure that Pharma faces today.

Companies were now required to demonstrate both the safety and efficacy of their medications, using a carefully developed, multistep process. Initial studies on toxicity in animals had to be followed by similar studies with informed human volunteers. Next, dosing studies and initial checks for human toxicity had to be completed. This was followed by several phases of ever-larger studies, to demonstrate statistically significant outcomes in general populations. Most importantly, the FDA no longer faced a sixty-day clock—a drug would only be approved after it was shown to be safe and efficacious.

While long opposed to regulatory oversight, Pharma has grudgingly come to accept this safety- and efficacy-assuring architecture. It does provide the industry with an advantage over much else in health care—once approved for introduction into commerce by the FDA, doctors and insurers are going to be satisfied that the medication works. The rest of medical interventions do not have that same standard, and it is up to insurers to police the evidence base. This regulation of efficacy and safety, however, adds huge upfront costs for Pharma, as Reinhardt outlined.

Pharma laments these costs associated with drug development, especially the arduous nature of large clinical trials.[5] There is a great deal of debate about the magnitude of those costs, with Pharma citing amounts greater than $2 billion per approved compound, and others suggesting smaller but still sizable amounts.[6] The policy point is that research is very expensive under this (appropriate) regulatory scheme. If the government or insurers reduce payments for medications, that will theoretically reduce research and, hence, the availability of new breakthroughs. The amount of reduction, however, is hotly debated.[7]

Once Pharma (or Biotech), as a business, has managed to get something approved, companies prolong their monopoly and market their drugs as aggressively as possible. Pharma shareholders should expect nothing less, but policymakers worry—correctly—that prolonged patents could lead to more costly drug expenditures. To partly address this issue, Congress passed the Drug Price Competition and Patent Term Restoration Act of 1984, also known, after its authors, as the Hatch-Waxman Act. Thanks to this new legislation, competing Pharma companies were better able to copy one another's drugs as they came off patents. In other words, the Hatch-Waxman Act made it easier to create cheaper, generic drugs in a competitive market.[8]

The 1938 and 1962 amendments to the Food, Drug, and Cosmetic Act, as well as the Hatch-Waxman Act, largely define the architecture of the regulatory oversight of medications. It is all federal law, and the states play only a very minor role. Under this regime, the path to success for drug manufacturers is to discover new, effective medications, and then to market them and keep a monopoly on them as long as possible. It is strikingly different from what we find in the rest of health care, and the path continues to evolve in the twenty-first century.

The Pharmaceutical Manufacturers' Path to Profit
PATENTS AND MARKETING

To maintain its monopoly over a branded product, Pharma attempts to delay the introduction of a generic competitor drug for as long as possible. The most time-tested way is to litigate whether the patent has indeed lapsed, thus challenging the new generic manufacturer. A critical offshoot of this strategy is to negotiate a settlement where the generic manufacturer is *paid to delay*. Increasingly, however, the courts view this as a potential antitrust violation, and the pay-for-delay practice may be substantially limited in the future.[9]

Newer strategies involve refusing to give generic manufacturers access to drug samples, so they can do bioequivalence testing, as well as patenting peripheral issues, such as new dosages, methods of administration, and new indications for use.[10] All of this is very hard-knuckled and contrasts sharply with the florid statements of "regard for human welfare" that most CEOs (not just in Pharma) espouse—but it is entirely reasonable from the point of view of maximizing profit and, hence, shareholder value. Pharma will do anything legally possible to prolong a patent, but once all avenues have been exhausted, the ensuing introduction of a generic drug is relatively rapid.

If anything, the marketing mission is even more hard-edged than patent prolongation. Today, pharmaceutical manufacturers' marketing teams have two different targets: the prescriber and the patient. The prescriber has long been considered the key target for ensuring that a medication would be used. Gerald Posner describes the beginning of Pharma's *detailing* to doctors in the 1950s, a strategy honed by Arthur Sackler, who is infamous for his eventual ownership (with his brothers Mortimer and Raymond) of Purdue Pharmaceuticals.[11] Arthur Sackler recognized that physicians could be influenced to prescribe a company's medication if marketing outreach was directly made to a physician's office. This involved providing background information on that drug, as well as small gifts or free lunches. While most physicians would deny that these blandishments were decisive in any way, they clearly worked for Pharma and have become very much a part of the health care landscape. Doctors who have a relationship with pharmaceutical salespeople, known as *reps*, or *detailers*, end up prescribing more of that detailer's brands.

The next step up from handing out gifts and information was to hire doctors, usually as consultants, to speak on behalf of specific medications at academic meetings or at conferences providing continuing medical education. Sometimes the physicians would become members of so-called speakers bureaus. Others would simply be consultants, available to provide advice to pharmaceutical firms on the variety of scientific and practice-related issues that might arise in the life cycle of a medication. Although these relationships can be quite substantial in monetary terms (no longer "small gifts"), physicians have long believed that they could dispel the notion of a conflict of interest by disclosing these financial relationships.

Those defenses were widely accepted for years. Then economist George Loewenstein published a series of empirical papers proving that disclosures of conflicts of interest are largely meaningless—patients and colleagues do not know how to interpret them. Furthermore, he has shown that small gifts do matter, as their receipt leads to actions on behalf of the small gift donor. In many ways, Loewenstein's research proves that managing conflicts of interest regarding Pharma marketing is impossible. This firm conclusion has, in turn, led to calls for the prohibition of such practices, rather than management of them.[12] These have been largely ignored by the medical profession, and certainly by Pharma. So marketing to doctors continues and grows.

The second prong of Pharma's marketing efforts goes directly to consumers, via advertisements that are intended to interest patients in certain treatments, presumably leading them to engage in a discussion with the prescribing physician. The 1962 amendments to the Food and Drug Act that outlined the role of *medication labels* also gave the FDA authority to regulate advertising.[13] Still, the FDA took nearly a decade to issue regulations for drug advertisements that required the ads to be neither false nor misleading, present a balanced view of the risks and benefits, and provide a summary of the risks, outlined in the drug label.

It took more than another decade before Pharma began to take advantage of these rules with ads that truly go *direct to consumers* (DTC). Taken aback by these DTC ads, in 1983 the FDA asked for a moratorium on further advertisements. In 1985, the FDA announced it was satisfied with the protections in place, and an extensive use of DTC print advertisements got underway. Broadcast DTC marketing was approved in the mid-1990s, and regulations on print ads were further eased in 2004, eliminating the need to present information on the entire label. The rapid growth of DTC advertising ensued.

Remarkably, the United States and New Zealand appear to be the only countries to allow direct-to-consumer advertising.[14] Medical ethicists and health policy experts have continued to raise questions about marketing that is oriented to physicians and its potential conflicts of interest, but DTC advertising has become widely accepted.

Lisa Schwartz and Steve Woloshin have done a thorough job of documenting marketing expenditures by Pharma.[15] They estimated that from 1997 to 2016, pharmaceutical marketing increased from $17.7 billion to $29.9 billion, with the largest increase being DTC prescription drug advertising, which rose from $1.3 billion to $6 billion. Meanwhile, marketing to health care professionals increased from $15.6 billion to $20.3 billion over the same period, of which $5.6 billion was for professional detailing and $13.5 billion for free samples (the idea behind the latter being that once patients get started on free samples, a valid prescription will soon follow). In addition, nearly $1 billion was spent on direct physician payments.

The breadth of Pharma's influence with real medical experts is breathtaking. For the last decade, the Centers for Medicare & Medicaid Services has maintained a reporting system on payments by Pharma and other for-profit companies to physicians, called Open Payments.[16] Anyone can type a doctor's name and the location of that practice into the website and get three years' worth of data on reimbursements. While working for insurers, I would often hear from physicians, many of them experts in their field, who were not happy about aspects of the pharmacy utilization review programs. Routinely, these doctors were well paid by Pharma, often into the hundreds of thousands of dollars per year for consulting and speaking fees. Presumably the Pharma dollars were at least partially influencing the views of these experts. If not, why would Pharma pay them so much?

The business interests of Pharma are clear, although they are not quite transparent to the average person. Pharmaceutical manufacturers bear the up-front costs of discovering medications and developing them through what is truly an arduous FDA regulatory premise. We can debate the cost of bringing a product successfully to market, but whether it is $1 billion or $2 billion, we can agree that the price is steep. So, firms fight to keep a patent-based monopoly as long as possible, and they intensely market it to prescribers and patients. They buy influence where they can through consulting relationships with expert physicians, many of whom see a great deal of value for their patients in these products. All of this makes good sense from a business point of view. Yet it might appear wasteful to some (myself included), who would prefer to see the medications stand on their own merits without so much (or even any) marketing.

NAMING THE PRICE

The brilliant advantage granted to a pharmaceutical manufacturer through its patent is that for at least a certain period, the manufacturer can name this drug's price. For the duration of a monopoly, the price is determined by the seller: both the initial price and then annual increases. To set these prices, the manufacturer probes what the market will bear—and the market has borne a great deal, as we will see. For over fifty years, these financial forces have been in place without regulation, and the situation has not changed greatly since the Hatch-Waxman Act passed in 1980. But in the twenty-first century, the push for more profit has dissipated any sense of moderation.

Most of the costs of production, once a drug is on the market, are small and stable, so pricing is a matter of profit maximization. This is most easily demonstrated by evaluating *launch prices*, or the initial price for a medication. Launch prices have been increasing for the last twenty years, and recent research shows that the median launch price increased 934 percent from 2006 to 2018.[17] Even for health care, known for its cost inflation, this is extraordinary.

What accounts for such a steep increase in the price of pharmaceuticals? Over the course of the late twentieth century, Pharma came to realize that insurers really cannot influence the launch price if a medication is effective and unique. Approval by the FDA brought not only a monopoly, but also the ability to name a drug's price, and that price could be high. Once a drug was approved and on the market, doctors would use it for the indications for which it was approved. Substantial demand was automatic, which could then be fanned by careful marketing.

Perhaps the key development occurred in 1991 when the path-breaking company Genzyme got approval for Ceredase to treat patients with Gaucher's disease. People who suffer from this disease have a deficiency of the enzyme glucocerebrosidase. As a result, fats build up in various organs, especially in bone marrow, the liver, and the spleen. Many of these patients are children, and Ceredase could literally save their lives.

Ceredase was derived from human placentas and essentially replaced the missing enzyme. In 1994, Genzyme began manufacturing Cerezyme, using recombinant DNA techniques. The disease was so rare, and the treatment so effective, that Genzyme justified a price of $150,000 per year.[18] Insurers could not refuse—without treatment, these children could die. Most of Pharma failed, at first, to understand the precedent set by Genzyme. Both insurers and pharmaceutical firms presumed that a drug that treated only a small number of people had to command a high price, given the costs of research and development for them. But slowly the broader lesson sunk in for Pharma. After all, a unique branded drug was indicated for and effectively treated a specific illness. Every drug costs a great deal to bring it to market. So why shouldn't every drug command a premium?

At the end of the twentieth century, many drug manufacturers were also hit by the generic wave. Critical insights into physiology from the 1960s and 1970s had given rise to a host of small-molecule drugs that treated many common conditions, such as diabetes and hypertension. The term *small molecule* typically means that the substances were synthetic chemicals. These are distinguished from *large molecules*, which are much more complex (often whole proteins) and designed to mimic actual biological entities. By the end of the twentieth century, many small molecule patents had lapsed, leading to a slew of generic conversions. As a result, finances tightened for Pharma.

The fiscal answer was inflation in the drugs' launch prices, starting early in the twenty-first century. There has been an even more rapid increase in launch prices since 2010, an increase that even the casual observer of pharmacy and pharmaceutical economics would recognize as a result of the hepatitis C breakthrough. The story of new, effective, and expensive therapies for hepatitis C deserves its own book, but I will distill it here.

Historically, hepatitis C was difficult to identify. Although the virus infected 3–4 million Americans and was frequently deadly, it had largely been untreatable up through 2010.[19] In 2011, two direct-acting antivirals, telaprevir and boceprevir, were introduced to the market, boosting cure rates to 70 percent, with many fewer side effects. Even better treatment was just around the corner: the approval of sofosbuvir in 2013. Many hepatologists had been anticipating this latter drug and had their patients waiting for treatment with it. They were not disappointed— cure rates exceeded 90 percent, and more than 95 percent of the affected patients were finishing the treatment. In many ways, this was the great medical breakthrough of the twenty-first century, until the mRNA vaccines for COVID-19 came on the scene.

But for our purposes, the story was the price. Gilead, the pharmaceutical company that owned sofosbuvir, decided that an extremely high price was warranted. Other competing breakthrough products were being developed, so the profits from sofosbuvir would have to be taken immediately. The cost for a twelve-week course of this oral medication was pegged at $84,000, which was shocking to many.[20] From a business point of view, this price was reasonable, as the company had perspicaciously bought the asset, owned the patent for a limited time, and faced real competition very soon. Gilead also made a delicate strategic decision: they realized that its high price might backfire on them from both public relations and regulatory perspectives. This was the prediction of several acute observers, who thought that the government or employer sponsors of health insurance would revolt at such a price tag.[21]

Nothing of the sort occurred. In many ways, sofosbuvir was a tough target for Pharma critics. While the cost of sofosbuvir was exceedingly high, the drug was also incredibly effective. There was good reason to believe that when compared with many other therapies, sofosbuvir was a bargain. Using cost-effectiveness measures to determine whether the real benefits aligned with the price tag, it was clear that even at $80,000 per treatment course, the cost per quality-adjusted life year (QALY) was only around $15,000 for the most prevalent genotypes of hepatitis C.[22] This is well below the "cost-effective" parameters of $50,000–$100,000 per QALY used by most health services researchers.

Payers complained that they simply could not afford these prices, and many state Medicaid programs had trouble absorbing the costs of this new treatment. Insurers put substantial utilization management barriers in place for patients infected with hepatitis C who sought treatment. Yet the hue and cry eventually died down, and the pharmaceutical industry was allowed to continue to name prices. Indeed, the lesson of hepatitis C and sofosbuvir was, do not stint on your launch price.

The hepatitis C treatment controversy provides an important insight about an employer's role in health insurance. Sofosbuvir is so cost effective because it cures the disease and prevents the ten to twenty years of disability that otherwise would occur. But an employer retains middle-aged employees for only four years (on average), and younger employees for an even shorter time.[23] Thus an employer does not reap the benefits of a healthy worker—someone else does. An employer's view is quite short sighted, being ill disposed toward a longer-term public health perspective. (I will return to this problem.)

There was one more important repercussion of ever-higher launch prices. They provided a signal to manufacturers whose drugs had been launched at lower prices years before yet still had patent life. These drugs could be "topped up" rapidly. The 2010s, in particular, have seen substantial annual increases in the prices of brand-name medications. Existing compounds are generally manufactured at the same cost as when they were first launched. So any price increases are pure profit for pharmaceutical manufacturers.

These high prices come with a catch, though, and a third prong of pharma marketing comes into play. Insurers and, in particular, employers have increasingly left some of the costs of health care to patients (also known as consumers), especially through high deductible health plans. If a patient with rheumatoid arthritis has a $5,000 deductible that must be fulfilled before insurance kicks in, that person might choose a cheaper treatment option, rather than pay $5,000 in out-of-pocket costs for the latest invention.

To encourage patients to use their newer, more effective, and more expensive drugs, Pharma began to donate money to private foundations, which then provided "assistance" to patients facing high deductibles or co-payments. These kinds of donations make good financial sense for Pharma. Suppose a patient with rheumatoid arthritis has a $5,000 deductible, and their doctor recommends a specialty drug, Humira, manufactured by Abbvie. A rheumatologist can refer that person to the Abbvie patient assistance foundation (to which, in 2015, Abbvie donated over $850 million),[24] which will then provide the initial $5,000 for the treatment. The remaining $75,000 is paid by the insurer/employer, a real bargain for Abbvie, since $75,000 comes in as revenue, at a cost of $5,000. The manufacturing costs for that one-year supply of Humira are well below $10,000.

By 2014, such assistance programs were available for over 300 drugs.[25] Medicare treats such payments as a kickback. Hence they are illegal for Medicare recipients. But almost all states allow them, and they are rampant in the employer-sponsored insurance market. In 2015, pharmaceutical *patient assistance foundations* (PAFs) gave away more than $5.7 billion to cover out-of-pocket costs. In terms of disbursements, nine of the fifteen largest charitable foundations in the United States were patient assistance foundations.

PAFs essentially tie the bow on Pharma marketing: they pay doctors who are doing the prescribing (or give them gifts), advertise directly, and fill in the gaps in insurance coverage. This enables pharmaceutical firms to take full advantage of their legal monopolies—the patents— to raise launch prices and cover yearly inflation costs. From a business point of view, for shareholders of the Pharma firm, all of these machinations form an appropriate strategy. But from a social point of view, this is a recipe for what many see as out-of-control drug prices.

The ever-higher prices do rankle patients and politicians, and Pharma must be careful about how hard it pushes for profits. As noted at the very beginning of this chapter, Pharma has one trump card in the debate over high prices—no profit equals no research into future discoveries. Pharma's argument is that if society wants a company to spend money on discovery up front, then that firm must be able to take advantage of its property rights once a drug is successfully brought to market.

But that argument only goes so far, and the public's concern about drug prices continues to grow. A recent Kaiser Family Foundation poll found once again that the biggest health policy issue for the public is the high price of drugs.[26] On that point, 88 percent of the public—including 77 percent of Republicans and 96 percent of Democrats—would favor reducing the prices of drugs by having the government negotiate directly with manufacturers on price. As voters, people worry quite appropriately that they will not be able to afford the medications they need.

Almost no other health policy issue has this kind of consensus. The research isn't clear about the exact sources of public dissatisfaction, but two issues stand out: the out-of-pocket costs of drugs (not everyone gets access to patient assistance foundations), and people in the United States pay much more for drugs than do citizens of other countries. Pharma's answer to this is what you might expect of any industry: a judicious use of money to support elected officials who will ensure that publicly held views do not become policy. More than two-thirds of the sitting members of Congress got checks from Pharma in 2020.[27] More importantly, Pharma is perhaps the most knowledgeable and precise distributor of campaign cash of all industries.[28]

Cost Control in Pharmacy Commerce
Pharmacy Benefit Managers

The above discussion is the story from the point of view of the manufacturers, but this book is about what employers and the government pay for health care—in this context, the costs they must pay for medications. Noticeably absent from this rather long introduction to pharmaceutical commerce is how the government and employers control costs. I will now turn to that topic.

On the governmental front, there has been relatively little action until very recently. The Centers for Medicare & Medicaid Services simply did not have the same leverage for drugs that it had regarding doctors and hospitals. The drug development process, onerous to Pharma, is overseen by the FDA. Patent law changes would require congressional action. While the CMS might influence changes in marketing, much of that also falls within the FDA, which has shown not much appetite for that. The CMS does apply anti-kickback laws to limit patient assistance programs, but not much more. As we will see in the next chapter, the CMS relied on the PBMs to effectuate cost savings in the Medicare Part D program, which began in 2003. So, for the rest of this chapter, I will concentrate on employers and PBMs.

Pharma has developed a playbook, which is based on steep increases in prices of medications and, hence, ever-higher costs to the health care system. While the public has become increasingly dissatisfied with this scenario, there does not seem to be a great deal of employer dissatisfaction. Self-insured employers continue to use their own cost managers and tolerate Pharma's persistent inflationary pressure. Understanding this seeming paradox requires a close examination of pharmacy benefit management.

Pharmacy benefit management is poorly understood by health policy experts, and there are few efforts to describe it in layperson's terms.[29] (An exception to the rule of opaque descriptions is Lawton Burns's *The Health Care Value Chain*, elucidating in detail what pharmacy benefit managers and group purchasing organizations do.)[30] It is dominated today by the three pharmacy benefit management companies: CVS Caremark (which now owns Aetna), Express Scripts (owned by CIGNA, a health insurer), and Optum (part of the UnitedHealth Group). These companies have, respectively, 32 percent, 24 percent, and 21 percent of the PBM market share.[31] They compete with many smaller PBMs. (This is another area with which I have some personal familiarity. For over a decade, I was in charge of CVS Caremark's health strategy and medical oversight, during which time we drove our market share from under 15 percent to greater than 30 percent.)

The PBMs' main role is to act as payer/insurer for drugs obtained by beneficiaries. Every employer hires not only an insurer to act as a third-party administrator (TPA) and deal with doctors and hospitals, but also a PBM to do the same work for medications. The only visible part of this division of labor for employees/beneficiaries is that they get two cards: one for insurance, and the other for medications. Even though their role isn't clear to the patient, the PBMs are deeply involved with each step of the medication's path from the manufacturer to the patient.

PBMs are not an ancient part of the health care scene; they first appeared in the 1980s. Original Medicare did not cover oral medications, and neither did a lot of commercial health insurance plans. Over time, however, pharmacy plans began to become a covered benefit, especially for trade union members. To help pharmacies adjudicate claims, several firms, led by Pharmacy Card System, Inc., invented the plastic benefits card. In the 1970s they used paper, turning to electronics in the 1980s to facilitate payments.[32]

At much the same time, several companies started to offer mail-order pharmacy services, trying to reduce the costs associated with filling a prescription by getting economies of scale through automation. By the mid-1980s, the first pharmacy benefit managers were combining these operations (claims adjudication at pharmacies and mail-order pharmacy alternatives) and offering services directly to self-insured employers. The mainline health insurers did not react, and, rather quickly, many employees had two forms of benefits—a pharmacy benefit and a medical benefit. Smaller PBMs merged, merged again, split, and then remerged, until the big three were formed by the middle of the 2010s.

Today their business model is complicated but rational.[33] The PBMs compete for business, based primarily on lowering the costs of medications for health care plans or self-insured employers. They also promise better service and a greater adherence to a medication regimen, but the competition for business usually comes down to cost. PBMs work to reduce costs in six major ways, although subsidiary initiatives are being added all the time, limited only by financial and business creativity.

The six key methods that pharmacy benefit managers employ to lower costs are worth spelling out. First, PBMs operate mail-order pharmacies, where they can offer lower prices through automation and economies of scale, compared with retail pharmacies. Mail order has not proven to be a huge growth engine for profits, as retail pharmacies have reduced their costs, but it remains as a component of the PBM business.

The second and third cost-cutting mechanisms that pharmacy benefit managers use are imported directly from insurance: cost sharing and utilization management. PBMs are the most disciplined users of co-payments, deductibles, and co-insurance to change consumer/patient behavior. Employing *tiering*, they create incentives to use the least expensive medications: first generics, and then less expensive branded drugs. They also use out-of-pocket costs to drive beneficiaries toward less expensive mail-order pharmacies or a restricted retail pharmacy network.

Third, they aggressively employ utilization management. Most drugs have very specific indications and dosage schedules, based on their original FDA approval. Often physicians will prescribe for off-label indications, but some of these prescriptions are either specious or mistaken. The PBMs maintain staffs of pharmacists and doctors who issue prior authorizations on expensive medications, in order to ensure that they are being used in compliance with evidence-based guidelines and FDA indications. The review mechanisms also push patients and prescribers toward equivalent generic medications.

These two functions are very successful, at least regarding the use of generics. The utilization of generic drugs is much higher in the United States than in European countries, and that practice is lowering drug costs.[34] There are also drawbacks to both functions, however. Out-of-pocket payments do force some people to walk away from prescriptions that they need. In 2019, the Kaiser Family Foundation reported that 24 percent of people had trouble affording their medications.[35] This, in turn, induces poor health, which insurance eventually must cover.

Utilization review enrages physicians and patients. Faced with a denial from a PBM, some patients will not pursue further treatment. Perhaps more importantly, doctors consistently cite prior authorization, particularly for medications, as one of the key factors driving burnout for them. This is particularly true in primary care. While tiering and utilization management work from a cost perspective, they can drive substantial adverse reactions by patients and doctors. These two factors are another example of the use of administrative burdens to effectuate policy (discussed in chapter 2).

The fourth major function that PBMs undertake is to source generic medications for their mail-order pharmacies. Once a medication loses its patent-created monopoly, many competitors jump into the market to create equivalent generic drugs. There are literally hundreds of these manufacturers in the United States, and even more overseas. Generic drug manufacturing is a huge industry in India, for example.[36] The various generic manufacturers compete largely on price.

Today, most wholesalers, pharmacy benefit managers, and retailers work together in one of three huge generic purchasing collaboratives.

They use economies of scale to drive prices down for generic medications, most of which today are bought overseas.[37] This use of market power has largely been successful. Since 2017, generic medication costs have continued to drop.[38]

Fifth, pharmacy benefit managers control costs by organizing and paying a network of retail pharmacies. In the simplest terms, this function resonates with insurers assembling a network of providers and choosing which doctors and hospitals they'll pay to provide care for beneficiaries. An insurer can exclude a hospital from the network if that hospital is demanding rates that are too high, in the insurer's eyes. The PBMs can do the same thing regarding pharmacies. If a PBM does not contract with a pharmacy, then beneficiaries are unable to use that pharmacy to fill their prescriptions.

The general view in the industry is that there are more pharmacies than the country needs, so leverage is in the hands of the pharmacy benefit managers. Even large chains are not immune. In 2011, Walgreens, then the largest of the retail pharmacy chains, took on the PBM Express Scripts in a contract dispute, refusing to accept Express Scripts' terms. Express Scripts then excluded Walgreens from its network. The result was widely seen as a debacle for Walgreens, reiterating the importance of owning a relationship with a drug plan's beneficiaries through their employer.[39] Independent pharmacies, like independent physicians' practices, feel especially poorly treated by the PBMs.

The situation in the pharmacy sector is more complicated than my analogy to network development would suggest. A PBM essentially inserts itself into the patient's visit to a retail pharmacy at the time a sale is made, taking advantage because pharmacies joined in early to the electronic exchanges of data. In that fraught moment, as a pharmacist keys in the necessary information, the prescription is bought from the retail pharmacy (who, in turn, has bought it from a wholesaler) by the PBM, who then charges the employer for the cost of the drug. At the same time, all of the out-of-pocket and prior-authorization logic plays out. In a health care industry not known for its embrace of digital technologies, this is a huge amount of information, sorted through in microseconds.

For a beneficiary at the pharmacy counter, all of these factors result in an adjudicated price. At the same time, the layers of co-payments, deductibles, and co-insurance are brought to bear. It is no wonder that neither a pharmacist nor a patient has any idea what the cost of a drug is going to be. Sometimes it is surprisingly low, but at other times it is intolerably expensive.

Pharmacy Benefit Managers and Brand Drugs

This sixth function of pharmacy benefit managers' efforts to reduce costs, those of branded drugs still on a patent, deserves its own section, given its prominence in today's debate over the cost of drugs. It is based on the development of *formularies*—that is, lists of drugs that will be covered by a pharmacy benefit.

Taking a step back, the PBMs have assembled independent expert doctors, pharmacists, and nurses who make up their pharmacy and therapeutics committees. These experts must approve all of the utilization management decisions and the co-payment tiering that the PBMs utilize. Such use of impartial, explicitly independent expertise is not found elsewhere in managed care. It is a reassuring requirement, as it means that a PBM's clinical decision making is attempting to be faithful to what experts consider to be the standard of care.

The pharmacy and therapeutics committees also oversee the formulary development process for a PBM from a clinical viewpoint. The list of approved drugs that a particular pharmacy can dispense represents a selection of medications, using only a subset of medications in a particular chemical or biological class when the other members of that class are essentially duplicates. Using a formulary to include some drugs, while excluding others, gives a pharmacy benefit manager leverage over manufacturers. The formulary/rebate strategy is the crucial tool with which the PBMs break down the costs of patented drugs. It is also very poorly understood.

Formulary strategy dates from the late 1980s. The nascent PBMs were aware that in most drug classes, there were several therapeutically equivalent alternatives. Putting only one on their formulary would obviously create more business for one manufacturer. Pharmaceutical firms took the bait, and negotiations for placement on a PBM formulary became commonplace.

In return for formulary placement, and under an exception to the federal law preventing kickbacks, a PBM can get a rebate from the manufacturer. This is basically a discount, except that it was transmitted to the PBM, not the payer (health plan or employer). The formulary strategy thus causes a gross-to-net phenomenon—the net for the manufacturer was calculated by applying the rebate to the original price. To provide a lower price for the ultimate payers (employers), the PBM shared the rebate with them.

In the past, the PBMs could keep a portion of those rebates, often on a risk basis. A PBM retained some of the pharmaceutical payment (rebate) after an agreed-upon guaranteed amount of rebate dollars went back to the employer (or health insurer). This was known as a *meeting the rebate guarantee*. Manufacturers did not like paying a rebate, but since they named the price, they could increase that price to keep up with the rebate amount. This kind of pressure, very akin to the cost/charge prices in hospitals, added further fuel to medication inflation.

Over time, competition ground down the amount of the rebate a PBM could keep. This led to contracts where 100 percent of the rebate was required to go to the customer. (The PBMs compete on offering the lowest net price to their customers, the employers.) By 2018, retained rebates were probably down to less than 2 percent,[40] and less than 1 percent in government-sponsored programs.[41] (I will discuss Medicare Part D, its drug program, in chapter 6.) Many observers complain that there is no independent analysis of this flow of funds.[42] Nonetheless, rebates really do amount to discounts, not secret payments to the PBMs, although pharmacy benefit managers have traditionally guarded the financial details of rebate arrangements. Moreover, the PBMs are always busy developing new business models (some with Pharma) that most employers have difficulty policing, such as the new group-purchasing vehicles.

I should note that employers like rebates. These funds are returned directly to their benefits teams in the form of a check and can be used to lower overall premiums or for other purposes. This is not to say that most employers are enthralled with pharmacy benefit management. The contracts are quite difficult to understand, and an employer's benefits team is generally even more dependent on the PBM consultants than is the case with the rest of health insurance. Few human resources department benefits managers would be able to explain the details of the various pricing mechanisms that the PBMs use to effectuate these six functions. But they do like having the flexibility that comes with a rebate check.

One more point about rebates is important. Most people have a health benefits policy with a pharmacy deductible, so they pay full price for a medication while they are in the deductible phase. If the rebates were applied at the point of sale (and some PBMs can offer this), then a patient would pay the rebated/discounted price of the drug while still within the deductible amount. But most employers prefer to have the rebates directed internally. Thus the price an employee pays while within the deductible is the *unrebated amount*, which, as we will see, can be considerably higher than the rebated price. Such prices no doubt increase the likelihood of patients' sticker shock, leading employees/patients to walk away without their prescription. The employer sees "free dollars" as the rebate checks come in, but there is little attention to the lack of adherence to a medication regimen such a process engenders.

To bring the PBMs' efforts to control the costs of branded and specialty branded medications to life, let us return to the hepatitis C story. The new hepatitis C medication, sofosbuvir, is considered a specialty drug. (*Specialty medications* are those that require specific handling or are very expensive—the definition is not sharp.) So the manufacturer ships it to specialty pharmacies, the largest of which are owned by the PBMs. This is the simplest part of the pharmacy commerce story—a manufacturer sells a drug to a specialty pharmacy, which is owned by a PBM; the pharmacy applies the PBM's management rules and cost-reduction techniques; and the pharmacy then sells that drug to an employer.

To illustrate the role of formularies and rebates with the hepatitis C example, I will fast forward to a year after the launch of sofosbuvir, when new and even more effective medications for the treatment of hepatitis C became available. One was a brand named Harvoni, a Gilead drug that combined sofosbuvir with ledipasvir. Another was Viekira Pak, which consisted of ombitasvir/paritaprevir/ritonavir and dasabuvir sodium, manufactured by Abbvie. Both had unsurpassed viral response and adherence performances. Experts on pharmacy and therapeutics committees would consider them to be equivalent. Both had prices above $70,000. So the PBMs went to work to reduce costs, since they are retained by self-insured employers (or health plans) only insofar as they can offer costs that are lower than those of their competitors.

First, the PBMs developed utilization management rules: the diagnosis of hepatitis C had to be verified, including the correct genotype (these drugs would not work as well for some genotypes of hepatitis C). Second, they would counsel the patient, to ensure that person adhered to the medication regimen (avoiding the need to do a costly retreatment if the patient did not finish the original course of the drug). Third—and most importantly—they would negotiate with the manufacturers. Since the drugs (Harvoni and Viekira Pak) were clinically equivalent (verified by the PBM's pharmacy and therapeutics committee), only one of these two would be necessary for the PBM's formulary. With the three largest PBMs having as much as 80 percent of the market, Abbvie and Gilead could not afford to be excluded from all of them. But getting on a PBM's formulary would require a price cut—that is, a rebate. The bigger the rebate, the lower the price for the client (an employer or insurer). Abbvie and Gilead faced tough choices and proved willing to give rebates in excess of 50 percent, a substantial lowering of the price of those drugs.[43]

In some ways, the unrebated price for these brand-name drugs is the charge price I mentioned for hospitals—without managed care, you pay the full cost. Employers (and most insurers) with aggressive PBMs get lower prices—that is, the rebated price. An uninsured person pays the full cost: for Harvoni, $80,000 for the course of therapy, as opposed to less than $40,000 for the rebated drug.

The same is true for cost sharing. A PBM rebate comes to a plan's sponsor after adjudication at the pharmacy, so the unrebated price is used to calculate the deductible or co-insurance amount faced by the patient. The underlying business deal between the PBM and the employer/insurer is sensible, but the outcome for the consumer/beneficiary/employee can be expensive and extremely confusing. Another way to look at it is that a sick employee needing branded drugs is subsidizing the premium costs of a healthy employee.

On this very complicated playing field, entrepreneurs and entrepreneurial thinkers at pharmacies, PBMs, and manufacturers continue to develop new ways to create a profit margin, often taking advantage of that very complexity. For example, manufacturers have created *patient assistance programs* to cover the costs of deductibles and co-insurance payments. Insurers and employers really dislike this, because when the price of a drug is adjusted at a retail pharmacy, the use of a patient assistance payment is (at least historically) not recorded. Thus a payer believes that the patient has paid for the medication out of pocket, and that person's remaining deductible amount is decreased. Since the use of deductibles or co-insurance is intended to make a patient a more diligent consumer by having skin in the game, a patient assistance foundation plan frustrates that impulse—and not just for medications.

The PBMs then respond. They adjust their contracts with pharmacies to record the use of patient assistance payments. They also modify the *accumulator*, where a patient's out-of-pocket payments are traced, and force that person's deductible back to its pre-assistance amount when a patient assistance program is used. Now the pharmaceutical manufacturer can keep "assisting" a patient, but that person's maximum deductible level—that is, the amount a patient has to pay before their drug insurance kicks in—is never reached. In other words, that person has to continue to pay for that drug out of pocket, ad infinitum, and thus has a strong incentive to not start or to discontinue a treatment using that medication. This issue will become more acute for drug manufacturers as more PBMs adopt accumulator adjustment programs. Even more sneaky, the PBMs are learning to take advantage of patient assistance foundations, automatically applying for Pharma manufacturers' co-pay assistance funds to reduce costs for beneficiaries, preventing these dollars from counting toward patients' deductible and maximum out-of-pocket limits before their insurance starts to pay. This program is known as a *maximizer*. All of this leads to confusion and surprise for patients at the drug counter.

Meanwhile, rebates help fuel the annual inflation amounts applied by pharmaceutical manufacturers. They contend that their prices are not the full reimbursement for their manufacturing costs, so they must continue to raise prices to increase their net profit. This complexity potentially creates a lack of transparency, and in relatively dark niches, business plans can spawn bizarre arrangements that are sensible for the players involved but would not conform to the dictates of rational drug policy development. Nor can employers really police these various business strategies—numbed by it all, they default to the prices charged by the PBMs.

Throughout this discussion of cost control in the pharmacy sector, I have sidestepped addressing government-sponsored programs. This is partly because the government was a latecomer as a pharmacy purchaser, at least through Medicare, only beginning to pay for oral medications about fifteen years ago. Medicare Part D deserves its own discussion, juxtaposed with Medicare Advantage, which is the story for chapter 6. But first I will assess what the PBMs are doing for employers purchasing commercial insurance and suggest what would be more sensible.

How to Reform the Pharmacy Commerce Mess

In at least one critical way, the solutions that employers have available for reducing the costs of medications are failing. In a recent Kaiser Family Foundation analysis, 82 percent of the respondents think the cost of prescription drugs is unreasonable.[44] To be clear, though, the problem of affordability is spotty. The same poll reports that 65 percent of them say that affording drugs is easy.

The problem is centered on people with a chronic disease, who are treated with large numbers of expensive medications and have relatively thin health insurance. A substantial minority are exposed to large out-of-pocket costs. Consistently over the last half decade, 28 percent of respondents have stated that they have difficulty affording their medications.[45] Faced with high uninsured costs at the pharmacy counter, many patients simply walk away, ignoring the advice of their doctor—who, in turn, is either unaware of the problem or powerless to address it.[46] More importantly, given the current strategies of the PBMs and manufacturers, these problems with unaffordability will only grow. Pharma's profit motive and the PBMs' rebate strategy combine to consistently drive up list prices, which people must pay when their insurance coverage is limited by out-of-pocket rules.

Employers are unlikely to drive for change. Given the overall complexity and lack of transparency by pharmacy commerce, the average human resources benefits team is in no position to advocate for different solutions. Meanwhile, pharmacy benefit managers annually publish their own data on cost increases their clients are experiencing. They suggest that employers are getting a good deal. For example, according to the PBMs, from 2016 to 2019, total cost increases in medications were less than 4 percent annually.[47] Their data are correlated by the Centers for Medicare & Medicaid Services' annual expenditure report: from 2016 to 2019, the annual increases in drug costs were (sequentially) 1.7 percent, 2.2 percent, 3.8 percent, and 5.7 percent. On the other hand, increases above 10 percent per year were the norm from 2013 to 2015.[48] Compare that with other, much more expensive components of health care, especially hospital services. Hospital cost increases averaged approximately 5 percent over the same period.

America's Health Insurance Plan [AHIP], the health insurer trade association, estimates that in 2021, 21.5 percent of an employer's health care dollar went to pay for prescription medicines, compared with 19 percent for in-patient hospital costs, 19.6 percent for hospital out-patient costs, 12.1 percent for doctor visits, and 6 percent for other out-patient care, with the remainder used for taxes, fees, and other expenses.[49] As a result, it is easy to understand how an employer might not realize the problem with rising pharmacy costs. But the pharmacy component of those expenditures continues to grow.

The PBMs' commercial approach also seems to be running out of gas. Further utilization management seems unlikely, as providers' pushback is growing stronger, and states and federal governments are taking note. Out-of-pocket rules are forcing patients off of their medications, leading to higher costs on the medical side of the equation. In most states, retail pharmacies are seeking legislative relief from the PBMs' control over their reimbursement. In particular, the PBMs long had contracts with payers that allowed them to keep the *spread*, or monetary difference, if their reimbursement to retail pharmacies was less than what they had guaranteed to the client. The majority of contracts prohibit that today, and regulators at state and federal levels want to outlaw spread pricing completely.

Meanwhile, generic prices are unlikely to go much lower, as the manufacturers' profit margins are, at best, thin today. For the first time, we are now witnessing the unavailability of some older drugs, as the reimbursement for them was too low to warrant continued production. Finally, the rebate program eventually drives up spending by individuals, essentially thinning out their health insurance still further.

There are other, new profit centers for the PBMs, however. They have taken advantage of the federal government's 340B Drug Pricing Program—a program intended to supply cheaper medications for low-income people—to derive new profits. (So has everyone else in the pharmaceutical supply chain.) Another new scheme is the use of group-purchasing organizations when buying medications from Pharma. But these, and all of the functions outlined above, can only thrive if the price of these drugs continues to go up, which eventually leaves some people unable to afford their medications. As commercial insurance thins, more patients will walk away from the pharmacy counter without filling their prescriptions.

What might work better? A survey of other leading economies could identify methods they use to keep pharmaceuticals affordable. But what we would find is that there is only one real answer: have the government negotiate the launch price and control inflation. And this method works. In 2020, Ezekiel Emmanuel and colleagues compared drug reimbursements in six countries similar to the United States.[50] They found that total per capita spending for drugs in the United States was $1,430 per year. Amounts in Australia, France, Germany, Norway, Switzerland, and the United Kingdom were all less than half that, with per capita costs in Australia and the United Kingdom being only $350. Moreover, these countries are using the same drugs to treat the same illnesses that we do in this country.

A report by the US House of Representatives' Ways and Means Committee staff reached the same striking conclusion.[51] Compared with Japan, Canada, Australia, and eight European countries, average pharmacy list prices in 2018 were $466.15 in the United States, compared with $124.45 in the other countries. Compared with the United States, prices for insulin were generally less than one-quarter in the other countries. Consider that a Humira prescription in the United States was $2,436.02, and in the other countries, $493.64.

The specific mechanisms employed by all of these other countries are remarkably similar. Prices are determined through direct negotiation or a calculation of maximum rates of reimbursement. Reimbursement is guided by objective means: either cost-effectiveness or reference standards. The same prices for medications are paid by all citizens, not divided into different levels of payers. Every pharmaceutical manufacturer is used to this kind of arrangement, as all of them do business in these countries. Some excellent health services research indicates that tying these negotiations to explicit reference prices or to calculated cost-effectiveness is crucial.[52]

Proof of the efficacy of using such an approach in the United States is available. The Department of Veterans Affairs currently conducts drug-pricing negotiations. Although some argue that the VA system only poorly approximates the rest of the American health care system, it's a fair place to start the comparison. The VA provides drug coverage for 9 million veterans in its outpatient medical clinics and mail-order facility. It negotiates directly with manufacturers, employing a formulary process similar to that used by the PBMs, but the results are much better. A recent analysis by the US Government Accountability Office revealed that the VA paid less than half of what the Medicare Part D program did for brand-name medications.[53]

The study points out that the VA uses a direct approach, buying from manufacturers and distributing medications through its mail-order pharmacy. Simplifying the handoffs enables the VA to blunt what is perhaps the greatest source of waste in commercial drug commerce: various distributors can buy low and sell high as prices increase, or reverse the field when branded drugs move to generics and are lower in cost. Slight delays in passing along savings, with this amount of money at stake, create great margins for the various links in the system. The VA sails past all of this.

Most Americans are open to the government exerting authority to reduce medication costs. A tracking poll published by the Kaiser Family Foundation in June 2021 showed that 88 percent of Americans think the federal government should negotiate for lower prices on medications, including 77 percent of Republicans.[54] This has remained the number one health priority for Americans over the last four years. Those who cannot afford their medicines may be the most vocal, but others are frustrated, too. Americans are also upset by the increasing complexity and lack of transparency around drug costs.

Could it really be a surprise, then, that when the Democrats came into office in 2021, they turned to drug prices? The Biden administration's proposed Build Back Better Act outlined the authority for Medicare to start to negotiate brand-name drug prices. It laid out careful steps, applying only to a limited portion of very expensive drugs. It also required that negotiations not begin until a drug had a reasonable period of time at the monopoly price set by the market. Politics intervened for almost a year. Then, surprisingly, formerly reluctant Senator Joe Manchin got on board with what eventually became the Inflation Reduction Act of 2022.

This act has begun a path for the government to lower drug costs by negotiating prices, but only in Medicare.[55] In 2023, drug companies will have to pay rebates if drug prices rise faster than inflation. In 2026, ten Medicare Part D drugs will enter into the negotiations, with fifty more targeted over the following three years. This incremental approach is what we would expect, given the history of government intervention. But in the end, by the early 2030s the federal government's approach and methods should begin to look like those in the United Kingdom or Australia. I will discuss the other details of the Inflation Reduction Act for Medicare Parts D and B in the next chapter. The key element here is that, after trying everything else, the federal government is now on the right course, given its need to control costs. But this program will only apply to those with government-sponsored health insurance.

One critical point deserves attention. When we consider the complexity of the drug pricing system, it's hard not to wonder if employers are really the best stewards of our health insurance benefits. They have accepted the PBMs' interventions, without demanding that prices be set by the government. This question will be sharpened now as the government starts to negotiate on a broader basis for Medicare beneficiaries. While overall inflation in the commercial market can be constrained by the current relationships between the PBMs and retail pharmacies, there will still be many people harmed by out-of-pocket costs—and their dissatisfaction is likely to grow. The potency of governmental negotiation, once its nose is under the tent, should lead those with commercial health insurance policies to ask why they can't access the government's leverage.

More importantly, governmental action will spur higher costs for private health insurance policies. The reaction of Pharma, no doubt, will be to cross-subsidize losses on the government's ledger with higher prices for commercial payers.[56] The PBMs may cope for a bit, but, if anything, they appear to be moving closer to Pharma, with huge profits coming from new group-purchasing entities that work directly with the manufacturers. Overall, governmental intervention for their insurance beneficiaries will make health care less affordable for employers—and their employees. The Inflation Reduction Act is thus another indicator of the value of a government-sponsored approach to health care insurance. The somewhat sad follow-up comment is, Why did employers not lobby for inclusion in the government's drug-pricing scheme? That failure, and their acceptance of the complex existing program for reducing medication prices, raises real questions about their stewardship of health care costs.

The bigger point for my thesis of an evolutionary path to socialized health insurance is that, in many ways, the area of pharmacy commerce, while completely different from that of hospitals and doctors, nonetheless demonstrates many similar themes. This story is evolving as we go into the mid-2020s, but let us return to the beginning of the twenty-first century to pick up the story of Medicare.

CHAPTER SIX

The Commercial Parts of Medicare: Parts C and D

―――――

TO UNDERSTAND THE INCREASINGLY powerful opportunity Medicare may provide for a more rational health insurance system, it's useful to unpack the history of the four components of this system. Parts A and B (traditional Medicare) function as part of the familiar fee-for-service system, reimbursing patients for hospital and physician services, respectively. Medicare Part C, now widely known as Medicare Advantage, is the managed care alternative to traditional Medicare. It is operated by private insurance companies, who take on risk for beneficiaries' health care utilization. Medicare Part D, the drug benefits system, is closely related to Medicare Advantage. It will take on a more central role in the discussion as I dig into the potential for health insurance reform and the development of managed care in the United States.

But first, we need some more details on traditional Medicare. Part A, originally established in 1965 by President Lyndon Johnson, presumed that there would be a national health system, funded by Social Security—that is, payroll taxes would go to a trust fund to pay for hospital insurance.[1] Part B was established at the same time—specifically, to provide coverage for regular physician visits. The Johnson administration had intended to finance Part B using the system proposed for hospital payments, but some legislators argued that expanding the program in this way might lead (rapidly) to socialized medicine. So, instead of relying on payroll taxes for funding, Part B is funded mainly by beneficiary premiums. Rather than a simple, expandable social insurance program, Medicare, from the start, was extremely complicated. Nonetheless, Parts A and B together are referred to as traditional Medicare.

Medicare's chops as a single-payer program were also hampered from the start by Congress's unwillingness to give Medicare any control over the development of hospitals or the practice of medicine. Instead, it was only an insurer. And as Uwe Reinhardt indicated, not only was it just an insurer, but its payment policies also specifically emulated those of the Blue Cross Blue Shield Association.[2] Medicare paid on a fee-for-service basis, with the usual and customary fees being charged.

This point cannot be made strongly enough. Traditional Medicare is a fee-for-service program, with all the inflation-engendering aspects of health care providers getting paid more to do more. The Centers for Medicare & Medicaid Services does control the price it will pay, which is much lower than that for commercial insurers. But the fee-for-service engine of overutilization will always underlie traditional Medicare. (As we will see, there may be ways to change that, going forward.)

Moreover, in traditional Medicare, the government itself did not do the paying. Instead, third-party administrators—usually private insurers—were hired to process claims on Medicare's behalf, to ease the minds of those suspicious of creeping medical socialism. This approach lasted for nearly forty years, until the passage of the Medicare Prescription Drug Improvement and Modernization Act (MMA) in 2003. The MMA was the largest administrative overhaul of the national health care system since its inception. While the MMA is mainly remembered for establishing Medicare Part D, this legislation also represented an important step in the modernization of the government's payment system. Instead of relying on private intermediaries, the MMA established Medicare administrative contractors (MACs) to handle payment for Parts A and B.[3]

The philosophical core of Medicare did not change with the arrival of MACs, who were still private health care insurers awarded a geographic area in which to process claims. But a key enabler is that MACs can decide what services should be covered, under a concept known as *local coverage decisions* (LCDs). The Medicare statute states that services must be "reasonable and necessary" in order to be covered, which is quite similar to the standard of effectiveness used by private insurers in their utilization management decisions. If a MAC wants to make a statement about not covering a particular service, the MAC must draft an LCD, hold a public meeting, and receive public comment before it can be adopted.[4] Often these policies are pursued in the face of lobbying by physicians or manufacturers with new devices or new procedures. The point is, though, that over time, even traditional Medicare came to adopt insurer mechanisms designed to promote value-based care.

Since MACs cover specific geographic regions and don't coordinate with one another, there is a good deal of regional variation in the procedures and products covered by Medicare. In response to growing confusion and the high costs associated with some regional coverage allowances, the CMS developed its own process for *national coverage determinations* (NCDs).[5] This national-level decision making is intended to expand coverage only when a new treatment is shown to be associated with an improvement in health outcomes for Medicare beneficiaries. Even though Medicare is not supposed to use cost-benefit analyses in its coverage decisions, MACs must enforce NCDs.

All of this is quite similar to what private insurers have been doing for years, but private insurers are substantially more restrictive and prescriptive.[6] The key point, however, is that coming into the twenty-first century, traditional Medicare was attempting to reduce unnecessary care, but not nearly as energetically as private insurers did. NCDs are relatively rare. To keep costs under control, the CMS primarily relied on its ability to name payment rates, doing very little to counter the volume-increasing incentives of the fee-for-service system. Rate control may even fan those incentives.

The unconstrained fee-for-service base for traditional Medicare does appeal to some. While organized medicine does not like the low fees paid by traditional Medicare, they do enjoy the relative lack of oversight. From a more politically left perspective, reformers who would advocate for Medicare for All appreciate traditional Medicare's exclusion of private insurers, eschewing the administrative costs they bring and the private profits in their underwriting function. In some ways this creates an odd coalition, which I will address in chapter 10.

Even though the Medicare program has a communitarian patina, beneficiaries in traditional Medicare can incur substantial out-of-pocket payments, just like participants in commercial private health insurance plans. Part A does not have a monthly premium, but there is a deductible for hospital care, pegged at $1,600 in 2023. Additional costs start to accrue after sixty days of hospitalization (specifically a co-insurance of $400 per day for days 61 through 90 of hospitalization in a benefit period). For Part B, there is an income-adjusted premium, ranging from $164.90 to $560.50 per month, along with a deductible of $226 in 2023.[7] As a result, out-of-pocket costs under traditional Medicare can be very high, and it is one of the few parts of the health care system today in which there is no out-of-pocket maximum. Not surprisingly, many beneficiaries relying on Parts A and B will buy supplementary insurance that covers portions of their out-of-pocket costs. Or increasingly, they turn to Medicare Advantage.

Medicare Advantage: Medicare Part C
Private Medicare Coverage in the Twentieth Century

Almost from traditional Medicare's founding as a passive, fee-for-service indemnity program, Medicare leaders began to experiment with private managed care approaches.[8] Even before passage of the HMO Act in 1974, Congress had authorized capitation payments for Medicare providers to reduce costs, but little happened until 1976, when some demonstration programs were launched. The experience with these programs was that there was less spending per beneficiary, but there was also a selection bias—healthier people were choosing the demonstration plans, so Medicare was arguably paying more for (healthier) people enrolled in managed care than those (less healthy) in the traditional program.[9] This is a chronic theme in managed Medicare.

Nonetheless, the Reagan administration proceeded with the development of managed care–oriented private plans in Medicare, pushing the passage of the Tax Equity and Fiscal Responsibility Act of 1982 (TEFRA). The HMOs were reimbursed at 95 percent of the adjusted average per capita cost (AAPCC), with other adjustments for demographic factors like age and sex. The reduced payment was meant to guarantee that Medicare did not overpay, but unfortunately, such relatively crude adjustments were still insufficient to stave off favorable selection effects. To address this widely recognized problem, private health care plans were asked to evaluate their finances and offer additional benefits to beneficiaries, to make the government's portion whole. The theory was that the government might pay more, but a beneficiary got more.

This was not necessarily a stable solution, but TEFRA and the rules that followed in 1985 birthed the modern Medicare Advantage program, where Medicare beneficiaries could decide to enroll in a Part C plan. They simply signed up for Part A, paid their Part B premium, and all services would then be rendered for an additional premium, which would be paid to a private plan. Additional benefits and more coordinated care attracted beneficiaries, and all of this was financed by the reduction in overall expenses associated with managed care.

As one might expect, Part C plans employed limited networks and undertook commercial plan–style utilization management, including prior authorization. Participating physicians had to be prepared to manage care. Some Medicare recipients were willing to accept such tradeoffs for the additional benefits the plans offered. Growth was slow but steady, accelerating in the 1990s as managed care caught fire in the commercial market, rising to 12 percent of all Medicare beneficiaries by 1996.

But during this period (roughly from 1985 to 1997), Medicare's risk assessment methodology simply did not hold up. Advantage plans could easily attract healthy individuals by offering low premiums and higher out-of-pocket payments or cost sharing. In addition, these plans were more prevalent in places where the average Medicare payments were higher, with the plans' sponsors essentially cherry-picking regional rate differences. Sick people avoided such plans, and those with a chronic disease might find that their established providers were not in network. For beneficiaries, there was a great deal of flexibility—they could switch as frequently as monthly, and the Part C plans had an out-of-pocket maximum, unlike traditional Medicare. Many beneficiaries loved their new managed Medicare.

Nonetheless, not savvy consumerism, but overpayment by the government was the defining policy theme for Part C. At least partly due to the rise of managed care in commercial health insurance, in the mid-1990s the per capita spending increase for private health insurance fell to 4 percent annually, while Medicare continued along at nearly double that clip.[10] This sense of Medicare being out of control, plus a warning that the Part A trust fund would be drained by 2003, led to congressional action.

The Balanced Budget Act of 1997 aimed to solve all the problems with Part C at once. First, it allowed preferred provider and provider-sponsored organizations (PPOs and PSOs) to participate in Part C. These were strategies that had been developed to manage care in the commercial markets. Second, efforts were made to get more precise estimates of a beneficiary's health status into the risk adjustment system. This was only perfected over the next five to seven years, when Medicare gained the capacity to get diagnostic data not only from hospitalizations, but also from ambulatory encounters. Third, Congress created incentives for managed care firms to do business in all counties, not just those with high AAPCC payments, and capped increases in areas with high AAPCCs at 2 percent. Making money was thus much more difficult.

The results were predictable. The Advantage plans first cut benefits, and then left the market. Over 30 percent of such plans closed over a four-year period. In 1998 there had been 6.3 million seniors in Part C, which dropped to 4.7 million by 2003.[11] This made a piercing impression on the insurance industry. The retreat of the managed care plans also made an impression on those opposed to the privatization of Medicare. Their take-home message was that fair payment would chill private payers' interest in Medicare, and traditional Medicare would remain ascendant. This is a theme that continues to play out today.

As the twenty-first century began, Republican members of Congress and the George W. Bush administration could not let the strategy of privatizing Medicare slip away. This political vision was the impetus behind the passage of the Medicare Modernization Act in 2003, which attempted to revitalize what was now to be known as Medicare Advantage. The MMA's vision was to bring private industry, and market incentives honed by competition, into the government's health care program. Unfortunately, for many reasons, it has proven to be the last significant example of Republican health policy development. (Republican-leaning health care experts continue to argue that a privatized Medicare, based on voucher payments for beneficiaries, would be the most efficient approach to Medicare.[12] This line of argument has little traction today.)

Its Resuscitation in the Twenty-First Century

Succinctly put, the MMA reflected the Bush administration's commitment to pay Medicare Advantage plans more per beneficiary than the government was spending in traditional Medicare, in order to resuscitate the Advantage program. Using a complex four-part formula, rates of payment rose, averaging more than 110 percent of traditional Medicare payments from 2006 to 2011.[13] New types of plans were allowed to participate, including regional PPO plans that could cover an entire state; special need plans (SNPs) intended for very vulnerable populations; and specific plans (known as *duals*) for those eligible for both Medicare and Medicaid.

The MMA also initiated competition between plans. Starting in 2006, plans had to bid for contracts on a county basis. Their bids had to cover required benefits and were to be judged against a benchmark: the county's historical costs for a traditional Medicare beneficiary. If a plan came in under the benchmark, then the plan would receive a rebate, 75 percent of which had to be devoted to better benefits or lower premiums. If the bid was over the benchmark, the difference had to be collected as additional beneficiary premiums. The result was a subtle mix of regulation and market incentive, since the bidding process became crucial to growth in plan memberships. The approach reflected the Bush administration's Republican brain trust's ideals. They brought market incentives to a program that was still assertively public. This was creative and bold policy making by any criteria. Increasingly, the base of Medicare Advantage was turned away from the fee-for-service system.

As might be expected, the Bush administration also improved risk adjustment. Now armed with more data from ambulatory visits and procedures, the Centers for Medicare & Medicaid Services, the successor to the Health Care Financing Administration, began to use Hierarchical Condition Category (HCC) coding. This new methodology was much more accurate, accounting for 10 percent of the variation in costs. In 2006, beneficiaries were required to stay in an Advantage plan for a year, creating greater actuarial stability. Tools were being put in place, based on the ability to gain ever-finer information electronically, to accurately pay for services used by enrollees in Medicare Advantage.

But the main point for the Bush administration was to get private insurers back in the game by paying them more. It worked. Payments relative to Medicare Parts A and B increased from 102 percent in 2003 to 114 percent in 2009. Insurers jumped back in, and the number of beneficiaries increased from 4.7 million in 2003 to 10.9 in 2010. Perhaps even more striking, the number of contracts (plans offered by insurers) increased from 157 in 2002 to 627 by 2009.[14] What looked to many like a dying program before the MMA, then became dynamic with its passage. Some, however, would say this was accomplished only by impoverishing traditional Medicare.

Nonetheless, the somewhat gratifying message from this survey of twenty-five years of Medicare Advantage through 2010 is that governmental design and regulation can manipulate and modify private insurers' participation in federally sponsored, privately operated insurance programs. Those suspicious of for-profit firms participating in government-sponsored programs might acknowledge this, especially given the continued growth of the Medicare Advantage program through 2022. Their counter, however, is that this only occurred because for-profit insurers stayed in the program, since it allowed them to earn inordinate profits.

The MMA and subsequent regulation of Medicare Advantage was not simply a matter of paying insurers enough to participate. The government induced insurers to accept a fixed budget, and then manage care in that geographic area using a variety of managed care techniques. These could include the payment of capitation to providers, especially in primary care; the use of narrow networks for providers; and utilization management. Insurers would either constrain costs or lose money.

This governmental oversight role applied not only to coverage and costs, but also to quality of care. In 2007, the CMS started the Star quality program ratings, first applying measures to the prescription drug program (which I will come to), and then, in 2008, with measures that were health plan specific.[15] I will go into the Star program in more detail later in this chapter, but suffice it to say now that a better Star performance yielded governmental bonus payments. Again, insurers follow the profit potential. From 2015, when the program had reached maturity, to 2021, the percentage of plans with four stars or better increased from 56 percent to 81 percent.[16] Insurers have clearly discovered that the return on investment when doing well on quality-of-care measures is quite lucrative.

This is another example of relatively straightforward governmental engineering to produce good outcomes, relying on insurers' profit incentives. Similar funding on quality-of-care measures is largely absent in commercial insurance, for both self-paid and fully insured individuals. For any insurer, the inequality of quality improvement efforts between Medicare Advantage and commercial plans is palpable, especially regarding the number of personnel and the amount of capital committed to this metric. Quality matters for government-sponsored health care plans in a way that it does not for commercial plans. Nonetheless, as I will show a bit later, this form of regulation may not necessarily produce better outcomes than traditional Medicare. And any regulation must be constantly updated to keep pace with developments by profit-seeking insurers.

Assessing the Medicare Advantage program over several decades leads to the somewhat reassuring conclusion that rational governmental manipulation of insurers' profit motive can produce decent health policy. But we can't jump to conclusions just yet. To best assess whether expanding Medicare Advantage could be an effective replacement for employer-sponsored insurance, three key measurements must be examined in more detail: cost, quality of care, and beneficiary experience. I get a bit ahead of the historical narrative by moving to assessments of Medicare Advantage today, but given the weight I expect the program to assume, as the potential vehicle for socialized health insurance, all the cards are best laid on the table at this point in the narrative.

Payment Today: The Coding Controversy

Eventually, the government's payments—perhaps overpayments—to health insurers in the Medicare Advantage plans had to be curtailed. The Affordable Care Act did that in 2010. The federal government's steps were rational and coordinated. Rebates decreased but could be topped back up with bonuses from good Star scores. A medical loss ratio threshold of 85 percent was set, to ensure that the majority of dollars went for medical care, not administration. Changes were made to the risk adjustment systems to counter plans' efforts to gain additional compensation through more intense coding. Out-of-pocket limits were created, distinguishing Medicare Advantage from traditional Medicare. Those limits in 2023 average $4,835 for in-network expenses, and $8,650 for in- and out-of-network combined.[17]

Rational reform again had its intended effect. On at least one set of measures, the percentage of Medicare Advantage payments, compared with traditional Medicare, had dropped from 114 percent in 2009 to 100 percent in 2017. The risk adjustment changes did not scare insurers away, but produced just the opposite reaction. The program has grown with increasing momentum. In 2020 it encompassed 24.1 million beneficiaries, nearly 40 percent of all Medicare recipients.[18] Over 80 percent of that enrollment was with the large insurers: United Healthcare, Humana, Anthem, CVS Health, Centene, Kaiser Permanente, or CIGNA. More than 60 percent of the beneficiaries were in zero premium plans, and overall premiums were slowly declining; 78 percent of the plans in 2020 had Star ratings of four or greater. Growth continues with predictions that, by 2030, 56 percent of the beneficiaries will be enrolled in Medicare Advantage.[19]

Nonetheless, payment by the government for Medicare Advantage plans remains an issue. Those suspicious of private insurers' involvement in the hallmark government-sponsored insurance program cry foul when the privatized Medicare program is paid more per beneficiary than traditional Medicare. Thus equivalence of payments has become an acid test. Data from the last five years suggest that payments through Medicare Advantage have again begun to outstrip those from traditional Medicare. Although rebates were decreased, bonus payments and ongoing risk adjustment strategies have made up for that. The Medicare Payment Advisory Commission (MedPAC) now asserts that Medicare Advantage plans are clearly being overcompensated by the current payment strategy.[20]

MedPAC argues that the profit margins for Medicare Advantage may have grown in the past decade, due to more careful use of beneficiary data, rather than by effective management of care to reduce costs by eliminating waste. Here, MedPAC points to increased risk scores over the past seven years, the result of insurers conducting more chart reviews to identify more diagnostic codes and get better reimbursement through risk adjustment.[21] Such reviews are intended to verify risk scoring by adding or deleting diagnoses. Therein lies a problem. In 2016, for example, only 1 percent removed diagnoses, and many more added new ones. These findings reiterate the need for careful regulation, as for-profit companies will maximize their profit margin wherever the rules permit it. Congress, following MedPAC's lead, has stepped in to mandate an automatic downcoding of Medicare Advantage submissions, at present by at least 5.9 percent.

Commercial insurers do not like MedPAC's implication that the government is spending too much, and that insurers are not playing fair. America's Health Insurance Plan, the health insurer trade organization, argues that the Medicare Advantage plans are approaching the issue of risk adjustment with integrity.[22] AHIP and MedPAC, as well as other academic assessors, continue to offer differing numbers and argue over their implications. What is important here is to realize that commercial insurers will explore every nook and cranny of a governmental program to improve their profit margin. They should, as their shareholders expect it. Meanwhile, the government will work to correct these incentives and push insurers toward the main job—to take out waste and reduce costs. That is what MedPAC continues to do: outlining how insurers should make a profit by managing care and eliminating waste, rather than taking the easier route of overcoding.

Part of the problem is the comparator: traditional, fee-for-service-based Medicare. Traditional Medicare has a different profit motive—do more, even if unnecessary—and diagnostic coding plays no role in that, even when such coding might be helpful in preventive efforts by identifying new medical problems and interventions. Nonetheless, those asserting that we need to curb Medicare Advantage overpayments have more compelling evidence.[23] These critics, as well as even-handed MedPAC, have specific solutions that the federal government should explore. Medicare Advantage must show its "advantage" by managing care, not by manipulating coding.

Increasingly, most agree. The Medicare Advantage industry group, the Better Medicare Alliance, has now advocated for annual audits using risk adjustment data validation techniques, as well as industry-wide requirements for best practices in home-risk assessments.[24] In a 2022 blog, Richard Gilfillan, Donald Berwick, and Richard Kronick have argued that Michael Chua and Kronick are probably correct in noting that overcoding could provide as much as $600 billion in over-payments for Medicare Advantage over the next eight years and suggest that these funds be reinvested in fixes for social determinants of health.[25]

MedPAC does not find this magnitude of overcoding, but the commission is certain that the problem is real. They have consistently recommended a risk adjustment model, based on two years of traditional Medicare and Medicare Advantage data; exclusion of data documented only on health risk assessments; and removal of the 5.9 percent limit on the reduction of differences measured between Medicare Advantage and traditional Medicare.[26] As the hue and cry continues, some portion of these reforms will take place. They must. As Michael McWilliams has pointed out, Medicare Advantage is on track to reach 69 percent of the Medicare population by 2030. At that point, there will be no way to use traditional Medicare as a benchmark, as the population differences will be too sharp.[27]

As 2023 began, the Biden administration reiterated its intent to undertake retrospective audits to determine overpayments to Medicare Advantage firms based on inappropriate designations of diagnoses, the *risk adjustment data validation* (RADV) audits.[28] This is causing a tremendous hue and cry, although the $4 billion the government hopes to receive in repayments represents only about 0.1 percent of the total amount of dollars going through the Medicare Advantage program over the decade. Insurers will continue to resist RADV methodology, even though they have lost a key round in court in 2021.[29] This is the kind of conflict one must expect with regulated profit makers, and the government appears to be equal to the task.

Perhaps more importantly, in terms of fair payment, the CMS is now proposing to incorporate the International Classification of Diseases' ICD-10 diagnosis codes into the HCC coding system. They also plan to eliminate certain codes they believe are subject to overcoding. MedPAC approves of both of these maneuvers, believing they can help even out the playing field with traditional Medicare.[30] These kinds of modifications, and the use of concepts such as autopiloted HCC codes and independent approved coders, can bring payment rates back into line.[31] This kind of constant adjustment is a sign of a healthy response by the government to ensure that a public program is fair and efficient. And it puts Medicare Advantage plans on notice—they must be prepared to manage care to turn a profit, and not rely on government overpayments.

The debate about the propriety of payments in Medicare Advantage has never really reached this degree of intensity in the general health policy literature. Gilfillan and Berwick have moved past just the risk-coding debate to suggest that the bidding process is unfairly favorable to Medicare Advantage plans, due to the CMS's calculation of traditional Medicare expenditures.[32] They and a group of other respected health policy advocates have made recommendations to the CMS that go well beyond what MedPAC has stated is necessary.[33] A third group of experts, organized by the Urban Institute, have yet another set of ideas for reform.[34]

These excellent arguments, as well as a lot of lobbying dollars, will determine what a Democratic administration's CMS will do to ensure equal footing for traditional Medicare and Medicare Advantage. Given the previous history of Medicare Advantage, I think the government will move to rein in risk coding, and perhaps readdress bidding. Then insurers will have to decide if the Medicare Advantage field is still profitable. I think it will be, but the profits will have to come from managed care relationships that eliminate waste, not from financial tactics. As I will discuss in chapters 9 and 10, this lining up of traditional Medicare and Medicare Advantage on an equal footing is crucial to which pathway Medicare for All eventually takes—traditional or Advantage. In any case, this debate over payments to Medicare Advantage is occurring now, which is propitious as employer-sponsored insurance enters its 2020s and 2030s stress test.

One other point is worth noting. Medicare Advantage is increasingly based in vertically integrated giants, such as the United Health Group, CVS Health, CIGNA, Humana, and Kaiser Permanente. Integrating their affiliated companies, particularly their pharmacy benefit management companies, can allow them to make a profit in those companies while showing smaller overall profit margins in the Medicare Advantage plans. Perspicacious researchers have latched on to this, although they lack comprehensive data to make their case.[35] Reporters have noticed,[36] and so, too, will the CMS. Keeping private payers in the Medicare program will require this kind of constant attention. If insurers want to integrate vertically into the health care system, they will have to tolerate much more transparency than they have in the past.

Payment for Providers

In a comparison of Medicare Advantage and traditional Medicare, one key issue I have not discussed is the payment rates for providers. Lower provider payment rates in traditional Medicare are the most effective way in which that program saves money. But the payers in Medicare Advantage are private insurers, not Medicare, and the federal government is not dictating terms for them.

One of the best-kept secrets in health policy is that Medicare Advantage plans pay rates that are very similar to the ones in Medicare. For years, I have asked hospital executives this question in background conversations, and they generally lament that Medicare Advantage payments basically shadow price traditional Medicare. But little was written about this until 2015, when Robert Berenson and colleagues published an article in *Health Affairs*, based on their survey of hospital and health plan executives, finding much the same thing.[37] Their respondents reported that the average payment by Medicare Advantage plans was just around 100 percent of that by Medicare, although Advantage plans more recently entering the market might have to pay more. Only in geographic areas with concentrated hospital markets might Medicare Advantage reimbursements get to 110 percent of traditional Medicare.

The reasons given for these relatively low rates, compared with the much higher rates paid by the same insurers in a commercial setting, were in many ways as interesting as the payments themselves. Hospital leaders cited the Medicare law, in particular Section 1866 of the

Social Security Act, which requires hospitals to accept Medicare rates for out-of-network care. This is critical for the Medicare Advantage insurers. A hospital does not need to contract with them for it to be in network. But when it is out of network, a hospital is only going to be paid at Medicare rates. The leverage this creates for Medicare Advantage insurers is enormous.

As a result, hospitals understand that they do not have much bargaining power with a Medicare Advantage plan. A Medicare Advantage insurance company network executive, negotiating with a hospital CFO, would point out that if an Advantage plan cannot include something close to Medicare rates, that plan will not be viable, and a beneficiary will have to use traditional Medicare, where there is no negotiating. Another possibility is that a beneficiary would simply be out of network, so again, the hospital would get Medicare payment rates. The same is true regarding doctor groups.

Some hospitals—those with substantial market power—are pushing back, albeit ever so slightly. For example, the Mayo Clinic has recently stated that Medicare Advantage patients from United Healthcare will no longer be scheduled for outpatient appointments if they are out of network. Mayo has suggested that this decision was based on COVID-19 issues—specifically, patient capacity. But the underlying rationale most likely is Medicare Advantage's low rates.[38] This dynamic will bear watching.

Medicare Advantage must cover not only hospital costs (Part A of traditional Medicare), but also those in Part B, including physicians' fees and medications. Part A is fairly straightforward: hospitals are reimbursed on a DRG basis. Part B is more complicated in many ways, but studies have suggested that reimbursements under Part B by Medicare Advantage are comparable with traditional Medicare rates.[39] (Part B drugs are especially complicated. Suffice it to say that any future Medicare program will have to presume that the government must negotiate the costs of Part B drugs, alongside those negotiated under Part D.)

In summary, Medicare Advantage thrives in large part on its ability to shadow Medicare reimbursement rates. Government-negotiated fees, plus managed care, produce very strong downward pressures on the costs of care. Medicare Advantage has this double punch: government rates, and incentives to produce value-based care. This insight bears on the attractiveness of Medicare Advantage as a replacement for employer-sponsored insurance. The negotiated fee part of this alone is considerable. The Kaiser Family Foundation estimated that private health insurance spending was $859 billion in early 2021. That amount would be $507 billion, or $352 billion less, if commercial insurers were paid at Medicare rates.[40] If employers had access to Medicare rates, then their share would drop from $474 billion to $280 billion, a 41 percent drop. The employees' share of premiums and their out-of-pocket costs would also drop, by $116 billion. These are numbers to keep in mind as I build toward predictions of what happens in the next two decades.

Quality of Care

Beginning in 2007, and fully functional since 2009, the CMS has published Star ratings, which supply rather comprehensive information on the performance of health plans, based on specific measures. The Star ratings were designed to serve two purposes: a public function, which gave potential beneficiaries information on which plan to choose; and a structural function, which rewarded plans with better quality scores. This creates a double incentive for Medicare Advantage firms to improve the quality of care.

The measures themselves derive from the forty-year history of research on quality in health care. They utilize three traditional domains: *outcomes*, *processes*, and *beneficiary experiences*.[41] For example, outcomes include blood sugar control for diabetes; processes involving colorectal cancer screening and fall risk reductions; and beneficiary experiences include health plan ratings and appeals that are upheld. This set of criteria is comprehensive from the point of view of measurable quality, although they have changed frequently over the last decade. So, too, have their relative weightings as the CMS endeavors to find the right mix of quality signals. While there are calls for improvement, most prominently for better risk adjustments around socioeconomic factors,[42] the validity of these measures is widely accepted.

Insurers take the Star measures very seriously. It is difficult to tell how much plan selection by individual beneficiaries is influenced by Star scores, and many experts think it is relatively little. On the other hand, there are very substantial quality bonus payments associated with attaining at least four-star status. Medicare Advantage plans covet these bonuses.[43] They can be used to fund supplemental benefits or reduce cost sharing for beneficiaries, but they can also be taken to the bottom line, with the caveat of meeting medical benefit ratios of at least 85 percent (see chapter 7 for more on medical benefit ratios). Plans generally find that there is a healthy return on investment associated with efforts to improve Star ratings. Unlike other capped areas of reimbursement, Star dollars have increased, from $3 billion in 2015 to $11.6 billion in 2021, or from $184 per member to $446 per member.[44]

A good deal of this increased payout is driven by an overall improvement in Star scores, with the number of plans with ratings of four stars or better increasing from 52 percent in 2015 to over 80 percent in 2021, even though the CMS annually stiffens its requirements. Some of this may be due to plan consolidation—that is, if an insurer has two plans and merges them, then the combined plan moves to the higher Star scores. Better data collection also plays a role.

But Star measures are not just a matter of administrative maneuvers. Most observers believe that creating the right incentives for quality will produce it. I can confirm that Medicare Advantage plans are decidedly more concerned about quality issues, at least around the discrete Star measures, than are employers' commercial plans. The return from an investment in quality of care is direct and clear on the Medicare side of the house.

The structure of quality-of-care assessments and improvements in Medicare Advantage is quite sound. Nonetheless, independent assessments of the quality of care through Medicare Advantage vary a great deal. An evaluation by the Better Medicare Alliance, the health plan–supported advocate for Medicare Advantage, is sunny. Their facts, however, are somewhat transparent. The alliance notes that Medicare Advantage scores are not just a matter of selection bias—that is, healthier people choosing the program. Instead, in 2018, Medicare Advantage beneficiaries had a 57 percent higher rate of serious mental illness and 16 percent higher rates of alcohol and drug abuse than traditional Medicare beneficiaries.[45] Even so, Advantage plan beneficiaries have 23 percent fewer inpatient hospital stays, 33 percent fewer emergency department visits, and a 5 percent increase in breast cancer screenings, compared with traditional Medicare beneficiaries. Overall, 92 percent of the Medicare Advantage beneficiaries were satisfied with the quality of care they receive.

Two recent academic studies funded by the Better Medicare Alliance reiterated these points. Kenneth Thorpe found that those with chronic conditions were more likely to choose Medicare Advantage plans,[46] attempting to correct the widely accepted contention that its members are healthier. Another study, by the consulting firm Avalere, showed that Medicare Advantage had more beneficiaries with chronic conditions and more members from racial/ethnic minorities who, in turn, tended to have higher social risk factors.[47] Nonetheless, health care service utilization was lower in the Medicare Advantage plans. While overall beneficiary costs were similar between Medicare Advantage and traditional Medicare, spending on preventive therapy and tests was 21 percent higher in Advantage plans, yet potentially preventable hospitalizations were 29 percent lower.[48] Another recent study revealed that for minority beneficiaries, Medicare Advantage programs were associated with significantly better outcomes for access and quality than traditional Medicare. I should note, however, that many of the studies on Medicare Advantage are sponsored by the insurance industry, and one has to be on guard for bias.

Independent academic assessments are not so uniformly reassuring. John Ayanian's team has recently published a dissenting view, focusing on nine clinical measures and comparing Medicare Advantage with commercial plans.[49] They found that four measures had improved vis-à-vis commercial plans, but four others had deteriorated over time. Overall, the comparison between Medicare Advantage and commercial plans was a wash. The authors' focus was only on clinical measures, and they left aside the incomparability of members' ages, but this study demonstrates that there is not unanimity in asserting that Medicare Advantage plans are of superior quality.

The study by Ayanian and colleagues contrasts with another recent analysis, showing that Medicare Advantage outperformed traditional Medicare in most studies comparing quality-of-care metrics.[50] Perhaps the best summary of research comparing quality in Medicare Advantage with that of traditional Medicare was published in late summer 2022.[51] These authors found few differences between the two programs, although Medicare Advantage did look better in terms of preventive services, identification of a primary source of care, and readmission prevention. Beneficiary satisfaction was very similar in both programs.

Thus Medicare Advantage programs cannot claim better overall quality, but there is no indication that the managed nature of their care is harming beneficiaries. In addition, there is at least some evidence that Medicare Advantage is closing gaps in health care equity. The Better Medicare Alliance documented that Advantage plan members with low incomes, and those in diverse populations, get better cost protection in Medicare Advantage.[52] Again, though, none of this is solid evidence. An investigation published just months later showed no differences in access, affordability, or use of preventive services in Medicare Advantage as opposed to traditional Medicare.[53]

Three more studies in late 2022 and early 2023 encapsulate the dispute over quality of care in Medicare Advantage and traditional Medicare. A thorough study of thirty-day mortality following acute myocardial infarction showed lower rates of mortality for Medicare Advantage beneficiaries in 2009, but no difference in 2018.[54] Another study showed that lowering the amount of avoidable acute care in Medicare Advantage plans was mostly a matter of shifting hospital care to short observation stays, which may have dubious quality implications.[55] A comprehensive review of utilization and quality of care indicated that utilization was lower and performance quality was the same as or higher than traditional Medicare.[56]

Thus I might conclude that as Medicare Advantage approaches traditional Medicare in terms of its share of Medicare beneficiaries, quality of care outcomes will blur. But another study, looking at situations in which providers had assumed a two-sided risk for their Medicare Advantage patients, showed that these at-risk providers outperformed traditional Medicare on all eight leading efficiency measures.[57] (These measures all involved the utilization of services, so they are not really what should be seen as quality of care.) This might mean that as we move more toward an active management model by providers of at-risk primary care, we will obtain the brass ring of greater efficiency.

The government is aware of all this back and forth on the quality of care in Medicare Advantage plans. The CMS is constantly modifying the Star measures. For example, in May 2020, the CMS increased the importance of the scoring (weights) for access measures and patient experience. They also shifted the cut points upward, creating a steeper incline to get a rating of four stars and above.[58]

More significant structural changes have also been suggested. Med-PAC believes that the current quality program should be enlarged. Most importantly, the commission argues that quality of care should be a zero-sum game. That is, all quality awards should come from the same overall budget, which essentially means those with poor quality ratings are paid less. MedPAC's proposed Medicare Advantage Value Incentive Program (MA-VIP) would radically reduce the number of measures in the Star programs and require that quality payments not increase the overall Medicare budget. MedPAC would also provide a continuous scale on quality measures and publicize those measures at the local market level.[59] So far, there has not been much appetite for this among politicians, but the discussion shows the healthy relationship of MedPAC to the CMS and Congress—specifically, the commission's ability to think through alternatives as the Medicare program evolves in a rational fashion. Eventually one must presume that the MedPAC recommendations will be instituted.

Perhaps even more importantly, leaders at the CMS have recently indicated their desire to move to a common and relatively simple set of foundational measures for the quality of care.[60] These measures would emphasize the prevention of chronic diseases and explicitly incorporate concerns about racial and gender equity. It is a long-needed set of reforms.

At this point, though, quality of care is a jump ball in the comparison of Medicare Advantage with fee-for-service traditional Medicare. Perhaps that should be reassuring. A managed program raises worries about stinting on quality while searching for efficiency, although this does not appear to be the case. On the other hand, we might wish that all the dollars the government is spending on quality bonuses were having a greater impact.

Beneficiary Experience

The other major feature of Medicare Advantage that has a bearing on quality is the enrollment process, which affects the overall beneficiary experience. Competing plans use telemarketing and web-based programs to alert potential beneficiaries to their options. But they also pay commissions to brokers and brokerage firms, who can funnel customers to them. These commissioned sales are greater than 80 percent of all sales.

The Commonwealth Fund evaluated the role that agents/brokers play in the signup process and found that 96 percent of Medicare Advantage plans have contractual relationships with brokers.[61] The brokers are all licensed through the states and certified through AHIP. Medicare has established specific marketing guidelines, which are modified annually. The responsibility for oversight falls to the individual plans, and failure to perform that oversight can result in penalties and sanctions, including exclusion from the program. More of this activity is moving online, but many beneficiaries still prefer personal relationships with individual brokers who speak their language and have command of the welter of choices around premiums, deductibles, and supplementary benefits. In many ways, this attention to education and oversight of the process contrasts sharply with the tools available to the average employee facing benefit decisions.

As might be expected, advocates for beneficiaries see room for improvement. The Commonwealth Fund report notes a few.[62] Most importantly, almost all of us are challenged by trying to make a rational decision about coverage when there are so many possible permutations of premiums, benefits, and out-of-pocket costs—to say nothing of the choice about a prescription benefit or use of a supplemental policy. The ability to obtain a plan that suits a person's needs clearly works best for those who are more highly educated and have more resources.[63]

Nonetheless, the current regulation of Medicare Advantage choices—and, in particular, the oversight of brokers—suggests that the CMS is serious about having beneficiaries behave as informed consumers. But today, once enrolled, there is little shopping by Medicare Advantage customers, as illustrated by data on plan comparison evaluations.[64] Yet satisfaction with Medicare Advantage marketing was decreasing in 2022, and there is an increased scrutiny of claims made by celebrity spokespeople.

The National Association of Insurance Commissioners (NAIC) would like to regain some authority to regulate marketing, as this was limited in the Medicare Modernization Act of 2003. NAIC cites misrepresentation, as well as fraudulent activity, resulting in improper enrollment.[65] Even the Better Medicare Alliance is asking for more regulation and oversight of third-party marketing companies. The CMS has responded with new proposed rules that would ban certain kinds of misleading advertisements and provide better information for potential beneficiaries.[66] Again, the government needs to step in to protect beneficiaries from aggressive profit-oriented tactics.

One other point on enrolling in Medicare Advantage deserves attention. Many Medicare Advantage policies are bought on behalf of employees with retirement health benefits by their employers: the group Medicare or employer group waiver (EGWP) plans. Commitment to retiree health has waned among employers over the last forty years, but it is still prominent in state and local governments, as well as in trade union contracts. Of the total 30.8 million people enrolled in Medicare Advantage in 2023, 18 percent were in group plans.[67]

In these plans, employers are paying the premiums, usually selecting one plan for their entire workforce. This phenomenon is not waning. Just the opposite is occurring—in late 2020, Medicare reported that group plans had increased their membership by 26 percent over the previous four years.[68] In most cases, employers have decided to shift from an arrangement based on traditional Medicare plus a supplemental policy to a Medicare Advantage chassis. All major health plans offering Medicare Advantage have a thriving group business, with lots of competition based on price and supplementary benefits (quality of care assurance is through the Star program). By late 2022, at least half of the employers offering retiree benefits did so with a contract for Medicare Advantage.[69]

This is important if we consider Medicare Advantage as a replacement for employer-sponsored insurance. Participating insurers offering EGWP Medicare products estimate their reimbursement from the CMS for a firm's employee population, design the plans, and (predictably) earn a profit margin from their management. If Medicare Advantage were an offering for all employees, or at least for employees in an age tranche such as 60–65, the same thing would happen. Actuaries would have to understand the complexities of the different risk represented by a younger population, but that is a capability firmly within their grasp. Group Medicare Advantage is thus a model for a Medicare Advantage for All program sold by private insurers to employers.

One other area of beneficiary experience that is currently under scrutiny is prior authorization. It is clear from a recent study that Medicare Advantage does deny coverage available in traditional Medicare.[70] While the overall impact is small—about $60 per beneficiary per year—the experience for an individual person can be harrowing, even given the concerns about Medicare oversight I previously discussed. The Office of the Inspector General at the Department of Health and Human Services has raised concerns about the evidence base that insurers are using.[71]

More importantly, perhaps, providers and patient groups have advocated for greater transparency and electronic processing of prior authorization requests.[72] Provider concerns about prior authorization continue to ramp up, with the AMA now stating that 33 percent of physicians report that prior authorization has led to a serious adverse event for a patient under their care. In response, the CMS has now promulgated draft rules to promote interoperability and faster decision making, again an indication that as problems arise, the government responds—if slowly.[73] The pressure on prior authorization is, in any case, much more important to the demise of employer-sponsored insurance than it is for Medicare Advantage.

In summary, Medicare Advantage, while quite operationally complicated, appears simple and rational when compared with much of what goes on in the commercial realm. There is strict oversight from the CMS, and there are incentives to provide quality of care. Beneficiaries very much like the program, and it does offer advantages over traditional Medicare: additional benefits, and lower out-of-pocket spending. Medicare Advantage plans may still cost more than traditional Medicare, but the CMS can correct that—and private insurers designing Medicare Advantage products will have to adjust to its regulations.[74] Most importantly, Medicare Advantage uses the capitation concept to encourage techniques that will remove health care waste: utilization management, narrow networks, primary care physician oversight of all care, and the lower reimbursement to doctors and hospitals that is part of Medicare. This is why some have started to argue that Medicare Advantage could reasonably replace employer-sponsored insurance.[75]

Drug Coverage in Medicare
Medicare Part D

The 2003 act that resuscitated Medicare Advantage also birthed Medicare Part D, the Medicare drug benefit. The authors of Medicare in the 1960s did not consider offering a drug benefit, as drugs were thought to be a minor part of overall health care costs. That soon changed, but most retired people were relegated to seeking drug coverage through a Medicare supplemental policy. In addition, by the 1990s, many employers who, at one time, offered retiree health benefits had retreated to just providing retiree drug benefits. As the twenty-first century began,

I have estimated that more than half of the pharmacy benefit management industry was devoted to such retiree programs, often based in the mandatory use of mail-order pharmacies.

The politics that came together to lead to the 2003 Medicare Modernization Act (officially known as the Medicare Prescription Drug, Improvement, and Modernization Act) were complicated, shadowed by the ongoing debate about the inclusion of drug coverage in Medicare.[76] In the final legislation, there were four critical components.[77] First was the administration of the program. The prescription drug benefit was not tied to Parts A or B, but instead was left entirely in private hands. While it was not clear exactly what entities would take up the role of managing the drug benefit when the legislation passed, pharmacy benefit managers and, to some extent, insurers rapidly shifted to full engagement. Part D was also designed to fit either with a Medicare Advantage plan or to be freestanding for those in traditional Medicare who wanted a drug benefit—the *prescription drug plans*, or PDPs.

Second, and relatedly, the government did not endorse federally negotiated drug prices, which was not surprising, given Part D's Republican heritage. Republicans, and many moderates, have long opposed governmental negotiation with pharmaceutical firms. Presumably these legislators have had visions of creeping socialism and threats to free enterprise. Yet these fears did not keep Medicare from eventually naming prices for hospitals, long-term care, and doctors. Nonetheless, in Part D, negotiation was left to the PBMs and insurers who had developed the plans, using the rebate methodology they had employed in commercial plans.

Third, Part D was to be risk based, like Medicare Advantage, with the government calculating payment rates that allowed the intermediaries (PBMs or Medicare Advantage plans) to profit if they controlled costs. This empowered the PBMs and Advantage plans to employ all the tools they had available for cost control: mail-order pharmacies; tiering, to get people to shift to generics; formularies, so rebates could be gained from branded drug manufacturers; utilization management, to reduce unnecessary or inappropriate care; and even spread pricing, through management of the retail network. As was the case with the

Medicare Advantage program, federal oversight was considerable—far greater than that applied by employers in their dealings with the PBMs. There was also a Star program, heavily oriented toward member satisfaction and a reduction of inappropriate denials of care.

The fourth major component was intended to address budget hawks' concerns about runaway medication costs and their potential contribution to the federal budget deficit. Part D offered only partial payments for medications: the plan was responsible for some of the costs; the federal government provided some payment directly; beneficiaries kicked in some funds; and even the manufacturers covered some of the costs. Payment responsibility shifted as costs mounted for any beneficiary. Prominent among these phases was the *donut hole* in the middle of Part D. After a certain amount of coverage, denominated in dollars spent, beneficiaries had to pay the full cost for medications for a period before *catastrophic coverage* kicked into place.

This biggest expansion in Medicare since 1965 was signed into law by President George W. Bush in December 2003. It combined a large dollop of beneficiary out-of-pocket spending with all the intricacies of the PBM world, and it was now heavily regulated. Surprisingly, it worked—by most measures.

PBMs and health plans decided to participate, beneficiaries signed up for what was a voluntary plan, and costs stayed well under the original estimates. The Part D program remained split between freestanding prescription drug plans (PDPs), for people who wanted a drug benefit but who had stayed in traditional Medicare, and plans annealed to Medicare Advantage policies (MA-PD plans). Very slowly over time, the PDPs' membership has dwindled, and the portion of the population in the MA-PD plans has grown.

An assessment on the tenth anniversary of Part D's implementation demonstrated progress in terms of broader coverage and constrained costs.[78] Membership had continued to grow, not only in the conventional program, where beneficiaries paid a premium, but also in the *low-income subsidy* (LIS) program, where beneficiaries had no premium and very limited out-of-pocket payments. In 2015, 72 percent of the people in Medicare had a Part D plan. On average, just over thirty stand-alone PDPs and fifteen MA-PDs were available to enrollees. Perhaps most importantly monthly premiums had moderated and even begun to decrease, diminishing to $37 per month for a PDP. The MA-PD premiums were also low, averaging $17 monthly.[79]

While the federal structure of the Part D plan has continued to evolve over the course of its fifteen-year history, by 2016 the standard plan design offered by most PDPs had crystallized. It is important to note that the architecture of federal payments determines the reimbursements to privately organized plans. A private plan estimates the federal payment and designs a program based on the use of generic and branded drugs (tiering) that it believes will drive a beneficiary to more cost-effective drug utilization. In other words, the federal rules determine the federal contribution, and the private plan then designs the details of its pharmacy benefit. These plans will vary in the tiering of medications and the cost sharing associated with them.

This approach has proven to be stable. Part D's overall spending increased from $44.3 billion in 2006 to $88.6 billion in 2015, a good deal below the initial estimates. In 2022, spending had increased to $119 billion, and there were 49 million beneficiaries. PDPs have stopped growing, but with the overall growth of Medicare Advantage, expansion continues in MA-PDs.[80]

The basic federal reimbursement structure for Part D plans remains complicated, even with filling in the celebrated donut hole as part of the Affordable Care Act. Through 2022, the Part D plans received payments that were based on the following federal formula.[81] There was an initial deductible of $480 for every member. After that, members entered a *coverage phase* for spending of up to $4,430 annually. In this phase, the government dictated that members pay a co-insurance of 25 percent, with the plan paying for the other 75 percent. Then came the *coverage gap phase*, which used to be the donut hole, of up to $10.690 in total drug spending, where members continued to pay 25 percent co-insurance. In this phase, the pharmaceutical manufacturers gave a 70 percent discount on branded drugs, and plans paid for 5 percent. Above that, in catastrophic coverage, Medicare paid 80 percent; plans, 15 percent; and members, 5 percent. Medicare's payment in this catastrophic phase was known as *federal re-insurance*. These rules defined the cost shares for the four parties: members, plans, manufacturers, and the government.

Reimbursements from the government and manufacturers form one aspect of the Part D plans. The second aspect—which had to be constructed actuarially, considering the statutory backbone—is the set of formulary decisions, utilization management parameters, drug tiers, co-payments, and co-insurance that a plan developed to define the relationship between the plan and its members. Essentially, the designer of a Part D plan takes the federal government's revenue estimate and designs a pharmacy insurance plan that manages the risk and leaves a small profit margin.

To do this today, plans have almost universally adopted five-tier programs (preferred and nonpreferred generics, preferred and nonpreferred branded drugs, and specialty tiers) and have various levels of both deductibles and co-insurance. Formularies have become tighter, and nearly one-quarter of their drugs are subject to prior authorization. In addition, burdensome cost sharing for drugs not in LIS plans has increased over time. For example, on average, co-payments have increased from $55 for nonpreferred brands in 2006 to $80 in 2015.[82] While there is an out-of-pocket maximum for Medicare Advantage, through 2022, the Part D drug program had no such cap.

The PBMs sponsoring Part D plans design such plans in the early spring of the year, before they are offered. The plans are then submitted to Medicare for review, so CMS regulators can assess if a plan is sound. At the same time, the plan's sponsor (a PBM or a Medicare Advantage insurer) is involved with manufacturers (about rebates and formularies) and the retail network (about reimbursement rates and quality of care incentives). All of this is part of the transparent exchange of information—at least between the CMS and a Part D plan—about the operation of that plan, so it can be formally approved for sale.

All of the decisions about formularies and utilization management must be approved by an impartial group of expert physicians and pharmacists called the *pharmacy and therapeutics committee* (its members have no ties to the industry), and then reapproved by the CMS. In this manner, the government can keep tight oversight of beneficiaries' welfare. This is in sharp contrast with the PBMs' unregulated administration of employer-sponsored plans.

The final aspect of a Part D plan, whether freestanding or part of a Medicare Advantage plan, concerns beneficiaries. Beneficiaries must first pay a deductible. In addition, they face five tiers of drugs, each with different co-payments. These tiers are designed to encourage the use of low-cost generics or lower-cost brand-name drugs. Beneficiaries must also know that only certain branded drugs are on the plan's formulary. These restrictive formularies fuel the rebate engine. Through 2022, as beneficiaries hit the level of spending that was formerly the donut hole, they usually had new co-insurance requirements that extended until their true out-of-pocket (TROOP) cost limit was met, after which there was usually a 5 percent co-insurance payment. This latter stage was known as the catastrophic phase. Through 2022, Part D plans still presented the possibility of people deciding that they could not afford the medications they need, as there was no limit on their co-insurance payments.

I have described these basic functions of the Part D plan through 2022 simply because the Inflation Reduction Act, passed in late 2022, has changed matters dramatically for Part D. While the drug negotiation aspects of the act are getting the most publicity, it also changes the responsibilities of who pays in each of the phases. Most importantly, the federal government has reduced its role in the catastrophic phase, putting the plan in charge of paying for the benefits. This is intended to increase plan management, so there will be more attention to tiering and rebates.

Again, the reason for these changes was mounting costs. As more drugs have increased in price, especially expensive specialty medications, the number of patients falling into the catastrophic phase has increased, as have the federal government's re-insurance payments— in 2022 they amounted to 45 percent of total expenditures, compared with 14 percent in 2006.[83] While the ever-greater use of generics has limited Part D expense increases to about 4 percent per year, most of this inflation has been driven by the high-cost drugs that all end up in the catastrophic phase. As the re-insurance dollars have poured in, the share of aggregate basic benefit costs borne by plan sponsors has decreased from 53 percent to 29 percent, undermining, from MedPAC's very reasonable point of view, the incentives to manage risk.[84] Another way to look at it is that in 2007, taxpayers were at risk for 24.9 percent of Part D costs, while in 2019, they were burdened with 61.2 percent of these costs. MedPAC's proposed solution was to increase a plan's risk in both the coverage gap and the catastrophic period, to ensure that plans have every reason to reduce costs. MedPAC suggested that plans cushion this change, temporarily, with other subsidies (such as expanded risk-corridor assistance, to limit the financial risks borne by insurance providers). With the Inflation Reduction Act, federal legislators heeded this sage advice.[85]

It appears that beneath MedPAC's interest in placing risk back into the private insurance program, which is the foundation of Part D, is its fear of concentration and collusion. MedPAC notes that five firms dominate the Part D picture (UnitedHealth Group, CVS Health, Centene, Humana, and CIGNA), with up to 90 percent of the beneficiaries in stand-alone PDPs being with one of these companies. As more and more people have gone into the catastrophic phase, rebates play a larger role, growing from 20 percent of a plan's liability in 2007 to 53 percent in 2018.[86]

This means that negotiations between a few large PBMs and large pharmaceutical manufacturers over rebates are a critical part of the Medicare drug program. The complicated structure of the manufacturers' role in the coverage gap creates opportunities for plans and manufacturers to overuse expensive branded drugs in their formularies, taking advantage of the federal subsidy.[87] In other words, through 2022, there was a strong likelihood that Part D plans had an interest in getting to the catastrophic phase, where the government would be picking up more of the total cost.

The increased plan risk in the Inflation Reduction Act addresses this.[88] Much less support in the catastrophic phase comes from the federal government, with the federal subsidy for branded drugs decreasing from 80 percent to 20 percent. The Part D plan is again on the hook for cost management, and the use of expensive brands in formularies becomes prohibitive. In addition, after 2025, there will now be a $2,000 hard cap on out-of-pocket spending. These are exactly the kinds of recondite changes that were recommended by MedPAC, changes that will have a real impact on costs and encourage sturdier management by the Part D plans. Such changes, plus the governmental negotiation provisions, will make the program run much more efficiently and effectively. From a health policy point of view, this is admirably exquisite regulatory change—just what our health care system needs.

From an individual beneficiary's point of view, the importance of the out-of-pocket limit cannot be understated. The Kaiser Family Foundation estimated that, in 2017, the out-of-pocket spending for medications for beneficiaries that were hitting the catastrophic threshold was more than $3,200.[89] People being treated for cancer, or with an autoimmune disease, have long faced strikingly high costs for their therapy.[90] For example, in 2019, Part D beneficiaries had out-of-pocket costs averaging $10,470 for eleven oral (hence Part D, not Part B) medications, with the median income for Medicare beneficiaries being $26,000.[91] The Inflation Reduction Act essentially fills this gap by increasing the demand on plan sponsors to manage care.

Next Steps for Medicare Part D Policy

The original Part D program was complicated, as might be expected, given the convoluted nature of medication commerce and the program's commitment to undertaking public goals through private firms. There is little doubt, though, that making medications affordable has saved lives. Reducing out-of-pocket spending leads to improved adherence to a medication regimen, and that, in turn, produces better health. In addition, Part D lowers the use of more expensive services by enabling early treatments of medical conditions.[92]

Over time, however, the high cost of specialty drugs has overwhelmed the basic Part D structure, and some fraction of beneficiaries have been burdened with costs they cannot afford. Guided by MedPAC and academic commentary, Congress has now rather nimbly modified the program to address emerging issues. The major elements of the Inflation Reduction Act are the changes in Part D noted above and coming negotiations over prices for the first ten high-cost medications, then twenty the next year, and so forth.

The government's move to dictate the prices it will pay for medications is a logical next step. While Parts A and B were originally set up to keep the government out of negotiations with doctors and hospitals, cost pressures built over time, and reasonable steps were taken to define appropriate compensation. Since then, various administrations, different mixes of Congress, and varied Department of Health and Human Services / CMS bureaucracies have proven to be quite capable of making decisions about appropriate compensation for doctors and hospitals, and they have kept it well under the level of compensation from private payers—without any breakdown of health care. The same will now be true for Medicare-defined compensation for medications.

Since at least the Clinton administration, pharmaceutical manufacturers had been able to parry suggestions about governmental negotiations on price. But today is different. The rise of specialty drugs—with breathtaking launch prices and, even more importantly, soaring annual inflation adding to their costs—is fundamentally a product of the last decade and a half. Specialty drugs have been heavily rebated, but those rebates occur post sale, so beneficiaries get no respite on their out-of-pocket payments. Over time, more forms of care become increasingly unaffordable for Part D beneficiaries.

The Inflation Reduction Act is just a beginning. It uses "negotiation" as the metaphor for price setting and applies this only to a relatively small set of mature medications. But if history is any indication, governmental authority to set prices will expand over time. The most straightforward expansion will be to address launch prices, the way most other countries do. Until that time, Pharma will persist in elevating the price it charges at the outset, putting further pressure on commercial payers. What we can be sure of is that the government will react—somewhat slowly, but steadily. The cost pressures on Medicare and Medicaid will allow nothing less.

Addressing launch prices is straightforward. The government would simply name a reasonable price for medications, most easily done by relying on a market basket of prices from other OECD countries, known as *reference pricing*. Even more accurate pricing would be based on the drugs' comparative effectiveness, produced by an organization like the Institute for Clinical and Economic Review (ICER), but that may too hot a political potato for now. The reference price idea is already obtaining some bipartisan support in Congress.[93] The critical issue though, as Pharma seems to thoroughly understand, is that the bulwark surrounding the pharmaceutical industry's control over medication pricing in the United States has been breached.

Full-blooded negotiation of drug prices by the federal government would not change much of the rest of Medicare Part D. The reference price would replace the rebate strategy used by the PBMs, but they could still administer the rest of the system. There is little doubt that Pharma would participate. The American market is too large to ignore, and this would simply level the playing field with the European countries that Pharma has done business with for years. If there are fears of dislocation, especially regarding innovation, the government can layer in the price changes in over time.

The other facet of the Inflation Reduction Act worth mentioning is that there is no protection for the private sector. As a result, Pharma will quickly learn the economics of cross-subsidies. Commercial insurers—and, even more importantly, employers—will face higher costs as Pharma stiffens its resolve in the face of lower profits from Medicare. Hospitals and doctors have done just that, so why not Pharma? That would make employer-sponsored insurance even less affordable, however, and would create more interest in government-sponsored options.

The purpose of this book is not to prescribe health care reform, but to describe our current system and suggest what might happen. The point here is that the system of medication commerce had come sufficiently off its wheels, and reform had to occur. The structure of Medicare Part D and its close relationship to Medicare Advantage facilitated these reforms. Governmental negotiation for medication prices was the next obvious policy choice, one that is very much in line with the history of Medicare, so its occurrence now, as we start to hit the costly cycle of aging baby boomers, was predictable.

Recapitulation

In summary, the private-sector portion of Medicare, Parts C and D, work rather well, taking advantage of the efficiency of the market to accomplish public goods. They can go wrong, however. For-profit companies are just that—they are in business to make a profit. They will garner that profit through great creativity, rigor, and hard work. Often these profits further the public's goals, but at other times they merely add inefficiencies. As a result, the government must stay one step ahead, or at least only a couple of steps behind. The modifications in Medicare's Parts C and D programs over the years show that reasonable oversight is possible. Governmental administrators can make adjustments as problems with for-profit contractors arise. Academic commentators, and especially MedPAC, create a pathway for policies that can lead to appropriate course corrections.

This chapter also reiterates the importance of an historical view. Caught up in the controversies of the moment, all programs appear to be imperiled. But seen over the course of years, issues such as negotiations over drug prices by the government, or adjustments in coding methods, appear to be part of the natural evolution of a privately sponsored program with governmental oversight. This is the path I am attempting to discern and describe in this book. On the risk adjustment issue, many of the key points of controversy were outlined by Joseph Newhouse in 1994.[94] So it is not surprising that this thorny issue still draws and deserves constant assessment. But the program survives— and thrives. Plan payment reductions have not stunted its growth.[95]

There is one more key point to be made about Medicare Parts C and D. They are assertively managed care programs, with a fixed budget.

The companies that offer them—insurers and PBMs—know that they have a fixed sum with which to care for patients, and a great deal of work goes into making sure that these funds are spent carefully and wisely. They must manage care and resist the profligate incentives of fee-for-service plans. That focus will be critically important as we move into the fiscal squeeze of the 2020s.

A related important point is that real managed care relationships at the provider level are much more likely to be cultivated and grow in governmental private/public hybrid programs than in the private self-insured sector. Self-insured employers are more prone to permit minimal management and oversight when compared with Medicare Advantage and the Part D program. The connection between self-insured employers and fee-for-service health care is sturdy. Just the opposite is true in Medicare's managed care programs. Thus a turn toward a government-regulated public/private program is also a turn toward the better management of care, which, I would argue, is the only way to afford health care over the next two decades.

CHAPTER SEVEN

The Affordable Care Act: Presumption of Coverage Combined with a Regulated Market

---

THE SAGA THAT IS THE AFFORDABLE Care Act, running from 2010 to 2021, puts the final pieces of this review of the evolution of the American health insurance system in place and sets the stage for a discussion about what will happen in the 2020s. The last decade has been tumultuous, especially for supporters of greater access for all. The Affordable Care Act was hastily put together, faced a variety of legal challenges seeking to cripple or eliminate major components, and then survived the energized but rather incompetent attacks from the Trump administration.

The ACA has survived and remains mostly intact, which has quietly ushered in a reformed view of the relationship of the government's role in health care, as opposed to what was the case at the beginning of the century. Compared with the situation roughly twenty-five years ago, the presumption that the federal government does guarantee coverage and regulate the quality of care is much better established. This shift—not perceptible in the week-to-week, month-to-month challenges to the ACA over the last decade—increasingly creates the foundation for a system of socialized health insurance in the United States.

The ACA did not eliminate private insurance. It did, however, establish two important points. First, the government has a responsibility to ensure that people have health care insurance. Second, the government, working with private contractors, can and will fill the gaps that the market creates. These same impulses were clear in the development of Medicaid, which I will discuss below, but the ACA, as a replacement for much of the individual health insurance market, was more assertive. After the ACA, it was clear that the government's role extended beyond the elderly and very low-income people.

The birth of the ACA is quite a story, well told elsewhere.[1] I will go into the details of the act's structure below, but from a bird's-eye view, it consisted of ten parts, or titles. To me, there are three key sections in the legislation. First, there was a complete reformulation of the troubled individual health insurance market, setting up new markets (exchanges), overseen by the government, to replace the existing private ones. This part of the act, Title I, also put in place employer and individual mandates. The former requires employers to provide a health insurance option for their employees. Individual mandates require every citizen to purchase health insurance. Both mandates are straight out of the playbook outlined by Stuart Altman in the 1970s,[2] and for many years they resonated with Republicans as much as they did with Democrats.

Title II of the ACA expanded Medicaid to people higher up on the income scale, but still too poor to afford insurance. These two titles have both proven to be very successful. The remaining titles contained several other policies, from panels to address costs to new nonprofit insurers—a collection of good ideas proposed by health policy experts that hadn't been able to get off the ground previously. Most did not get off the ground in the ACA, either.

The passage of the original act has been followed by remodeling, some by the Supreme Court, and the rest by the Trump administration. The successful parts, from the point of view of enduring policy—Titles I and II—still stand largely intact today. Many of the remaining provisions have been rolled back or have had little impact on overall health care policy.

In a short-term political context, the passage of the ACA appeared to be part of an increasingly desperate scramble to get the correct

Democratic majority together to vote for expansion. But from a broader historical perspective, it's clear that the ACA represents several important and progressive steps in the long march toward greater coverage for those unable to afford health insurance: the movement toward socialized health insurance. The title of Jonathan Cohn's book on the ACA, *The Ten Year War: Obamacare and the Unfinished Crusade for Universal Coverage*, reflects the mixed emotions that many advocates have about Obamacare.[3] This beleaguered sentiment, however, undervalues the substantial progress the act represents in our shared assumptions about the government's role in health insurance, especially as it sets up further adjustments in the 2020s.

A change in the government's post-Obamacare commitment to the nation's health also has crucial implications for the other major funders of health care: private employers and state governments. For employers, the big question should be, To what extent has the federal expansion begun to erode the assumptions that underlie the role of business in financing health care? Specifically, is it time to turn that role completely over to the government, especially in view of the storm clouds with cost highlighted in chapter 4? For states, similar questions arise, made more salient by the highly prized value of federalism in Medicaid, which, in the past, has allowed some states to restrict access to care to avoid taxing their citizens.

The federal government, over the course of fifty years, is clearly headed toward the viewpoint in Massachusetts, where voters think everyone should have reasonable access to health care, rather than in Texas, which has chosen to eschew such broad responsibility. Democrats were back at widening access again in 2021–2022, while the Republicans, under President Donald Trump's urging, merely paused rather than rolled back reform—another indication of progress in the crusade mentioned by Cohn. Obamacare is just another symptom of a bigger role for the federal government in health insurance and the slow expansion of access to it.

This circumstance also has substantial implications for the subsidiary thesis of this book: private health insurance, bought by employers, is unlikely to survive. The ACA did not undermine private health insurance, as some predicted it might. There are two simple reasons why. First, the ACA—in particular, its exchanges—did not solidify for years. In the first five to seven years of Obamacare, the long-term future of the exchange market was in doubt. That is no longer the case. Second, the cross-subsidy problem in employer-sponsored insurance required more time to worsen, with the crunch really arriving in the 2020s.

But we are getting ahead of ourselves. Much of the ACA is about coverage for the low-income population without employer coverage. I will now turn to that topic, first by introducing Medicaid.

A Primer on Medicaid: Health Insurance for Low-Income, Elderly, and Disabled People

Medicaid's expansion was one of the two most important parts of the ACA. The arc of reform in Medicaid illustrates and reinforces the evolution of the American health insurance system over fifty years, one in which the federal government's role has ceaselessly grown, alongside an increasing commitment to universal access. The ACA is the most recent acceleration of this phenomenon and must be understood in that context. So, before examining what happened with the ACA in 2009, we must return to the mid-1960s and the start of Medicaid.

Medicaid was born at the same time as Medicare.[4] Its operation was completely distinct from that of Medicare, however, in that it was based, like most of the welfare programs to which it was tied, on federal collaboration with individual states. From the beginning, Medicaid incorporated state flexibility into its design.

Federal legislation articulated its overall architecture. Title XIX of the Social Security Act set forth the federal requirements for coverage, based on specific eligibility parameters.[5] First, and most importantly, there were the categorically needy—primarily low-income families, in particular dependent children and their caretakers—who relied on the Aid to Families with Dependent Children program. (I should note that a good deal of Medicaid is meant to support services for the elderly and disabled that are not covered by Medicare, in particular long-term care.

In an effort to focus this book somewhat, I will not go into long-term care financing in any detail. I regret this omission but believe it is necessary.)

The level of coverage for the categorically needy was set by income and controlled by the states. Many states initiated coverage only when a family's income was less than 50 percent of the federal poverty level. This latter point is important in two ways. First, the history and structure of Medicaid have always emphasized a state's choice—that state's commitment to the health care for its low-income population dictates the breadth of the program. Second, the program evolved over the course of the twentieth century—from one based on complicated categories to one based on simpler legislative definitions regarding income levels, where it stands today. The underlying point, though, is that Medicaid was not originally synonymous with universal access: needy enough people qualify and those not quite needy enough do not. The states defined "needy."

Almost from the outset, there was steady movement in terms of finding more people who qualified as "needy enough." Just a few years after the initial enactment of Medicaid, the federal government passed the Social Security Amendments of 1967, creating the early and periodic screening, diagnosis, and treatment program (EPSDT)—a comprehensive program for evaluating a child's development.[6] EPSDT was an early harbinger of things to come. Through the 1980s, even as the country began its hard turn toward income inequity and the abandonment of the middle class, the federal government added requirements for health care insurance for pregnant women and then for children. By the early 1990s, all states were required to cover health care for pregnant women and children up to age 6. Federal dollars were matched with state dollars, so expansions of the program did put a pressure on state budgets.

States could have done more than what was required by the federal government. From the outset, in addition to the *mandatory categorically needy* categories, states were allowed to cover a second segment, consisting of the *optional categorically needy* and the *optional medically needy*. The former were people who, while they still had low incomes, did not meet the mandatory thresholds. The latter involved those who qualified at a low-income level once their medical expenses were debited from their gross income. These optional programs meant that a state like New York might opt to cover more people, and a state like Alabama, fewer. States evolved in fifty different directions. Some of them reasoned that, if the federal government was going to provide matching funds, why not get a dollar's worth of coverage for an outlay of fifty cents? Other states simply wanted to hold on to their fifty cents.

There was also flexibility in terms of the benefits that could be covered. The backbone of Medicaid programs was a list of mandatory benefits maintained initially by the HCFA and then by the CMS. These included inpatient and outpatient hospital services, physician services, and the EPSDT services cluster. By 2017 the list had expanded to include services for family planning, nurse-midwifery, and smoking cessation.[7] Stalwart benefits—such as prescription drugs, home health services, prosthetics, and hospice care—were and continue to be optional for states, a stark indicator of the partial coverage aspect of Medicaid. Today, all states cover prescription drugs, but they do not have to cover all of them. If they do agree to cover all medications, they then get a special price: the best price offered elsewhere in commerce.

Federal funding for all these benefits is complicated, addressing the differences between states. The government's portion is determined by the federal medical assistance percentage (FMAP) and generally matches the amount a state spends. By statute, however, the formula is designed to provide more funds for states that have lower per capita incomes. Mississippi currently claims the highest FMAP, at 77.76 percent.[8] The FMAP is thus means tested, with those states with perceived lesser means (in terms of per capita income) receiving more assistance from the federal government in terms of coverage for those with low incomes.

The historical key to Medicaid is its essentially federal nature, so it differs greatly from the completely national Medicare product. Given this, as the federal grasp on health care tightens as we move down the path toward socialized health insurance, we should see a simplification of the Medicaid benefits structure and some homogenization and expansion of eligibility criteria. That is exactly what the ACA did.

Those are the Medicaid essentials: mandatory and optional categories of beneficiaries; mandatory and optional benefits; and varying levels of federal matching funds. Layered on that are complementary programs of various sizes and stripes. The most important one is the Children's Health Insurance Program (CHIP), passed in 1997.[9] CHIP was designed to broaden coverage for children in a manner that is not based directly on income eligibility. Instead, it is a series of block grants that give states much greater flexibility in their plan designs. By 2017, CHIP was operational in forty-nine states, covering children in a financial situation that is up to at least 200 percent of the federal poverty level (FPL), and, in nineteen states, up to 300 percent of the FPL.[10]

Perhaps just as important as the boosted coverage, CHIP dramatically changed the process of enrollment, compared with traditional Medicaid. As Cindy Mann and Deborah Bachrach note, with the advent of CHIP, asset tests were dropped, verification burdens lifted, and traditional visits to the welfare office eliminated. During welfare reforms the year before CHIP passed, traditional welfare's Aid to Families with Dependent Children (AFDC) was replaced by Temporary Assistance for Needy Families (TANF). This had heralded the changes for Medicaid as it evolved from a welfare program toward health insurance.[11]

As if there was not enough diversity in state Medicaid strategies, Section 1115 of the Social Security Act preceded the Medicaid-enabling legislation by three years, giving the federal government the ability to work with states on imaginative programs to test new approaches to welfare.[12] Over the years, Section 1115 waiver programs have been used by administrations from both major parties to test drive new directions in Medicaid—for Democrats, most frequently to extend coverage, and for Republicans, to reduce coverage. Recent high-profile waivers have been to impose work requirements in several red states, programs that have largely been shown not to work.[13] But through much of the 1980s and 1990s, the Section 1115 waivers were oriented to new organizational approaches—in particular, managed care.

Given the history of the rise of managed care in the 1990s, we should expect that prepayment, with its promise of lowering costs while preserving quality, would have been infused into Medicaid. Many states were interested in just that and followed the waiver route. They were forced to, because traditional Medicaid had installed the principle of allowing a free choice of providers, frustrating the basic tenets of managed care. (*Any willing provider laws* are ubiquitous at the state level. They were the initial set of impediments that organized medicine put up during the managed care tensions in the 1990s.)

Waivers had eroded the managed care prohibition in Medicaid to the extent that by 1996, as many as 40 percent of beneficiaries were in managed relationships.[14] The Balanced Budget Act of 1997 opened the floodgates, removing the need to seek a waiver to put a managed care program in place and allowing states to use for-profit HMOs. Perhaps more importantly, the federal government no longer insisted on a choice among HMOs, so states could hire an exclusive managed care firm, although both the states and the federal government continued to prefer some competition and choice. This enabled states to utilize bidding for contracts from numerous competitors. States were allowed to turn the administrative difficulties of financing health care for the impoverished over to a managed care provider. This was an attractive alternative for many state officials. Medicaid embraced the notion of governmental oversight of private contractors early on. Nor has the federal government ever seriously considered limiting the use of managed care by the states. In addition, many states welcomed the opportunity to delegate and cap their financial risk.

Medicaid never backed off from managed care the way the rest of the health care system did in the early twenty-first century. States continued to experiment with a variety of prepaid programs for the various categories of beneficiary classes. The Kaiser Family Foundation estimated that by July 2020, 72 percent of Medicaid beneficiaries were in a comprehensive managed care plan.[15] Thirty-five states use nothing but managed care for their Medicaid population. Only Vermont, Wyoming, Alaska, and Connecticut (a strange quartet) have no managed care programs for Medicaid.

The lion's share of the arrangements between states and their insurance contractors are based on full-capitation contracts, which the federal government oversees to ensure actuarial propriety. Programs oriented toward children and pregnant women, the TANF population, are more likely to be in capitated plans, as their costs are predictable. Yet even the programs for seniors and the disabled are moving toward capitation. From a benefits viewpoint, behavioral health, pharmacy benefits, and long-term care services were traditionally kept out of managed care, but that is increasingly unlikely to be the case from here on in. For example, forty-one states now have long-term services and supports under a managed relationship, including California, Texas, Florida, New York, Pennsylvania, and Illinois.[16] The appeal of managed care transcends typical red/blue state divisions. In 2021, 52 percent of the $728 billion spent on Medicaid went to managed care organizations.

I should add one more note on managed Medicaid. While insurers who contract with the state are on a capitated budget, they generally do not engage primary care doctors to manage patient care. In most cases, the financial backbone of these Medicaid programs entails fee-for-service charges, but fee-for-service at discounted rates. In addition, these plans engage in tight utilization management. Physician and nurse organizations that take capitated payments for Medicaid beneficiaries and manage health care to eliminate waste are relatively rare.

Managed care contracts enable state authorities to escape the uncertainty of running a fee-for-service program, exchanging it for one with a fixed budget. The flip side of this comfort is disquiet over the quality of care. Could providers on a fixed budget be scrimping on care?

What empirical evidence there is has not uncovered evidence of fundamental deficiencies. Thorough reviews in the 1990s and, more recently, in 2017 have suggested that care in managed Medicare was no worse than fee-for-service.[17] In addition, opening Medicaid up to managed care in the late 1990s was accompanied by an increase in federal oversight, with the creation of specific expectations under Section 1932 of the Social Security Act.[18] Today the required components of a managed quality of care strategy are voluminous, focusing on procedures for ensuring access and monitoring performance.

The health insurer trade organization for managed care, AHIP, sees ongoing improvements in the quality of care in managed Medicaid, and the Kaiser Family Foundation largely corroborates this view.[19] Medicaid plans are putting more measures into place and designing new and more precise quality-of-care initiatives.

These conclusions are not definitive, and there have been some studies suggesting that Medicaid's managed care plans produce a worse quality of care than fee-for-service-based plans.[20] More to the point, the striking thing about quality of care in managed Medicaid plans is how relatively little information is available. Assiduous federal and state regulatory programs would seem to offer some comfort, but the results have not been well documented.

Another factor relating to the quality of care is Medicaid's parsimonious compensation for services, which have never approached those of other programs. Medicare pays hospitals and doctors much less than commercial insurance programs, and reimbursement levels for Medicaid are still lower—considerably so.[21] In 2019, in fee-for-service Medicaid plans, physicians' fees were 72 percent of those paid by Medicare (although that was an increase, compared with 2012). Medicaid's managed care now seems to pay on a similar basis.[22] While reimbursements in a few states are actually more than those paid by Medicare, most are well below that level, with Rhode Island in the basement, at 37 percent of Medicare payments.

Two additional points should attend the discussion of provider payments. Medicaid programs have many sources of supplemental payments, and these are often used to support hospitals, which employ physicians. Those dollars are not included in the assessment of fee schedules. There can also be significant variations across medical specialties.

Nonetheless, paying so much less for hospital and physician services through Medicaid sends a complex message about the program. In particular, it prompts the question, Will high-quality providers stay in the program? As might be expected, the result of poor pay is that some physicians do not feel a civic duty to participate. If they are not going to be paid appropriately, their thinking goes, then there is no sense in accepting new Medicaid patients, as payments for these individuals do not cover the full costs of their care. All the data bear this out. For example, in 2015, while 90 percent of physicians were taking on new patients with commercial insurance plans, only 70.8 percent would accept new Medicaid patients. General / family practice doctors had an even lower acceptance rate, at 68.2 percent, and only 35.7 percent of psychiatrists would take on new Medicaid patients. Low payments might not be the only reason providers do not participate in Medicaid plans, but it is certainly a considerable factor.[23] There are some indications that these numbers rose through the last decade, however, as the ACA's Medicaid expansion advanced. Recent reports suggest that 17 percent of primary care practices don't take Medicaid, although these tend to be small independent practices in urban areas with higher household incomes.[24]

One of the greatest steps toward health care equity would be equity in payments among the government-sponsored programs. As it is, low-income people, who are disproportionately Black and Hispanic, face greater barriers to health care, due to Medicaid's lower payment rates. This brute fact is often overlooked in discussions of health care equity. In any such discussion, it would seem that equal payments for the care of people from all income levels should loom large.

In 2010, Medicaid presented a complex picture. History revealed incremental gains in coverage for those with low incomes from 1965 to 2010. Medicaid evolved from a welfare program to a more conventional form of health insurance. In some ways, this can be seen as strong progress in the development of a better social safety net, since an administrative burden was lifted. Pamela Herd and Donald Moynihan make this point about Medicaid in their book, *Administrative Burden: Policymaking by Other Means*.[25] Their discussion of the recent history of Medicaid reforms in Wisconsin demonstrates how simplifying enrollment processes can increase benefits, and how putting hurdles in place is really poor policy making.

Medicaid did remain distinct from commercial plans and Medicare on many fronts. It had become heavily managed, compared with commercial insurance, and lacked the universality of Medicare. Medicare was similar to a guaranteed right to health care for those over age 65.[26] Medicaid did not evince that same commitment. But the ACA would address much of this.

President Obama Begins Obamacare

The mixed bag of Medicaid, as well as 44 million people with no health insurance (14.5 percent of the population),[27] greeted the Obama administration in 2008. Why did President Barack Obama choose to pursue health care reform, given the long list of policy chores he faced after George W. Bush's eight years in office? Obama knew that health care would take a lot of the oxygen out of the federal government, perhaps displacing other priorities. Yet he surmised that other big initiatives, such as immigration reform or climate change, might have been even harder to address, and he argued that health care reform was the issue that could change the day-to-day lives of more people.[28]

In his memoir of his time in office, Obama notes the inspiration he felt when he met Laura Klitzka at a health care town hall. At age 35, she had breast cancer, was undergoing arduous treatments, and had bills she could not pay because she was nearing the lifetime limits of her husband's insurance policy. She had to ponder whether more treatment was worth it. Obama was clearly moved. He describes how Klitzka "smiled wanly as we watched Peter [her husband] doing his best to keep track of the two young kids playing on the floor."[29]

Obama's choice of the person whose plight motivated him resonates with the major theme of this book. He could have chosen a homeless person who had never signed up for Medicaid, or a person working a minimum wage job who could not afford a health insurance plan. Instead, he chose someone with employer-sponsored insurance, through her spouse, who was reaching its limits—she was about to become underinsured.

From a cold business perspective, it was a market bind that was potentially ruining Laura Klitzka's life. Lifetime limits or annual limits on a health insurance policy had long been considered a very valuable tool for actuaries, who were attempting to estimate and control long-term risk. Health insurers used these limits, just as property insurers did. Most people are well served by their employer-sponsored insurance. But some, like Mrs. Klitzka, are not.

An even more potent tool for controlling health insurance risk was the ability to deny insurance to people with preexisting conditions. If Mrs. Klitzka had eventually received additional therapy and her cancer had gone into remission, she would then have been haunted by the problem of identifying a new insurer if she or her husband switched jobs. She would have a risk of disease recurrence, much more so than a person without her medical history, and thus might incur higher costs of care in the future. If an actuary can exclude that kind of risk, there is more predictability in overall policy costs for a plan's sponsor. This kind of thinking is perfectly reasonable from an insurance point of view, but terribly harsh from a human standpoint.

Obama's reaction to the Klitzkas' quandary was not an isolated one. More Americans were clearly getting uncomfortable with restricted access to health insurance. What had long been an acceptable business practice was slowly becoming unacceptable. This was not a matter of "common decency," which had permitted these kinds of insurance mechanisms for seventy years. Rather, it was a matter of changing what constituted decency in health care. Over time, a sense of entitlement to medical care, as a person or a citizen, had begun to feel right to more Americans, and it evolved into a more general consensus that was embodied in aspects of the Affordable Care Act.

The sense of entitlement to health care as part of one's reasonable expectations as a citizen remains even firmer today than in 2010. Polling data show that bans on preexisting condition clauses are supported by over 70 percent of Americans, while the ACA itself is seen favorably by 55 percent of Americans (slowly but surely up from 46 percent in 2011).[30] This cumulative progress should come as no surprise. While Medicare itself seemed equivalent to an astronomical Big Bang, historians have outlined the long progression toward its passage. The Medicaid story is even more compelling in terms of incrementalism, as coverage grew over the forty-five years from its inception in 1965 to 2011. With each extension of these critical federal programs, the sense of access to health care as part of our social compact has grown.

The general answer to "Why now?" may be unformed or anecdotal. But "now" in 2010 seemed like the right time to many, and even more so in 2020. But this growing consensus, this essential change in ideology, was not entirely smooth. The ACA only came into being after a great deal of political intrigue, and it has largely survived still more legal and political battles over the last decade, emerging mostly intact. Crucially, though, for the purposes of the arguments in this book, the ACA has set the next foundation for a further evolution in our health care system. That evolution leads to a broader federal role that will eventually prompt the retreat of conventional employer-sponsored health insurance, with continued expansions of coverage for those with low incomes. To understand how the ACA can catalyze that change, it is necessary to go into some detail on the ACA's structure, which is vast and, in many places, arcane. To simplify that task, I will look at the ACA as it stands today, without having to recount its birth, infancy, or adolescence, except where it helps us understand the direction in which we are headed. Even when simplified to today's ACA, an overview is still a major task.

Boiled down, it is rather simple. As Paul Starr puts it, the ACA was "a two-pronged expansion of coverage through Medicaid and private health insurance, all on a slow timetable that stretched beyond the next two elections."[31] The expansion of Medicaid followed the program of the previous three decades: lowering the income levels for qualification, and further reducing out-of-pocket cost barriers. The private insurance portion of Medicaid also echoed the past, containing a new set of heavily regulated insurance plans that replaced the increasingly unstable individual insurance market—definitely a nod to the Clinton program nearly twenty years before.

Starr points out that these new state-based health insurance exchanges were the Senate's idea. The House had wanted a federal insurance program relying on Medicare pricing, known as the *public option*. Its advocates' hopes were that a Medicare public option could siphon off the employer-sponsored market, in addition to revamping the individual insurance market. Their aspirational goal was to eventually produce a federal payer for all of health care. They missed their goal by one vote in the Senate. But, I predict, they have anticipated the future.

The public option was a step too far for 2010, but it was not a radical new idea. John McDonough points out that the concept of running a federal competitor to employer-sponsored insurance, relying on the ability and willingness of the federal government to set lower rates of reimbursement, had been floated by Karen Davis in 1991. It was updated by Jacob Hacker in 2007, by which time the costs of paying providers under Medicare had really diverged from commercial insurance.[32] (I discuss this further in chapter 10.)

In any case, the Senate-inspired Obamacare health care exchanges were not Medicare based, so they did not have a built-in pricing advantage. They relied on private insurers' negotiations with providers. That, in turn, had implications for their networks, which would come to look like Medicaid networks. And that colored employers' view of the exchanges. The details of these main aspects of the ACA are important as we try to understand how the health insurance system will evolve.

The (Sensible) Structure of the Affordable Care Act
Title I: The Exchanges

The ACA is a simple matter of coverage expansion in a private exchange market and in Medicaid, but the details bring that simple formulation to life. Title I leads the way. John McDonough has carefully outlined Title I of the ACA.[33] As a proud Bostonian, he sees the public exchange portion of the ACA as an extension of the Massachusetts exchanges, which were initiated in 2006. He refers to this as a three-legged stool.

The Massachusetts program relied on a comprehensive reform of the individual market. This is the first of McDonough's legs. Throughout the 1990s, health economists, led by Katherine Swartz,[34] had examined the overall travails of individual and small group markets and pointed out the differences between states. Most states allowed individual actuarial ratings of applicants, meaning much higher premiums for those who were sick. Preexisting condition clauses would allow insurers to demur providing any coverage, or policies could be offered with severe restrictions on an annual or a lifetime payout.

But some states began to see the disaster these kinds of restrictions could represent for some people, especially those who were sick and not currently receiving benefits through their workplace. In the early 1990s, New Jersey and Massachusetts began to eliminate preexisting condition clauses, requiring that insurance be available to everyone, regardless of their health status—a reform known as *guaranteed issue*.[35] *Community rating*, a notion as old as states' oversight of Blue Cross plans, was the next step. This was applied across the individual insurance market, thereby eliminating individual actuarial ratings.

As Massachusetts made these reforms in the individual market and expanded Medicaid, its citizens received very high levels of insurance coverage, with improvements in their health care outcomes. The next step was to address better coverage for those without plans sponsored by large employers, creating a new individual and small group market-place, known as the *connector*. Thus the first leg of the Massachusetts stool was a broad reform of the individual insurance market, with the addition of the connector (exchange).

To finance this guaranteed issue reform, its state government also needed to require everyone to buy insurance (or so the reformers thought). Otherwise, the individual insurance market would consistently be troubled by moral hazard, with only the sick buying insurance, thus creating inadequate risk pooling and driving up premiums. This was not a theoretical issue. Guaranteed issue reform alone definitely drove up premiums, and several states rescinded their original guaranteed issue legislation when faced with much higher average premiums. Thus an individual mandate, complemented by a less controversial employer mandate, was the second leg of McDonough's reform stool.

The third leg consisted of assistance for those seeking health care coverage, in order to help maintain affordability. In Massachusetts, these subsidies took the form of premium support and restrictions on cost sharing.

McDonough, and many others, thought these three key elements would be mutually reinforcing. If any of the three were to be removed, the stool might topple.[36] That turned out to not be the case, as reforms eventually proceeded without an individual mandate, but this outline accurately characterizes the assumptions on which Title I of the ACA was based. This was the structure that became law in 2010, and it gained regulatory detail over the next six years under the Obama administration.

The ACA was further shaped by four years of a Republican-dominated Congress, motivated to restrict governmental involvement in citizens' lives. Republicans never presented any alternative vision of a health system, however. In a world where Republicans as well as Democrats endorse bans on preexisting conditions, it's difficult to imagine a future for health care reform that doesn't prohibit regressive underwriting, as well as offers premium support—the two key legs of the metaphorical stool that make individual health insurance affordable. Still, Republicans chipped away at Title I of the ACA, especially the individual mandate.

The stool is an apt description, but it also overlooks some of the critical changes Title I made in how private insurers did business. The ACA substantially modified private insurance's legal foundation, turning insurance companies into something that more clearly resembled public utilities.[37] Not only were actuarial mainstays like preexisting conditions, rescission, and lifetime limits eliminated, but coverage for a broad range of conditions was also required, and caps were placed on out-of-pocket spending. In fully insured plans, limits were placed on profits by mandating that *medical loss ratios* (the amount spent on the provision of care, as opposed to administrative costs or profit) had to exceed 80 or 85 percent, depending on the plan—although this provision did not apply to self-funded plans. Many plans also had to provide coverage for preventive services, without cost sharing.

The details are enormously complicated, especially in that some ERISA plans were considered to be grandfathered in, while others were not. Moreover, their grandfathered status could change with alterations in the benefits an employer offered. The insurance industry adapted to these changes and never missed a stride in their earnings or share values, a point I will return to looking forward into the 2020s.

Both the self-insured and fully insured group markets had new foundational rules, but companies and clients adapted to them. The transition was remarkably placid. All these new rules were consonant with an expanded view of what a citizen could expect from health insurance.

The peaceful nature of the changes in the private insurance market contrasted with the atmosphere in the new exchange markets, which were tumultuous for the first five to eight years of the ACA's history. The exchange structure itself was relatively straightforward, with states able to either run their own exchanges or take advantage of federal administration. There were to be four product levels—bronze, silver, gold, and platinum—corresponding to the actuarial value of the plan, with bronze set at 60 percent and platinum at 90 percent. Premiums were lower for the bronze plan, while cost sharing was much higher. Most of the focus was on the individual insurance market, but each exchange had to set up a small business health options program, as the marketplace for employers with fewer than 50 employees has always been intimately related to that for individual-plan purchasers.

The architects of the ACA, buttressed by CBO estimates, expected enrollment in the exchanges to grow to over 25 million people, with about 80 percent of them receiving subsidies.[38] Such growth never occurred. The opening of the exchanges in October 2013 was marred by a set of website design problems that took nearly a year to fix, casting some doubt on the federal government's ability to operate a health insurance program.

More importantly, though, the exchanges were a soft target for intervention by the hostile Trump administration, which arrived in 2017. The appeal of the exchanges' products to low-income individuals was based on a series of mechanisms, taking the form of subsidies, to reduce premiums and out-of-pocket costs. Insurance plans were required to reduce cost sharing for those under 250 percent of the federal poverty level, with the federal government compensating them for the cost of this support. This support was known as *cost-sharing revenues* (CSRs).

The Trump administration decided that this guarantee of federal support, the CSRs, was not part of the ACA text, so these payments ended in early 2017.[39] This new and unforeseen mandate caused panic among insurers. Many of the major commercial insurers, Aetna and UnitedHealthcare among them, had already exited, and the others had to wonder if the market could remain stable. The next step by the Trump administration was to eliminate the tax penalties enforcing the individual mandate, creating further anxiety among those who thought all three legs of the stool were needed to maintain the exchange market.

But advocates for coverage who operated many of the exchanges saw a clever solution to the loss of the CSRs. They came up with a plan to use tax credits for premiums to replace the lost cost-sharing revenues, manipulating the benchmark of the silver plan. Plans thus remained affordable even for those at or near the low-income level. (Some very thoughtful analysts of the ACA now think it is time to replace this *silver-loading* phenomenon, but during the Trump turmoil, silver loading was crucial.)[40]

In the end, the individual mandate did not really matter. This outcome had been foretold in a *New England Journal of Medicine* article in 2016, highlighting that subsidies for the exchange market and expansions in Medicaid eligibility were really the critical elements of the law.[41] They were right. By 2020, the jury was generally in: there had been little loss of coverage attributable to the ending of the individual mandate.[42] Several states have restored this mandate at the state level (notably, California and Massachusetts),[43] but all others are doing fine without it.

With ten years of history, and now seven years of implementation, the product of Title I is quite stable. The Congressional Research Service reviewed the health of the exchanges in early 2023 and found that Democratic states on the West Coast and in the Northeast continue to operate their own exchanges, while most of the rest of the country relies on the federal exchange.[44] The federal government projected expenditures of $2.31 billion on exchange administration in 2023, most of which can be recaptured in user fees.

The exchanges and their qualified plans are well integrated with Medicaid and CHIP, so eligibility is coordinated. The Trump administration had narrowed the start of the open enrollment period from November 1 to December 15, but the Biden administration has reopened this. Overall enrollment has been steady. The Trump team managed to decrease the number of enrollees from 12.2 million in 2017 to 11.4 million in 2020, but it is rebounding under Biden and in the wake of the COVID pandemic. In 2022, enrollment stood at 13.8 million people.[45] In 2023, enrollment is greater than 16 million. With regard to access, the out-of-pocket maximum has increased from $6,350 in 2014 to $9,100 in 2023, apace with health care inflation.[46]

The exchange market works for beneficiaries. And it works for insurers. In the mid-2010s, there were constant fears about insurer participation, but in 2023, 93 counties had one insurer, 771 counties had two, 881 had three, and 1,396 counties, including many of the most populous ones, had more than three choices. No county was without an insurer. There was competition, and the premiums were stable.[47] The Kaiser Family Foundation reported that from 2020 to 2021, the median premium increase was 1.1 percent.[48]

Premiums and cost sharing tell the story. For plan year 2022, the average benchmark plan premium was $368 per month for an individual, down from $411 in 2018. For someone with a household income at 150 percent of the federal poverty limit, the net cost was zero. To give this data some context, the federal poverty limit in 2021 was just over $27,000 for a family of four, so 150 percent is just over $40,000.[49] The exchanges are viable today in a way that could not have been predicted eight years ago. And all the major insurers are back in the program.

The point is that the exchange products should be seen as a regular bargain. Sensible reform, based on the private administration of health insurance in a public program, behaves admirably and is relatively immune, in the medium to long term, from political interference. The ACA exchange market has started to have the feel of an accepted part of our health care landscape.

One more word about the exchange markets. Insurers must be fully qualified by the exchange itself, and their benefits are carefully regulated. The plans are efficient and have lower payments for providers than commercial insurance. As the exchanges survived through the 2010s, Medicaid specialist insurers (such as Molina and Centene) became more prominent in the exchanges. Their networks were narrow, excluding expensive hospitals and physician groups. This has persisted as the bigger commercial insurers and Blues plans have come back to the exchanges. The Medicaid playbook is widely in use.

This connection between Medicaid's managed care and the exchange program should not be overlooked, especially as we think about the future. Employers were not interested in the ACA markets for the first five years, due to the tumult surrounding the act. Today, the exchange insurers are stable, but their networks of providers are generally like those in the Medicaid networks. This is not true in all geographic areas; provider cost can be high because of lack of competition. Moving to the exchanges, with lower provider participation rates, is not attractive for employers until their costs rise more severely—or until an alternative is available that has the federal government dictating reimbursement, with a comprehensive network of providers.

The status of ACA as we move into the 2020s was thoroughly assessed in "What's Left of the Affordable Care Act? A Progress Report."[50] The title sounds much more pessimistic than the article's conclusion, which is that over 80 percent of the statute has been implemented and can now be considered part of the foundation of health care policy in the United States. Title I, especially, had high survival marks.

Title II: Medicaid Expansion

Title I's key complement is Title II, the expansion of Medicaid. Comparatively, it was very straightforward, with various qualifying conditions slowly giving way to income-linked criteria. Title II of the ACA completed that evolution, making everyone with an income below 138 percent of the federal poverty level eligible to enroll. The additions were primarily nonelderly, nonpregnant, childless adults.[51] These eligibility criteria were neatly knitted with the exchange criteria, which kicked in for incomes above 138 percent of the FPL, going up to 400 percent.

The federal government was to foot the bill for this expansion: 100 percent in the first three years, then incrementally down to 90 percent, where we are today. Other elements of Title II supported this overall approach: an increase in drug rebates from 15.1 percent to 23.1 percent on branded drugs in Medicaid; more funding for CHIP; a decrease in disproportionate share payments to hospitals, considering the increased Medicaid funding; and the development of new adult health quality measures. The ACA, by combining Medicaid and the exchanges, was a coordinated effort to reduce the number of uninsured in the United States: the very low-income are all covered by Medicaid, and those close to that earnings level by the exchanges.

The ACA also changed the methods of determining eligibility and ushered in a much more conventional approach to a benefits package. The act created a *modified adjusted gross income* (MAGI) approach for individuals meeting certain criteria, thus doing away with the resource and assets test, which had been such a staple of the administrative burden for those applying for Medicaid.[52] MAGI plays a large role in simplifying the onerous application process for Medicaid, which, in the past, had been used by states to reduce enrollment.

The ACA also extended the use of the *alternative benefit plan* (ABP), which had first been added in 2005. Coverage under an ABP must include the essential benefits that private insurance plans were required to cover under the ACA.[53] States that chose to implement the expansion of Medicaid had to provide an ABP. Again, the ACA was pushing Medicaid toward equivalence with commercial insurance.

American health care reform occurs incrementally. Many were not ready for what Titles I and II intended: a clean step leading toward the end game of universal coverage. So it was no surprise that twenty-six red states joined in a suit contending that Medicaid expansion of this sort was unconstitutional. They relied on an obscure Supreme Court doctrine concerning the coercive nature of federal grants.[54] The more prominent part of the suit focused on the unconstitutionality of the individual mandate. The federal Eleventh Circuit Court of Appeals decision in the case rather summarily dismissed the claim. The court found that the Medicaid program was essentially voluntary in terms of state participation—it could not be coercive.

But that is not what the Supreme Court decided. In *National Federation of Independent Business v. Sebelius*,[55] the individual mandate passed muster as a constitutional exercise of governmental taxing powers, but the court found Medicaid's expansion to be coercive and allowed states to opt out of the federal mandate. Underlining the incrementalism theme, Chief Justice John Roberts described a middle path between the conservatives' dissent that would have invalidated the entire expansion, and the liberals' view that would have allowed it in all states.

Advocates for universal coverage were understandably distraught by the decision. Sara Rosenbaum, put it succinctly: "The cause of [today's] gross health inequity is not the ACA, but rather the US Supreme Court's 2012 decision in *National Federation*."[56] But the (ever-diminishing) middle of the political spectrum could reasonably conclude that Roberts had strained to find a compromise.

The years since have borne this out, demonstrating an evolutionary vector in the direction of health care coverage. While twenty-six states originally joined the lawsuit against the ACA, today only ten states remain on the sideline. They are mostly very conservative states in the South, including the large populations in Texas, Florida, and Georgia.[57] North Carolina is now moving toward expansion. Over time, the hospitals in these remaining holdout states will create a demand for Medicaid expansion as they slowly lose the higher profit margins associated with employer-sponsored insurance. For now, the logic of health care coverage continues to percolate. The Biden expansions, as part of the response to COVID, are evidence of that.

Medicaid expansion is now about two-thirds complete. The cost over the ten-year period of 2011 to 2021 increased from $427 billion to $748 billion. Enrollment increased from 56.3 million in 2011 to 86.3 million in 2021, with the average spending per enrollee essentially flat—health care for the newly enrolled being less expensive than that for the large disabled population already resident in the program.[58]

With the COVID pandemic and the employment fallout it caused, Medicaid's growth has been even greater, increasing by 21.2 million people since February 2020 and topping 92.3 million in December 2022.[59] The repercussions for access to care and overall health have been overwhelmingly positive. A 2020 compendium of the literature on Medicaid's expansion revealed that participants' utilization of care and their health outcomes improved substantially, disparities were diminished, and provider capacity increased.[60] Another collection of research studies established the positive impact of Medicaid's expansion on state budgets.[61] None of these results are unexpected once people have access to health care—Obama got it, and so does most of the public.

The Biden protections for Medicaid recipients, essentially making it impossible for states to terminate Medicaid coverage once it was initiated, came to an end in 2023, with the end of the pandemic period.[62] On the other hand, the Inflation Reduction Act locks in broader support by the government on the exchanges. In light of this, the administration is working hard to advise people whose Medicaid coverage lapses about reenrollment, as well as their options in the exchange markets. This illustrates both the dynamic relationship between the exchanges' population and Medicaid recipients, as well as the changing status of coverage. The important structural point is that a Democratic administration now has many more levers to assist people to get health insurance than it did fifteen years ago, before Obamacare.

Other Positive Results

The impact of the synchronized punches of Titles I and II on people's lack of health insurance is impressive. When Obama was elected in 2008, there were 44.2 million uninsured people in the United States, climbing to a high of 46.5 million in 2010, or 17.8 percent of the nonelderly (not covered by Medicare) population. By 2016, that number fell to 26.7 million people, or about 10 percent. During the Trump administration, there was an uptick to 28.9 million people, decreasing to 27.5 million in 2021 as (1) the Biden team began taking down the nettlesome obstructions that the Trump administration had put around enrollment, and (2) the American Rescue Plan Act (ARPA) and its COVID relief package has expanded Medicaid to those at an FPL of 150 percent.[63] By early 2022, the uninsured rate stood at 8 percent.[64]

There are several ways to analyze who remains uninsured. Benjamin Sommers, the former deputy assistant secretary for health policy, has perhaps the simplest take. He identified several key factors associated with the uninsured in 2018: 50 percent were eligible for ACA subsidized coverage, half through Medicaid and half in the Exchanges; 9 percent were in the Medicaid gap in states that had not expanded Medicaid; 16 percent were undocumented (not citizens); and 16 percent earned more than 400 percent of the FPL.[65] This means that all of the above have access to health insurance, with the exception of noncitizens and the leftover gap populations in thirteen states. I will use these insights in chapter 9 in examining the next steps regarding universal access. But the important point here is that the current situation could not be more different than that pre-Obama.

John Holahan and colleagues have outlined alternatives for taking the next steps, building off ARPA's enhancement of the tax credit on premiums.[66] Without descending into the depths of the coverage discussions, they argued that the Biden administration could provide ACA subsidies to people in nonexpansion states by extending coverage in the exchange marketplace to those with incomes falling below 100 percent of the FPL; could do this and enhance premium subsidies using the ARPA model; or could do the latter and also add new cost-sharing relief. The theme is simple—get those left out by their states' refusal to expand Medicaid (Title II) by allowing them coverage using Title I tools. The most generous option would cost $335 billion over ten years and cover 5 million very needy people, without unconstitutionally forcing states to adopt this Medicaid program. It would also cost slightly less than Medicaid expansion itself. Their proposal helps show the next incremental steps toward coverage that can be considered as I move to predictions about the 2020s.

The important point is that with the ACA, the country has taken considerable strides toward universal access. Getting to the portion of the last 10–15 million in the US population, made up of noncitizens, will be difficult, although there are some cogent proposals in that regard.[67] The government must also address the administrative burdens that hold back some of our poorest citizens from seeking health insurance. Clearly, though, for the remaining 20–25 million low-income Americans who want and need health insurance, that goal is in sight, with clear policy steps outlined for accomplishing it.

As a way to fund all these new benefits, the government did pay providers less. Title III, known as Improving the Quality and Efficiency of Health Care, was essentially a series of cuts in Medicare payments for providers and Medicare Advantage plans. The providers complained and went back to the commercial insurers to retrieve these losses. The Medicare Advantage plans also complained but managed to cope with it. Revenues of $450 billion were projected over the 2010–2019 decade, and almost all aspects of this title were implemented. (Later in this chapter I will return to the establishment of the Center for Medicare & Medicaid Innovation, which was also part of Title III.)

The other revenue engine was Title IX, which imposed a series of taxes. The big ones stuck. Title IX imposed new levies on both earned income and unearned income for the wealthy, bringing in more than $200 billion over ten years. A tax on health insurance remained in place for some time, but the health insurers persistently lobbied against it, and it was suspended in 2017. The Cadillac tax—meant to tax very high-cost insurance policies, in order to get employers to shop appropriately for coverage—remained controversial, was delayed, and was eventually buried in 2019. Thus ended any effort to address a health benefit tax break. Much the same thing happened to the tax on medical devices.

The net federal subsidies to accomplish closure of the coverage gap are unexpectedly low. The focus is again on a population less than 65 years of age. The CBO predicts that by 2033, the costs for Medicaid and CHIP will increase from $388 billion in 2021 to $528 billion in 2031. The expenditures for the marketplace/exchange program will increase from $99 billion in 2021 to $169 billion in 2031. Thus the total subsidy would grow to $697 billion in 2031.[68] This is certainly an enormous amount, especially because the Medicare load to the federal government's burden is not being added in here. But, with these numbers, Obamacare appears to have gotten the difficult half of the country's uninsured population covered for somewhat less than $100 billion per year, or around 2.5 percent of total health care expenditures.

Coverage in the United States may never be universal. Our experience with the individual mandate has demonstrated that. Some people may not opt to buy health insurance. Noncitizens will probably continue to have trouble getting government-subsidized insurance. But making reasonably priced health insurance coverage available to all citizens is certainly possible. Every lesson we have learned over a sixty-three-year arc from 1960 to 2023 suggests that we are headed in that direction.

The Relatively Unsuccessful Bits of Obamacare

To finish the review of the rest of Obamacare, I can use one of the best expressions from Texas: "all hat and no cattle." The remaining titles of the Affordable Care Act contain several brilliant ideas from Democratic health policy thinkers, but they have amounted to very little (with the exception of Title VII on medications). These parts of the law provide important lessons in what to avoid in health care reform going forward.

Some are relatively small lessons. Title IV was a well-meaning effort to buttress the dilapidated public health infrastructure in the United States. Public health has historically been a state investment in America, with over 90 percent contributed by the states.[69] State spending has been flat or decreasing for much of the past decade as states struggle to fund Medicaid. The impoverishment of our public health system had been a huge contributor to the storm of the COVID pandemic.[70]

The ACA did not help much. By 2012, it was clear that Congress was going to chip away at its $2 billion per year appropriation, with under $1 billion making the cut in the years 2015–2019.[71] The lesson for public health advocates should be to separate public health from health care coverage and find ways to cut the costs of health care, in order to create room for public health—admittedly not a gentle prescription. In addition, public health must be nationalized. Leaving the states in charge means that our public health system will continue to underperform. The COVID pandemic might have helped underline all this.

Another set of reforms in the back half of the ACA, focused on reducing the costs of health care, all came to naught. The Independent Payment Advisory Board fiasco is a great example. Back in the dawning days of 2010, moderate Democrats had continued to lobby for a "MedPAC on steroids." They wanted an independent (but not too independent) panel of experts who could develop ways to improve the quality of our health care and reduce costs. Their view was that smart people could come up with viable ideas, especially to reduce costs.

The result was the Independent Payment Advisory Board (IPAB), which was not organized immediately, but would be birthed as Medicare costs rose. From the outset, IPAB was hobbled by a prohibition on proposals that rationed care; raised either taxes or premiums; or changed Medicare's benefit, eligibility, or cost-sharing standards. Provider groups (hospitals, doctors, Medicare Advantage plans) were protected from any further cuts. Even with all that, by the time John McDonough was writing in 2012, he was able to recount plenty of incoming fire against IPAB from every interest group, particularly by providers and pharmaceutical firms who worried that relatively independent academics would force through a variety of cost-cutting initiatives that would reduce overall profits for firms involved in health care.[72] So they joined the cry to "keep bureaucrat hands off of my Medicare." They argued that Medicare, viewed as an entitlement, should be free from expert-driven cost cutting. After an initial slowdown probably attributable to Obamacare, Medicare's annual growth rates began to spike in the mid-2010s. IPAB's threat became real. So, too, did the opposition, with the final denouement being outright repeal in 2018.

IPAB's fate calls attention to decisions about the cost of care and the utility of interventions. IPAB was intended to make transparent decisions about the value of specific therapies, in order to indicate which ones should receive payments. Unfortunately, introducing a refreshingly rational and public approach like this is a difficult thing to do in the United States. Any pharmaceutical firm or provider group worth its salt would be able to organize protests and raise concerns about rationing. They would have relied on well-intended patient advocacy groups to lobby their legislators. Notably, almost all of these advocacy groups overwhelmingly rely on Pharma and other producers for their financial support. But they are effective, and they consistently wave the flag of government-imposed rationing.

As a result, in the United States, determinations about cost-effectiveness are made more readily—and quietly—by private companies. It is not clear this is a good thing, but private firms, especially insurers and PBMs, make decisions about the cost-effective use of resources all the time. In the government-sponsored programs, transparent decision making about these kinds of issues is a nonstarter. Put another way, a PBM running a Medicare Part D program can make cost-effective decisions about care options in a way a fully government-run program might not be able to.

The final part of the back third of the ACA concerned the development of new insurers, largely because the Democratic base harbored considerable hostility toward private insurers. Two programs in particular attempted to birth new forms of insurance. The first was the Community Living and Assistance Services and Supports Act (CLASS). It was intended to be privately funded but run by Medicare. Beneficiaries were to pay premiums and then receive assistance when becoming disabled or requiring long-term care.

The motivating concept underlying CLASS was the desire to allow people with relatively minor disabilities to remain at home. Unfortunately, it was saddled with unrealistic expectations from the outset. First, because it came from the political left wing, the premiums had to be minimal for low-income individuals. Second, because this legislation needed support from moderates, CLASS was meant to be self-sustaining, with no governmental subsidy. It did not take long for the CMS to realize that this combination was impossible. Late in October 2012, the Obama administration simply let it drown, saying CLASS could not be implemented, since self-sustenance was not possible with the available premiums.

The other ACA adventure in cultivating new insurance plans was the co-op program. Out of a concern about equity, the ACA helped create nonprofit health plans that were governed by their members, reflecting back on the first HMOs in the Pacific Northwest. Since greedy investors were excluded from participation, and since the new plans were community-based, the hope was that they would be strong competitors in the exchange marketplace, with appropriate values. Twenty-three co-ops joined the field in 2014, but by 2020, only three were left.[73] There were lots of reasons for their failure. The more progressive voices in health services research declared that the Obama administration ended up playing politics, cutting the co-ops' funding when they needed it most. The loss of risk-corridor funding was another blow (a travail for all of the exchange market, which I have not had time to address).[74] Many private insurers also got out of the exchanges, but most have come back in. As a result, the marketplace is stable today, without the co-ops.

Given these experiences in the ACA, is it reasonable to presume that the government's best option is to leave insurance work up to the insurance industry, especially if the plans are overseen and governed in the same way Medicare Advantage plans are today? That might be an overly broad conclusion to draw at this point, but the appropriate role for private insurers is a critical consideration as I address the prospect of health care reform in the 2020s.

Some Returns from the Other ACA Titles

Within the general failures of Titles III–X, there were a couple of bright spots. First, there was Title VII, primarily the Biologic Price Competition and Innovation Act (BPCIA). The BPCIA followed in the footsteps of the Hatch-Waxman Act and set forth a process for biosimilar drugs, the off-patent replacements for patented specialty biologic drugs. A discussion is too lengthy to include here, but suffice it to say that after nearly a decade of gestation, the BPCIA is starting to work, and biosimilars are lowering costs for branded medications.

The final part of the ACA that will play a role in the health policy of the 2020s—if only as a lesson about how the federal government should effectuate reform—is the Center for Medicare & Medicaid Innovation (CMMI). Building on what was seen as the success of state-based waivers under Section 1115, the authors of the ACA wanted to give the federal government the ability to innovate directly. The CMMI was that vehicle.

The ACA directed the CMMI to test new models for care that reduced health care costs and improved its quality, paying for value rather than volume.[75] Importantly, the ACA freed the CMMI from congressional approval of new programs and eliminated some budget neutrality rules that had hampered demonstration programs in the past. But the CMS's actuaries were still required to certify savings before a program could jump to broader implementation. Furthermore, like all demonstration programs, the CMMI's efforts faced problems with limited timelines and specific outcome measures.[76] Nonetheless, the CMMI did represent a novel approach to effectuating change in our health care system, but the limitations on governmental demonstration programs can permit only limited optimism about real breakthroughs.

The CMS, led at the outset of the Obama administration by Donald Berwick, was committed to the CMMI, and the program assumed a high profile from the start. The first leader of CMMI under President Obama was Rick Gilfillan, followed later by Patrick Conway. Both were seen as being highly intelligent, visionary, and committed. While most of the Trump administration's team was interested in how to torpedo the ACA, the Republican CMMI leaders—first Adam Boehler, and then Brad Smith—were well-known entrepreneurs, very committed to cost-effective yet high-quality care. So the CMMI has not lacked good leadership.

The CMMI had its ups and downs in the mid-2010s, but the health policy community has retained a great deal of enthusiasm for the program. Yet Smith, the last Trump-appointed director, provided a sobering assessment as he departed.[77] After ten years, the CMMI had launched fifty-four models or programs, but only five resulted in substantial savings, and even fewer led to improvements in health care quality. Several programs had lost billions of dollars.

Smith found a number of systematic faults. Almost all the programs had been voluntary efforts to coax providers away from fee-for-service charges and toward capitated payments. Most physicians were only interested in upside risks and would abandon the project when initial profits failed to materialize. Demonstrations of the sort the CMMI funded always depended on estimated goals, or benchmarks, and these can be difficult to assess. Moreover, benchmarks can be spongy, as care patterns change over the course of a program. Smith noted how the program for bundling payments for a joint replacement could not keep pace with changes in actual medical practices. Orthopedists were aggressively shifting procedures to an outpatient setting, a circumstance not contemplated in the program's original bundle. So the CMMI had, and continues to have, a very difficult time developing precise assessments for its interventions.

Perhaps more importantly, the CMMI was also at the mercy of efforts by providers to manipulate codes to enhance payments. For much the same reason, the demonstration projects were vulnerable to adverse selection by providers, who could voluntarily enroll the subset of their patients who might contribute positively to the program. In other words, physicians working in a fee-for-service model could select when participation was advantageous. Finally, the CMS adjudication systems were not supple. The CMMI often could not sort out the claims that should be in a demonstration program from those that should not.

On the other hand, Smith helpfully provided eight fixes that could be applied to the CMMI's demonstration projects, which would help address the problems he outlined. But the real question is, Are these relatively small and discrete demonstration projects going anywhere? Perhaps the market is moving faster. Managed care has infiltrated Medicare and Medicaid. More providers are developing capabilities to accept full capitated risks, which obviate the need for gentle steps away from fee-for-service costs. And managed care companies and large provider groups are getting more creative with care management. (I will discuss this dynamic further in chapter 8, when I review accountable care organizations.)

The subsequent jobs of these CMMI leaders are indicative of the shift of expert knowledge to corporations. Gilfillan went on to be the CEO of Trinity Health. Conway is an executive with the UnitedHealthcare physicians' group. Both Boehler and Smith are back with venture capital, funding new companies that aim to remake health care. It seems like the market is picking up the challenge, maintaining the same focus as the CMMI, but guided by profit, which could be more sustaining.

Assessing the Place of the ACA in the Evolution of Our Health Care System

With a dozen years of hindsight, I can outline four key legacies of the ACA. First, it accelerated some evolutionary changes that were already underway in commercial health insurance. The exchanges remade the private health insurance market nationally, building on approaches some of the states had already taken. The ACA also asserted greater federal control over employer-sponsored self-insurance, as well as fully insured programs. It did away with restrictions on health care that were related to insurance practices, such as preexisting conditions. It also carefully limited cost sharing—that is, out-of-pocket spending—and established minimal benefits packages.

This set of reforms represents a true sea change in the way we, as a country, view and experience private health care insurance. Whether it is employer-sponsored or bought by an individual, health insurance is no longer merely a commercial contract. Through the ACA, Americans have recognized the need for people to have genuine health insurance coverage. A right to health care, while often discussed, was never a part of private insurance until the ACA prohibited the use of traditional ways in which insurers cut people out. These changes also brought new costs to employers and limited the ways in which they could stint on coverage for their employees.

The ACA limits the worst impulses of employer-sponsored insurance programs. In so doing, though, it removes many of the regressive policies that could make insurance affordable for employers, even as they pay the heavy cross-subsidy costs. In that way, the ACA slowly but surely accelerates the financial demise of employer-sponsored insurance.

Second, the ACA provided the pathway to nearly universal access. Titles I and II use the development of new public exchanges for low-income workers and the expansion of Medicaid to massively extend the reach of federal health insurance programs. If we put aside residents who are not citizens, and that small number of people who can afford health insurance but do not want to buy it, Obamacare more than halved the number of those without health insurance, due to poverty.

It also provided clear pathways for increasing the availability of health insurance still further. Universal coverage for those who want health insurance is within reach. These fiscal and structural steps are not isolated. Rather, they build on the historical evolution of Medicare and Medicaid.

The presumption of universal health care coverage, set forth by the ACA, has clear implications for employer-sponsored insurance. Employers have a mandate to provide insurance, and that is strengthened as the government slowly closes the gaps for those citizens without insurance. Employers will not be able to walk away from providing health care insurance, and the federal government will have to cooperate with employers as they find health insurance benefits, under the current conditions, to be too expensive. Employers will need government-set provider rates of reimbursement and a much stronger push toward managed care.

Third, the ACA endorsed—and eventually demonstrated—the durability of private firms undertaking the operation of public insurance functions, while adhering to comprehensive regulations regarding the quality of health care and the integrity of benefits. Again, this builds on forty years of development in Medicare and Medicaid. In this sense, the ACA can be seen as the next incremental step in the federal government's progress toward the overall regulation of health care, using private companies as the vehicle and allowing them to seek a profit through innovation.

Significantly, a public option to compete with employer-sponsored insurance was seen as a step too far in 2010. So the ACA did not make Medicare reimbursements available for all. Instead, Medicaid was expanded, along with its sub-Medicare payment rates. More importantly, private insurers, in their exchange markets, used their Medicaid networks and, as best they could, kept the provider payment rates low. These moves create further pressure on providers who participated in the programs to seek greater rates of payment from the employer-sponsored sector of commercial insurance.

Finally, theoretically attractive solutions based on expert advice, such as from IPAB (MedPAC on steroids) and the CMMI (waivers on

steroids), were somewhat disappointing. Comprehensively rational solutions do not appear to be useful in American health care policy. Incrementalism foils them.

All this expansion of coverage and the government's role in it did not
appear to prompt inflation, as some might have predicted. Instead,
the ACA appeared to substantially reduce the rates of increase in both
governmental and commercial costs. National health care expenditures grew only at 3.6 percent in the period from 2010 to 2018, versus 6.9 percent in 2000–2009.[78] From 2010 to 2018, Medicare spent
$667 billion less than predicted at the start of that period.[79]

What does this mean for reform in the 2020s? The lessons extend
from the birth of Medicare and Medicaid in the 1960s through today's
ACA, so they seem somewhat durable. Four are significantly important.
First, no major structural government interventions will occur unless
there is a durable Democratic Congress (with reasonable majorities)
and a Democratic president. In the years after the first George W. Bush
administration, Republicans have developed little—if any—real policy.
Moreover, their impulse to focus first on "small government" does not
conform to the evolving health care ideology. Health care is slowly being treated more and more as a right, and taking away entitlements is
very hard. From a statistical point of view, if not a current political one,
a Democratic constellation is quite possible over the next three presidential elections.

Second, any further health care reform measures seem likely to take
advantage of the existing institutions—in particular, the managed
forms of Medicare and Medicaid, as well as the exchanges. These programs signal clear pathways to universal access. More importantly, an
alternative to the wounded program of employer-sponsored insurance
can be found in existing governmental programs. Employer-sponsored
insurance will continue to produce stories like that of Laura Klitzka,
whose insurance was simply not adequate. (Sadly, Mrs. Klitzka died of
breast cancer in 2013.) Such cases will create a continued impetus for
change.

Third, reformers will have difficulty removing private insurance from
the field of play. The fledgling efforts to develop a public option failed.

So, too, did the co-ops, which were intended to be humane nonprofit insurers. Most advocates for broader access lump together employer-sponsored insurance and private insurers, and they try to eliminate both. The point here is that the real evolution of governmental programs could be in cooperation with private insurers—employer-sponsored insurance could fade, but private insurers probably will not.

Fourth, should (as I would predict) employers begin to find that, in the future, health insurance has become unaffordable and seek access to government-sponsored programs, the federal government will have to find the right mix of reimbursement rates and provider participation. Allowing businesses to buy into Medicare Advantage solves the problems for the employer/employee sector. So does a single-payer option, based on traditional Medicare. But Medicaid and the Exchanges currently depend on sub-Medicare reimbursement rates. Will providers continue to participate in these programs, unless they are required to by federal law? Probably not. As the federal government moves more assertively into the role of rate setter, it only makes sense that rates would be homogenized.

Rate homogenization addresses another key issue in health care: equity. A great deal of the inequality we find in health care—for people of color and those with low incomes—can be traced to differences in rates of payment (although systemic racism should not be discounted). A single government-regulated pay policy does much to address that.

Homogenization means that the level of payments must be reduced for many providers, unless we can push managed care programs through fast enough to eliminate health care waste. These are the issues we face, which have grown more immediate today as a result of the progress made by the ACA in rationalizing our health care system.

CHAPTER EIGHT

Entering the 2020s

THE EVOLUTION OF THE UNITED STATES' health care system, ranging from the passage of Medicare and Medicaid in the mid-1960s through 2020, reveals not only the vigor of the government-sponsored programs, but also the way in which they are undermining the viability of employer-sponsored insurance. This slow evolution is not easy to recognize, but a close evaluation of where employer-sponsored insurance stands today reveals that these weaknesses are real. In addition, new phenomena—symptoms of the stress in the system—suggest intermediate-term instability that must eventually call for reform. Fortunately, there are also some developments occurring today that will be especially useful to a new system that relies on managed care and government-dictated rates of payment to secure viable health coverage for all in the future.

The Current Picture of Employer-Sponsored Insurance

The birth of employer-sponsored insurance was somewhat of an afterthought, based on labor economics after World War II and propelled by a tax deduction that is enormous, but is widely overlooked. From a solidly Republican point of view, that kind of tax subsidy is unconscionable, allowing sloppy and unfocused spending because it dulls market incentives. The emergence of ERISA's role only made matters worse, eliminating a good deal of what otherwise might have been beneficial state regulation for large employers. Self-insurance under the ERISA regime created broad immunity from state-based oversight. Employers have taken on all the financial risk of illness but have done little to manage it. They have been abetted by insurers, who simply applied their none-too-delicate underwriting principles and assigned employers to a fee-for-service world that was built for providers' profits, not for the pursuit of good health.

Today, the on-the-ground administration of employer-sponsored plans encapsulates these inherent deficiencies. The decisions around health care insurance fall to the human resources department, which oversees all benefits and employee training/development. In my experience, few HR professionals come out of an insurance or health care background, and most learn the nuances on the job.

Periodically (usually every three years), the human resources team and their consultants assess the market and develop requests for proposals (RFPs), to which the competitors respond. These engender (again in my experience) spirited competition, largely based on projected costs. The human resources team then decides which contractor to use for the next three years. But an employer rarely sees reductions in costs, and only limits on increases, since there is a presumption of inflation.

It is difficult to dislodge an incumbent, as change can agitate employees. A firm's human resources team has many roles, but the critical one is the development and retention of talent.[1] Often, regarding benefits, this means avoiding complaints by limiting changes—and that includes using any of the tools typically employed to reduce health care costs. The HR team needs to balance more rigorous cost control against employee complaints. The latter trumps cost control, and rigorous cost control frequently engenders employee dissatisfaction.

Today, employers choose preferred provider organizations or high deductible health plans with PPO features 78 percent of the time.[2] Employees seem to expect that they will pay ever-higher out-of-pocket costs, but they dislike any perceived service interruption. Since human resource departments want to avoid employee agitation, PPO or HDHP plans fit neatly with that set of intentions. The result is that an employer-sponsored plan will glide along with 5–6 percent inflation, with the only employer-based cost control mechanisms being to raise out-of-pocket spending by a covered employee or increase that employee's premium contribution.

This aspect of employer-sponsored insurance defies explanation. For twenty years, the choice by employers, and its acceptance by employees, has been to thin the insurance policy rather than manage care more effectively. The fee-for-service system is taken as a given, as the real management of care might cause employee dissatisfaction. Utilization management is tolerated, but employers ensure that it is seen as the "insurer" (really the third-party administrator) who instigated this process. Somehow, the wallet issues of premium contributions and out-of-pocket spending do not cause the same degree of irritation. As a result, the annual cost of premiums went from $5,791 for a family of four in 1999 to $22,463 in 2022.[3] That is the abiding reality for commercial self-insured health insurance in this century.

Perhaps the most critical issue is that employer-sponsored plans are locked into the fee-for-service culture. Sturdy management of care requires the capitation of payment, and a restricted network of doctors and hospitals that accept responsibility for ensuring that only necessary care is rendered. Thus there must be a commitment to value-based care. The concept of a restricted health care network grates on employers and employees alike and appears to be largely off the table. Without much impetus toward managing health care, the commercial model essentially atomizes the patient population, freezing them into a lowest-common-denominator, fee-for-service world.

That fee-for-service program not only has the inflationary engine of provider-induced demand, but also suffers from ever-higher payment rates as providers successfully cross-subsidize the lower governmental reimbursement rates with higher commercial rates. As the federal role in health care grows and brings with it much lower rates of payment to hospitals and doctors, these providers argue that their only move is to make up for that deficit by getting more in payments from commercial insurers. Perhaps providers would do so even with what they might view as adequate government payments. But the result is the same. Getting more requires additional leverage, fueling ever-greater consolidation in the health care system and creating increased inflationary pressure in the commercial insurer segment.

Many policy analysts—and most health economists—see the cross-subsidy concept as a specious excuse. They believe that hospitals and doctors would maximize their revenues from commercial payers even if governmental payments were higher. This may be the case. The more important actuality, though, is that providers can negotiate with commercial payers but not governmental ones, so they focus their attention appropriately, without recognizing that the disparities they are creating are eventually unsustainable.

Some (very few) employers have tried to move beyond this by directly contracting with hospitals. Boeing is a well-known example. With large concentrations of employees at assembly plants and other installations in Seattle, St. Louis, and Charleston, South Carolina, Boeing has bypassed its insurers and negotiated agreements with local hospital groups, seeking steep discounts.[4] This effort has been oriented more toward fee-for-service discounts than the actual management of care, but the company's resolve and energy are impressive.

Most employers, however, do not have the benefit of a heavy concentration of employees in a metropolitan area. As a result, they cannot get the attention of physician groups or major hospitals. Nor would those providers normally be prepared to undertake the administration of various contracts with different employers. (Boeing uses a national Blues plan to do this work.) The rarely emulated Boeing experiment is the exception to the rule. The employer health insurance market remains disaggregated and is relatively swollen with costs. Narrow surgical networks maintained by entrepreneurs have recently begun to get some traction, based on steep price decreases that providers are willing to take. Such "travel for surgery" programs bear watching.

But overall, we must ask, Can the status quo persist? Market dynamics suggest that we are approaching an end game. Large hospitals and big physician groups cannot really negotiate with the government's health care plans (Medicare and Medicaid). The only place to go for increasing their profits is the employer market. This they do, forcing up payment rates with each negotiation to allow cross-subsidization of their business interactions with the government. Still, there is competition between hospitals, and insurers can offer some hospitals more patient volume in return for a lower unit price. But that requires a narrow network, and employees who are used to free choice in a PPO plan without managed care will balk at that.

Perhaps more importantly, the large providers—hospital systems and their physician groups—are slowly but incessantly moving to prevent the formation of narrow networks by aggregating ever-greater shares of the hospital and doctor markets under one roof—and onto one pen in terms of signing contracts.[5] Market dominance enables physicians to demand a high price for their services, insulating an integrated system from pressure to move beyond fee-for-service charges, at least for now.

The disparities these dynamics produce in terms of payment rates are startling. Averaging several estimates in the health policy literature, the Congressional Budget Office found that in 2022, commercial insurers paid 182 percent of Medicare allowances for inpatient services, with estimates rising as high as 231 percent. For more lucrative outpatient services, commercial insurance, on average, paid 240 percent of the Medicare rate, with estimates as high as 293 percent.[6] One might reasonably ask, How much longer can employers tolerate this?

Commercial insurers are not blameless in this game.[7] Insurers, emulating hospitals, use consolidation to increase their market leverage and negotiate lower physician payment rates. While a stronger market position for the insurer can reduce payment rates for hospitals and physicians, it is less clear that this has a significant impact on premiums.[8] One must conclude that a lot of the lower price goes toward insurer profits. There is evidence, however, that the big insurers are not going to get any bigger, as the federal government has indicated that future major mergers would be blocked.[9] Second-tier insurer mergers to create another first-tier insurer, however, such as the one between Centene and Wellcare in 2020, are not off the table. Vertical integration—for instance, between health insurers and PBMs—has also been allowed to go forward.[10]

While key experts are exhorting the government to evaluate, monitor, and (when necessary) bring antitrust laws to bear across the health care spectrum,[11] the provider market is the center of attention today. Deloitte, the health care and benefits consulting firm, has reviewed the evidence and predicts far more consolidation by hospitals and doctors. It noted that the top ten hospital systems now control 24 percent of the market, with their revenues growing at twice the rate of the rest of the market.[12] In a fee-for-service, commercial insurance world, there is no safer bet for a hospital than to raise its market prominence. Higher payment rates allow a hospital, and its affiliated doctors, to cross-subsidize payments from the government. Governmental reimbursements, however, are immunized from the ill effects of market domination.

But this strategy must ultimately be doomed. Broader coverage by Medicaid and the exchanges can provide some payments for patients who were previously uninsured and could not afford their needed health care. Over time, however, the growth of government-sponsored programs creates pressure to lower the rates of payments still further. At some point, additional consolidation and a greater disparity between payment rates reach a limit, beyond which employers will be unwilling to pay.

From another perspective, what other levers can employers pull if they want to reduce inflation in their health care benefits? Most are not prepared to negotiate with providers the way Boeing has, and moving out of a traditional fee-for-service format would create frustration among their employees. The benefits from a move to managing health care in a narrow network of providers would probably be reaped after a few years, but corporations do not look that far into the future, especially their human resources departments. HR teams understand that the company's employee population is transient, averaging about four years with one employer, and much less among those workers under age 40.[13] In this timeframe, which applies to the HR department as well as to the company generally, the career-enhancing aspects of bold action without an immediate return are minimal.

This abiding reality makes lodging responsibility for health care and public health with employers an especially bad idea, as most interventions aimed at promoting better health care require years, not months, to reap results. The same is true for any major shift to a narrow-network capitated plan, which will create lots of benefits disruptions. People are citizens, and humans, for a lifetime, but employees often remain with a particular employer for only a limited time. So we should expect health care decisions by employers to be short sighted.

Benefits managers pull a much more expedient lever: trimming employer costs by increasing the burden of premium sharing or out-of-pocket payments for employees. An insurer can also offer greater utilization reviews and closer scrutiny of claims submissions. These will work to lower overall costs, but they will also add administrative costs and create burnout in the provider class.

Furthermore, the strategy of thinning employer-sponsored insurance is reaching a limit for two reasons: ERISA/ACA requirements on actuarial value; and overall health care inflation, compared with workers' wage inflation. The ACA restrictions on ERISA plans not only prohibited overall coverage ceilings (for example, old plans might reimburse health care costs of up to $500,000, but after that, a beneficiary was liable), but they also create a cap on out-of-pocket spending. In 2023, this cap was $18,200 for a family plan. In addition, ERISA plans had to have a floor of a 60 percent actuarial value—and most would emulate a silver plan, which has a 70 percent actuarial value.[14] The *actuarial value floor* limits the amount for out-of-pocket payments that can be built into a plan.

The Trump administration attempted to blunt this requirement, advocating for so-called skinny plans, but the ACA rules have generally held up. The pressure remains, however, as plenty of employers would like to offer much skimpier coverage. Litigation presently in the federal courts is challenging the government's interpretation of the interaction between the ACA and ERISA, which requires plans to have reasonably broad benefits.[15] (Litigation landing in right-leaning federal district courtrooms represents the biggest challenge to the slow, progressive push of health care oversight.)

Premium contributions, which have far outstripped employees' wages, have also been limited by the ACA. Again, the numbers are telling. The average wage index increased from $29,230 in 1999 to $58,130 in 2021, a 100 percent increase,[16] while the average premium for family coverage increased from $5,791 in 1999 to $22,221 in 2021, a 283 percent increase.[17] For an individual plan, the total premium for single coverage increased from $2,196 to $7,739, or 252 percent.

The Affordable Care Act addressed this issue by creating limits on employee contributions, based on an employee's wage. These were modified in 2021 by the Internal Revenue Service. The new rules require that the premium contribution for the lowest cost, self-only coverage an employer offers not exceed 9.83 percent of an employee's household income.[18]

Still, the costs for employees are substantial. More importantly, they are not evenly distributed, as they primarily fall on the sick. The whole point of health insurance is that it is rational when events are distributed randomly—for example, I am not sure if I, or my child, is going to develop cancer, so I insure against those uncertain costs. That is also the basis for the theory-of-justice argument on behalf of health insurance—in John Rawls's original position, people would opt for insurance as the fair approach.[19] When people are underinsured to the extent they had (and have) become, the economic/moral rationale for health insurance falls apart.

That remains the case today. When out-of-pocket costs are, on average, such a significant part of household spending, and with random (ill-health) events requiring some people to spend a huge part of their savings on filling gaps in their health care coverage, the fairness and financial rationality of the system suffers. A report published by the Commonwealth Foundation points out that only 62 percent of adults are either very or somewhat confident that they can meet their health care costs.[20] The report also indicates that out-of-pocket spending is concentrated, with the top 5 percent of out-of-pocket spenders accounting for 46 percent of these costs.

The paradox is that this problem troubles those who are employed and have insurance, as opposed to the low-income segment of the population. The protections in and coverage provided by the Affordable Care Act and Medicaid appear to be working. Instead, thin commercial insurance is the issue. A Commonwealth Fund Survey in early 2020 applied pre-COVID numbers to this problem.[21] Among adults aged 19–64, 43.4 percent were inadequately insured—defined as out-of-pocket costs totaling 10 percent or more of household income. Fully a quarter of the adults in employer-sponsored plans are underinsured, and the number of those who have a policy deductible of more than $1,000 has doubled. The consequences are worth quoting: "Among those who reported any medical bill or debt problems, 37 percent said they had used up all their savings to pay their bills . . . and one-quarter were unable to pay for basic necessities such as food, heat, or rent."

A recent comprehensive analysis revealed that 17.8 percent of Americans had medical debts that were in collection status, with the mean amount being $429.[22] The debt situation was much worse in states that did not expand Medicaid through the ACA. (Medical debt overall decreased after the ACA came on line in 2012.) Another recent study has shown how increased medical debts intensify the grind of other social determinants of health on those at or near low-income levels.[23] The design of the ACA and the expansion of Medicaid have gone a long way to protect these individuals from medical debt. The same cannot be said of employers' health benefits coverage, except where it has been regulated by the reach of the ACA. Indeed, ACA controls on out-of-pocket spending and premium contributions should put an end to a further thinning of employer-sponsored insurance. Even with this promise, however, underinsured patients have become the top reason for bad debts incurred by providers.[24]

The evidence of commercial health insurance's thinning persists, even as we have generally come through the perturbations caused by the COVID pandemic in what were once rather steady trends in the costs of health care. An analysis in early 2022 suggested that growth in health care expenditures would be only moderate in the decade of the 2020s, with the percentage of GDP attributable to health care remaining rather steady, at just under 20 percent.[25] Michael Chernew (the chair of MedPAC), however, has pointed out that these statistics reflect a GDP that was depressed by COVID, noting that there will be meaningful growth in the proportion of overall economic activity absorbed by health care.[26] He also signals that all of these predictions are built on a deflation in what Medicare pays hospitals and physicians. That, in turn, puts pressure on employers.

That pressure is apparent in a 2022 report on national health care spending.[27] Federal spending on health care in 2021 did decrease, after the huge increase in 2020 as the pandemic intensified. The federal share of health care spending was still at 34 percent, with households chipping in 27 percent, and private businesses only 17 percent. The big increases were in private business spending, at 6.5 percent, and out-of-pocket spending by household members, at over 10 percent. All these numbers continue to support the unsustainable dynamic among the various insurance sectors.

In this light, experts have dredged up an old solution: comprehensive price regulation by the government.[28] In a twist, some see a heavy governmental hand as just what is needed to support affordability.[29] Advocates point to Maryland and its comprehensive experiment with all-payer rate settings for hospitals. Maryland is the only remaining state with such a program, although thirty years ago, nearly a dozen states supported this kind of initiative. Advocates, however, neatly overlook that Medicare largesse is what provides the foundation for rate setting in Maryland, and that the market strives to escape such regulation, rather successfully.[30] As a result, calls for price caps seem rather muted, although they do bear watching. A review of Rhode Island's affordability standards did suggest a slowdown in overall health care spending.[31]

So, what is the next move for employers? The inflation engine of fee-for-service costs continues to grind, and any steps the government takes to control costs contribute to this vortex. A further thinning of health care benefits is increasingly closed off by the Affordable Care Act. Thus costs borne by employers must rise. The trigger event that would bring the employer-sponsored insurance system down is a new open door to federal health care coverage. Inadequate coverage by employers can increase the call for a broader availability of federal programs. Employers might be allowed to opt into Medicare: the *public option*. Or they might be allowed to contract with a Medicare Advantage plan, thereby utilizing Medicare's lower payment rates. Perhaps initially, this would be available only for older employees, starting with those aged 60–65.

If that door were opened, the base for commercial insurance cross-subsidies would slowly diminish, as some employers would choose the federal program, creating new pressure for higher payment rates to providers from the remaining employers. A vicious (although advocates for public health care coverage might see it as virtuous) cycle is engendered, creating more pressure for access to federal plans. Indeed, the federal health insurance plans have evolved in a direction where public/private meta-utility programs (like the exchanges or Medicare Advantage) are easily used as an alternative to traditional employer self-insurance. That trigger event has not occurred, but the pressure increases each month as we move through the 2020s.

Such an outcome might be avoided if employers stepped up to insist on new health care formats that would foster value-based care and eliminate waste, thus reducing their costs. This prospect was what caused some interest in the combined efforts by Amazon, JPMorgan Chase, and Berkshire Hathaway to develop care alternatives, known as Haven. The outcome unfortunately proved the limitations of employer-based innovation. After about three years of effort, the Haven program was shut down. While many enthusiastic startups, and even traditional insurers, continue to bring new products to the market that are meant to engender value-based care, it is difficult to see real progress. Meanwhile, employers themselves remain quite bullish about their ability to handle the challenges—definitely disagreeing with my predictions about the future of health insurance.[32]

That central conundrum, the (un)affordability of an employer-sponsored plan, is not alone in contributing to a sense of gloom. The atomistic, unregulated aspects of employer-based health insurance coverage bind it to fee-for-service charges in PPO or HDHP settings. Weak PPO/HDHP control of fee-for-service costs spawns a whole series of other problems as I look at our health care system in 2023. At least four of these symptoms of our ailing system deserve further exploration: (1) the plight of primary care, (2) the ascendance of utilization management, (3) a lack of transparency, and (4) the surprise bill phenomenon. They characterize our health system today and are all arguably products of the problems resident in the employer-sponsored insurance sector. At the same time, there are some developments that provide at least some hope for a more efficient and just health care system.

Symptom One: Troubled Primary Care

First, there is the problem of primary care—we do not pay enough for it and do not value it sufficiently. To understand why requires understanding how we set the compensation for physician services in a fee-for-service world. The ultimate responsibility for the amount we pay various physicians falls to the American Medical Association. In chapter 2, I reviewed how Medicare had moved to rate setting for physicians in 1992, endorsing the Resource Based Relative Value Scale payment program, tied to the current procedural terminology coding system. The RBRVS was a wholly new, revolutionary way to value physicians' work, representing a hard turn away from the usual and customary methods of applying historical rates. From the mid-1990s on, the CMS would control the physician payment spigot for Medicare. But not the distribution.

According to the AMA, the relative value scales consisted of three main elements: the nature of the work, practice expenses, and malpractice costs. Geographic differences in care have been added as a fourth key characteristic. Of these, the nature of work was most intensively studied, as William Hsiao and his team consulted tirelessly with medical society experts to describe exactly what work went into performing various examinations, procedures, and surgeries.[33] It was a health services research tour de force, and—even more amazingly—was endorsed and implemented by the CMS.

Unfortunately, the RBRVS program did not particularly value the management of care a primary care physician, especially a gatekeeping primary care doctor, might have to do. Nor did Hsiao and his team have a chance to correct this oversight. Instead, the RBRVS program's update was handed to the American Medical Association, which astutely had set up the AMA/Specialty Society RVS Update Committee (RUC) to take the handoff.[34] Since the AMA was never a friend of managed care, the updating remained focused on a single method of payment: one fee paid for one service

Today RUC is made up of representatives from every specialty society, but the core committee consists of twenty-three practicing doctors, as well as representatives from the AMA and the AMA-owned current procedural terminology (CPT) apparatus.[35] As CPT codes are developed for new procedures, they are fed into RUC, which makes a recommendation on their value for the CMS. The latter accepts those recommendations more than 90 percent of the time. RUC, like lots of other parts of medicine concerned with economics and finances, is accused of being nontransparent, and even secretive.[36]

This can be problematic, because RUC's output is foundational. Every doctor's office and all insurers rely on the CPT codes and their valuation by the CMS. Recently, a couple of leading health policy researchers have turned their attention to the crucial decisions that RUC makes on the work aspect of care. They found that RUC tends to overvalue the time and effort of surgeons, leading to inaccuracies that are biased toward procedure-oriented work.[37]

This kind of RUC discretion, combined with the inherent conflict of interest as fee-for-service-based doctors (many doing procedures) develop their own payment rates, should raise serious questions about RUC. Specialty societies recognize the importance of RUC presentations and prepare accordingly to support what they see as the value of their type of health care. They understand that their profits are based on generous fees associated with the codes they develop.

A set of technocratic solutions have been proposed, focusing on using better time stamp data from electronic medical records to get accurate estimates of issues as simple as how long the procedure takes, as well as to incorporate quality data.[38] But the big question should be, If we want to move away from fee-for-service charges, why not just uproot this evaluation process and lodge it in CMS, with firm instructions to reevaluate how cognitive services (those services that do not involve a procedure, but, rather, a diagnosis and perhaps a prescription) and, in particular, primary care doctors, are paid? Why is that not the kind of innovation the Center for Medicare & Medicaid Innovation can do?

This solution is basically what six primary care doctors from Georgia advocated in a suit they filed, hoping to get better primary care physician representation, and a more open RUC process, by declaring RUC to be a federal advisory committee under the Federal Advisory Committee Act. Their underlying motivation was a better valuation of primary care work, which, by the time they sued in 2012, was pegged at one-twelfth the time of ophthalmologists doing cataract surgery.[39] As a *New England Journal of Medicine* article pointed out, the RBRVS was meant "to correct payment distortions that produced large income disparities among specialists. This objective has not been achieved. . . . Cardiologists and radiologists have incomes up to 2 to 2.5 times those of family physicians, general internists, and psychiatrists."[40]

So how is this connected to employer-sponsored insurance? The reliance on fee-for-service payments, which is an important side effect of the lax management of employer-sponsored insurance, keeps in place a valuation program that frustrates the development of primary care as the essential fulcrum for managing health care. PCPs are paid too little and have too much responsibility.

The Centers for Medicare & Medicaid Services has not been assertive about changing the locus of authority regarding physician reimbursements, even though it claims to be committed to paying for value, not procedures. CMS leaders recognize that there are very few models of paying for value in health care that do not have a primary care doctor at the center, working assiduously with patients to ensure that interventions really demonstrate value. But that has not translated into efforts to replace RUC.

In the meantime, the number of overworked and underpaid new physicians choosing a career in primary care continues to dwindle in the United States. In 2019, the Kaiser Family Foundation estimated that more than 14,000 primary-care physicians were needed to eliminate existing shortages.[41] Unfortunately, persistent fee-for-service charges will continue to incentivize medical students—who often have sizable student loan debts to repay—to pursue careers in more procedure-oriented and, therefore, more lucrative fields.

High expectations, limited time, and low pay are the key elements of the current malaise. A 2021 article has insightfully captured the situation, focusing on three realities of primary care.[42] First, the electronic medical record system yokes PCPs to a set of administrative tasks, including dealing with insurers about prior authorization, that overwhelm a full-time primary care doctor. As much as twenty additional hours of work per week are needed for bureaucratic tasks after thirty-two hours of patient care. All of this is seen by PCPs as useless administrative work, divorced from managing patients' care or from healing.

Second, managed care in the 1990s gave rise to *value-based payments*: performance measures that now seem detached from real value, but which require real time to meet. Third, the rise of consumerism, with patients using their portal into electronic medical records to request advice and obtain help with insurer issues, creates more real-time work for a PCP. The major point is that there is too much to do and not enough time in which to do it, given the number of patients who must be seen to make a primary care practice viable. The only real answer is payment reform.

The prestigious National Academies of Sciences, Engineering, and Medicine weighed in on the primary care problem/potential fix debate. The Committee on Implementing High Quality Primary Care issued a final report in mid-2021, subtitled *Rebuilding the Foundation of Health Care*.[43] The new report helpfully defines primary care as promoting integrated whole-person health by relying on interprofessional teams residing in the community of care and emphasizing equity. To facilitate this practice, the authors find that new payment models are crucial, ones that rely on interprofessional teams, knitted together by digital health care. The essential first action is to shift from fee-for-service rates to modified capitation, with an emphasis that funds flow to a primary care team. The next critical action is for CMS to step in to control the assignment of values, with RUC participating in an advisory capacity. Increasing the amount of health care dollars going to managed primary care plays a crucial role throughout the report. Most health policy experts agree with this assessment.

The government, particularly the CMS, continues to evince a recognition that the fee-for-service system needs to be curtailed, and that fostering a strong primary care base is an essential part of that. As noted in the previous chapter, the Center for Medicare & Medicaid Innovation has launched several demonstration projects. The most important of these is the series of comprehensive primary care (CPC) initiatives. These have had some impact, but the overall situation continues to worsen.[44] The Commonwealth Fund cites a recent national survey showing that in 2002, 6.5 percent of health expenditures went to primary care, which had decreased to 4.7 percent in 2019, while in European systems, that number is 14 percent.[45] In addition, fee-for-service charges that pay for high-volume programs provided more than 90 percent of doctor compensation.[46]

The fee-for-service system is slowly killing primary care. We need the financial support and real empowerment that comes with capitated funding, with primary care providers (doctors or nurses), working with a team of clinicians, as the main focus of patient care. The government should drive this. The fee-for-service-based, employer-sponsored segment certainly has not. Instead of being the center of the managed health care system we need, primary care is attenuating before our very eyes.

Symptom Two: Overreliance on Utilization Management

The continued dominance of fee-for-service programs leads to the second poster child of our dysfunctional health care system today: utilization management. Insurers left to deal with the flood of unnecessary services induced by fee-for-service incentives from employer-sponsored insurance have only one clear alternative—to review proposed medical interventions and approve them, based on their conformance to evidence-based medicine. From an insurer's viewpoint, this is rather straightforward.

The incentive in a fee-for-service system is to do procedures, even when generally agreed indications of the need for such interventions are not met, as procedures produce income. Only a few doctors (if any) do procedures just to get paid for them, but they will push the margins of what a patient needs, given the financial incentives. *Utilization review*, *utilization management*, and *prior authorization* are the names for the process where insurers will not approve a payment unless a patient's doctor has submitted clinical materials that justify the intervention. A lot of this review is prospective (before the procedure is done), but there is also retrospective analysis and denial in certain situations (discussed in chapter 3).

Prior authorization is essentially a clinical process. Insurers constantly check through high-volume or high-cost procedures or interventions and determine the level of evidence necessary to demonstrate that the indications called for in the medical literature have been met. For example, before bariatric surgery, an insurer would ask, Is the patient's body mass index sufficiently high, and is there a documented failure of a more conservative therapy (diet)? If the answer is yes, then the surgery is approved.

The first step in the development of any utilization management program is the perception/suspicion that there may be a large portion of procedures that do not meet the criteria. For example, in terms of bariatric surgery, too many people who are not sufficiently obese (from expert medical literature's point of view) are nonetheless having this surgery performed. The second step is typically a pilot program. By applying specific criteria, how many surgeries are (properly, according to the literature) averted, and how much reviewer and administrative time is involved? The third step is a formal return on investment (ROI) analysis—that is, how many surgeries are averted, times the cost of those surgeries, divided by the costs of the utilization management programs?

The problem with this formula is that, from several points of view, an ROI does not account for a physician's or a patient's perspective, but only focuses on insurers and their clients (employers). First, almost all physicians and patients feel that insurers have no right to be substituting their judgment for that of the treating physician. This is set forth as a matter of principle, but in practice an insurer is generally only interested in the received wisdom of the published literature, not the opinion of an individual doctor.

Second, most physicians can barely countenance that there is a problem with overutilization, despite overwhelming evidence to the contrary. Third, and somewhat more compellingly, the costs of gathering the information necessary to fulfill an insurer's criteria fall on physicians and their office staff and are not incorporated into the insurer's ROI. There are real costs that are borne on the provider's side, with no means of compensation.

Once an insurer denies a service, appeal rights (including an appeal to an impartial third party) and required timeframes for response are almost universally available. This process is highly regulated by Medicare for Medicare Advantage members. Regarding commercial insurance, most corporate-sponsored plans are self-insured, and there is little regulation by state laws. ERISA oversight of a plan sponsor / third-party administrator, however, is rather rigorous. The appeal rights are generally a matter of a contract, falling within the parameters set by ERISA, which then is enforced by the US Department of Labor.

No matter whether this process involves a Medicare plan or a commercial one, appeals take further time and effort on the part of providers and patients, leading to greater agitation on the part of the patient and higher costs for the provider. If too many appeals are successful, the ROI for the insurer drops, so the program may be abandoned. An insurer's reasoning is strictly financial, once it is clear that these criteria for the utilization management process have clinical integrity.

Insurers are certain that their criteria have integrity. They firmly believe that there is more than enough low-hanging fruit (in terms of overutilization) to avoid getting into controversial clinical areas. Recent studies of utilization criteria have produced differing assessments of how these criteria conform with evidence-based guidelines. A review from authors associated with Tufts Medical Center and Genentech found that 55.6 percent of insurers' clinical protocols were more stringent than corresponding clinical guidelines.[47] They also noted a good deal of variation in the criteria from company to company. On the other hand, a recent analysis of PBM criteria by the Institute for Clinical and Economic Review, the comparative effectiveness think tank, appeared to give high marks to most pharmacy benefit management companies for compliance with the guidelines.[48] Most recently, an econometric analysis has confirmed what most insurers already know—their averted costs are often ten times the administrative costs of the management program.[49]

Utilization management, particularly prior authorization, continues to grow in depth and scope.[50] Avalere documented that from 2014–2020, utilization management increased for all twelve therapeutic categories they evaluated, ranging from 41 percent for psoriasis to 309 percent for multiple myeloma.[51] Moreover, every insurer uses its own program features, so a physician's office staff has numerous different formats to follow, depending on the type of insurance a patient has.

Sometimes the process can be as simple as step therapy: having a patient try a cheaper alternative before switching to a more expensive drug. At other times, records and radiographs must be compiled, especially for big-ticket procedures. Physicians must spend time on the phone themselves (in addition to efforts by their office staff), especially on peer-to-peer communications. Physicians detest the whole process, which is a major pain in today's medical practices. For insurers, it is a vital part of their effort to reduce costs for their clients. Competitively, a strong prior authorization program is critical to their health insurance sales. The literature clearly documents the reductions in medical procedures and interventions that insurers accomplish with utilization management.[52]

The literature also clearly shows that doctors believe prior authorization delays care and thereby harms patients.[53] But numerous studies have failed to make the connection between a delay and adverse patient outcomes, even though (as pointed out in chapter 6) a third of the surveyed physicians believe they have had patients harmed by delays.[54] It stands to reason that such harm should be rare, as in almost all circumstances, there are either regulatory or contractual requirements that determinations be made within a specific period of time (usually one to two weeks), and that there should be an opportunity for expedited review (usually 24–72 hours). This accommodates most treatment situations. At least in terms of Star measures for Medicare, the penalties for failing to adhere to defined turnaround times are sufficiently severe that they induce insurers to set up specific teams to address Medicare appeals.

Nonetheless, every active health care provider experiences the hassle factor of prior authorization and questions why it is necessary. And there is no doubt that the process costs providers and their organizations real dollars.[55] None of this goes into an insurer's calculation of the return on investment for new utilization management ideas. In addition, all forms of utilization management lead to physician burnout, which is becoming an ever more serious problem.[56]

The only real and thorough solution is to address fee-for-service charges and the incentives driving overutilization. The contrast with a system in which a provider accepts capitated risk is stark. In these situations, an insurer turns off its prior authorization requirements. Once the capitation amount is negotiated, the insurer has no risk. As a result, prior authorization would have no return on investment. A capitated provider must weigh the benefits of a procedure and its costs, and thus has every incentive to render only that care which the weight of medical evidence outlines as necessary.

While there are many proposals for greater transparency in prior authorization processes, especially about creating greater efficiency through standardization, as well as using electronic/digital programs for inputting data, the simple truth remains: problems with prior authorization are problems with fee-for-service health care plans. Thus organizations like the AMA and affiliated state medical societies would instead prefer to pursue legislation making utilization management programs more difficult to pursue or more costly for insurers.[57] But these organizations are not addressing the root cause, which is unnecessary patient care, provided through a system that profits from more procedures.

Employer-sponsored insurance is once again in the middle of the problem. Most of the utilization management impetus is aimed at fee-for-service, commercially insured accounts (Medicare utilization management is more muted). The fee-for-service engine in commercial insurance is especially revved—the average case or procedure is worth so much more than in Medicaid or Medicare. So temptations to operate at the edges of clinical evidence are more pronounced. Employers value utilization management, as it does save them money. Thus employers' voices have been quite silent in the ongoing hue and cry about the problems associated with prior authorization.

Today, there are more calls for a restriction on the use of utilization management by providers, and the CMS has recently set forth new criteria for Medicare, Medicaid, and the exchanges that emphasize electronic processing.[58] But nothing similar is planned for commercial insurance, which is where the real problem lies. With increasing costs, we can expect an increased use of prior authorization and utilization management, with all the negative repercussions this has for practicing doctors. In moving toward the end of 2023, insurers concerned about the regulation of utilization management have begun to cut back on some of their criteria. But these are most likely their "low yield" criteria. Being competitive in commercial insurance will continue to require ample utilization management.

Symptom Three: An Absence of Transparency

Both the third and fourth irrational aspects in our health care system are also derived from employers' passivity and their acceptance of fee-for-service health care plans. Number three is a lack of transparency in pricing any and every service in health care, especially in hospital/ insurer relationships. A local hospital or hospital system usually contracts with each of the commercial insurers offering coverage in the area—at any one time that would include a local Blue Cross plan, maybe a few regional insurers, most of the five or six major national insurers, and some of the national Medicaid plans. The hospital and the insurer lock horns and develop a deal. Usually neither party likes the deal, but that is what we expect in negotiations.

The parties do agree on one thing, however. Neither the hospital nor the insurer wants their competitors to know the rates that are being paid. Insurers prefer not to let competitors know the terms of the good deal they negotiated, or let their customers know what a bad deal they accepted. Hospitals do not want smaller insurers to chase after the rates they must give to larger-market-share insurers, nor do they want other hospitals to be able to shadow these more favorable rates.

Sadly, there is one thing providers and insurers can agree on: hide their rates. The result is that the eventual consumer—a self-insured employer or an individual beneficiary—has no idea how much anything costs (although an employer can audit claims after they occur).

The same opacity is not true for federal reimbursements, either when Medicare is the payer or when Medicare Advantage plans shadow the Medicare fee-for-service price. The rates the government pays are made public, and Medicare rates provide the one signpost with which other negotiations can be put into context. Commercial insurers always pay more, but one striking aspect is the variation in the amounts. Different insurer rates for common conditions can range up to 300 percent more than those of the lowest payer (usually Medicaid).

From a systems point of view, a lack of transparency is senseless. Economists have models to predict what would happen with open information sources. Uwe Reinhardt wrote that transparency would lead to lower overall payments, or at least a drive toward the Medicare benchmark.[59] That should benefit payers. For hospitals and hospital systems, seeing the better rates that larger systems receive might strengthen the hand of smaller hospitals' negotiators. Some cagy policy experts will counter that transparency could create incentives for ever-greater consolidation (profit envy, leading to merger discussions). But providers already have ample incentives to bulk up. Whatever the effect, neither hospitals nor insurers have advocated for transparency.

Nor is opposition to total transparency limited to hospitals and insurers. Physicians are in much the same boat, especially aggregated physicians working for hospital systems or in large medical groups, a situation that increasingly is the norm. At least one big reason for a practicing physician to join an integrated group is the prospect of higher reimbursement rates because of the leverage an integrated system has, compared with an individual doctor or a small group practice. Additionally, procedures and treatments might now be done in a hospital facility, rather than in a doctor's office, again with much higher reimbursement rates. Making these types of large "facility fee" payments visible to competitors does not serve a physician's interest.

But transparency would certainly be helpful for consumers, whether they are employers providing health insurance or individuals facing out-of-pocket costs. Employers today buy market intelligence information on competing insurers from a benefits consulting firm—the spread sheeting I have referred to previously. If those data were made public, especially in machine-readable files, then some entrepreneurs would aggregate this information and make it available relatively inexpensively. Seeing the remarkable differences between reimbursement rates should feed an interest in narrower networks, which is critical in a move from a preferred provider organization to an HMO. Narrow networks restrict choices but allow much more aggressive negotiations.

At least that is the way administrations as diverse as those of Presidents Trump and Biden have seen it. The Trump administration, in an admirably cogent health policy intervention, required hospitals (in 2021) and insurers (in 2022) to make their prices available to the public. This was sold to the public as allowing rate shopping, and the CMS is now building a regulatory format to enforce it.[60] For now, hospitals are attempting to ignore these requirements.[61] But as insurers build the electronic architecture to do their own obligatory reporting, it is hard to understand how the hospital industry can continue to evade publically revealing their prices.

The good news is that today, many different organizations are busy capturing data from files posted by hospitals and insurers. There is every reason to believe that by the end of 2023, any hospital or any insurer will be able to access data on what providers are paid by insurers. Thus one of the major services of health benefits consultants—their estimates of rates of payment in various provider networks—will become superfluous. More importantly, the covers will be pulled back on our country's predominant fee-for-service payment schemes.

Full transparency will have substantial implications, insofar as it shows what a crazy welter of prices the combination of commercial health insurance and fee-for-service systems have built, including cost/charge differentials. Medicare, when setting its reimbursement rates, will look strikingly competent in comparison. Moreover, the Medicare rates of payment will look all that more attractive to employers.

Some of this information has long been available, at least within insurers. For at least the last decade, entrepreneurs have sold "transparency" digital tools to employers, making available information on the different rates that an insurer pays to different providers for the same procedure. For example, this tool could reveal that an outpatient MRI might vary fivefold in price, depending on the location. The use of comparative data, combined with a stiff deductible on health insurance policies, was meant to induce consumerism, as it has, with some limited success. But this is not the kind of transparency the real buyers—employers—need to do their shopping.

The other main cost category, in addition to hospitals and doctors, is drugs. Here the issue is even more fraught. Every American who gets a prescription is aware of the mystery that is pharmacy pricing. As you stand at the pharmacy counter, you can never guess what the cost will be (for all the reasons discussed in chapter 5). The PBMs, insurers, and pharmacies face their own Trump-inspired transparency rules,[62] which the industry is attempting to delay.[63]

But the writing is on the wall, and transparency will lead to a real appetite for reforms in drug pricing—creating, I suspect, more momentum toward federal negotiations of drug prices, at least for government-sponsored programs. Additionally, drug prices negotiated by Medicare would help greatly clarify overall prescription drug commerce by setting a realistic reference price. Wholesalers, pharmacies, and the PBMs will probably have to adhere to that reference price as they do their own negotiations in the employer-sponsored arena. The many PBM regulation bills that are being considered by Congress in 2023 heavily feature transparency requirements.[64]

The most important audience for transparent hospital, physician, and drug prices will be employers' executive-level managers, or C-suite. Employers probably have always been a little suspicious of the deals they get with their insurers and their PBMs, mediated as they are by consultants. Few directors of employer-sponsored health benefit plans have a deep understanding of the various pricing and utilization dynamics in their company's insurance benefits—hence a dependence on consultants. Their bosses might sense that. These firms will no doubt be surprised by what they are paying, and what others are paying.

Employers are slowly but surely coming to the realization that the health benefits system they have does not make sense. Part of that budding awareness has to do with unavoidable cost pressures (see chapter 4). Another part is the remarkable evolution of government-sponsored programs, which slowly are appearing more and more rational. A third part has to do with the increasing number of signs signaling that our current commercial health care system—driven by profit incentives on all sides into a variety of strange mutations—is going in the wrong direction. A reasonable CEO might ask, In a rational system, why would price transparency be controversial? That person might also ask, Why have we not pushed for transparency ourselves? Why have we had to rely on the government to bring this about?

From my viewpoint, it is hardly surprising that the push toward transparency has been promulgated by the federal government, not by employers. Rational change in our health care system almost entirely comes through government intervention.

Symptom Four: Surprise Bills

Surprise bills are a fourth example of the kind of strange mutation that employer-sponsored fee-for-service health care has spawned. The commonly accepted paradigm for a commercially insured beneficiary is as follows: a patient has a medical problem, goes to the hospital, gets treated, and health insurance provided by the employer pays for it. For example, suppose a person has chest pains, goes to a hospital's emergency department, and the team there diagnoses a myocardial infarction (heart attack). That individual then gets admitted to the hospital, a doctor does an angioplasty on their coronary vessels, the patient stays in the hospital for a few days, and then goes home with medications. Insurance theoretically pays for it all.

But what insurance actually pays is its share of the hospital's bills and the various invoices from the individual doctors. The cardiologist most likely is not affiliated with the hospital and, even if employed there, invoices separately from the hospital's charges. So a lot of bills come through over the next few weeks, all summarized in the insurer's explanation of benefits (EOB). The EOB is generally incomprehensible to the patient/consumer (although insurers continue to work to make it more straightforward). Nonetheless, let us presume the best of situations occurs: the deductible amounts, co-payments, and co-insurance amounts are clear, and the patient pays whatever is necessary, according to the nature of these employee benefits.

This scenario assumes that the insurer has previously contracted with all the providers involved—in this case, the hospital, its staff doctors, and any independent physicians who treated the patient. Through 2000, this was a reasonable assumption. Some doctors (especially in New York City) would not contract with insurers, would warn patients about the situation, and would bill a patient directly, leaving it up to the patient to deal with the insurer—truly an indemnity situation.

In Medicare, an agreement to contract with the insurer was known as *accepting assignment*, and in the mid-1980s, Medicare made it clear that it would not accept *balance billing*—that is, a patient being billed additional amounts above its set rates. Commercial insurers did not have the same ability to bind doctors to a contract, and states have varied rules on balance billing.[65] Historically, most doctors *participate*—in other words, they have a contract with the insurance company that is setting the rate payments. *Nonparticipating providers* are those without commercial contracts with insurers.

Over the last twenty years, nonparticipation has become a financial strategy. Depending on the state, if an insurer does not have a contract with a provider, that provider performs a medical service, and a patient accepts that service, then in many cases the individual patient is liable for paying for the service. The financial strategy pursued by the provider is to present an astronomically high bill, thereby creating a bind for the patient. This is meant to force or shame the insurer into paying the provider at a rate much higher than the typical fees paid to in-network or participating doctors (but probably less than the initially submitted astronomical bill).

It is one thing when a well-known specialist in New York informs a wealthy patient that they are responsible for payment. It is another thing when a patient does not know whether a doctor is in network or out of network, so that doctor's role and the potential bill are somewhat hidden. Now let us go back to the patient with a heart attack. That person was seen by an emergency medicine doctor in the emergency department, as well as by an anesthesiologist when the angioplasty was performed. The relevant hospital-based doctors (emergency department, anesthesia, radiology, and pathology) historically were independent practitioners who contracted to provide services to the hospital. Over the 1980s through the early 2000s, more and more physicians were employed directly by hospitals. But many still remained independent, and some aggregated into large physician organizations.

The physician-staffing companies, as well as individual doctors, began to realize that they could go *non-par*, or charge higher rates than insurers would pay and then seek reimbursement for those higher rates from the insurer, accompanied by a threat to bill the patient if the insurer wouldn't ante up. Most patients would have assumed that these doctors were part of the hospital's overall service and would never really think to explore the doctors' corporate status. (Consider our patient example, in the midst of being treated in the emergency department, trying to discern if the doctor was going to balance bill for an additional amount.) This is the background for surprise medical bills.

The American health care system is fee-for-service based and profit driven, so balance billing and nonparticipation have grown in importance. Insurers were battling the issue in the first decade of the 2000s, but as the financial rewards became clear, more capital found its way into the situation. One example is EmCare, the physician-staffing division of Envision Healthcare, which employs 25,000 clinicians today, particularly hospital-based emergency medicine doctors, anesthesiologists, hospitalists, and others. Private equity has heavily invested in Envision, as well as other physician-staffing firms.[66] A lack of transparency around billing helps hide much of this story, but a recent investigation of TeamHealth, another large for-profit provider group, by ProPublica shows how nonparticipation and balance billing threats can increase payments dramatically for large physician groups.[67]

The doctors themselves, as well as their professional organizations, maintain that this is entirely fair and claim that these arrangements reflect the lengths they must go to in order to get a reasonable payment from insurers. From a business point of view, it is a for-profit system on all fronts, with everyone maximizing their profits. Our fee-for-service health care system creates these opportunities, and commercial insurance is unable to shut them down. Medical financial transactions are generally opaque, and entrepreneurs step in to take advantage of the situation. There is no problem explaining it from the market's perspective.

From a patient's point of view, however, it is a different story. Our heart attack patient is faced with a bill for $5,000, not covered by insurance, for the services of an emergency medicine doctor during a two-hour stay in the emergency department. Any reasonable person would see this surprise bill as a travesty. The patient may never have met the physician on the other end of this bill, and in many cases, patients simply can't afford to pay. This does not happen, however, to Medicare patients. Surprise billing is solely a creature of commercial insurance.

After over twenty years with insurers, providers, hospitals, and states failing to solve this problem, the federal government has finally reacted and enacted new legislation, the No Surprises Act. It is intended to protect consumers, forcing insurers and doctors to work out billing issues through alternative dispute-resolution measures.[68] In many ways, this act reiterates my observation that federal health care regulators will slowly but surely address deficiencies in our health care system. The No Surprises Act neatly fills the gaps in state-based protection schemes, overcoming the ever-present ERISA preemptions.[69] Once again, the federal government is stepping in to solve a problem in the fee-for-service commercial insurance arena.

There is still a lot of wrangling left as these regulations take shape, and lots of money is on the table—20 percent of emergency medicine department visits and 16 percent of hospitalizations today have a surprise bill. The AMA and the American Hospital Association are both suing the Biden administration over the regulations published to effectuate the No Surprises Act.[70] The critical issue will be which standard of payment the government endorses as the starting point for negotiations—the provider's charge, or the insurer's fee schedule.[71] Even while this litigation proceeds, the act is nonetheless having its intended effect. Research by AHIP (the health insurer trade association) and the Blue Cross Blue Shield Association suggests that more than 2 million surprise bills were avoided from January to February 2022, with the promise of 12 million more being deflected in 2022.[72]

For us, the point is not that a solution is finally taking shape, but that surprise billing occurs at all. It is a symptom of reliance on current commercial insurance, based in a fee-for-service system, and profit-seekers' constant search for better returns. While surprise bills are a matter of concern for employers who use commercial health insurance plans, no such thing can happen with Medicare. It is a fitting paradigm for twenty-first-century employer-sponsored insurance, where the federal government must step in with a solution, even when the problem has little to do with federal payments. Satisfyingly, that solution seems to be working.

Some Hope on the Horizon
Growth of Accountable Care Organizations

There are several explanations for the diminished interest in capitation-based managed care as the twentieth century moved into the twenty-first century. Twenty years ago, information technology was not seen as being able to provide enough data to allow physicians to manage patients' health care. Others argued that balancing costs and quality of care was just too hard, and malpractice suits against managed care providers led to a general rout of capitated arrangements.[73] Yet neither of these viewpoints necessarily explains the persistence of primary care–based, capitation-supported providers, especially in California. Both of the factors cited above played a role, as did providers' and commercial insurers' comfort with fee-for-service arrangements. For providers, consolidation allowed them to increase payments to themselves without eliminating waste.

But health policy advocates of both conservative and liberal stripes did not give up on managed care, understood as financial incentives for providers to redesign their health care practices, so that more of it was value-based. For example, in the second term of the George W. Bush administration, leaders at the Centers for Medicare & Medicaid Services began to experiment with hybrid models of risk and fee-for-service payments for providers, starting in 2005 with Medicare's physician group practice (PGP) demonstration pilot program. Based largely on disease management criteria, the PGP failed to move the dial on costs.

So Medicare turned to the idea of an *accountable care organization*, or, as it is ubiquitously known, an ACO. The term was coined by Elliott Fisher, and he and Mark McClellan have been its leading academic/policy proponents. McClellan, in particular, has been evaluating, cajoling, and championing ACOs in the nearly fifteen years since he left the Bush administration, after serving at the CMS and the FDA. Leavitt Partners, led by former governor of Utah and former Department of Health and Human Services secretary Mike Leavitt, has played a similar nurturing role. The Leavitt team defines an ACO as an organization made up of providers, or providers and hospitals, who develop care management programs to oversee clinical care, coordinate that care over the various care sites, and manage its care population through the use of health information technology.[74] An ACO thus encompasses a lot of the aspects of managed care, without being tarred as a managed care organization.

As might be expected, the Affordable Care Act played an important role in expanding the reach of accountable care organizations. This legislation established the Medicare ACO program for fee-for-service (traditional) Medicare. The CMS (mainly the CMMI) developed the blueprint, launching the Pioneer ACO program in January 2012, and the Medicare Shared Savings Program (MSSP) a few months later. Now, with over a decade of experience, the MSSP is the foundation for the development of ACOs. The main incentive to participate in the MSSP has been that doctors involved in an ACO could avoid penalties under the parallel merit-based incentive payment system. By the beginning of 2017, there were 561 ACOs under contract.[75]

From the start, ACOs had some trouble gaining financial traction. Many of them were integrated delivery systems, steeped in fee-for-service charges. Without a unitary mindset around managing care and increasing value-based care, it was difficult to understand how they would succeed in substantially cutting Medicare costs. Those ACOs consisting only of physician groups had a better chance to succeed, as they did not carry the contrary incentive of keeping hospital beds full. The initial, thorough evaluation of the program's first three years showed just that, although even the savings by the physician-only groups were not large.[76]

Over the last five years, there has been, if anything, shrinkage in terms of the number of MSSP ACOs. Nearly 60 percent of them involve only upside risk, although the number of those interested in also taking downside risk is slowly growing. (Managed care, as a capitated payment, is, by definition, both an upside and a downside risk.) The saving per capita for ACOs continues to grow, albeit modestly.[77] Meanwhile, the CMMI spins out sibling programs aimed at slightly different market segments, but only a few of these have resulted in much of a savings (the ACO Investment Model being a good example).[78] Perhaps most tellingly, a recent simple analysis by the Gist Health Care consulting group showed that cumulative savings from the MSSP program from 2013 to 2019 accounted for 0.06 percent of the total Medicare spending over that time period.[79]

But the ACO movement is not really losing energy.[80] Some of the slack in enrollment is due to the COVID overhang. Perhaps more importantly, the ACO movement is slowly indoctrinating physicians, in particular, in learning to understand how to manage their patients' health care to improve outcomes. The ACO Investment Model, for example, offered capacity-building investments. In addition, the CMS funded the development of the Health Care Payment Learning and Action Network (HCP-LAN) which has formalized descriptions of payment models, and shows that today, more groups are taking downside (category 4) risks. The ACO concept has taken root much more deeply in Medicare Advantage than elsewhere. This is not unexpected. Nor are the disappointing results to date in terms of commercial, or employer-sponsored, ACOs. Many commercial insurers have programs where they are setting up ACOs, but in my experience, that commitment is thin, and interest in it less so.

The real impact of ACOs is occurring elsewhere. From interviews I have done over the last year for another project (on primary care), it is impressive to see how much learning about managing health care, in order to ensure that more of it is value-based, has occurred as a result of an initial experience with ACO structures. The lessons acquired from traditional Medicare are now being used by ACOs, which are moving to participate in Medicare Advantage plans, taking on risk in working with insurers.

It may be unfair to focus just on MSSP and the federal government. Commercial payers continue to contract with ACOs, as do some Medicaid programs.[81] From personal experience, I can state that most insurers' focus on ACOs is rather thin, unless (like Humana or UnitedHealth) they own primary care groups. A recent empirical analysis of commercial ACOs at Elevance, the large Blue Cross Blue Shield plan, corroborates this impression. While ACOs may have some impact on the quality and cost of care, it is quite small.[82] Medicaid ACOs have had trouble getting traction, often because of their difficulty in coordinating with for-profit managed care programs.[83] Nonetheless, the CMS has pushed ahead, with its leadership firmly behind expanding accountable care, as they define it.[84] (Tellingly, though, in the CMMI's 2022 *Report to Congress*, its number one accomplishment was a prior authorization program for ambulance use that saved over $1 billion!)[85]

The CMS is enhancing the ACO program in traditional Medicare. Now known as ACO REACH, it features a greater emphasis on demonstrations of equity, as well as on much greater risk taking by the participants.[86] The MSSP program has long had several tracks, graded on the basis of the amount of upside and downside risk that the ACO was willing to take. In addition, traditional Medicare beneficiaries could be assigned to a risk pool, based on their association with a primary care provider in the ACO, either on a retrospective (previous year) or a prospective (coming year) basis. The aggregated costs associated with these beneficiaries, and carefully risk-adjusted expected costs, would create the risk parameters for the ACO.

The ACO REACH program goes all the way to capitated risk: either capitated risk for PCP services, or full capitation for all the costs for the assigned beneficiaries. To experienced care managers, it looks like Medicare Advantage, without an insurer as the intermediary and with heightened concerns for social determinants of health and enlightened governance.[87] The details of assignment, risk evaluation, and payment are dauntingly complex but quite sophisticated, from an actuarial viewpoint. A participating ACO will have to reach quality of care measures (which include equity) and manage care to reduce costs. In many ways, ACO REACH can create a managed care platform for traditional Medicare, one that eliminates the private insurer. For those who harbor concerns about fee-for-service plans but support Medicare for All, this is a potential solution—provided it would be possible to determine how employers might be able to shift into it as an alternative to employer-sponsored insurance (a discussion for chapter 10).

The ACO movement is a signal event for America's health care system. It emphasizes value-based care—health care that is rendered with concerns about its cost and quality. This movement is training many physician groups, and some integrated systems, to consider the benefits of removing health care waste from the system. But its flaw is that it is meant to coexist with fee-for-service systems. I think that, in the back of the minds of many of its proponents, it is a transitional phase. Perhaps ACO REACH is the next step. For now, though, the biggest benefit of the Medicare Shared Savings Program may be that it has prepared a larger subset of physician groups to get ready to take real risk under Medicare Advantage.[88] Indeed, many of the groups trained in the ACO program are looking at Medicare Advantage collaborations.

The Rise of Digital Health

There are some other cogent and hopeful developments in health care financing and delivery in 2023. Energy and capital for these aspects of health care are heading in positive directions, which gives me some hope for a better structure going forward. Two are particularly worth noting, largely because they fit with a vision for the future based on managed care that is overseen by the government: digital health and investments in primary care.

According to the definition of *digital health* by the nonprofit Healthcare Information and Management Systems Society (HIMSS), "Digital health connects and empowers people and populations to manage health and wellness, augmented by accessible and supportive provider teams working within flexible, integrated, interoperable, and digitally-enabled care environments that strategically leverage digital tools, technologies and services to transform care."[89] This may be a bit too much of a mouthful, but it does capture the breadth of the digital health concept. First, it is relatively simple and generally low cost. A digital intervention is not a $20,000 drug or a $15,000 outpatient procedure—it is meant to be delivered for pennies or just a few dollars.

Second, digital interventions are usually oriented toward chronic diseases and are meant to supplement primary care. This industry is built on the perceptions that people need to be reminded and cajoled to take care of themselves; that this part of their care has been over-looked or omitted by overworked primary caregivers; and that a digital intervention can change behaviors. Just as digital marketing can successfully get people to buy things, the same techniques can be used to get people to take care of themselves.

Third, most of digital health easily accommodates a risk model for payments. Digital health providers or purveyors sell their products—which feature an explicit goal of reducing the costs of disease—to at-risk employers or to insurance companies. The return on investment they offer is that the cost of the intervention is less than the costs of treating the disease. So digital health generally fits in neatly with an at-risk model of care, where it complements the efforts of providers to address chronic diseases. For a modest outlay of X dollars per member per month, health care costs totaling more dollars per member per month can be avoided.

For example, AmericanWell, or Amwell, is a telemedicine company, developed over the last fifteen years with the view that more patients could be reached and cared for using a digital appointment.[90] The concept makes sense, as many costs could be avoided—especially the costs of brick-and-mortar office space—if visits could be done remotely. In addition, there has long been a belief that making a doctor's appointment as convenient as possible would lower the threshold of engagement for people who need health care. But it really took the COVID pandemic for people to realize that telemedicine was a viable alternative to in-person patient visits. As the pandemic worsened in 2020, roughly 30 percent of all visits with doctors occurred using telemedicine technology.[91] In some areas of health care, especially mental health, its use has persisted at very high levels.

The federal government (for Medicare/Medicaid) and state regulators (for commercial insurance) are currently considering how to cultivate telemedicine. During the pandemic, many of the rules about the interstate practice of medicine were suspended. The question now is, Should they be reinstated? Telemedicine is more efficiently performed when a practicing doctor can be in any state, not just the one in which a patient is located, but state licensing laws have previously prohibited this type of interstate medical practice.

No matter what the eventual outcome of these regulatory deliberations is, the genie is out of the bottle, and insurers and integrated systems are racing to provide both virtual primary care and, in some instances, specialty care. While the volume of virtual visits has decreased dramatically since the height of the pandemic, companies like Amwell, Teladoc, and other large telemedicine firms are gearing up for a growth in visits, and insurers—as well as large retailers and integrated systems—are developing programs for both virtual urgent care and virtual primary care.

The latter might be crucial. One can easily imagine that telemedicine-based primary care can be integrated with face-to-face encounters, making it more available for a greater number of people.[92] Combined with other aspects of digital medicine, this presents the possibility of much better oversight for patients, especially for those who are fragile from chronic diseases and thus represent the greatest risk for unnecessary hospital stays and exacerbated illnesses. An at-risk primary care practice could readily incorporate low-cost telemedicine to improve its patients' engagement.

A second example of digital medicine is at-home and at-work monitoring of chronic diseases. Devices to detect basic physiological functions, as well as the activities of daily living, are becoming smaller, more precise, and much cheaper. Some common and widely acknowledged monitoring programs can now be drawn into a digital health world and become much more effective. For example, over the last fifteen years, several companies have developed technology to enable a glucometer (a device used for years to measure blood sugar levels in people with diabetes) to communicate with an outside receiver. Livongo was a company that thought bigger and deeper about this, not only receiving the glucometer signals, but also creating a support mechanism that used digital reminders and text messages or phone calls from a nurse or a technician, especially when the readings were persistently low or high. In the past, this sort of counseling would have fallen to primary care doctors. They would have had no real-time information like this, or, perhaps, not enough time to do the monitoring. As a result, an important moment for an intervention would have been missed.

Livongo's market pitch was that better care and, therefore, better control of diabetes leads to lower overall costs.[93] This exemplifies the wellness/preventive medicine approach that informs so much of digital medicine. It is clear that a program of this sort is a good fit with a health care system depending on primary care oversight for a patient with a chronic disease. Such a system searches for low-cost ways to *prevent* illness, rather than waiting and addressing complications with expensive procedures.

Another example of digital health care is digital therapeutics, which rely on interactions with a smartphone to treat patients, particularly those with behavioral health issues. Sleepio, for instance, offers a subscription service for patients with sleep disorders.[94] The company is built on research that has shown how digital interactions and training, all based on cognitive behavioral therapy, work as well as or better than the array of medications prescribed for insomnia.[95] Sleepio's product is priced on a per member per month utilization schedule, aiming to be lower cost than branded medications. Thus an employer or an insurer can cut drug costs, and ensure better treatment for patients, if they are willing to endorse a digital medicine approach. Such interventions are another tool in attempts to control unnecessary costs, since medications to treat insomnia (known as sleepers) are expensive, dangerous, and often overused.

In summary, digital medicine conforms nicely with a health care system interested in the lowest possible costs for treatment. A digital infrastructure provides a much more attractive price point than a reliance on expensive professionals or high-priced branded drugs. Competition from other digital therapeutic companies, not encumbered by the monopoly of drug patents, keeps prices low. Thus they have a tight fit with managed care. The point has recently been made that digital interventions are problematic in fee-for-service medicine, largely because these interventions entail huge administrative costs when billed as discrete, individual services.[96]

Digital medicine allows us to imagine a world based not on fee-for-service and costly hospitals, procedures, and drugs. Rather, its focus would be on prevention, wellness, and control of chronic diseases. Adding a much broader array of data from transparency laws, as well as the probability of analytics based on the much faster tool of artificial intelligence, to this mix would create the promise of a new era in medical management.

People are noticing this—particularly venture capitalists. There is an enormous amount of money flowing into digital medicine. Over $14 billion went into both new and relatively established companies in 2020, and in 2021, the same amount was invested in just the first six months.[97] Since that time, this push has slowed some, along with the nation's economy. Clearly, though, investors are sold on the premise, and this funding momentum means that there will continue to be progress in a real amelioration of chronic diseases using digital formats. Some leading investors and health care veterans foresee a revolution in the American health care system, based on digital medicine. I am not quite that bullish, as there is still a good deal of strong empirical work to be done to establish that true savings and quality improvements are there. But I do see digital medicine developing hand in hand with capitation-based primary care.

I should also note that digital medicine is one place where employers have led the way. They have endorsed the potential reduction in health care costs by buying these kinds of programs for their employees, even while the rest takes place in fee-for-service programs. Medicare Advantage plans have also been avid users of digital medicine.

Investment in Primary Care

From the point of view of venture capital, the only rivals to digital medicine for investment dollars are doctors' practices, particularly those of primary care physicians. For years, venture capital has been interested in specific medical specialties, especially those of hospital-based providers. Dermatology has also been attractive, for several reasons. There are relatively few dermatologists. They do a good deal of cash business, as many patients will pay out of pocket for cosmetic procedures that are not covered by insurance. And their minor, medically necessary surgical procedures are well compensated by most insurers. Telemedicine can make dermatologists more efficient and aggregate geographically disparate practitioners. Moreover, control over dermatopathology lab samples can be very lucrative.[98] The cash flow there, and the labs' potential for aggregation, draws investors.

The same is true for hospital-based physicians (emergency medicine, radiology, hospitalists, and pathologists). Rolling up small mom-and-pop groups into a large contracting entity gives that agent a now-familiar leverage with insurers. Taking advantage of a non-par status and using highly remunerative surprise billing are additional fill-ups. Compared with these kinds of opportunities, primary care has been a late bloomer. But it appears that a lot of capital is starting to see a role for primary care in a rational health care system.

The thesis for venture capital's investment in primary care is severalfold. Aggregation is possible, in that there are a large number of primary care practices willing to join larger organizations. Aggregation itself is relatively inexpensive. And the growing role of primary care physicians in managed care is likely to make these providers more valuable over the next decade. These conditions have been or are in the process of maturing.

Venture capital investments cannot seriously be based on a fee-for-service future. While aggregation helps with leverage, it would take a lot of leverage to substantially increase primary care fees. In fee-for-service plans, payments to primary care physicians are just too low (barring a hostile takeover of the RUC, which seems unlikely unless the CMS did so). Rather, if primary care can become the cockpit for a system structured on capitated risk, then decision making by PCPs becomes the crucial element in the creation of a profit margin. The PCPs would be paid more, and thus become more valuable, enhancing the original investment. More importantly, most investors will not just want to acquire primary care groups, but also their contracting and care management assets, taking capitated risk from insurers.

Many advocates for better health care through primary care capitation would probably be shocked (and even upset) that its progress could be catalyzed by profit-seeking venture capitalists. Another path might have been preferable, but exhortation and governmental experiments with accountable care organizations have not really moved the ball. A pathway to building up primary care through venture capital may be a good bet for accomplishing the transformation of the US health care system into something that promotes health.

Through 2022, venture capital seems to have been increasing its involvement in primary care. One report suggested that as much as $2.6 billion in 2020 and $1.8 billion in the first half of 2021 had been invested in primary care.[99] But these totals broadly overlap with the estimates for digital health care, in that many primary care startups have a strong digital infrastructure and use telemedicine components in their care. Nonetheless, specific venture capital investments are clear. For example, Carbon Health and Crossover are both aggregating primary care providers by using telehealth and marketing them, either through a membership fee (Carbon) or as a solution for self-insured employers in providing primary care for their workforce (Crossover). To give a sense of the magnitude of private capital interest, Crossover had raised $281 million, mostly in late 2020 or early 2021.[100] Both have signaled a willingness to move into capitation. But both have also suffered decreased valuations as we have migrated into the chilly financial climate of 2023.

Even more on point, CityBlock uses its primary care base and its own communications platform, entitled Commons, to acquire risk contracts from Medicaid insurers. CityBlock employs a team-based approach to follow patients, close gaps in their health care, and identify and intervene on behalf of patients who are becoming more fragile. Founded in 2017, CityBlock has raised more than $600 million thus far.[101]

Iora Health was one of the original companies attempting to manage care through the PCP cockpit formula. At Iora, the team surrounding primary care physicians includes nurses, behavioral health specialists, and, in particular, health coaches. Iora moved nearly exclusively to contract for taking Medicare Advantage risks from insurers. The company's providers then manage the beneficiaries' health care to create a profit margin under this capitation. Iora raised nearly $350 million, and then was bought by another venture-funded entity, One Medical, for $2.1 billion in 2021.[102] A third example is Aledade, an enabler of value-based care. Aledade does not "own" primary care providers, but it gives them the tools to manage chronic diseases. The list of similar organizations is long—and growing.

In reviewing the nascent intervention of venture capital into the evolution of primary care, several astute observers noted that the core assumptions of most of these companies, and their investors, were similar: all offered comprehensive and tailored care, and they focused on populations, using a capitation-funding mechanism.[103] In 2023, the valuation of publicly traded companies such as Clover Health or One-Medical has decreased substantially, but venture capital money continues to flow into smaller private companies.

Another salient issue is that the new generation of primary care startups is eager to treat patients enrolled in Medicare Advantage plans and ensure that these patients are retained within those plans. This enables the PCPs to take a long-term view of a patient's health, which is a necessary component in the dynamics of managed care. Over a period of several years, they can carefully treat chronic diseases and prevent illnesses, thus reaping the benefits of better health *and* profit margins on capitation. They are also quite interested in directly contracting for traditional Medicare patients through the ACO REACH program. Such primary care groups do not mind (and might even prefer) sidelining the for-profit Medicare Advantage insurers and taking a higher percentage of premiums.

The hectic changes in an employer's setting (employees coming and going, employers switching health plans) prohibit such a long-term strategy. The average employee stays in the job for a little over four years,[104] and the tenure of any one insurer in a commercial contract can be less than that. The duration of stays in Medicare Advantage plans is approximately twice that long, especially as patients grow older, and they are even longer in traditional Medicare.[105]

In 2022, the integration of digital care and the rise of primary care managers for chronic diseases are key strategic developments in health care. Larger organizations are emulating the entrepreneurs. For example, UnitedHealth Group's Optum division has been on a multiyear campaign to buy primary care practices and primary care organizations. Optum now has more than 50,000 doctors on its payroll, many of whom are primary care physicians.[106] The specific division in Optum undertaking this strategy, known as OptumHealth, has revenues of more than $40 billion.

Humana has taken a similar path, although on a smaller scale, and it continues to pour funds into other primary care support structures, such as its $100 million investment in Heal, which is a startup that specializes in at-home care.[107] There is a palpable movement toward the holistic management of patients, based on the premises that better health care can lower costs, and that primary care provider groups can make reasonable profits on the elimination of health care waste. If anything, the COVID pandemic has hastened this process, literally opening many eyes to the pragmatic value of virtual care.

Perhaps most importantly, these strategic impulses in digital health and primary care management thrive in Medicare Advantage relationships. The ready capitation of Medicare Advantage premiums and the value obtained from managing care make Medicare Advantage plans the key target and laboratory for such developments. For many insurers, this is an advantageous strategy: gain more Medicare Advantage participants and manage their health care to remove waste. Programs like ACO REACH, which can convert traditional Medicare into a managed product, accomplish the same goal.

Yet a word of caution is in order. There are many who raise concerns about this vertical integration in health care, such as when an insurer like UnitedHealth/Optum or CVS Health/Aetna begins to buy primary care practices.[108] Commentators are especially worried about what this means for the hospital industry.[109] Even more concern is raised about the role of private equity—specifically, whether private equity–backed providers are simply doing more fee-for-service procedures and charging more.[110] Sherry Glied and Thomas D'Aunno have pointed out that private equity firms can make a profit by improving efficiency or by taking advantage of arbitrage opportunities—the latter is rife in health care (such as in surprise billing).[111] So concern is warranted. Any funding in health care should be focused on relatively long-term returns, and arbitrage opportunities are usually limited, as the financial demise of several physician-staffing companies indicates.[112] Looking abroad is also important. A recent report from the United Kingdom suggested a decline in the quality of care with privatization.[113]

Pathway toward Reform

In summary, as we enter the 2020s, the dinosaur that is our nation's employer-sponsored insurance plans lurches on toward an uncertain future. It remains locked into an unmanaged preferred provider organization, with a fee-for-service chassis, that is mediated by commercial insurers who no longer see this business as the critical part of their overall enterprise. These insurers must negotiate with large hospital systems and their physician employees, who all seek ever-greater increases in their fees, to offset the much lower payments they get from government-sponsored health insurance plans.

Demographics, with the aging of the American population, are clearly no friend to this circumstance. Governmental rates of payment cannot increase by much. So providers continue to consolidate, trying to get a last squeeze out of any leverage they have vis-à-vis the commercial insurers. Businesses caught up in this cannot help but reduce employee benefits if they want to control costs, and they are eventually hemmed in by the Affordable Care Act. From the employees' viewpoint, they have insurance, but it is thin, and health care costs that are not covered by it can be bankrupting. The average person does fine, but at the edges are those who cannot afford care.

The side effects of this downward spiral are enormous. Insurers looking to reap an advantage turn to more-restrictive utilization management, a process that creates inefficiencies and costs for providers, which they can only recoup by negotiating for higher rates. A fee-for-service structure spawns a variety of other organizations aiming for easy profits. But these profiteers also often cause unseen costs, given the lack of transparency in pricing and the negotiated arrangements that all the players seem to tolerate. In this environment, primary care–based health insurance policies, and the exacting tasks associated with managing chronic diseases and eliminating wasteful interventions, are cultivated less and less.

Yet beneath the health care dinosaur's feet, the mammals are starting to thrive. The combination of digital health and at-risk primary care programs provides a potent alternative. Their innovators are drawn to public programs that foster managed care. As a result of the evolution in the government's role, the rebirth (of sorts) of capitated payments, and a better use of technology, real change could be in store for health care.

I must emphasize the "could be" in the last sentence. There are still many who think that employer-sponsored insurance is just fine. Insurance groups like AHIP present data about how satisfied workers are with their health benefits.[114] The health policy consulting firm Avalere, in a project sponsored by the US Chamber of Commerce, posits that employer-sponsored insurance had a very robust return on investment.[115] This ROI is based largely on the returns from wellness programs, which seems unpersuasive, given the data I have reviewed, but it is not out of line with mainstream thinking. And leading firms, like JPMorgan Chase, continue to explore new benefits programs. So there must be many who see no approaching precipice.[116] But for those who find some resonance in the historical analysis I have presented up to this point, the next two chapters explore the movement, down one of two alternative paths, that could lead rather rapidly to socialized health insurance.

CHAPTER NINE

The Evolution of American Health Insurance: A Future with Medicare Advantage for All

———

THE HISTORICAL RECORD and empirical facts I have laid out about our current health care system are widely accepted by most health policy experts, though many would disagree with my major conclusions—employer-sponsored insurance cannot endure; and we are progressing slowly toward a socialized system of health insurance, where the government outlines the policy, sets the rules for administration, oversees quality of care, and dictates reimbursements. What is not clear is how those further steps on the path to socialized health insurance will occur. The Chinese proverb, "Do not try to make predictions, especially about the future," resonates with any student of policy.

But there are few alternatives, and the same forces that have existed for years would seem to impel us toward one of two possibilities. Either the government begins to offer a single form of insurance for everyone—the single-payer Medicare for All—or it finds a role for private intermediaries, as it has for Medicare Advantage and the Affordable Care Act exchanges, while still setting the structure and rates of payment. In my mind, both alternatives represent the tenets of *socialized health insurance*—that is, health care is a public good, controlled by the government. The former is usually considered a clean replacement of private insurers with a single government-sponsored program. The latter relies more on market incentives, allows profit-making companies to develop solutions, and offers an incremental solution.

A strong case can be made that the best thing to do would be to tear up what we have and start over. Liran Einav and Amy Finkelstein have recently done so in *We've Got You Covered: Rebooting American Health Care*.[1] But that is not a luxury I think we have. Reform must be a matter of evolution.

In this chapter I will outline a further evolution of the market-utilizing form of socialized health insurance, Medicare Advantage for All. In the next, I will review the purer single-payer format. Both have considerable advantages, which tie in neatly with their deficiencies. Which alternative plays out depends a good deal on unpredictable politics. My point is that either way, we are headed into a socialized health insurance future. But first I will summarize the forces that have made the path to this future so certain in my mind.

Recapping the Argument

The reason the path to socialized health insurance is so clear is that employer-sponsored insurance is financially unsustainable. Commercial health insurance, never the subject of rational planning, has blundered along toward the dead end of uncontrolled costs. Long-term social and economic trends have driven this evolution, trends sufficiently sturdy enough to appear irresistible at this point.

The first such trend is the aging of the American population. There will be greater medical costs as people in our society grow older, the workforce shrinks in proportion to the number of older nonworkers, and younger generations shoulder the burden of supporting the elderly. Without a real upswing in productivity, which seems unlikely, more tax dollars will be required to support health care for the elderly, and the health care industry will need to become more efficient.

At the same time, political decisions made over the last two decades have contributed to much larger deficits at the federal level. Policymakers and economists generally agree that continued deficit spending to address all the new federal outlays cannot be a realistic strategy.

Deficits today lead to harder decisions about spending in the future. The government could simply tax everyone more (even much more). But the historical record suggests that there is a relatively low possibility for imposing new taxes in our current political culture. Moreover, how much of any new revenue would be used for health care, as opposed to other needs, such as infrastructure or means to address global warming?

Together, an aging population and higher deficits create a strong likelihood of increasing downward pressure on health care spending as we move into the later 2020s and the 2030s. The only two ways to reduce health care costs that I have identified are to set lower rates of payment or manage care. Employer-sponsored insurance is increasingly incapable of setting rates and has been unable to promote managed care. On the other hand, government-sponsored programs do set rates of reimbursement. In addition, by relying to some degree on private insurers, the government has fostered managed care.

What is more important here is that the employer-sponsored and the government-sponsored health insurance domains are intimately linked in a fashion that spells disaster for employers. As cost pressures build on the government, it cuts out more unnecessary care practices and lowers rates of payment. Thus profit-driven providers must turn to the "softer" employer-sponsored programs, many of which are based on fee-for-service charges. Their profits drive higher costs for employers. Governmental pressure, fueled by an aging population and long-term deficits, is unrelenting, which increases cost pressures on the employer-sponsored part of the ledger.

These cost pressures grow as the prominence of the public programs expands. The main government-sponsored programs, traditional Medicare and Medicaid, have been supplemented in this century by the unexpected surge in popularity of Medicare Advantage, the emergence of Medicare Part D drug benefits, and the federal exchange program (as part of the Affordable Care Act). In addition, Medicare is being supercharged as more baby boomers enter its age bracket, and Medicaid expansion in the last decade has been nothing short of breathtaking.

Putting some numbers to this growth in the government's role regarding health care helps make my point. The Office of the Actuary at the CMS summarizes the role of governmental and employer payers on an annual basis.[2] In 2021, health consumption expenditures were $4.3 trillion. Medicare accounted for just under $901 billion, and Medicaid, $734 billion. Private health insurance totaled $1.21 trillion, but this number is somewhat misleading. When breaking down the private revenues spent on health care, businesses only paid $731 billion. Households made up the rest, including the out-of-pocket costs for insured individuals (cost sharing), the amount employees pay as a percentage of their employer's health care plan (employee premium contributions), and the amount paid by individuals and families to purchase their own policies. Thus Medicare, Medicaid, and individual employee payments have begun to dwarf the amount paid by businesses.

The other major trends that help me foresee the future evolution of US health care relate to the overall complexity of our health care system. The physician workforce is decidedly moving toward an employment model and away from traditional individual practices or small-group private corporations. This is significant, as smaller medical practices could only thrive in a fee-for-service business model—and they could not accommodate managed care. Meanwhile, the hospital industry is rapidly consolidating into large multiple-hospital systems, often employing many doctors.

Heft creates a better negotiating position. As long as employer-sponsored insurance exists, consolidation (with some integration) is the primary financial strategy for hospitals and their cadre of doctors, since large systems can increase their compensation amounts through leverage used against commercial insurers. Governmental payers, on the other hand, do not negotiate. This means that the hospitals' strategy is limited over time—there is only so much cross-subsidy for the government's lower rates that private payers can absorb. (Once again, I use "cross-subsidy" to mean the inequity of governmental and private payments, not as a justification for the hospitals' strategy.)

Consolidation could potentially have a salutary effect on our health care system, as it could promote managed care. Isolated hospitals and independent physicians have had to remain in fee-for-service programs in order to stay in business. As an alternative, an organic integration of health providers, in the form of integrated systems, can much more readily accommodate changes in financing, particularly a move from fee-for-service charges to capitation. Taking capitated payments was the original reason for much of the integration and consolidation of hospitals in the 1990s, before hospital leaders realized that it could also be used for leverage in fee-for-service negotiations. If cross-subsidization falters, as I suspect it must, reverse engineering will allow these integrated organizations to take capitation payments and remove health care waste—thus following their original impetus.

Those are the key trends in the health care arena of the twenty-first century, at least up to this point: an aging population, deficits, maturing federal/private insurance structures, a growing overall federal role in health care, consolidation/integration of hospitals and doctors, and a set of changing health care workforce attitudes. They provide the context for the next two decades.

Meanwhile, the unhealthy dynamics in employer-sponsored insurance programs continue along the same path they have followed since 2000. In a way, employers have always been accidental tourists in the health care system. Their role was birthed because of tax incentives and then isolated from governmental oversight by the unintended (or at least unanticipated) consequences of the Employee Retirement Income Security Act. Employers were left on their own and employees' costs for health care were subsidized by a tax break based on what was paid toward health benefits.

Benefits managers, responsible only for their company's own employees, have found it difficult to develop innovative policies to manage health care. Their default is to go along with the advice of benefits consultants and insurers and accept a program based on preferred provider organizations. The major lever for employers in reducing health benefits costs had been their ability to increase their employees' share of the costs of care, up to the maximum allowed by ERISA. That escape hatch is now blocked by the more stringent Affordable Care Act.

At the same time, the bill for an employer's portion of those costs increases each year. An employer's insurers—more accurately, their third-party administrators, or TPAs—have as their most powerful tool (at least theoretically) the ability to negotiate for lower rates with providers. The aggregation of numerous employers into a single bargaining unit should create a powerful lever for an insurer. But provider consolidation is meant to stymie that leverage by insurers. In many circumstances, an integrated health care system is in the driver's seat.

As our country's population ages and deficits grow, the government's resolve to pay less stiffens, and the pressure on employer-sponsored insurance increases. What else can employers do? The ability to force workers to make more out-of-pocket payments has now been blocked by ERISA and ACA actuarial rules; insurers' utilization management programs are growing even more unpopular and, as they expand, are losing the return on investment for insurers; and coding wars, with both sides armed by artificial intelligence tools, will reach a standoff. There are only a few ways to reduce costs, and the natural avarice of providers (no criticism is meant here, as I expect all of the health care players to be profit maximizers) simply drives up employers' expenditures on health care. The spiraling vortex of cross-subsidization eventually must reach some limits.

One of the hardest questions in health policy is, Why have employers not been more aggressive and progressive? There are coalitions of employers, including the National Business Group on Health, that have identified cost as the greatest problem in employee health care and have pushed to address it. But this has not led to demands for managed care or strong opposition to provider consolidation. Given that, and the growing depth of the problems that beset employer-sponsored insurance, it seems to be too late to expect progressive employers to solve these problems. The answer will be to turn to the more dynamic and consumer-friendly federal programs, as odd as that might sound.

The Alternative of Government-Sponsored, Privately Administered Insurance for Employees

The federal government seems to have developed a talent for private/ public partnerships that use insurer expertise and make good health care plans fully available on a local basis for consumers. This is especially true of Medicare Advantage, although aspects of this federal/private hybrid approach can be seen in the exchanges and Medicare Part D's freestanding drug plans. As I look to the 2020s and 2030s, I anticipate the failure of employer-sponsored health insurance, as companies will not be able to bear the cost pressures. Governmental programs could be a relatively easy off-ramp for both employers and employees.

The first question is, Which one to choose? Some astute observers thought the markets created by the Affordable Care Act, the exchanges, would be a low-cost alternative for employers. Under the ACA, employers face a mandate to either provide health insurance or subsidize access to the exchanges. So why have employers not turned to the exchanges?

The exchanges were very slow to develop, hampered at the outset by an enrollment process that had all the negative connotations of the phrase "government designed." Insurers participating in the exchanges faced a series of regulatory and financial hurdles, some of them created by the Trump administration, that chilled employers' interest. Major insurers then walked away. But slowly a subset of insurers, mostly based in Medicaid's managed care programs, began to find that the underwriting for these programs was stable, and profits were reasonable. At that point, however, the exchanges looked like an extension of Medicaid, and employers did not have much interest in moving their employees into that vehicle, especially because the cost pressures they faced in 2015 were not nearly as severe as those they will be facing in 2030. So an exodus to the exchanges never occurred.

The other key point about exchanges is that the government is not the paymaster. The rates of reimbursement to providers are the result of negotiations. Private insurers in the exchanges generally use their Medicaid networks and try to pay Medicaid rates. Their argument to hospitals and doctors is that the exchanges' population would be uninsured if not for the exchanges—so getting paid even Medicaid rates is better than nothing. The same argument would not work, however, if previously commercially insured employees were a part of the exchanges' population, as cost pressures from consolidated providers would increase. Even short of such a development, exchange insurers today often have trouble negotiating what they would consider to be reasonable rates with hospitals. This means that the premiums in some regions could be prohibitively high, especially for those without a cross-subsidy.

The alternative federal plan, Medicare Advantage, avoids many of these problems. Most importantly, Medicare Advantage parrots Medicare rates (and appears to be able to continue to do so), so noncontracting hospitals would only be paid at those Medicare rates. Secondly, Medicare Advantage is based on capitation, so it will more naturally be a framework for developing managed care.

In addition, Medicare Advantage plans are now ubiquitous throughout the United States and compete with one another based on the quality of health care, benefits, and out-of-pocket costs. The federal government's oversight is sharp, and private companies funding these insurance products are very aware that the government is not afraid to use sanctions to ensure compliance. Quality of care data, in the form of Star ratings, are transparent. Consumer information on these plans is overseen carefully, to ensure truth in advertising. Brokers must be licensed and are monitored. None of this is perfect, but the government has the levers to effectuate positive change as problems are identified. Looked at over the last twenty years, Medicare Advantage is dynamic.

Within an insurance company, attention to detail and regard for the beneficiaries' welfare is palpably stronger in Medicare Advantage, compared with commercial plans.[3] Decisions made regarding prior authorization requirements and other utilization management plans are scrutinized by the government, and overturns on appeals constitute a very important Star measure. So insurers are much more careful in their utilization of prior authorization and any other denials of care. In addition, these plans are local. In the bidding process, an insurer must qualify for a particular geographic area, and plan designs must be actuarially stable. Medicare Advantage plans—especially the national ones—are the growth engines for most large insurers. Insurers understand the need to carefully follow the rules outlined by the federal government, as they cannot afford to be sanctioned.

In many metropolitan areas, Medicare Advantage plans resemble the Clinton administration's proposed competing managed care plans envisioned by Alain Enthoven—an efficient mix of market incentives and governmental oversight. The plans are private but are funded by the federal government. The difference between the Enthoven model and one based on Medicare Advantage is that the government plays the role of consumer—or, really, the consumers' watchdog. Enthoven had hoped that employers could act in this fashion, but as we have seen, the expertise in corporations is just too thin to play such a critical role.

Moreover, the employers' agents—the commercial insurers—are rather hands off, as they really do not take on risk and only have relatively small profit margins on their ERISA-based work. If a plan's costs grow dramatically, they fall to the risk bearer—the employer. Today, the energy and emphasis in a major insurer is oriented toward Medicare Advantage, where the insurer does have risk. Even in the relatively short time (fifteen years) I spent in the insurance industry, the insurance companies' shift from interest in national accounts (large, self-insured employers) to the Medicare Advantage team has been palpable.

Beneficiaries in Medicare Advantage plans have several critical advantages over those in self-insured employer plans. First, and most importantly in terms of affordability, they access the much better rates Medicare obtains from providers. Insurers negotiating for Medicare Advantage rates shadow price traditional Medicare. Some integrated systems will not accept those lower rates, but Medicare Advantage plans are required to have reasonable networks, and they do. Unlike commercial insurance, out-of-network services are paid at Medicare rates.

Second, in Medicare Advantage, benefits are carefully regulated and a lid is placed on out-of-pocket costs. In 2021, these were set at $7,550 for in-network expenses. In traditional Medicare, however, there is not a maximum limit on out-of-pocket spending. The list of benefits in a Medicare Advantage plan must be approved by the CMS on a prospective basis and essentially must conform to the standard of care—so-called skinny benefit plans are not allowed.

This contrasts with ERISA-qualified employer plans, which, even after the ACA's reforms, have a great deal of control over their benefits structure. As costs continue to rise, much more attention is paid to approved benefits, with some employers interested in eliminating coverage for whole classes of drugs, such as gene therapies or specialty drugs for specific conditions. There is no doubt that many of these therapies and medications are overpriced—hugely so—but they are legitimate treatments, falling within the standard of care. Nonetheless, ERISA plans can simply omit them from their benefits structure. This is rare, but probably will be less so going into the 2020s.

The foregoing demonstrates a critical conundrum in employer-sponsored insurance. An employer's impulse regarding cost control is at odds with what we have seen as the emerging ideology of health care coverage. Employers skin down their insurance benefits, so some percentage of their employees simply cannot afford care. Or, as costs get pushed higher, employers will eliminate benefits that some sick people really need. Most citizens find this behavior reprehensible. It can occur without outcry only because it is hidden in the employee benefits industry. But that cannot last.

The third major attribute of Medicare Advantage over self-insured plans is that its relative transparency and regulatory oversight mean market aberrations (or exuberance), such as huge profits from surprise billing, are simply not possible. Insurers are very careful about their coding when interacting with the government. Abuses related to issues like risk adjustment draw the attention of the CMS and the Justice Department, and corrections in these processes are made relatively rapidly. The veteran regulators at the CMS are savvy, and they are backed up by the intellectual firepower of MedPAC, which constantly reviews areas of potential inefficiency or excessive profit taking by insurers. The government can also depend on the muscle of the Justice Department. As any veteran insurance plan person or health care lawyer will agree, much greater care on all issues is accorded to federally sponsored plans, compared with commercial ones.

Fourth, and perhaps most importantly, Medicare Advantage fits in well with models of risk taking using gate-keeping primary care groups (see chapter 8). An insurer offering a plan must be geographically based and has to assemble a reasonable local network. This contrasts sharply with the lack of local grounding for employees covered under a self-insured plan, where the default least-common-denominator approach is an insipid PPO plan. In commercial insurance, beneficiaries are homogenized into a regional network and benefits structure that must work for many employers.

Here the difference between employer-sponsored plans and Medicare Advantage ones is sharp. The choice of a primary care physician and integration into a specific care network are explicit features for Medicare Advantage beneficiaries. This allows plans to emphasize the use of PCPs in particular organizations, especially for new enrollees during open enrollment periods. A Medicare Advantage plan is able, with this local grounding, to formulate a contract, based on a percentage of the premiums, with a local primary care group that is prepared to manage risk.

No wonder many new, innovative primary care groups prefer working solely with Medicare Advantage plans and Medicare beneficiaries. The care is local, the capitation fees are transparent, and they are free from insurers' oversight of their medical practices, since PCPs have a budget to guide them. In addition, the average duration of time a beneficiary is in a Medicare Advantage plan is almost double the duration under an employer-sponsored plan—so a primary care group has the time to be able to manage chronic diseases and profit from that management. Thus almost all of the innovations in managed care today feed off Medicare Advantage.

This coevolution of Medicare Advantage and PCPs focusing on risk, and the potential for profits from managing care, is not lost on large health insurers. UnitedHealth Group's Optum organization now employs more than 50,000 doctors, many of whom are in primary care groups. These groups are interested in obtaining as many Medicare Advantage contracts as they can, complementing their primary care management with insights from advanced analytics.[4] Humana is doing the same thing, with an even greater emphasis on Medicare Advantage.[5] Large retailers have made assertive moves into the actual provision of care. For example, CVS Health purchased Aetna and developed Health Hubs at retail pharmacies. Walmart has its new Walmart Health brand, and Walgreens is now the owner of VillageMD.[6]

Over time, these companies have been incorporating models like those developed by innovative and focused primary care groups—Oak Street Health, ChenMed, and Iora Health—into the care programs they design and use as the basis for their Medicare Advantage business. Venture capital also likes this model and is voting with their dollars to support startups in primary care. These kinds of primary care–based Medicare Advantage plans would be well positioned to enroll new beneficiaries if Medicare began to accept those under age 65. Thus some health care experts have begun to advocate for a public option, based on Medicare Advantage.[7]

Others have reached the same diagnosis about the failure of employer-sponsored insurance but suggest a different curative therapy. Regina Herzlinger and Barak Richman have concluded that current employer-sponsored insurance programs do not serve employees well.[8] Their solution is to give employees cash, in the form of a health reimbursement account (HRA), taking advantage of changes in the use of HRAs that were pushed by the Trump administration. A related proposal would allow exchange plans to be purchased by employees.[9] This is certainly creative, but one must have a lot of faith in an employee's ability to make a smart purchasing decision without the overarching apparatus of Medicare Advantage's consumer protections.

Medicare Advantage has the strengths of government-negotiated rates, the integration of primary care–managed global budgets, and strict governmental oversight that puts for-profit insurers in the role of a regulated utility but still allows the introduction of profit-driven innovations. Since our political system values incremental reform and free choice by key constituents, the simple move of opening up Medicare Advantage plans to employees over the age of 60 would give employers an opportunity to begin to use this governmental program if they so desire.

My bet is that employers, and their employees, would be very interested in this product. Incrementally dropping the age of eligibility would allow a phased, gradual rescue for sinking employer-sponsored health insurance coverage. A long view, based on sixty years of evolution in the US health care system and a relatively long ten- to twenty-year future horizon, leads to the conclusion that replacing employer-sponsored insurance with an evolving program like Medicare Advantage is a viable policy option.

One more point deserves mention. Over the last thirty years, the administrative costs of the American health care system have repeatedly been lamented and criticized. The elimination of such costs drives much of the impetus for traditional Medicare for All—a single-payer plan—which I will discuss in more detail in the next chapter.

Be that as it may, fine-grained analyses of this administrative burden focus on the claims submission process and the complexities of utilization management.[10] McKinsey & Company (a consulting firm) pegs administrative costs at $950 billion, spread among private and public payers, as well as doctors and hospitals.[11] To take one-third of this total out, they recommend instituting centralized automated claims clearinghouses, greater interoperability, standardized quality reporting, and streamlined medical policies.

Each of these possibilities would be quite tractable as more commercial insurers migrate to a Medicare Advantage chassis, especially one based on capitated payments to primary care doctors. Utilization management costs would go away, and claims submissions could be done in a uniform fashion, which would be dictated by the CMS. While many insurers would still be participating, they would have to conform to federal standards, just as they do today with Medicare Advantage's quality of care reporting. These points have all been made by Sachin Jain,[12] but they bear repeating as outlines for what I see as the most likely reform of our health care system. Replacing government-sponsored insurance with Medicare Advantage should reduce—perhaps radically—administrative costs.

Potential Weaknesses of Medicare Advantage

Medicare Advantage plans can be improved. Most experts agree that their compensation per member is currently too high—higher than in traditional Medicare. In 2022 and 2023, the debate over governmental reimbursements to Medicare Advantage plans has reached a particularly fervid pitch. Perhaps the most insightful addition to the arguments is the summary offered by Paul Ginsburg and Steven Lieberman.[13] They point out that all parties appreciate the support Medicare Advantage gives to a reliance on capitation in order to obtain value. Weighing the competing points of view carefully, they tend to agree with Berwick and Gilfillan that overpayments in Medicare Advantage, based on risk coding, are not tolerable and have to be curtailed. They believe MedPAC has pointed the way, and the CMS's policymakers have the tools necessary to right the payment ship. In early 2023, the CMS had taken bold steps, moving to the new ICD-10 disease classification program and eliminating certain codes that appeared to be overused. This raised the ire of insurers and physician groups working in capitated Medicare Advantage plans, who then pushed successfully for a stepwise integration of these changes.

As a historical perspective, in the 2010–2015 timeframe, overly high reimbursement rates had successfully been reduced. That will occur again as we move to the mid-2020s, due to revisions in coding, better audits, and (perhaps) changes in the bidding structure. Anyone concerned about the costs of American health care—and federal budget deficits—cannot support a Medicare Advantage program that is overpaid and insurance companies that are overprofiting. From the insurers' point of view, they will have to adapt and put new efforts into the elimination of health care waste.

As with all debates about governmental resources, political motives lurk just beneath the surface in discussions about Medicare Advantage overpayments. Single-payer advocates believe that on a level playing field, private insurers will lose interest in Medicare Advantage. That is one of the key developments to watch over the mid-2020s. If that is the case, then a second pathway to Medicare for All—the single-payer option—becomes much more likely.

Moving beyond the issue of costs, many see a higher quality of health care in Medicare Advantage, while others believe it is quite similar to what exists in traditional Medicare.[14] This is a very active debate in health policy today. Perhaps most telling is MedPAC's rather bleak complaint that it can no longer really judge the quality of care in Medicare

Advantage.[15] The answer should be to focus on a very specific, not too numerous set of measures, such as the ones CMS's leadership has recently endorsed.[16] As I look to the future—one with primary care doctors, buttressed by digital medicine, taking capitation and managing health—Medicare Advantage presents the appropriate chassis. It has a clear edge over traditional Medicare, which could remain mired in fee-for-service programs unless there are some significant changes.

If Medicare Advantage is the vehicle leading to socialized health insurance, governmental oversight of it will have to be nimble and swift. This view resonates with that of Sherry Glied and Thomas D'Aunno.[17] Their target is venture capital and its search for arbitrage in health services. They point out that unless regulators are agile, for-profit companies will find ways to take advantage of the health care system's complexity and opacity to gain inappropriate profits. They chose venture capital-supported anesthesia groups that use surprise billing as one example, but there are many others. Most of the kinds of abuse reviewed by Glied and D'Aunno are in the employer-sponsored insurance sector, but their point is well taken. Government must be up to the task of regulation if it is to allow for-profit firms to have central roles in the American health care system.

That premise goes to a much more fundamental problem that some see with Medicare Advantage. Many health care reformers and advocates for patients look dimly on for-profit health care. In particular, they find it galling that many insurance company executives can make huge amounts of money while putting policies in place that, at least at face value, restrict access to care. The average person would probably agree with them.

The American College of Physicians (ACP) certainly supports this position, forcefully stating their suspicion of—and even opposition to—for-profit influences in health care.[18] Arguing from the first principle of patient welfare, the college's position paper arrives at the conclusion that health care in the future should either be through a single governmental payer or a public option in a regulated insurance market.[19] This argument is cogent, but I would add one point. While most of the problems the ACP and others seek to solve are similar to those I have outlined in this book, these organizations seem to overlook the point that physicians themselves are profit seekers. Hospitals, and their employed physicians, are nonprofit in name, but most financial analyses of their operations fail to reveal a clearly charitable nature. They act much like any other profit seeker. One of the biggest problems we must address is the overuse of resources in a fee-for-service system that is driven by physicians and hospitals. Eliminating private insurers because you are opposed to profit taking in health care overlooks the other elephant in the room.

Be this as it may, if you agree with the point of view espoused by the ACP, relying on private insurers in Medicare Advantage plans as the foundation for our health care system just does not sit comfortably. The ACP prefers to have a prohibition on for-profit payers, rather than tight regulation.

I will turn to a single-payer program, such as the one the ACP advocates, in the next chapter. But the challenge the ACP presents to a system that allows private insurers, such as Medicare Advantage, is rather straightforward. The government must be able to regulate insurers. Historical evidence suggests that it can. But insurers must also recognize that an unalloyed search for profits will corrode the country's health insurance program. It is in insurers' enlightened self-interest to orient their programs toward the elimination of health care waste and improvements in the quality of care for beneficiaries. To the extent that they can do so, they will preserve their role in socialized health insurance.

The Tipping Point for a Medicare Advantage Future

The big assumption underlying my prediction of a substantial change in American health care during the 2020s is that inherent demographic and financial pressures help make the relative deficiencies of current employer-sponsored insurance plans obvious to all. The crucial subset of this "all" is the employers themselves. Would private employers turn to a government-sponsored program?

Such a turn is not without precedent. In the early 2000s, many employers had insurance programs with drug benefits for retirees. Once

Medicare Part D became available, they shifted rapidly to employer group waiver programs that allowed their retirees to use Part D as the core of their benefits. This migration caused a stunning shift in the pharmacy benefit managers' business model.

The same is true of group Medicare Advantage plans. Employers who, in the past, had offered retiree health benefits using Medicare's supplemental plans now use the Part D program to provide that benefit. If the government wanted to make a Medicare Advantage–type program or Medicare Part D available to those under age 65, there are reasons to believe that employers would be interested. They would not reject it out of hand on political grounds, as they are using similar governmental programs today.

For employers, the main issue will be cost. Employers' concerns about health care inflation are sufficient enough for them to begin broaching the subject of governmental intervention. A recent Kaiser Family Foundation survey of business leaders found that more than 80 percent moderately, considerably, or strongly agreed that health care costs were too high, citing fee-for-service programs, provider consolidations, and medications as the key drivers.[20] More importantly, 87 percent believed that the cost of health care would become unsustainable over the next five to ten years, and 85 percent believed there would be a need for a greater governmental role in health care coverage and its related costs. So there is at least some feeling within the business community that eventually the cost question will lead to a broader governmental role.

If history provides any lessons, the federal government's initiative would be incremental, opening the door to a migration toward Medicare Advantage in a fashion that would be stepwise and optional. No one would be forced into a single system. Rather, businesses could choose to make the program available to some segment of their employees below the age of 65.

The Biden administration, at least to some extent, has broached the subject, advocating for lowering Medicare's eligibility age to 60, as a buy-in proposal.[21] Insofar as details are available, however, the Biden proposal is not really a buy-in as much as it is simply an extension of

Medicare, with new federal outlays for health care coverage. Nonetheless, the tone the administration has used is incremental, and that is important for hospitals and physicians. These key providers will have to adjust to the loss of (higher) commercial reimbursements, so they need the migration of employers to the proposed Biden plan to be relatively slow.

This point about incrementalism by using an age-tranche concept is critical. Any move from a commercial insurer's plan to Medicare decreases revenues for the providers, as they are paid less. Moving the entire commercial insurance population to Medicare in one fell swoop would be catastrophic for most hospitals and many medical provider groups, which could see an immediate 15–20 percent drop in revenues. (As I will discuss in chapter 10, single-payer advocates would cushion this drop by relieving doctors of a lot of their administrative costs.) A progressive approach where a new, five-year age tranche of beneficiaries would be eligible on a periodic basis gives providers some time to adapt. When such incremental steps occur, financial pressure on the remaining commercial contracts worsens—a circling down the drain for the employer-sponsored market would increase in velocity.

Moving employer-sponsored beneficiaries to Medicare Advantage–type plans should not be a free lunch for employers. One financing option would be to raise taxes on income to pay for the new Medicare beneficiaries. That would be appealingly progressive, in the economic sense of that term. With higher income taxes, those with low incomes would pay proportionately less. Yet even the most progressive economists might see the political value of keeping the costs of health care benefits centered on employers. Employers would probably pay for a new "Medicare Advantage for those less than age 65" plan, just as they do today for many Medicare Advantage–based retiree plans.

The move to Medicare Advantage–type plans could thus be accomplished without new taxes on corporate or individual incomes. Instead, the transition could be effectuated by keeping the employer mandate for health insurance in place and giving employers an option to use Medicare Advantage–type plans to provide coverage for their employees, rather than ERISA-regulated plans. Keeping employers in the game reiterates the concept of incrementalism. The employers' historical role would persist, to the extent that they would pay the costs for their employees' Medicare Advantage–type plans. But the government would oversee the benefits and administration of the insurance product.

Would employees be interested in such plans, especially if, during an open enrollment period, they had a choice between a Medicare Advantage–type plan and a typical commercial plan? The critical elements for employees are the plan's list of benefits and the extent of their out-of-pocket costs. In a Medicare Advantage–type plan, these issues are highly regulated by the CMS, with benefits being relatively broad (basically in keeping with the current standard of care) and out-of-pocket costs being capped. A Medicare Advantage for All program would therefore eliminate many of the concerns about underinsurance that are becoming so important in employer-sponsored insurance plans. The average worker could be very happy to be on a Medicare Advantage–type plan.

Would employers find this a reasonable alternative? As always, it comes down to cost. Medicare Advantage eliminates underinsurance, which should increase employer expenses. Yet some simple math suggests that a Medicare Advantage–type plan would be a bargain for employers. Let us start with the current approach for a self-insured employer plan. For an individual (not a family) plan in 2022, an employer paid approximately $6,800 for an HMO or a PPO plan. For an individual policy, an employee contributed between $1,200 (HMO plan) and $1,500 (PPO plan), for a total cost of roughly $8,000 to $8,300.[22]

Commercial insurers do have certain ways to shave costs, some of which might be lost in a Medicare Advantage framework. ERISA's avoidance of state-mandated benefits probably shaves off about 5 percent of total costs by not having to comply with these mandates. Let us assume that cost difference will go away. Utilization management might net another 5 percent reduction in overall costs in a commercial plan. But Medicare Advantage also has utilization management, although it is quite a bit more dilute. I have estimated that, at most, this has about half the effect of its use in a commercial program.[23]

Coding issues will save a commercial insurer another 5 percent, but providers are much more careful about coding games for government-sponsored programs, so we might discount these savings. Case management, disease management, and wellness initiatives do not provide much value from a cost point of view, but they are present in both commercial and Medicare Advantage plans. Taking these all together, the initiatives that a third-party administrator (the insurer) provides for an employer-sponsored plan means that the true cost of the policy for an employer plus an employee—without the efforts of the TPA/insurer—is on the order of $8,600 to $8,900. (In my analyses of single-payer insurance in chapter 10, commercial health insurers are given very little credit for any of these savings—their contribution just applies to administrative costs.)

Now consider the discounts on provider costs that Medicare obtains, compared with commercial insurers. I believe that, over time, there will be a further movement for Medicare to negotiate prices for drugs. Since it is difficult to estimate when this might occur, I will assume that employers' prices for medications would be similar in commercial plans and the new Medicare Advantage–type plans. (This is a substantially conservative assumption.)

The real benefit of using Medicare Advantage–type plans is the discounts on fees that are paid to providers. More than two-thirds of the costs of commercial health care insurance are in hospital and physician services. The discount for hospital services in government-sponsored plans is approximately 50 percent, and the discount for physician services is about 30 percent.[24] Applying these discounts to the numbers outlined above results in the costs of an HMO benefits plan decreasing from $8,600 to less than $6,280. This is less than the amount an employer paid for the cost of insurance ($6,800), while an employee paid $1,200. As I argued in preceding chapters, Medicare discounts on the costs of provider services swamp any cost-reduction benefits derived from commercial health insurance. The discounts essentially make up for all the management costs by a TPA/insurer and also cover an employee's contribution to the premium.

This is a relatively coarse analysis, simply showing the effect that provider payment discounts in Medicare have on a commercial health insurance plan. More-technical versions of the role of provider discounts in lowering costs and premiums are available, such as from the Urban Institute.[25] Designing a Medicare Advantage–type plan for under-65-year-olds would have to account for a variety of other factors, including premium contributions (Medicare Advantage beneficiaries still pay the Part B premium), out-of-pocket costs, and the plan's profit margin. A Medicare Advantage–type program would also involve utilization management, with narrow networks and a required, limited choice of primary care doctors.[26] But the blunt effect of the governmental rates is what will entice employers.

A Medicare Advantage–type plan for employees brings governmental regulations on benefits and cost sharing into the employer sector. It provides thicker insurance, doing so at a competitive price (through lower compensation for providers). Since the plan would be tied to the government's own fiscal concerns, companies should be able to rely on this formula going forward.

A Medicare Advantage–type plan for employees between the ages of 60 and 65 might not work for all employers and employees, but many would find it attractive—especially from a cost perspective. As some employers join in, the cross-subsidy pie would get smaller, and costs would go up for those who remain in the employer-sponsored plans. Walmart might jump right in. Google may continue with its very extensive commercial plan. But over time, as more companies like Walmart join in, Google will be left footing the bill for the ever-increasing costs in commercial plans as providers get more stubborn in their negotiations, in order to make up for the loss of commercial revenue from those who have switched to Medicare Advantage–type plans for their employees.

An important asset of a new Medicare Advantage program for tranches under age 65 is that it facilitates the medical management of chronic diseases. Group Medicare members are reliably long-term members—on average, for more than ten years. This gives a primary care group plenty of time in which to address risk. Perhaps as importantly, major insurers are familiar with the group market and can readily modify their tools, ranging from actuarial expertise to marketing infrastructure, to step in and offer plans to a new set of potential beneficiaries in the 60–64 age group.

One further issue is the tax treatment of health benefits. The exemption for health care benefits is perhaps the biggest tax break in the United States, estimated at more than $250 billion in 2019.[27] This is not a benefit for corporations per se. Rather, it helps individual employees, who do not pay taxes on the benefits they receive in terms of health insurance. These benefits could be easily monetized and then taxed. (From an employer's point of view, this is simply a business deduction, like wages, a point that Jon Gruber has helped me understand.) This tax break is regressive, in that it benefits the wealthy more than it does low- or middle-income employees, as the rich have more substantial benefits but higher tax rates. No doubt this is one of the few things on which the political right and left agree.

Economists, including liberal economists, would welcome the removal of this exclusion. It would provide as much as $250 billion in new federal revenues, and the taxes would be applied in a progressive fashion. But even liberally inclined legislators do not endorse mucking around with the tax exemption for health benefits. One reason is that it is poorly understood—barely recognized in most discussions of health policy. Another is that any revision would impose new taxes on workers, including the middle class. Changing the exemption would especially be anathema for unions, who have brought health care benefits to their members as a tax-free boon. So I will proceed as if there is no alteration in the tax status of employee health care benefits. (Note that a single-payer format would claim the savings, as these programs are based on new income or payroll taxes. More on this in chapter 10.)

In summary, the government could make Medicare Advantage–type plans available for employees under the age of 65. This change requires almost no substantial structural remodeling of the overall health insurance market. These plans would probably be attractive from a cost and a benefits / quality-of-care point of view. Some employers would opt in.

This is one path to socialized health insurance. As more age tranches for enrollment are made available over time, Medicare Advantage–type plans would replace commercial insurance. The government would determine the payment rate for providers, and it would set forth the parameters of the policy, including the beneficiary's costs and the range of benefits. Private insurers would remain in the game—seeking profits, just like physicians and hospitals would. Administrative costs would be decreased with a simplified and standardized revenue cycle for developing and paying bills, although not to the extent that a traditional Medicare for All (single-payer) plan would. And it would be incremental, easily bolted onto the existing health care system and able to grow over time. Medicare Advantage–type plans are based on a risk chassis, so they should promote the growth of managed care, particularly capitation-taking primary care.

How Would the Key Players in the Health Care System React to a Broader Role for Medicare Advantage?

Medicare Advantage for those less than age 65 is not a new idea. It has been circulating for years, especially as a proposal for first responders, who often retire before they turn 65.[28] The unions that represent these public employees know group Medicare Advantage well, and would no doubt opt to use that vehicle for coverage. Prominent health policy experts with a broad background have already begun to advocate outrightly for more extensive use of Medicare Advantage to effectuate health care reform.[29]

If a new Medicare Advantage program goes into place, and some percentage of the affected 22 million 60- to 64-year-old employees switch from their employer-sponsored health care plans to Medicare, what would providers do? Their first response might be to panic. This shift in payers would mean that as much as 10 percent of the hospital business would go from being paid $1 to 50 cents; for doctors, that $1 sinks to 70 cents. These are substantial revenue losses, and if adding the first tranche proceeds well, then the 55- to 60-year-olds are next, and so on down the line.

The response of a typical hospital CEO most likely will be rate re-lated: get paid at commercial rates by the Medicare Advantage plans. That will not be easy. The use of Medicare payment rates for Medicare Advantage recipients who are not in network has been a durable fea-ture of US health policy for years. The CMS team developing legisla-tion entitled "Medicare for Some Under 65" will know they have to maintain the Medicare rate cudgel, as will any legislator voting for this.

A subsidiary response, probably led more by doctors than by hospi-tals, will be to do more—more tests, visits, and procedures—to in-crease their revenues. The medical management scheme in Medicare Advantage plans will resist this. On the other hand, it is likely that both traditional Medicare and (even more so) the remaining commercial in-surance plans will absorb the spillover effects from ramping up the in-tensity of care under fee-for-service reimbursements. (As I will discuss in chapter 10, the most thorough analyses of single-payer insurance do not anticipate provider-induced demand for increased revenues.)

The eventual response by providers, however, must be to move from doing more to make more to doing less to make more. In other words, they will take capitation and reduce health care waste as the major source for their profit margin. This is what the small primary care groups that are currently taking on risk are doing. This is not a new concept, but now there will be added force as the cash cow of employer-sponsored insurance starts to disappear.

The federal government, or at least the CMS, has long recognized that, going forward, managing care to make it value based is critical for a sol-vent health care system. The Centers for Medicare & Medicaid Services have attempted to foster such behavior through the Medicare Shared Savings Program and through CMMI demonstrations. Gauging the suc-cess of such programs, however, is complicated.[30] But at the very least, a stronger foundation for health care management is taking shape.[31]

What is clear is that insofar as an integrated system participates in the MSSP or other initiatives from the CMMI, it is hedging its bets ap-propriately about the future shape of health care financing. Whether or not a system's leaders are still committed to fee-for-service plans, they must be thinking about strategies for the future, and their concerns about the long-term viability of commercial insurance must play into that, even if those concerns are not fully articulated. Many, it would seem, are quietly preparing for the future I am setting forth here. Others will ride the fee-for-service horse for as long as possible.

If group Medicare Advantage for employees begins to unfold, the negative spiral of cross-subsidy will worsen as integrated systems attempt to get ever-larger rates from a diminishing base. Smart integrated systems will understand this and realize that their only option is to manage care in order to gain a profit. They can develop the same kind of primary care management programs that Humana and United-Health/Optum are building.

One could argue that integrated systems are well placed to succeed in a value-based environment. They can accept full capitation as payment, negotiating with insurers for a percentage of the premiums. Any training they internalized from MSSP or other CMMI-inspired ACO projects can stand them in good stead. Integrated systems can also get out from underneath an insurance company's oversight of care, including all utilization management and coding disputes, once they own the risk. But they will have to eliminate unnecessary care procedures and turn their backs on fee-for-service incentives. This will be difficult, but the majority of physicians and hospital leaders have been espousing the virtues of value-based care for years. The move to accommodate a broader Medicare Advantage program will merely be the tipping point.

Employers are the next set of stakeholders to consider. They will be charged an actuarially accurate average cost for each employee, an amount that will probably be substantially less than what they were paying on a self-insured basis. They will like the savings. But employers will reasonably have other questions. How much inflation will occur? How effective will the administration of the program be? How will their employees perceive this change? With regard to inflation, an employer's concern most likely will be, If I am no longer in charge or in control, and the government is, would I see costs skyrocketing? The best predictions are based on past performance, and there the record is clear. From 2008 to 2021, Medicaid's per enrollee spending increased by just under 19 percent; for Medicare, by approximately 37 percent. Private health insurance over the same period increased by just over 54 percent.[32] Being able to control the rate of payment by fiat is the single best tool in moderating health care costs, at least until that care is seriously managed.

A more sophisticated answer to the question about inflation should be based on competition. This new market for replacing commercial insurance plans should be large, so one would expect a reasonable amount of competition between Medicare Advantage firms, which, in turn, would hold costs down. Today, that certainly seems to be the case.

The Kaiser Family Foundation noted that there were 2,034 Medicare Advantage plans in 2017, rising to 3,550 in 2021.[33] This rapid increase suggests that the market is dynamic, and new entrants are finding their way to it. Kaiser estimated that in 2021, the average Medicare beneficiary had access to thirty-three different Medicare Advantage plans, up from nineteen in 2017. It is hard to characterize this as a lack of competition. And from inside an insurance company, it certainly feels like there is a lot of competition—the annual bidding process and results in enrollment are watched closely, and there are winners and losers.

The group Medicare Advantage landscape is dominated by the large national insurers: UnitedHealthcare, Humana, Aetna, Elevance, and CIGNA, with Centene and Molina moving in. Local Blues plans are also beginning to get active in the group environment. Plans from national insurers and Blue Cross would compete with one another for this business, ensuring an active and competitive market. So employers would have both the record of Medicare cost increases and the fact of ample competition to rely on as they consider the viability of a group Medicare Advantage plan as an alternative for their older workers.

Competition should also improve quality. A group Medicare Advantage policy is generally equivalent in quality to a commercial policy, and it is highly regulated by the federal government. Group Medicare Advantage benefits are broad, out-of-pocket costs are restrained, and the program is readily articulated through a primary care gatekeeper, in a highly managed format. Employees might have to adapt to tighter provider networks and a limited choice of primary care providers. But in return, they would have much less out-of-pocket spending and broader benefits.

In summary, as this new group Medicare Advantage program would be put into place, providers would have to cope, but they would have time to do so. Employers would get to make common sense decisions, balancing costs and proposed changes in their employees' health care benefits. The incremental, and voluntary, aspects of a group Medicare Advantage program are very attractive.

Would a Dominant Medicare Advantage Plan Be Appealing, and Would It Be Equitable?

Consumers prefer Medicare Advantage plans to commercial plans. J.D. Power tracks this sort of information on an annual basis. In 2022, on a scale of 1,000 points, the top Medicare Advantage plan (Kaiser Foundation Health Plan) scored 844, with the industry average being 809.[34] The lowest-rated plan, Centene, came in at 773. The ratings for commercial plans were much worse. The best plans, mostly Kaiser plans in various states, were in the 734–795 range, and the mean, by region, generally fell in the 705–740 range.[35] These findings are durable over time, with the best-rated commercial plans not rated as highly as the mean score for Medicare Advantage plans.

The same result is generally found regarding comparisons between Medicare Advantage and fee-for-service traditional Medicare. In a 2017 study, enrollees reported a better overall experience with Medicare Advantage.[36] The Better Medicare Alliance (BMA), the industry group supporting Medicare Advantage, also polls patients. Given the funding source for the BMA, one must take its publications with more than a grain of salt, but in early 2021, they reported that in their poll of 1,200 seniors, 98 percent of the beneficiaries were satisfied with their Medicare Advantage plan, and 97 percent with their provider network.[37]

These satisfaction scores are impressive. But perhaps a more important question is, Are Medicare Advantage programs equitable? Do they treat sick patients and healthy patients in a similar fashion? Do people of color get fair treatment, or does the program evince many of the same racist qualities that are found in health care generally?

On the point of care for the very sick, experts on Medicare and long-term care have had some doubts. They are concerned that Medicare Advantage plans have incentives to unload sicker patients, even though Medicare pays higher capitation fees for the sick (risk-adjusted payments). These authors have shown how high-cost patients tend to leave Medicare Advantage plans proportionately more often.[38] The same appears to be true for those receiving home health care.[39] While some studies show that Medicare Advantage plans provide more-efficient but equally high-quality care,[40] these observations cannot account for the "forced" exit of sicker patients,[41] which is certainly something we would not want in a well-functioning health insurance plan.

How would Medicare Advantage plans accomplish such targeted, and regressive, disenrollment? Let us presume that there is no evil intent, but also that the Medicare Advantage plans will seek a profit. They do run narrow networks and make more use of utilization management than traditional Medicare, although both of these impulses are regulated. Nonetheless, as beneficiaries get sicker, they might try to hold on to one specialist, or avoid administrative hassles, by going back to traditional Medicare. In addition, different Medicare Advantage plan designs could be carefully targeted by an insurer to enroll a comparatively healthy population.

These moves could be countered, however, by regulation. One idea would be to penalize plans for disenrollment; another would be to rate all Healthcare Effectiveness Data and Information Set (HEDIS) scores by the severity of the Hierarchical Condition Category coding score of the relevant patient population.[42] MedPAC, scanning and assessing the literature, will presumably pick up on these threads and recommend regulatory change, if indicated.

The other question one must ask is, Do Medicare Advantage plans offer a similar quality of care to people of all races? There is not a lot of research on this question, although a team at Brown University has developed some insights.[43] They have shown that Black people and, in particular, people of Hispanic origin are much more likely to be enrolled in Medicare Advantage plans, compared with traditional Medicare. The same has been true for people who lived in neighborhoods with greater social disadvantages. So it would appear that the enrollment process in Medicare Advantage is not discriminating.

Nonetheless, Medicare Advantage Star ratings do not necessarily identify racial equity in outcomes. Black and Hispanic people had simulated Star ratings that were significantly lower than white beneficiaries.[44] There is a broad recognition that more research of this sort is necessary—now more than ever.[45] Fortunately, the current administrator of the CMS, Chiquita Brooks-LaSure, appears to recognize this and is creating a strategic vision that emphasizes health equity while advancing access.[46] This should infuse the government-sponsored programs, including Medicare Advantage. Our country, in its health system, has failed to recognize the harm that comes from embedded racism, and this needs to be addressed. Today, governmental programs are leading that effort.

Is There Anything Similar to a Medicare Advantage-Based Socialized Health Insurance Program?

Those concerned about reform might be reassured if they saw a similar system functioning elsewhere: private plans, with some beneficiary choices, competing for enrollees but carefully regulated by the government, and all plans paying providers (doctor and hospital services) uniform rates. That is a fairly close description of what happens in Germany today.

The Germans have a federal system, with close collaboration between their federal government and their states.[47] This program essentially has universal coverage, with insurance provided for nearly 90 percent of the population through 109 sickness funds, which are nonprofit but nongovernmental health insurance plans. Individuals choose the sickness fund through which they want coverage. The other 10 percent have private insurance, which is purchased by wealthier individuals.

Germany's federal government regulates the funds, but it is not involved in the delivery of care. The states and sickness funds negotiate with providers, mostly at the state level, regarding fees. Ultimately, there is one state schedule for all providers, so all doctors and hospitals are paid the same amount for similar services, which is not dissimilar to the federal government's payment schedule for Medicare in the United States.[48] Most of the payments are for fee-for-service charges, although there is a good deal of interest today in payments for performance.

In theory, the sickness funds use different insurance structures to compete against one another for value. Most commentary seems to suggest that this competition does not amount to much.[49] But the sickness funds do collect the employers' and workers' contributions and have begun to employ more integrated payment schemes between doctors and hospitals. The core of Germany's program—independent insurers who are heavily regulated by the federal government and spend risk-adjusted amounts on behalf of beneficiaries—is very similar to what a Medicare Advantage–dominated program would entail in the United States. The big difference is the for-profit status of most Medicare Advantage insurers in America. The German system and a similar system in Switzerland (which does allow nonprofit health insurers to be owned by for-profit parent companies) both demonstrate that a socialized health insurance system can still leave providers, hospitals, and insurers in private hands.

The comparison with Germany's system has a bearing on one question that seems to be asked in international health policy circles: Are the sickness funds promoting innovation? In the United States, we would expect insurers to continue to develop new models of care (like the Optum development regarding primary care) and integrate digital tools to help eliminate health care waste. They have to be creative and compete, or their profit-seeking status will come under even more scrutiny.

To Summarize the Case

A program like Medicare Advantage could be a bridge that takes beneficiaries out of the crippled employer-sponsored health insurance regime. It would be directed by the government but would allow companies to innovate. The program would be affordable as well as tractable, in that financing issues would rely on underwriting/actuarial estimation mechanisms that the government already employs. The beneficiaries' out-of-pocket spending would be limited, and the benefits package would be broad and evidence based. The program could be readily annealed to risk-bearing primary care, which most experts, for years, have agreed is the best way to ensure efficient and high-quality health care. It could be put into place incrementally, using age tranches brought in over a period of time. Competition between competing firms should fuel innovation in eliminating health care waste.

A steady transfer of formerly commercially insured beneficiaries to Medicare Advantage would slowly decrease the revenue from the remaining commercial insurance plans, making hospitals' fee-for-service financing impossible. Integrated systems would have no choice but to become accountable care organizations—that is, to take on risk and reduce waste. The overall 30 percent drop in reimbursements that would occur in a move to Medicare rates will have to be made up by driving 30 percent of the health care waste out of a capitated budget.

There may be some residual private insurance plans, with some employers committed to them. That is the case in Germany, where about 10 percent of the population has a private insurance plan. But those who are privately insured in the United States would not have access to the governmental rates. Their health insurance plans would be very pricey, keeping the number of enrollees, one must suspect, quite small.

In many ways, this is a reasonable prediction, given the deteriorating base for employer-sponsored insurance and the fifty-five-year progression of federal health care plans, culminating in today's Medicare Part D, exchange, and Medicare Advantage programs. It punches the ticket in terms of what is politically feasible. Most importantly, it would rely on incremental change, which is a critical part of our history of health care reform.

The big question about a future with Medicare Advantage becoming our socialized health insurance vehicle is, Can it survive and prosper if providers are paid at fair rates? Richard Gilfillan and Donald

Berwick attribute Medicare Advantage's growth not to better care, but to overpayment by the government, leading to unseemly profiteering.[50] They probably know that this has not been entirely true historically, especially because there is general agreement that Medicare Advantage and traditional Medicare neared parity in the Obama administration, in which both of these individuals served.

But their focus is on today and the future. Paying insurers at more than traditional Medicare rates cannot make sense as we face the fiscal future that is at the center of this book, which drives my prediction about the extinction of commercial health insurance plans. To some extent, the onus is on the government to demonstrate that it can regulate for-profit entities and adjust the Medicare Advantage program as necessary to avoid excess and unfair profiteering. But to some extent, for-profit insurers must realize that they are moving into a socialized health insurance future, and that health insurance is a public good. They will need to bend their mindset toward supporting that public good, just as much as they concentrate on returns on shareholder value.

Make no mistake, though, Medicare Advantage for All is socialized health insurance. Providers would be paid according to the government's fee schedules. The nature and extent of the health insurance policy would be directed by the government, with that package being the same for anyone in the Medicare Advantage for All program. The march of improvements in governmental programs and changing public assumptions about access to health care have enabled progress in this final step toward socialized health insurance. The behavior of providers under a fee-for-service system, and the diffidence of employers' benefits managers and commercial insurers, facilitated it.

But that is not the final word. Another camp wants to move assertively away from profit making and toward a program where the government pays for health care—a more full-blooded socialized health insurance. A single-payer format is the dominant alternative structure discussed today. In the next chapter, I turn to that set of proposals and assess how it holds up against an incremental Medicare Advantage model.

CHAPTER TEN

Medicare for All: A Single-Payer System

UP TO THIS POINT, I have argued that the march of socialized health insurance is as much a matter of the structural weaknesses of the employer-sponsored insurance model as it is a change in political views, although it is expedited and made possible by the shifting norms and expectations we, as a country, have about access to health care. In this socialized medicine future, the government would control or sponsor all of the health care insurance, defining the benefits, the beneficiaries' experience, and the costs. The government would also set the rate of payment for doctors, hospitals, pharmaceutical firms, and the rest of health care. The path outlined in chapter 9, socialized health insurance based on a Medicare Advantage–type plan, would not occur due to an earthquake, hurricane, or explosion of reform, but simply through the expediency of allowing employers to buy much cheaper government-sponsored insurance.

No one is really advocating for socialized health insurance through Medicare Advantage today. To me, this seems sensible and in keeping with the incremental path to health care reform we have been on for the last sixty years. But most people do not see a coming crisis in employer-sponsored insurance, and for-profit insurers themselves have no interest in advocating for Medicare Advantage to replace their employer products, even though, as I have suggested, much of the focus in those companies today is on their government-based plans.

On the other hand, the pathway to socialized health insurance does have strong advocates. For years, the left-leaning portion of the Democratic Party, as well as many physician and nurse advocates, have argued that we, as a nation, would be far better served with a single-payer, Medicare For All program that would replace other forms of insurance—at the very least, employer-sponsored insurance, Medicaid, and the exchanges. Their arguments have gained ground and seeped rightward, closer to the Democratic Party's center. Their main goal is universal access—those low-income individuals who are currently uninsured, as well as noncitizens, would be swept into the program, with their health care costs covered. There would be no (or very little) out-of-pocket payments, no private payers, and full coverage for all cost-effective health benefits.

If one accepts the demise of the employer-sponsored insurance sector and cannot tolerate a Medicare Advantage–based system with its private payers, then Medicare for All is the alternative. It deserves close examination.

Health Care Reform into the 2020s

As we begin to move into the middle part of the 2020s, the advance of socialized health insurance is really not on the table. Quite unexpectedly, the elections in 2020, after a great deal of tribulation, almost resulted in an alignment for health care reform. Democrats controlled the White House, the House (barely), and the Senate (even more marginally). The discipline of Speaker Nancy Pelosi and Chuck Schumer notwithstanding, the Biden administration could not do whatever it wanted, as it needed every Democrat elected to the House and Senate on board. Moderates (like Senators Joe Manchin and Kyrsten Sinema) frustrated the administration's efforts to bring about substantial health care reform. Nonetheless, there were attempts—and some results.

The Biden administration received a lot of advice. Health care policy experts (academic and nonacademic), who could only keep their heads down during the Trump years, sprang forth with a variety of new ideas and proposals. There were few surprises in these suggestions, given that there is a good deal of consensus on the overall set of problems—much of this book has been spent reviewing those. But examining the main suggestions illustrates how the debate over the government's role in health care has evolved to this point.

John Ayanian has succinctly set out these issues as a series of crucial questions.[1] Who remains uninsured, and how can they be covered? Who remains underinsured, and what can be done to make coverage more affordable for them? How much health care spending can the United States afford? How can racial, ethnic, and socioeconomic equity in health outcomes be achieved?

Ayanian and *JAMA*, the *Journal of the American Medical Association*, organized a series of essays by leading experts in health policy, in part to answer the questions posed above. As one might expect, the papers go in many directions, but Ezekiel Emmanuel helpfully summarized them into five themes.[2] The first was that the federal government must exert downward pressure on high health care prices. Second, the health care system must become more efficient, reducing waste. Third (and derivative from the first two), drug prices need to be addressed. The fourth was to effectuate system-wide changes, specifically by supercharging the Center for Medicare & Medicaid Innovation and accountable care organizations, forcing the acceptance of managed care. Finally, Medicaid needed attention, with much more of an emphasis placed on better outcomes and greater equity.

Add to these another list, assembled by Bob Kocher and Rahul Rajkumar: (1) payment systems should encourage multiyear investments in health; (2) payment models must be aligned across payers; and (3) the administrative burden in revenue cycles and quality of care measurements must be reduced.[3] These recommendations encapsulated what Democratic health policy experts thought was needed as the new Democratic majorities in Congress considered health care reforms. But few comprehensive proposals were put forward, the presumption being that changes would be incremental.

Faced with lower horizons as a result of the very tight Senate majority, the Biden administration nonetheless pursued health care reform that resonated with the above-stated imperatives. The administration's proposals were the backbone of the House of Representatives' effort: HR 5376, the Build Back Better Act (BBBA). The major health elements of the BBBA were highly recognizable as incremental extensions of existing policy in the Affordable Care Act, Medicaid, and Medicare Part D, as well as in drug negotiations. A few of these finally made it into law as part of what was eventually passed, the Inflation Reduction Act.

Regarding the ACA and Medicaid, one could see the pincers of the act's Titles I and II again in play. New subsidies for ACA health insurance policy purchases had gone into place as part of the COVID relief bill, the American Rescue Plan Act (ARPA): the upper-income threshold was removed and the value of premium subsidies / tax credits increased. The BBBA would have extended these. Perhaps more importantly, the BBBA contemplated lowering the affordable coverage provision, which determines an employee's cost share, from 9.61 percent to 8.5 percent until 2025. The Kaiser Family Foundation estimated that these provisions would have lowered the number of uninsured by 1.2 million.[4]

Along the same lines in the BBBA, and targeted toward those states that have not expanded Medicaid, the federal government would have fully subsidized the purchase of benchmark health insurance plans. This provision would have allowed coverage for another 2.2 million people. The cost of these two provisions over the next decade would have been about $125 billion.

The BBBA's Medicaid expansions were just what one would expect, given the history of that program. Over a ten-year period, another $1.2 billion would have been spent to ensure that postpartum care in all states would run for twelve months. CHIP coverage would have been made uniformly continuous for twelve months, despite income fluctuations that might otherwise interrupt it. These changes would have represented the continued federalization and homogenization of the Medicaid program. (The increased subsidies did make it into the Inflation Reduction Act, extended until at least 2025.)[5]

The BBBA was also intended to reduce drug prices—specifically, by waiving the prohibition against the federal government negotiating the prices. These proposals also became part of the Inflation Reduction Act. The government did get the authority to negotiate prices for ten drugs in Medicare Part D in 2025, fifteen in 2026 and 2027, and then up to twenty. But this applied just to Medicare, only for drugs that lack generic or biosimilar competitors, and small molecule drugs that had been on the market for at least nine years (thirteen years for biologics).

This effort to control drug prices might seem small, but it is not. Medicare is now building its own PBM, and once that pharmacy benefit structure is in place, it can be expanded as fiscal reality demands. Perhaps as importantly, there is a rebate back to Medicare for any drug whose price rises faster than the rate of inflation in the consumer price index, or CPI. The Biden administration would have liked this aspect to apply to all payers, but the final law only applies it to Medicare (Medicaid already has a similar rebate provision). It is a big step. Overall, the Congressional Budget Office estimates these drug savings to be more than $230 billion for the federal government over ten years.[6]

The Biden team has taken the expected incremental pathways: tightening the drug side in a manner not dissimilar to what Medicare did with hospitals and doctors thirty years ago; and continuing further use of the ACA's very viable Titles I and II. These could be accelerated and strengthened when the Democrats again have the House, Senate, and presidency in firm control. This course of action is in line with many of the recommendations from health policy experts.

The progress made by the Biden team anticipates how Medicare Advantage–based socialized health insurance would move toward universal access. Medicare Advantage is characterized by a relatively extensive benefits plan, with a premium payment that is income weighted (for Part B). It has protections for out-of-pocket payments both in medical insurance and, now, drugs (Part D). It utilizes traditional Medicare payments for providers, while providing a foundation for health care management as a capitated payment.

For Medicaid and the exchanges to match this, they would have to move to a standardized essential benefits plan. This is exactly the evolutionary direction of the Medicaid program: moving to what is called an *alternative benefits plan*, or ABP. The benefits plan in the exchanges is very similar.[7] Much of the fight with Republicans and Republican-leaning federal district court judges has been to keep that benefits package broad, prohibiting so-called skinny plans. Having a single benefits plan, and governmental control over the structure of health insurance, brings uniformity to the system, which allows a rather dramatic simplification of the revenue cycle, thereby lowering administrative costs.

The other prospect (discussed in chapter 7) is to continue to increase the income threshold at which Medicaid becomes available, while also increasing the subsidies for those in the exchanges. The big step here is to provide coverage for those people in the nine states that currently have not expanded Medicaid who otherwise would qualify for Medicaid in the other forty-one states.[8] This will take a substantial Democratic congressional majority and a Democratic president, but that is within the realm of possibilities. The pathway is very clear.

Closing the gaps between Medicare Advantage, on the one hand, and Medicaid and the exchanges, on the other, is the key link between socialized health insurance based on Medicare Advantage and universal access. Some other steps aimed at uniformity are also important. The patient protections in Medicare are more extensive than those in Medicaid and the exchanges, so they would have to be extended. Bringing a single federal process to bear for payment and the oversight of utilization management would greatly simplify this administrative burden, cutting costs along the lines suggested by McKinsey & Company.[9] For the foreseeable future, there might be state-to-state variation in the criteria used by Medicaid as opposed to Medicare—such as different criteria for accessing treatment for hepatitis C—which would not be completely socialized health insurance. Over time, however, one would expect these to homogenize. That is the nature of health reform as we have seen it in the United States: it takes more time to get to the eventual goal.

Incremental change can mean two steps forward and one step back. There are still individuals, especially adults in nonexpansion states, who should have Medicaid coverage. Moreover, as the COVID emergency ended, so, too, did the continuous-coverage provisions of the Families First Coronavirus Act, which allowed many families to stay on Medicaid without experiencing changes.[10] This might remove as many as 20 million people from Medicaid, some of whom will not make it back to either the Medicaid umbrella or to coverage under the ACA's exchanges. This, in turn, will drive the uninsured rate up from the historical low of 8 percent in 2022. Such developments do not make the path to socialized health insurance seem inevitable.

That is why the straight path to socialized health insurance through a single-payer format is becoming more prominent, even if that was not part of what health policy experts were recommending to the Biden administration.

The Single-Payer Mindset

Historically, advocates for a single-payer format, known widely and simply as "Medicare for All" (I will refer to it as *traditional Medicare for All*), did not use arguments based on practicality, political viability, or even fiscal probity. Their leading contention was that, first and foremost, health care is a right, and everyone should have access to it. A just health care system can come to no other conclusion, and neither can any interpretation of the various health care professions' moral commitment to their patients. Medical ethics—both at the level of providers and patients, as well as the health care industry's stance toward patients in general—dictates that all people should have access, regardless of their ability to pay.[11] As such, a single-payer format has a moral commitment to universal access: all of the insured and all of the uninsured. Medicare for All celebrates egalitarianism in a way that a market-based program, no matter how regulated, does not.

As I have made clear, this book, in part, is about what happens as employer-sponsored insurance fails and what replaces it. For single-payer advocates, the evolution of health insurance, and the rise of federal payers, is in many ways irrelevant. The goal of a single-payer system is coverage for all and, as a matter of justice, equal treatment for all beneficiaries/citizens/patients. Thus the historical evolution of the US health insurance system, and the political/economic reality represented in that evolution, demur to the moral imperative–based view of a single-payer system.

Previously, this view was admirably pure, but also quite unrealistic. That is no longer the case. Political attitudes have changed sufficiently for a single-payer format, and its moral backing, to now be part of health policy discussions. To that point, serious politicians are proposing the sweeping changes necessary to create a single-payer system. In addition, more policy analysts and economists have awakened to its merits.

The intellectual basis for this emerging populism in health care can be found, at least in part, in the recent surge of economic research into income distribution in Western economies. The thesis is that the last forty years of American history are best understood as seeing the general impoverishment of the working class and a concentration of wealth in the hands of the very rich. This analysis, which is certainly nothing new to Marxists, has gained momentum and urgency from empirical work by Thomas Piketty and other economists, who take as their turning point 1980, with the ascendance of the Reagan administration. I touched on this literature in chapter 4 and will just lightly review it here in terms of Medicare for All politics.

Piketty finds very similar trends in the United Kingdom and France: a tremendous leveling of income in the period after World War II up to the late 1970s, and then a rapid reconcentration of wealth over the next forty years.[12] He traces changes in tax structures and legal oversight of the economy to reveal why and how wealth has become so concentrated, and why so much social comity has been lost. Some health policy experts use this irrefutable reality of wealth concentration as the lens for understanding health care over the last fifty years.

The impoverishment of the middle class fuels, or should fuel, a general populism aimed at reining in income inequity produced by unregulated market activity. That is the Bernie Sanders / Elizabeth Warren message in the left wing of the Democratic Party, specifically giving rise to the "tax the rich argument" made by Emmanuel Saez and others (see chapter 4). In health care, this gives rise to efforts to reduce inequality by making sure everyone has good health insurance, as well as to animosity toward the most prominent for-profit players: the private insurance companies and pharmacy benefit managers.

A single-payer strategy is admirably honest. In a nation like ours, it is reasonable to assume that only the government can address inequality in access. Following Branko Milanovic's view in *Capitalism Alone*, Western liberalism means market dominance—with some occasional, spasmodic restraints on profit seeking by the federal government, aimed at curbing inequality or addressing financial hurdles that citizens face.[13] A single-payer system is based on this view of governmental intervention—specifically, that much of the market must be banished from health care to eliminate the inequity that reigns today. So the concept of a single payer and universal access are conceptually married.

While commitment to health care for all gives a single-payer program its moral superiority, over the last twenty years that has been twinned with an efficiency argument. Put simply, a single-payer system has much lower administrative costs. With these lower costs, more money would be available to broaden access to and thicken the benefits of health care insurance, thus delivering universal access.

A single-payer health care plan is also practical. Other countries that are like ours, such as Canada, operate in this fashion. People there speak the same language we do; share a similar, although somewhat colder climate; and, most importantly, have a capitalist democracy paralleling ours. A single-payer system works there, so it could—and should—work here. It isn't just some liberal ideal. It is obtainable, and penny pinchers will have to agree that it is more efficient. I will now examine this latter part of the argument in more detail.

Financial Analysis of the Single-Payer Proposal

For those with a more fiscally conservative bent, the efficiency-based argument for Medicare for All (as a single payer) is compelling. It has been made repeatedly over the last thirty years, such as by David Himmelstein and Stephanie Woolhandler, who have also been tireless advocates for a single-payer plan as the founders of Physicians for a National Health Program. Their most recent rendition of the United States / Canada comparison appeared in 2020 in the *Annals of Internal Medicine*.[14]

The Canadian health care program is rather straightforward in terms of financing. The provincial governments pay for health care, using global budgets for hospitals. They also make fee-for-service payments to doctors, but the provincial penetration for doctors' charges varies from 45 to 80 percent.[15] So at least some portion of the reimbursements to physicians is in private hands in each province. That contrasts with how charges for drugs are handled, as there is a nationally negotiated deal with pharmaceutical manufacturers.

As a result of these arrangements, there is no cross-subsidization between private and public insurers for hospital services. There is relatively little submission of individual bills (doctors being the chief exception). Nor is there much utilization management, or concerns about coding. Services are broadly covered, and there is no cost sharing by recipients. In addition, there is almost no analysis of the actuarial risks of discrete groups (such as employer groups), or any insurer's sales functions. So there are very few costs associated with insurance company administration. Providers readily get their bills paid, so there is little cost to them.

Private insurance does exist in Canada, and nearly two-thirds of Canadians have this type of insurance. It is generally reserved for excluded services, such as vision and dental care, rehabilitation, and private hospital rooms (as well as private doctors).[16] In the aggregate, the role of private insurance is not small, probably forming over 30 percent of overall expenditures.[17] This is notable. Single-payer programs in the United States generally do not envision out-of-pocket payments being sufficiently large enough to require anything near this degree of private insurer participation. As a result, Medicare for All would generally go beyond Canada in eliminating for-profit insurers.

Given the structure of Canada's health care system, one would expect its administrative costs to be lower—and they are. In calculating administrative costs as a part of overall expenditures in the United States versus Canada, insurance overhead is pegged at 7.9 percent in the United States versus 2.8 percent in Canada; hospital administration costs at 26.6 percent versus 13.1 percent; and physicians' administrative costs at 21.8 percent versus 10.8 percent.[18]

The dollars add up quickly. US administrative costs are estimated at $812 billion, and $628 billion of that could be saved if we had a single-payer program. (The amounts estimated by advocates such as Himmelstein and Woolhandler are not dissimilar to those calculated by McKinsey & Company,[19] which was discussed in chapter 9.) This is an impressive sum. All those administrative costs would go a long way toward getting the perhaps 15 million citizens and legal residents of the United States who are now uninsured into appropriate health care coverage.

Doing these kinds of calculations is not easy, so there is some sponginess in the numbers. A lot of data sources must be amalgamated, and, given the above authors' political views, one must assume that these estimates most likely are near the maximum end of the range, in terms of dollars saved. Physician data, in particular, rely on surveys which, in the United States, are generally crippled by a socially acceptable response bias—US doctors hate insurers' oversight and thus are willing to exaggerate the costs they experience. But directionally, their analysis makes real sense. We can take as a given that a single-payer program has lower administrative costs than our current approach, and probably less than a Medicare Advantage for All program, although there would be arguments about the breadth of differences.[20]

There is one caveat. Most single-payer proposals simply change the flow of funds siphoned from private insurers and employers to the government—in particular, to traditional Medicare. These proposals often presume that fee-for-service charges remain in place. While ridding the system of for-profit corporations (like insurers), the device manufacturers and pharmaceutical companies would still remain. More importantly, so would the fee-for-service-based, essentially for-profit doctors and hospitals (which, although often incorporated as nonprofits, usually act like profit seekers). A single-payer format might be able to control per-unit pricing and administrative costs, but if a fee-for-service backbone remains, the system could gear up to do more of everything (utilization management being presumably eliminated), and costs might rise.

Single-payer advocates have foreseen this potential criticism.[21] Researchers have examined historical precedents, finding only a small increase in utilization of health care services in other countries that have moved to universal coverage. Moreover, by citing the number of unoccupied beds in hospitals, researchers take comfort in the evidence that there is not much excess demand. Advocates believe ambulatory visits might rise 7–10 percent, which is far lower than the predictions of 20–30 percent by skeptics.[22]

Until recently, very little work has been done to assess the various moving parts of the single-payer format—lower reimbursement amounts, reduced administrative costs, and little if any insurer oversight—that are constructed on an essentially fee-for-service environment. In 2020, Christopher Cai and fellow researchers summarized studies of the economic impact of single-payer proposals, finding twenty-two papers over the last thirty years that fit their rather stringent criteria for breadth and objectivity.[23] Unexpectedly (especially for someone like me, with a background in private insurance), twenty of the twenty-two papers suggested overall savings with a single-payer format—provider-induced demand did not outstrip the administrative savings. But in the appendix, which identified all twenty-two studies, only one was in a peer-reviewed article, published over thirty years ago, with a group of authors headed by Himmelstein and Woolhandler. So a skeptic still could have had grounds for questions.

That skepticism is harder to maintain today, however, in light of the objective Congressional Budget Office's publication of twin reports on a single-payer system in 2020 and 2022.[24] The first analyzes the costs of the program, using five permutations that involve differences in reimbursement rates (all notably above current Medicare rates, but nowhere near commercial ones) and beneficiaries' out-of-pocket costs. The proposals would increase federal spending on health care by $1.5 trillion, rising to $3 trillion in 2030 (presuming a five-year introduction of the program, beginning in 2025). But overall national health care expenditures would range from $300 billion more to $700 billion less, with most models showing an overall decrease. As expected, this decrease comes from administrative cost savings and lower payment rates.

The CBO admits to a high degree of uncertainty in its estimates, primarily in how providers and patients would react to the changes. In broad terms, alterations in payment rates to the lower-cost version that was modeled by the CBO (which still are not as low as those in Medicare) would net around $500 billion per year, and administrative cost savings are estimated at $400 billion. Utilization cost increases range from $200 billion to $400 billion. The assumption is that all residents, except for 2 million of the 10 million undocumented noncitizens, would be covered.

The utilization assumptions are worth noting. The CBO anticipates that the supply of health care would be increased by demands for it, because (1) patients would have more coverage and lower out-of-pocket costs, (2) providers would have more time freed up from administrative chores, and (3) some providers would opt out and charge higher prices. But demand would outstrip supply, putting a partial lid on utilization. Moreover, the CBO presumes that at lower rates of payment, providers would generally supply less. Under every scenario, there would be congestion in the health care system, due to the excess demand.

This assumption about provider behavior is critical. Reviewing studies on the elasticity of supply as a result of changes in payment rates, the CBO estimates that elasticity is positive—that is, as payment rates go down, there is less supply. Faced with a loss of higher payments by commercial insurers, hospitals—and especially doctors—would do less, rather than try to do more, and they would also increase the intensity of their coding. Critics of fee-for-service incentives would certainly expect a burst in provider-induced demand and upcoding. Nonetheless, the CBO's review is even handed and evidence based.

In many ways, the CBO's analysis clearly makes the case for efficiency in a single-payer format, in that overall health expenditures would decrease. Adding this to the moral imperative of universal coverage, the advantages of Medicare for All—a single-payer plan using fee-for-service traditional Medicare—are considerable. The only remaining problem is how to get there. Our health care system evolves incrementally, but a single-payer system typically involves rather rapid change. Is that possible?

The Single-Payer Revolution

So the next question about a single-payer format involves politics, not economics. How we get from where we are today to a more efficient (and equitable) state in the future? For some employees and employers, Medicare Advantage can be neatly characterized as a stepwise development in the federal government's expanding financial role, which is in line with the incremental evolution of health care insurance in the United States. A single-payer system would be different—and quite a substantial leap. That leap, however, might not seem as great as it did fifteen years ago, before Obamacare. We have evolved, as a country, to accept a larger governmental role, and we have also reached more of a consensus about our expectations for health care coverage. For example, the preexisting condition clause is now gone. Nonetheless, a move to Medicare for All is hardly incremental.

Recently there were two bills in Congress that set forth a single-payer program: HR 1384, sponsored by Representative Pramila Jayapal, and S2119, sponsored by Senator Bernie Sanders. In addition, Senator Elizabeth Warren outlined a related plan as part of her campaign for president. These plans differ in some details. For example, the House bill has a two-year transition period, and the Senate bill has a four-year transition from where we are now to a full single-payer program. Still, that is rapid action, given how we have seen our health care financing system evolve to the present day.[25] The CBO has noted that the five-year development phase it modeled, from 2025 to 2030, would be very difficult to achieve. So perhaps the Senate bill, with its longer transition period, seems more realistic. Otherwise, though, the House and Senate versions are quite similar.

Senator Warren's approach was somewhat different, and the dissimilarities are illustrative. Warren's proposal during the 2020 elections would have entailed an employer Medicare contribution tax, equivalent to 98 percent of what they currently pay, on average, for health care premiums. The remainder—the costs of coverage for the uninsured and coverage to replace workers' premium contributions, as well as their out-of-pocket spending—would have been financed by general corporate taxes and taxes on the wealthy. She did not touch the tax break on health care benefits.

Senator Sanders, on the other hand, would put in place a new 7.5 percent payroll tax, as well as a 4 percent individual income tax (the House bill is very similar). Sanders was apparently spending more time with economists—he endorsed progressive taxation. That is, he believed that any difference between current corporate health care spending and the new payroll tax would flow to workers, in the form of higher wages. These higher wages would enable workers to pay the new income tax. (This demonstrates a good deal of faith in efficient markets, for a socialist.) Sanders did put a floor on the income tax increase—only people earning more than $29,000 would pay it, and he topped up the health care revenues with estate and wealth taxes. Since the government would be footing the full bill, the foregone tax on health benefits would end—the replacement wages would be taxed, another source of revenue for the federal government.

The contrast between the proposals by Sanders and Warren shows that there are a number of routes in putting together the federal dollars needed to fund a single-payer health care system. But the policy cores of these programs are identical. Both create something resembling the Canadian single-payer program (although it would be operated federally in the United States, not by provinces/states), and they take advantage of savings from lower overall administrative costs. They also utilize the same basic financial tool discussed in the analysis of a transition to Medicare Advantage for All: reliance on Medicare pricing (as well as lower administrative costs).

Nor are Representative Jayapal and Senators Sanders and Warren afraid of new taxes. They see it as a matter of justice to address the inequity in our current tax structure, where low-wage workers pay overall taxes proportionately similar to that of the very rich, as a percentage of their wages/wealth. Warren's plan was designed to keep a promise of no new middle-class taxes. Sanders is willing to tax the middle class, trusting that additional wages would flow to workers from companies who no longer had to directly pay for their employees' health insurance.

The numbers can work, at least insofar as financing a single-payer program is concerned. Traditional Medicare for All proposals entail new taxes to cover the rest of the uninsured. On the other hand, a Medicare Advantage–based rescue plan for employer-sponsored insurance does not provide new coverage, so no new taxes are needed. An expansion of coverage would rely on further steps along the paths already outlined—extensions of the exchange programs and Medicaid.

The practical problem with the Medicare for All proposals is not the numbers, but politics and history. Medicare for All represents a tremendous amount of change for a system that has evolved only incrementally in the past. The congressional single-payer bills envision a transition period of two to four years, but that transition probably would mostly involve planning, although perhaps some intermediate changes could be marbled in, starting with the exchanges and Medicaid. In each of these proposed programs, private insurers would be eliminated, and the government (that is, the existing Medicare intermediaries) would start administering health care payments. Taxes would be increased to accomplish this. Commercial insurers would eventually close up shop, everyone would be issued Medicare cards by the CMS, and we would have a single-payer system.

Proponents of a single-payer Medicare plan are not wedded to fee-for-service reimbursements, even though most analyses, including by the CBO, presume that payment architecture will continue to exist. Abdul El-Sayed and Micah Johnson outline the two main alternative formats in *Medicare for All: A Citizen's Guide*.[26] The first is fee-for-service plans, with ongoing experiments in value-based health care services and encouragement of accountable care organizations. The other option is global budgets (at least for hospitals), similar to the Canadian system. A related approach to global budgets would be even broader—paying providers (presumably hospitals and doctors) to accept such a budget for all services. Think of the latter as an overall imposition of capitated payment.

El-Sayed and Johnson acknowledge that providers would take a haircut on payment rates, but they would have to spend much less on administrative tasks and could provide more medical care. Doctors would also be relieved of insurance companies' oversight. This theme of physicians' greater enjoyment of their medical practices without the interference of insurers is found throughout much of the literature on a single-payer program. It is certainly true that the administrative time spent in dealing with insurance companies' oversight is associated with burnout among clinicians.

Both administrative proposals—the retention of fee-for-service rates or the use of global budgets—have some practical problems. On the fee-for-service front, one would have to leave an entire revenue cycle in place, in order for providers to bill for individual services. If providers are at all profit motivated—and I presume they are and will be—they will continue to get advice on how to optimally code. Thus the government will have to be prepared to audit charges and use its own software to ensure that the coding is proper. Keeping the revenue cycle and its potential for encouraging the use of aggressive coding will mean more administrative costs, chewing into the efficiency of a single-payer program, although it appears that the CBO took this into account.

Concerns about overcoding link with concern about the CBO's assumptions regarding supply elasticity. With a fee-for-service plan, one can maximize income by doing more and coding more. A single-payer program entails no utilization management, so, presumably, the utilization of services that may have little value could proliferate. Putting utilization management back into place (traditional Medicare does some utilization management in its local and national coverage decisions) could help stem this possibility, but once again, that means higher administrative costs.

Global budgets, however, would handle this kind of inflation in services. For example, under a global budget, a hospital would receive a set amount of money, whether a surgeon does one or five spinal fusions. But global budgets at this scale—and instituted at this speed—will be daunting. We have little real experience with large integrated hospital systems doing business on a global budget. The only thing close is Maryland's all-payer hospital program, but that is built on nearly fifty years of hospital rate setting in the state.[27] Most commentators on the Maryland experiment have cited the importance of the slow evolution, and local control and knowledge, that are associated with the budgets that most Maryland hospitals operate under at the present time. In addition, the Maryland program only involves hospitals. It allows unrestrained fee-for-service charges in physicians' practices and ambulatory settings. It is not difficult to envision how fee-for-service physicians would increasingly turn to an outpatient setting to perform procedures if only hospitals were saddled with a global budget.

An all-provider global model would be even more challenging. Under it, all physicians and hospitals would have to be assigned to integrated groups and then split a global budget. This means one thing for Johns Hopkins University's hospitals and its medical faculty, while it would be a wholly different situation for Tampa General Hospital and the private practice doctors who admit patients there. Most metropolitan areas do not have a sufficient degree of vertical integration to cope with comprehensive global budgets. Where this architecture does exist (some cities do come to mind), it has been the result of a slow evolution. In addition, it would be incumbent on the CMS to develop a large bureaucracy to track data and allocate payments, changing these global budgets on at least an annual basis. The current staff at the CMS is relatively small, with (for-profit) intermediaries doing most of the payment work.

Moreover, global budgets would be imposed on new organizations that have only a modest experience with them. A two- to four-year transition period seems like a short time in which to develop this kind of expertise. The pace of development for Medicare for All decisively contrasts with a Medicare Advantage for All program that would build incrementally from its existing base and thus would have developed a facility with global payments and attributions of risk. Working under a global budget should be our goal in health care, but it should evolve incrementally, growing from experiments with smaller, globally capitated primary care groups.

El-Sayed and Johnson acknowledge that the federal government might not be too good at this, citing the botched rollout of the Healthcare.gov website in the lead-up to the Affordable Care Act's exchanges.[28] They take heart from what happened in 1966, when the federal government rolled out the new Medicare program in eleven months. What they neglect to acknowledge, however, is that this program relied on existing payers and was resolutely based in a fee-for-service system, since everyone wanted as little change as possible, except for a new payer. They also fail to recognize that initiating an enrollment website is rather simple, compared with imposing a universal global budget.

El-Sayed and Johnson point to the Kaiser Permanente organization, which has a global budget and works through a big organization with numerous hospitals and doctors. What they omit from their discussion is that the Kaiser program is based on nearly eighty years of evolution and has an insurer arm that spends a good deal on administrative costs, with actuaries identifying risks and accountants divvying up the capitation. Moreover, Kaiser can afford it—since they have a closed system, they do not substantially participate in cross-subsidizations of Medicaid and uninsured patients. Finally, it would be difficult to spread the Kaiser Permanente program throughout the country in two to four years. Even Kaiser Permanente has not spread nationally, even though it has tried to over the last thirty years.

The ground is more familiar for the other major health care expenditure: pharmaceuticals. Single-payer advocates propose using Medicare to conduct these negotiations, perhaps based on reference drug pricing from other countries. This is sensible and will probably evolve to be part of any alternative to employer-sponsored insurance. The difference is that in a single-payer program, this happens immediately. Again, the contrast with our history of health care reform in the United States is stark. The Inflation Reduction Act relies on incremental and limited first steps in Medicare's negotiations with pharmaceutical firms. The Biden proposals also contemplate negotiating just for a subset of expensive drugs, and only after these medications have had a long, nonnegotiated price run-up. In 2017, employer-sponsored health insurance paid for 42 percent of prescription drug costs; Medicare, 30 percent; Medicaid, 10 percent; and other payers, 4 percent. People paying out of pocket contributed 14 percent.[29] The federal load is considerable, but less than one-half of the total. A single-payer system would have to take on the entire budget.

The other big political hurdle for traditional Medicare for All is paying for it. The tax bill will be enormous. In chapter 9, I outlined a way for Medicare Advantage for All to infiltrate the commercial insurance sector through a voluntary program that allows corporations to pay their way into the program. Once this begins to occur—and it can be metered out through the mechanism of age tranches—it should gather steam as the remaining employers using commercial health insurance programs face ever-higher demands from providers. But a single-payer, traditional Medicare for All system does not have the same path, so it must depend on big tax increases.

Returning to the CBO's assessment, based on the year 2030, they estimated that federal subsidies, with no change in the laws, would be $2.82 trillion. Single-payer scenarios increase that amount to between $4.33 trillion and $5.82 trillion.[30] This range of estimates is similar to those developed by John Holahan and Linda Blumberg.[31] They evaluated Senator Sanders's proposed single-payer program in 2018. Their review suggested the need for $32.6 trillion over ten years, which was remarkably similar to the analysis done by the Mercatus Center at George Mason University, which estimated about $32 trillion.[32] The Sanders plan was considerably more generous than that outlined by the CBO.

Advocates for a single-payer format outline a number of taxation paths to pay for the program. While it is clear that, at least from a historical perspective, Americans (especially the wealthy) are undertaxed, the new revenues necessary to foot a single-payer system's bill are impressive. The Committee for a Responsible Federal Budget, which is an assertively bipartisan organization, notes that to fund a single-payer program, we would need either a 32 percent payroll tax, a 25 percent income surtax, a 42 percent value-added tax, a more than doubling of current income taxes and corporate taxes, or an increase in the national debt of 108 percent of GDP.[33] This would require quite a Democratic majority in the House and Senate, with a committed president.

The outcome, however, would be spectacular. Universal coverage itself is a goal we should all be supporting. In addition, the CBO predicts greater longevity and labor productivity in our country's population, leading to an increase in the GDP of up to 1.5 percent. Who does not support that? Yet the price tag for a single-payer system is high, and occurs suddenly.

Possibilities for an Incremental Development of the Single-Payer System

The problem with single-payer traditional Medicare for All is pace. Our health care system evolves slowly. We are reaching a tipping point with regard to the dynamics of employer-sponsored insurance, but it is still hard to imagine the rapid legislative effort necessary to institute a single-payer plan. To some extent, single-payer advocates have identified this problem and searched for an incremental approach.

For example, a few advocates on the Democratic Party's left have allowed for the preservation of Medicare Advantage, leading to some mixed models. Jonathan Oberlander has helpfully described Medicare for All's pure and hybrid varieties.[34] "Pure" refers to the version by Senators Warren and Sanders, with a true single payer. A sole insurer, Medicare, would replace all private health care insurance. "Hybrid" follows the proposal by then senator from California and presidential candidate, now vice president, Kamala Harris, who would preserve Medicare Advantage and allow competition with traditional Medicare.

Oberlander also outlines a third leg, a public option, referring to yet another candidate in the 2020 Democratic presidential race, former mayor of South Bend, Indiana, now Transportation Secretary Pete Buttigieg. Buttigieg would have allowed people to either keep their current coverage or join a Medicare-like public option. This idea eventually became an element of the Biden campaign's platform. To the extent these nuances are comprehensible to the voting public, in 2020, a public option was favored by 67 percent of voters, whereas 57 percent supported Medicare for All.[35]

The *public option* is not a new concept. Suhas Gondi and Zirui Song have provided a straightforward definition of the term's two elements.[36] "Public" refers to public financing (akin to Medicare), with the government taxing recipients progressively and determining the benefits and premiums. "Option" means consumers could either choose this plan or some private insurance plan that they would purchase or receive through their employer. The idea is that the government would get into the health care insurance game as a competitor with private insurance companies, rather than just being the monopolist for those over the age of 65. The public option format is most often associated with traditional Medicare.

Karen Davis outlined the concept in the 1990s.[37] Helen Halpin and Peter Harbage developed the concept of a public option on a health care exchange chassis, treating the public plan like one of the competitors in an Enthoven-inspired managed competition scheme.[38] That proposal was meant to inform Californian efforts to reform health care under Governor Gray Davis.

But the most widely acknowledged advocate of the concept today is Jacob Hacker, who outlined "an affordable government insurance plan built on Medicare's infrastructure" in 2001.[39] Both Hacker and Halpin recount the development of a public option over the course of the first decade of the twenty-first century, its strengths being scalability and options about who and what is covered. Many Democrats sought to have it incorporated into the Obamacare legislation. It failed at the last moment—foiled by Senator Joe Lieberman and the impending arrival of Senator Scott Brown (see chapter 7).

A public option, and its advocates, did not go away. Many liberal democrats continued to rue its absence from the Affordable Care Act, thinking it could be the critical bridge toward a single-payer system. They believed that Medicare would be preferable to private insurance, even for employers—if only they could make it available. So a public option was not gone, or forgotten, even after the ACA was passed without it.

A public option did fit neatly into the health exchanges. For people, or even small businesses, moving over to an exchange from the individual market and signing up for traditional Medicare would have been a straightforward and attractive option. Funding could have flowed through the federal government in much the same way as it did for the other products on the exchange. So traditional Medicare for All could have infiltrated the individual market.

In late 2020, the Biden health policy team further developed a public option concept and then stretched its boundaries as part of the Unity Task Force discussions with the Bernie Sanders team after Biden garnered the Democratic presidential nomination. As Hacker outlines, the Biden team's public option would have had no deductibles and would have covered primary care without cost sharing; been operated directly by the federal government (no Medicare Advantage); and paid Medicare-negotiated prices, including federally bargained drug prices.[40] Anyone could have signed up for it, including workers with employer-sponsored insurance—companies could even have signed their workers up and paid premiums on their behalf to the federal government.

But the key point was "option." No one was forced to join, and the program could be scaled over time, creating something that could be politically palatable. Presumably, employees would retain their existing tax treatment regarding payments for health benefits: tax free for a worker, rather than being taxed as income. A public option scheme thus offered a segue to Medicare for All. In some ways, it was an alternative path to socialized health insurance.

Two important themes about a public option format emerge here that play directly into the notion of catalyzing change over the next two decades. The first is the relationship of a public option to employers and employees. While it was often seen as a gap filler for those who needed help getting insurance on the individual market, advocates of a public option now see employees as being eligible to participate in it. The advantage of including employees is that a larger program, especially one with more middle-class workers, becomes a much more permanent policy change. More importantly, a public option addresses the need that employers will have for a less costly alternative to commercial health insurance. To make this work as an employer option, the government would have to design a process for assessing the costs of employees' health care and then charging their employers for that. There would be some administrative costs, but the government appears to have this actuarial expertise. (Note that in Medicare Advantage for All, this capability already exists.)

The second crucial element is that a public option complements the existing structure of the ACA. In chapter 7, I outlined how Titles I and II of the ACA can be expanded to fill gaps in coverage for low-income people. To a large extent, universal coverage (except for undocumented noncitizens) and universal access (even for those hearty individuals who do not want health care insurance) is possible with the current ACA levers. A public option is not necessarily needed for coverage purposes, as the closing jaws of Titles I and II can effectuate that. Instead, it is about replacing employer-sponsored insurance.

At this point, I should note the general animosity traditional Medicare for All proponents have toward Medicare Advantage. As Hacker states, "The public plan would be government insurance, not private plans regulated by government (currently known as Medicare Advantage plans)."[41] The "currently known" part of this sentence somehow makes the Medicare Advantage program appear ephemeral. That is how many progressives see the program. They crave the administrative efficiency of a single-payer format, with all health care dollars going to patients, not to "greedy" insurers. Nor do Medicare Advantage advocates see single-payer proponents as fellow travelers—for now, they are content to stick with the over-age-65 tranche. The proponents of each of what I call "alternative pathways" treat themselves as mutually exclusive.

It will not be easy for public option advocates to rid the health care economy of private insurers. Washington State's experience with a public option underlines this point. In June 2020, Michael Sparer carefully outlined the politics surrounding Governor Jay Inslee's effort to establish a public option as a support (in part) for his presidential run.[42] What Inslee got as a result of negotiations with the state's legislature was a public option that consisted of private health plans on a state exchange, which capped providers' rates at 100 percent of Medicare. But it was not the publicly administered plan that Inslee apparently intended.

Washington State now has five Cascade Select plans, providing a standardized benefit with lower deductibles.[43] These plans cap provider reimbursements at 160 percent (not 100 percent) of Medicare. They pay no less than 101 percent of the allowed costs for care, and 135 percent of Medicare rates for primary care. The two Blues plans in Washington State have refused to participate, but commercial insurers (including United Healthcare) are on board. The lesson here is that where you start with a public option is one thing, but where the political process takes you is another. Meanwhile, Colorado inaugurated a Colorado Option in the 2022–2023 open enrollment period.[44] And several bills in Congress continue to call for a public option.[45]

Public option infiltration does address the incremental problem faced by a single-payer system. But two other strategic administrative issues stand in the way. The first is the conversion from a "Big Bang" introduction of single payer into the infiltration/incremental approach. A single-payer structure keeps providers relatively whole by combining lower rates of governmental payments and relief from administrative inefficiency. But the administrative costs in most renditions of a single-payer format go away immediately. For instance, the staff doing prior authorization work in a doctor's office will no longer be needed. But the replacement of a small number of commercial insurance patients with single-payer ones does not allow that administrative load to be readily lightened, so the new patients are simply paying less. This could complicate the behavior of providers and not conform to the CBO's views about the elasticity of supply. (On this point, I can find few economic analyses on which to rely.)

The other administrative issue is the role of managed care. Advocates of a one-time conversion to a single-payer system have outlined how global budgets and managed care could be incorporated into the new payment program. One of the key benefits of Medicare Advantage for All is that it makes use of both managed care and lower governmental payment rates to reduce costs. A public option Medicare for All program would be (at least in most renditions available today) an assertively fee-for-service one. Some advocates are not worried about this. For example, the American Public Health Association, in its very trenchant advocacy for a single-payer system, notes that fee-for-service is also the norm for other single-payer programs, and the association is not worried about the loss of managed care.[46] Be this as it may, allowing the further development of managed care in a single-payer structure seems only prudent. El-Sayed and Johnson acknowledged this in their book on the future of single-payer health insurance, discussing the use of global budgets.[47]

There do appear to be some ways to integrate managed care and public option incrementalism. In particular, some current programs operated by the federal government could be adapted to allow managed care incentives into a public option approach for employers. The leading example is ACO REACH, the new accountable care program for traditional Medicare (discussed in chapter 8).[48] Like other ACO formats operated by the CMS, it assigns patients either retrospectively or prospectively to a primary care physician's practice and then provides the practice with a budget for that patient. This budget is in the form of a capitated payment, either for primary care services or for global capitation. It enables well-organized primary care practices to manage care, eliminate health care waste, and earn a profit by ensuring that this care is value based. The ACO REACH program also integrates specific quality of care measures and administrative requirements, both aimed to address populations of patients who have previously lacked access to care. ACO REACH essentially converts fee-for-service Medicare into capitation, with all the attendant needs for managed care that this implies.

The ACO REACH program is intended to be used by a variety of organizations, including federally qualified health care centers. But it has also attracted some of the conveners and managers of at-risk primary care groups, such as agilon health and Aledade. Eventually, one could imagine organizations like Optum and Humana participating. There is no need for an insurer function in ACO REACH, since the government addresses the assignment of patients and payment rates.

Managed care is facilitated by a for-profit intermediary, such as agilon health, but at much lower percentages of premiums than insurers expect. With a very low administrative overhead, the fee-for-service format of traditional Medicare is converted into a managed care product.

One could imagine the ACO REACH product annealed to a public option program within the CMS. A public option law would allow employers to opt in. They could then work directly with at-risk primary care providers. An employer would pay the federal government (CMS) for enrolled employees. The CMS would then pass on most of that premium (such as the 97.5 percent already given to ACO REACH) to an organized provider group, which would then manage care, paying specialists and hospitalists at Medicare rates. This would be administratively efficient, incorporate managed care, and take advantage of Medicare reimbursement rates. This possibility does not have the oversight apparatus that is a feature of Medicare Advantage, but that could be added. Today, the CMS appears rather confident of its ability to perform oversight for ACO REACH, and providers appear to be comfortable taking on risk for these Medicare beneficiaries.

The scenario for employers requires an organic relationship between them and the provider groups, which are now developing. A large primary care group—COPIC, in Columbus Ohio—is working with agilon health to develop managed care capabilities. They are also collaborating with JPMorgan Chase to offer managed care for its employees. Together, they would be a natural pairing for a public option that integrates providers with employers.

As more public option utilization occurs, experience would develop and demonstrate the efficiencies associated with limited administration and, most likely, the reasonable management of care. It would take place as an incremental run-up. This evidence would then be an argument for a full conversion to a single-payer system. Some advocates may find this unnecessary, but America's history in the evolution of health care financing is quite incremental. ACO REACH might not be the right pathway, but its development does signal that there will be opportunities to innovate, using a public option format, in a way that can segmentally bring beneficiaries to a Medicare for All program—a program that emphasizes value-based care.

Finding an incremental pathway will not appeal to some proponents for single-payer Medicare for All. They are (admirably) motivated by a commitment to universal access and, in many cases, outraged by the profit impetus in health care. But they need more votes to get this kind of (rather massive) legislation passed. In the meantime, public option approaches might be advisable to expedite this eventual goal.

From the point of view of a practical solution to the rapidly approaching conundrum of employer-sponsored insurance, Medicare Advantage, made available over time to employers, is much less radical than a single-payer program. It also helps facilitate the additional steps we need to take to get to universal access. Our history of health care reform has been assertively incremental, fueled all along by a slowly expanding impulse to ensure that people have reasonable coverage. As a solution to the crippled employer-sponsored sector and the injustice of low-income individuals' lack of access to health care insurance, a steady move to Medicare Advantage, combined with a stepwise expansion of the exchange subsidies and Medicaid availability, can stay in these incremental swim lanes, with a clear pathway to getting the overwhelming majority of the US population into a health insurance program that is adequate and equitable. It is a program of socialized health insurance in which the government designs the insurance policy, oversees its quality of care, makes changes as necessary, and defines the payments for providers.

Medicare for All, as a single-payer program, would move there faster. It would be propelled by the impulse to provide just and equitable coverage for all, and it could be much more efficient. The real question, though, is whether the case is strong enough to motivate enough voters and their legislative representatives. The answer today would be no. The sticker shock is likely to be too great. But I could be reading the political tea leaves too narrowly, as a single-payer case has become stronger over time.

Concluding Thoughts

I have tried to write this book as a careful observer, and only hesitantly as a prognosticator. I have made four crucial observations. First, the federal programs for health care insurance have grown and matured in a continuous fashion, and they now offer real promise for closing the remaining gaps in access to health care. Second, these efforts are supported by changing social values and assumptions. Increasingly, people see health care as a right, not a purchased good. Third, with appropriate governmental oversight, private insurers can have a role to play in the administration of public health care benefits, and they will bring market incentives that promote innovation. Fourth, the growth of federal health care insurance, and the relative lethargy of employers as payers, has brought employer-sponsored insurance to a point where it increasingly becomes unaffordable.

These observations lead to my prognostication. Employers will seek access to governmental programs, once these are made available. Two pathways for this are possible. In the first, the government will open up Medicare Advantage programs to private employers, who will get a bargain by paying premiums to the government, rather than to commercial insurers. This will further drive cost headwinds toward those employers who persist in using private commercial insurance, thus leading more of them to move to governmental programs. As the government comes to oversee more of the nation's health care, it will continue to close the remaining gaps that remain in access and have incentives to develop (1) a uniform administrative structure, (2) a homogenizing revenue cycle, and (3) similar cost control programs in Medicare, Medicaid, and the exchanges. In many ways, this is a continuation of the same evolutionary path that we have been on for sixty years. The result is Medicare Advantage for All.

Medicare Advantage for All still leaves the profit-making private insurers in the game. In today's debates, some find this unacceptable, fearful that these corporations will take inappropriate and undue profits out of health care costs—money that could be used to treat patients. On this point, I am reminded of Senator Sanders's summary about his own plan (quoted by Jonathan Oberlander): "The ongoing failure of our health system is directly attributable to the fact that—unique among major nations—it is primarily designed to . . . maximize profits for health insurance companies, the pharmaceutical industry, and medical equipment suppliers."[49] Sanders just left out the doctors, the nurses, the hospitals, the rest of the provider community, and everyone else involved in the health care business.

But Sanders has a point. The government would have to be capable of assessing situations, like today's trend toward overcoding, and adjust the program appropriately. A historical analysis suggests that the CMS is capable of such assertive oversight. In addition, for-profit insurers would be well advised to recognize the increasingly public role of health insurance and cease placing profit first. History shows how private insurers have had trouble controlling their profit seeking, failing to understand that they have a role as trustees of equitable health care.

The alternative to Medicare Advantage for All, traditional Medicare for All (a single-payer system), is much better recognized. Its power is simplicity: no more multiple payers, and much lower administrative costs. Both paths take advantage of the rates that Medicare pays. But the single-payer format would have an advantage in terms of much less administration. Its drawbacks are related to its simplicity. That simplicity can take root only with sweeping legislation, doing away with the very large corporations that have long been a part of American health care and putting substantial new taxes in place. A second problem is that a single-payer structure does not naturally support managed care—in many renditions it adheres firmly to a fee-for-service concept. But prompting value-based care is critical for health care's future. There are some ways to incrementally move toward a single-payer system. They involve the use of a public option, perhaps starting in the exchange market, and then moving on to employers. This could potentially be annealed with global payments and, hence, managed care.

Perhaps the most likely future, then, is for the government to open up both pathways to Medicare for All: its traditional and Advantage forms. This would be rather straightforward, enabling employers to buy into a governmental program, using either Medicare Advantage's retiree-style plans, or a public option for traditional Medicare. This would allow these two approaches to compete against one another. And it would permit the government and the health policy community to assess costs and quality of care over time. That might give legislators the confidence to move forward with the massive effort to completely replace private insurers with a single payer. Or they may be satisfied with what they see in the oversight of Medicare Advantage for All by the federal government.

What does seem certain is that these paths will be pursued. The foundation for commercial, employer-sponsored health insurance is crumbling under too much cost pressure. This should not be seen as a crisis or a shameful event, but rather as an opportunity. There is every reason to believe that whatever path to Medicare for All we pursue, the result should be broader coverage and better care for patients. Anyone in health care—and any reasonable citizen—must be moved to action by the thought of patients despairing about how to pay for their next treatment. We have seen that President Obama was. Under a completely socialized health insurance program, no matter what its format, our health care system will be transformed with a much better focus on justice and a commitment to the welfare of individual citizens.

NOTES

Preface

1. Munira Z. Gunja, Evan D. Gumas, and Reginald D. Williams II, *U.S. Health Care from a Global Perspective, 2022: Accelerating Spending, Worsening Outcomes* (New York: Commonwealth Fund, January 2023), https://doi.org/10.26099/8ejy-yc74.

2. Eric C. Schneider, Arnav Shah, Michelle M. Doty, Roosa Tikkanen, Katherine Fields, and Reginald D. Williams II, *Mirror, Mirror 2021—Reflecting Poorly: Health Care in the U.S. Compared to Other High-Income Countries* (New York: Commonwealth Fund, August 2021), https://doi.org/10.26099/01dv-h208.

3. Jonathan Cohn, *The Ten Year War: Obamacare and the Unfinished Crusade for Universal Coverage* (New York: St. Martin's, 2021).

4. Ezekiel J. Emanuel, *Reinventing American Health Care* (New York: Public Affairs, 2014).

5. Charles E. Lindblom, "The Science of 'Muddling Through,'" *Public Administration Review* 19, no. 2 (1959): 79–88, https://doi.org/10.2307/973677.

6. Donald M. Berwick, "*Salve Lucrum*: The Existential Threat of Greed in US Healthcare," Viewpoint, *JAMA* 329, no. 8 (2023): 629–630, https://doi.org/10.1001/jama.2023.0846.

7. Troyen A. Brennan, *Just Doctoring: Medical Ethics in the Liberal State* (Berkeley: University of California Press, 1991).

Chapter 1. Why Health Insurance Is Tied to Employment

1. Katherine Keisler-Starkey and Lisa N. Bunch, *Health Insurance Coverage in the United States: 2019* (Washington, DC: U.S. Government Publishing Office, September 2020), https://www.census.gov/content/dam/Census/library/publications/2020/demo/p60-271.pdf.

2. Micah Hartman, Anne B. Martin, Benjamin Washington, Aaron Catlin, and the National Health Expenditures Accounts Team, "National Health Care Spending in 2020: Growth Driven by Federal Spending in Response to the COVID-19 Pandemic," *Health Affairs* 41, no. 1 (2022): 13–25, https://www.healthaffairs.org/doi/pdf/10.1377/hlthaff.2021.01763.

3. KFF [Kaiser Family Foundation], "Vast Majority of Large Employers Surveyed Say Broader Government Role Will Be Necessary to Control Health Costs and Provide Coverage," press release, April 29, 2021, https://www.kff.org/health-reform

/press-release/vast-majority-of-large-employers-surveyed-say-broader-government
-role-will-be-necessary-to-control-health-costs-and-provide-coverage-survey-finds/.

4. There are many excellent works on this history, notably Herman Miles
Somers and Anne Ramsay Somers, *Medicare and the Hospitals: Issues and Prospects*
(Washington, DC: Brookings Institution, 1967), and Paul Starr, *The Social Transfor-
mation of American Medicine* (New York: Basic Books, 1982). Much of it is succinctly
summarized by the Institute of Medicine. All are cited in M. J. Field and H. T.
Shapiro, eds., *Employment and Health Benefits: A Connection at Risk* (Washington, DC:
National Academies Press, 1993), https://www.ncbi.nlm.nih.gov/books/NBK235989.

5. Starr, *Social Transformation*, 86.

6. Pamela Martin and Anne Neville, *The Corporate Practice of Medicine in a
Changing Healthcare Environment* (Sacramento: California Research Bureau,
April 2016), https://sbp.senate.ca.gov/sites/sbp.senate.ca.gov/files/CRB%202016%20
CPM%20Report.pdf.

7. Debra L. Roth and Deborah Reidy Kelch, *Making Sense of Managed Care
Regulation in California* (Oakland: California Healthcare Foundation, November 2001), https://www.chcf.org/wp-content/uploads/2017/12/PDF-MakingSenseMa
nagedCareRegulation.pdf.

8. Martin and Neville, *Corporate Practice of Medicine*.

9. Gerald Posner, *Pharma: Greed, Lies, and the Poisoning of America* (New York:
Simon & Schuster, 2020).

10. Posner, *Pharma*.

11. U.S. Bureau of Labor Statistics, "Employee Tenure in 2020," news release no.
USDL-22-1894, September 22, 2020, https://www.bls.gov/news.release/pdf/tenure
.pdf; David Altig and John Robertson, "Falling Job Tenure: It's Not Just About
Millennials," *Macroblog, Federal Reserve Bank of Atlanta*, June 8, 2015, https://www
.atlantafed.org/blogs/macroblog/2015/06/08/falling-job-tenure-its-not-just-about
-millennials.aspx.

12. Stuart Altman and David Schactman, *Power, Politics, and Universal Health
Care: The Inside Story of a Century-Long Battle* (New York: Prometheus, 2011).

13. Altman and Schactman, *Power*, 86.

14. Most of this discussion follows Mary Ann, Chirba Martin, and Troyen A.
Brennan, "The Critical Role of Erisa in State Health Reform," *Health Affairs* 13, no. 2
(1994), https://doi.org/10.1377/hlthaff.13.2.142.

15. Liran Einav, Amy Finkelstein, and Ray Fisman, *Risky Business: Why Insurance
Markets Fail and What to Do About It* (New Haven, CT: Yale University Press, 2022).

16. Wilk v. American Medical Association, 895 F.2d 352 (7th Cir. 1990).

17. Goldfarb v. Virginia State Bar, 421 U.S. 773 (1975).

18. Arizona v. Maricopa County Medical Society, 457 U.S. 332, 338 (1982).

19. Imani Telesford, Shameek Rakshit, Matthew McGough, Emma Wager, and
Krutika Amin, "How Has U.S. Spending on Healthcare Changed Over Time?,"
Peterson-KFF Health System Tracker, February 7, 2023, https://www.healthsystem
tracker.org/chart-collection/u-s-spending-healthcare-changed-time/.

20. Robin A. Cohen, Diane M. Makuc, Amy B. Bernstein, Linda T. Bilheimer, and Eve Powell-Griner, *Health Insurance Coverage Trends, 1959–2007: Estimates from the National Health Interview Survey*, Report no. 17 (Hyattsville, MD: National Center for Health Statistics, July 2009), https://www.cdc.gov/nchs/data/nhsr/nhsr017.pdf.

Chapter 2. What Do Health Insurers Do?

1. "HEDIS and Performance Measurement," NCQA [National Committee for Quality Assurance], https://www.ncqa.org/hedis/ [accessed September 21, 2023].

2. J. G. Navarro, "Net Promoter Score (NPS) of Businesses in the United States in 2021, by Industry," Statista, January 11, 2023, https://www.statista.com/statistics/1223117/customer-satisfaction-nps-by-industry-us/.

3. Benjamin Sommers, Atul Gawande, and Katherine Baicker, "Health Insurance Coverage and Health—What the Recent Data Tells Us," Sounding Board, *New England Journal of Medicine* 377, no. 6 (2017): 586–593, https://www.nejm.org/doi/full/10.1056/NEJMsb1706645.

4. Steffie Woolhandler and David U. Himmelstein, "The Relationship of Health Insurance and Mortality: Is Lack of Insurance Deadly?," *Annals of Internal Medicine* 167 (2017): 424–431, https://doi.org/10.7326/M17-1403.

5. Saurabh Bhargava, George Loewenstein, and Justin Sydnor, "Choose to Lose: Health Plan Choices from a Menu with Dominated Option," *Quarterly Journal of Economics* 132, no. 3 (2017): 1319–1372, https://doi.org/10.1093/qje/qjx011.

6. Amitabh Chandra, Evan Flack, and Ziad Obermeyer, "The Health Costs of Cost-Sharing," Working Paper no. 28439, National Bureau of Economic Research, Cambridge, MA, February 2021, revised April 2023, http://www.nber.org/papers/w28439.

7. Cristina Boccuti and Marilyn Moon, "Comparing Medicare and Private Insurers: Growth Rates in Spending over Three Decades," *Health Affairs* 22, no. 2 (2003): 230–237, https://doi.org/10.1377/hlthaff.22.2.230.

8. Kathleen Dianne Schaum, "Medicare Payment Systems: A Look Forward and a Look Back," *Advances in Wound Care* 2, no. 10 (2013): 593–597, https://www.ncbi.nlm.nih.gov/pmc/articles/PMC3865626/.

9. William C. Hsiao, Peter Braun, Nancy L. Kelly, and Edmund R. Becker, "Results, Potential Effects, and Implementation Issues of the Resource-Based Relative Value Scale," *JAMA* 260, no. 16 (1988): 2429–2438, https://jamanetwork.com/journals/jama/article-abstract/374679.

10. David C. Chan, Johnny Huynh, and David M. Studdert, "Accuracy of Valuations of Surgical Procedures in the Medicare Fee Schedules," *New England Journal of Medicine* 380, no. 16 (2019): 1546–1554, https://www.nejm.org/doi/full/10.1056/NEJMsa1807379.

11. John W. Urwin, Emily Gudbranson, Danielle Graham, Dawei Xie, Eric Hume, and Ezekiel J. Emanuel, "Accuracy of the Relative Value Scale Update Committee's Time Estimates and Physician Fee Schedule for Joint Replacement," *Health Affairs* 38, no. 7 (2019), https://www.healthaffairs.org/doi/abs/10.1377/hlthaff.2018.05456.

12. Donald M. Berwick and Andrew D. Hackbarth, "Eliminating Waste in US Health Care," *JAMA* 307, no. 14 (2012): 1513–1516, https://jamanetwork.com/journals/jama/article-abstract/1148376.

13. William H. Shrank, Teresa L. Rogstad, and Natasha Parekh, "Waste in the US Health Care System: Estimated Costs and Potential Savings," *JAMA* 322, no. 15 (2019): 1501–1509, https://jamanetwork.com/journals/jama/article-abstract/2752664.

14. Marty Makary, *The Price We Pay: What Broke American Health Care—and How to Fix It* (New York: Bloomsbury, 2019).

15. Allen B. Kachalia, Michelle M. Mello, Troyen A. Brennan, and David M. Studdert, "Beyond Negligence: Avoidability and Medical Injury Compensation," *Social Science & Medicine* 66, no. 7 (2008): 387–402, https://www.sciencedirect.com/science/article/abs/pii/S0277953607004741?via%3Dihub. I now believe that this estimate is near the high range.

16. M. Liu, X. Yuan, J. Ouyang, J. Chaisson, T. Bergeron, D. Cantrell, V. Washington, Y. Zhang, and S. Nigam, "Evaluation of Four Disease Management Programs: Evidence from Blue Cross Blue Shield of Louisiana," *Journal of Medical Economics* 23, no. 6 (2020): 557–565, https://pubmed.ncbi.nlm.nih.gov/31990232.

17. Timothy M. Dall, Rachel C. Askarinam Wagner, Yiduo Zhang, Wenya Yang, David R. Arday, and Cynthia J. Gantt, "Outcomes and Lessons Learned from Evaluating TRICARE's Disease Management Programs," *AJMC* [*American Journal of Managed Care*] 16, no. 6 (2010): 438–446, https://pubmed.ncbi.nlm.nih.gov/20560687.

18. Akinori Hisashige, "The Effectiveness and Efficiency of Disease Management Programs for Patients with Chronic Diseases," *Global Journal of Health Science* 5, no. 2 (2013): 27–48, https://www.ncbi.nlm.nih.gov/pmc/articles/PMC4776791/#ref4.

19. Lyle Nelson, "Lessons from Medicare's Demonstration Projects on Disease Management and Care Coordination," Working Paper no. 2012-01, Congressional Budget Office, Washington, DC, January 2012, https://www.cbo.gov/sites/default/files/112th-congress-2011-2012/workingpaper/WP2012-01_Nelson_Medicare_DMCC_Demonstrations_1.pdf.

20. Soeren Mattke, Hangsheng Liu, John Caloyeras, Christina Y. Huang, Kristin R. Van Busum, Dmitry Khodyakov, and Victoria Shier, "Workplace Wellness Programs Study," *Rand Health Quarterly* 3, no. 2 (2013): 7–15, https://www.ncbi.nlm.nih.gov/pmc/articles/PMC4945172.

21. Zirui Song and Katherine Baicker, "Effect of a Workplace Wellness Program on Employee Health and Economic Outcomes: A Randomized Clinical Trial," *JAMA* 321, no. 15 (2019): 1491–1501, https://jamanetwork.com/journals/jama/fullarticle/2730614.

22. Zirui Song and Katherine Baicker, "Health and Economic Outcomes up to Three Years After a Workplace Wellness Program: A Randomized Controlled Trial," *Health Affairs* 40, no. 6 (2021): 951–961, https://www.healthaffairs.org/doi/pdf/10.1377/hlthaff.2020.01808.

23. Julian Reif, David Chan, and Damon Jones, "Effects of a Workplace Wellness Program on Employee Health, Health Beliefs, and Medical Use: A Randomized Clinical Trial," *JAMA Internal Medicine* 180, no. 7 (2020): 952–960, https://jamanetwork.com/journals/jamainternalmedicine/fullarticle/2765690.

Chapter 3. Health Care in the 1990s

1. Troyen A. Brennan, *Just Doctoring: Medical Ethics in the Liberal State* (Berkeley: University of California Press, 1991), 212.

2. Ryan J. Ross, Vanessa C. Forsberg, Bernadette Fernandez, and Katherine M. Kehres, *Federal Requirements on Private Health Insurance Plans*, Report no. R45146 (Washington, DC: Congressional Research Service, August 2018, updated March 2023), https://fas.org/sgp/crs/misc/R45146.pdf.

3. Peter D. Fox and Peter R. Kongstvedt, "A History of Managed Health Care and Health Insurance in the United States," in *The Essentials of Managed Health Care*, 6th edition, ed. Peter R. Kongstvedt (Burlington, MA: Jones & Bartlett Learning, 2013), 1–36, on p. 11, http://samples.jbpub.com/9781284043259/Chapter1.pdf.

4. The later options were point of service (POS) plans, with in- and out-of-network providers and lower cost sharing if patients stayed in network; and high deductible health plans with a savings option (HDHP/SO). See Gary Claxton, Matthew Rae, Emma Wagner, Gregory Young, Heidi Whitmore, Jason Kearns, Greg Shmavonia, and Anthony Damico, "Section 4: Types of Plans Offered" and "Section 5: Market Shares of Health Plans," *Employer Health Benefits: 2022 Annual Survey* (San Francisco: Kaiser Family Foundation, 2022), 71, 74, https://files.kff.org/attachment /Report-Employer-Health-Benefits-2022-Annual-Survey.pdf.

5. Howard Bauchner and Phil B. Fontanarosa, "Waste in the US Health Care System," Editorial, *JAMA* 322, no. 15 (2019): 1463–1464, https://jamanetwork.com /journals/jama/article-abstract/2752663.

6. Ellen M. Morrison and Harold S. Luft, "Health Maintenance Organization Environments in the 1980s and Beyond," *Health Care Financing Review* 12, no. 1 (1990): 81–90, https://www.cms.gov/Research-Statistics-Data-and-Systems /Research/HealthCareFinancingReview/Downloads/CMS1191139dl.pdf.

7. Kimberly Amadeo, "The Rising Cost of Health Care by Year and Its Causes," The Balance, updated October 21, 2022, https://www.thebalance.com/causes-of -rising-healthcare-costs-4064878.

8. Alain C. Enthoven, *Theory and Practice of Managed Competition in Health Care Finance* (Amsterdam: Elsevier Science, 1988).

9. Alain C. Enthoven, "The History and Principles of Managed Competition," *Health Affairs* 12, Suppl. 1 (1993): 24–40, https://www.healthaffairs.org/doi/full/10 .1377/hlthaff.12.suppl_1.24.

10. Francesca Gino, "The Rise of Behavioral Economics and Its Influence on Organizations," Harvard Business Review, October 10, 2017, https://hbr.org/2017/10 /the-rise-of-behavioral-economics-and-its-influence-on-organizations/.

11. Saurabh Bhargava, George Loewenstein, and Justin Sydnor, "Choose to Lose: Health Plan Choices from a Menu with Dominated Option," *Quarterly Journal of Economics* 132, no. 3 (2017): 1319–1372, https://doi.org/10.1093/qje/qjx011.

12. George Loewenstein, Troyen Brennan, and Kevin G. Volpp, "Asymmetric Paternalism to Improve Health Behaviors," *JAMA* 298, no. 20 (2007): 2415–2417, https://jamanetwork.com/journals/jama/fullarticle/209557.

13. Scott D. Halpern, Benjamin French, Dylan S. Small, Kathryn Saulsgiver, Michael O. Harhay, Janet Audrain-McGovern, George Loewenstein, et al., "Randomized Trial of Four Financial-Incentive Programs for Smoking Cessation," *New England Journal of Medicine* 372, no. 22 (2015): 2108–2117, https://www.nejm.org/doi/full/10.1056/nejmoa1414293.

14. Charles E. Lindblom, "The Science of 'Muddling Through,'" *Public Administration Review* 19, no. 2 (1959): 79–88, https://www.jstor.org/stable/973677.

15. Paul Starr, *Remedy and Reaction: The Peculiar American Struggle over Health Care Reform* (New Haven, CT: Yale University Press, 2013), 86.

16. Stuart Altman and David Schactman, *Power, Politics, and Universal Health Care: The Inside Story of a Century-Long Battle* (New York: Prometheus, 2011).

17. Robert Moffit, "A Guide to the Clinton Health Plan," Heritage Foundation, November 19, 1993, https://www.heritage.org/health-care-reform/report/guide-the-clinton-health-plan/.

18. Bhagwan Satiani and Patrick Vaccaro, "A Critical Appraisal of Physician-Hospital Integration Models," *Journal of Vascular Surgery* 51, no. 4 (2010): 1046–1053, https://www.sciencedirect.com/science/article/pii/S0741521409023088.

19. Lawton Robert Burns and Ralph W. Muller, "Hospital-Physician Collaboration: Landscape of Economic Integration and Impact on Clinical Integration," *Milbank Quarterly* 86, no. 3 (2008): 375–434, https://www.ncbi.nlm.nih.gov/pmc/articles/PMC2690342.

20. Scott Allen and Marcella Bombardieri, "A Healthcare System Badly Out of Balance," *Boston Globe*, November 16, 2008, https://archive.boston.com/news/local/articles/2008/11/16/a_healthcare_system_badly_out_of_balance/.

21. Thomas M. Selden, Zeynal Karaca, Patricia Keenan, Chapin White, and Richard Kronick, "The Growing Difference between Public and Private Payment Rates for Inpatient Hospital Care," *Health Affairs* 34, no. 12 (2015), 2147–2150, https://www.healthaffairs.org/doi/10.1377/hlthaff.2015.0706.

22. Austin B. Frakt, "How Much Do Hospitals Cost Shift? A Review of the Evidence," *Milbank Quarterly* 89, no. 1 (2011): 90–130, https://pubmed.ncbi.nlm.nih.gov/21418314.

23. Eric Lopez, Tricia Neuman, Gretchen Jacobson, and Larry Levitt, "How Much More Than Medicare Do Private Insurers Pay? A Review of the Literature," KFF [Kaiser Family Foundation], April 15, 2020, https://www.kff.org/medicare/issue-brief/how-much-more-than-medicare-do-private-insurers-pay-a-review-of-the-literature/.

24. "Healthy Marketplace Index," Health Care Cost Institute, September 2019, https://healthcostinstitute.org/hcci-originals/healthy-marketplace-index/hmi.

25. Claxton et al., "Section 5," *2022 Annual Survey*, 74.

26. Samuel H. Zuvekas and Joel W. Cohen, "Fee-for-Service, While Much Maligned, Remains the Dominant Payment Method for Physician Visits," *Health Affairs* 35, no. 3 (2015): 24–34, https://www.healthaffairs.org/doi/full/10.1377/hlthaff.2015.1291.

27. Laura Tollen, "As Commercial Capitation Sinks, Can California's Physician Organizations Stay Afloat?," California Health Care Foundation, November 7, 2016,

https://www.chcf.org/publication/as-commercial-capitation-sinks-can-californias
-physician-organizations-stay-afloat/.

28.   David Dranove and Lawton R. Burn, *Big Med: Megaproviders and the High Cost of Health Care in America* (Chicago: University of Chicago Press, 2021).

Chapter 4. Twenty-First-Century Numbers

1.   Richard Jackson, "America's Demographic Future," Concord Coalition, May 21, 2020, https://www.concordcoalition.org/special-publication/americas-demographic -future/.

2.   Jonathan Vespa, "The U.S. Joins Other Countries with Large Aging Populations," *The Graying of America: More Older Adults Than Kids by 2035*, U.S. Census Bureau, March 13, 2018, revised September 16, 2018, and October 8, 2019, https:// www.census.gov/library/stories/2018/03/graying-america.html.

3.   MedPAC [Medicare Payment Advisory Committee], *Report to the Congress; Medicare Payment Policy* (Washington, DC: MedPAC, March 2023), 16, figure 1-6, https://www.medpac.gov/wp-content/uploads/2023/03/Mar23_MedPAC_Report_To _Congress_v2_SEC.pdf.

4.   National Research Council, *Aging and the Macroeconomy: Long-Term Implications of an Older Population* (Washington, DC: National Academies Press, 2012).

5.   National Research Council, *Aging and the Macroeconomy*, 18.

6.   Robert Gordon, *The Rise and Fall of American Growth* (New York: Princeton University Press, 2016).

7.   National Research Council, *Aging and the Macroeconomy*, 47.

8.   Dudley L. Poston Jr., "3 Ways That the U.S. Population Will Change over the Next Decade," PBS News Hour, aired January 2, 2020, https://www.pbs.org/newshour /nation/3-ways-that-the-u-s-population-will-change-over-the-next-decade/.

9.   MedPAC [Medicare Payment Advisory Committee], *Report to the Congress: Medicare and the Health Care Delivery System* (Washington, DC: MedPAC, June 2015), 40, https://www.medpac.gov/document/http-www-medpac-gov-docs-default-source -reports-june-2015-report-to-the-congress-medicare-and-the-health-care-delivery -system-pdf.

10.   MedPAC, *Medicare and Health Care Delivery*, 43.

11.   MedPAC, *A Data Book: Health Care Spending and the Medicare Program* (Washington, DC: MedPAC, July 2023), 20, https://www.medpac.gov/wp-content /uploads/2023/07/July2023_MedPAC_DataBook_SEC.pdf.

12.   Paul N. Van de Water, "Medicare Is Not 'Bankrupt,'" Center on Budget and Policy Priorities, updated February 13, 2023, https://www.cbpp.org/research/health /medicare-is-not-bankrupt/.

13.   Boards of Trustees, *2023 Annual Report of the Boards of Trustees of the Federal Hospital Insurance and Federal Supplementary Medical Insurance Trust Fund* (Washington, DC: Boards of Trustees, March 2023), https://www.cms.gov/oact/tr /2023.

14.   Adaeze Enekwechi, Gretchen Jacobson, and Cori Uccello, "Addressing Medicare's Finances Is Still Urgent: A Framework for Considering Options," *Health*

Affairs Forefront (blog), *Health Affairs*, June 29, 2022, https://www.healthaffairs.org/do/10.1377/forefront.20220627.360838.

15.   U.S. Bureau of Labor Statistics, "Databases, Tables, and Calculators, 2010–2023," https://www.bls.gov/data/ [accessed September 21, 2023].

16.   Melinda B. Buntin, Salama S. Freed, Pikki Lai, Klara Lou, and Laura M. Keohane, "Trends In and Factors Contributing to the Slowdown in Medicare Spending Growth, 2007–2018," *JAMA Health Forum* 3, no. 212 (2022): e224475, https://jamanetwork.com/journals/jama-health-forum/fullarticle/2799212.

17.   Letter from Phillip L. Swagel, director, Congressional Budget Office, to Sheldon Whitehouse, chairman, Committee on the Budget, United States Senate, March 17, 2023, https://www.cbo.gov/system/files/2023-03/58997-Whitehouse.pdf.

18.   MedPAC, *A Data Book*, 5.

19.   Chris Farrell, "Medicare Could Be Insolvent in 2024: How to Prevent It," Next Avenue, March 1, 2021, https://www.nextavenue.org/medicare-could-be-insolvent-in-2024-how-to-prevent-it/.

20.   Congressional Budget Office, *The 2023 Long-Term Budget Outlook* (Washington, DC: Congressional Budget Office, June 2023), https://www.cbo.gov/publication/59331.

21.   Neil Irwin, "America May Need to Start Caring About the Deficit Again," Axios, June 29, 2023, https://www.axios.com/2023/06/29/cbo-federal-deficit/.

22.   Thomas Piketty, *Capital in the Twenty-First Century*, trans. Arthur Goldhammer (Cambridge, MA: Harvard University Press, 2013).

23.   Emmanuel Saez and Gabriel Zucman, "The Rise of Income and Wealth Inequality in America: Evidence from Distributional Macroeconomic Accounts," *Journal of Economic Perspectives* 34, no. 4 (2020): 3–26, https://pubs.aeaweb.org/doi/pdfplus/10.1257/jep.34.4.3.

24.   Laurence Ball and N. Gregory Mankiw, "What Do Budget Deficits Do?," Working Paper no. 5263, National Bureau of Economic Research, Cambridge, MA, September 1995, https://www.nber.org/papers/w5263.

25.   Melanie Lockert, "What Is Modern Monetary Theory? Understanding the Alternative Economic Theory That's Becoming More Mainstream," Business Insider, updated, https://www.businessinsider.com/modern-monetary-theory-mmt-explained-aoc-2019-3/ [accessed September 21, 2023].

26.   Francesco Purificato and Diane Flaherty, "Modern Monetary Theory: A Debate," Working Paper no. 279, Political Economy Research Institute, University of Massachusetts Amherst, February 2012, https://peri.umass.edu/publication/item/457-modern-monetary-theory-a-debate/.

27.   Olivier Blanchard, *Fiscal Policy Under Low Interest Rates* (Cambridge, MA: MIT Press, 2022).

28.   David Cutler, "Health Care in a Time of Deficit Concern," *JAMA Health Forum* 4, no. 3 (2023): e230930, https://jamanetwork.com/journals/jama-health-forum/fullarticle/2802970.

29.   Advocacy Resource Center, "Issue Brief: Corporate Practice of Medicine," American Medical Association, 2015, https://www.ama-assn.org/sites/ama-assn.org

/files/corp/media-browser/premium/arc/corporate-practice-of-medicine-issue-brief
_1.pdf.

30. Carol Kane, "Recent Changes in Physician Practice Arrangements: Private Practice Dropped to Less Than 50 Percent of Physicians in 2020," Policy Research Perspectives, American Medical Association, 2021, https://www.ama-assn.org /system/files/2021-05/2020-prp-physician-practice-arrangements.pdf.

31. Ronald G. Wheeland, "MedPage Today News: The Waning World of the Solo Practice," MedPage Today, December 2, 2017, https://www.medpagetoday.com /resource-centers/advances-in-dermatology/medpage-today-news-waning-world -solo-practice/1751.

32. Christopher Cheney, "3 of 4 Physicians Employed by Health Systems, Hospitals, or Corporate Entities," Health Leaders, April 25, 2022, https://www .healthleadersmedia.com/clinical-care/3-4-physicians-employed-health-systems -hospitals-or-corporate-entities/.

33. Blake Madden, "The Future of Physician Employment and the Physician Practice," Workweek, April 28, 2022, https://workweek.com/2022/04/28/future-of -physician-employment-and-physician-practice/.

34. AAMC [Association of American Medical Colleges], "Nation's Physician Workforce Evolves: More Women, a Bit Older, and Toward Different Specialties," https://www.aamc.org/news/nation-s-physician-workforce-evolves-more-women-bit -older-and-toward-different-specialties/ [accessed September 21, 2023].

35. Carol K. Kane, "Policy Research Perspectives: Recent Changes in Physician Practice Arrangements; Shifts Away from Private Practice and Towards Larger Practice Size Continue Through 2022," AMA [American Medical Association], July 2023, https://www.ama-assn.org/system/files/2022-prp-practice-arrangement.pdf.

36. Lisa Klinger, "What's the Difference between Actuarial Value and Minimum Value under the ACA?," Leavitt Group, April 8, 2013, https://news.leavitt.com /employee-benefits-compliance/whats-the-difference-between-actuarial-value-and -minimum-value-under-the-aca/.

37. Matthew Rae, Rebecca Copeland, and Cynthia Cox, "Tracking the Rise in Premium Contributions and Cost-Sharing for Families with Large Employer Coverage," Peterson-KFF [Kaiser Family Foundation] Health System Tracker, August 14, 2019, https://www.healthsystemtracker.org/brief/tracking-the-rise-in -premium-contributions-and-cost-sharing-for-families-with-large-employer -coverage/.

38. Gary Claxton, Matthew Rae, Emma Wagner, Gregory Young, Heidi Whit-more, Jason Kearns, Greg Shmavonia, and Anthony Damico, "Section 6: Worker and Employer Contributions for Premiums," *Employer Health Benefits: 2022 Annual Survey* (San Francisco: Kaiser Family Foundation, 2022), 79, https://files.kff.org/attachment /Report-Employer-Health-Benefits-2022-Annual-Survey.pdf.

39. Claxton et al., "Section 2: Health Benefits Offer Rates," *2022 Annual Survey*, 45.

40. Claxton et al., "Section 8: High Deductible Health Plans with Savings Option," *2022 Annual Survey*, 129, 131.

41.   Claxton et al., "Section 7: Employee Cost-Sharing," *2022 Annual Survey*, 107.

42.   Sara Berg, "Help Cut Burdens of High Deductible Plans," AMA [American Medical Association], November 17, 2020, https://www.ama-assn.org/delivering-care /patient-support-advocacy/help-cut-burdens-high-deductible-health-plans/.

43.   Claxton et al., "Section 6," *2022 Annual Survey*, 78.

44.   Elise Gould, "State of Working America Wages 2019: A Story of Slow, Uneven, and Unequal Wage Growth over the Last 40 Years," Economic Policy Institute, February 20, 2020, https://www.epi.org/publication/swa-wages-2019 /#:~:text=The%20median%20wage%20in%202019,time%2C%20full%2Dyear%20 worker/.

45.   David U. Himmelstein, Robert M. Lawless, Deborah Thorne, Pamela Foohey, and Steffie Woolhandler, "Medical Bankruptcy: Still Common Despite the Affordable Care Act," *American Journal of Public Health* 109, no. 3 (2019): 431–433, https://ajph .aphapublications.org/doi/10.2105/AJPH.2018.304901.

46.   Lunna Lopes, Audrey Kearney, Alex Montrero, Liz Hamel, and Mollyann Brodie, "Health Care Debt in the U.S.: The Broad Consequences of Medical and Dental Bills," KFF [Kaiser Family Foundation], June 16, 2022, https://www.kff.org /report-section/kff-health-care-debt-survey-main-findings/.

47.   MedPAC [Medicare Payment Advisory Committee], *Report to the Congress; Medicare Payment Policy* (Washington, DC: MedPAC, March 2020), 465–466, https:// www.medpac.gov/wp-content/uploads/import_data/scrape_files/docs/default -source/reports/mar20_entirereport_sec.pdf.

48.   Anthony T. LoSasso, Kevin Toczydlowski, and Yanchao Yang, "Insurer Market Power and Hospital Prices in the US," *Health Affairs* 42, no. 5 (2023): 615–621, https://www.healthaffairs.org/doi/10.1377/hlthaff.2022.01184.

49.   MedPAC, *Medicare Payment Policy* [2020], 465–466.

50.   David Dranove and Lawton R. Burn, *Big Med: Megaproviders and the High Cost of Health Care in America* (Chicago: University of Chicago Press, 2021).

51.   MedPAC, *Medicare Payment Policy* [2023], 71–73.

52.   Congressional Budget Office, *The Prices That Commercial Health Insurers and Medicare Pay for Hospitals' and Physicians' Services* (Washington, DC: Congressional Budget Office, January 2022), https://www.cbo.gov/system/files/2022-01/57422 -medical-prices.pdf.

53.   Nancy Beaulieu, Michael Chernew, and J. Michael McWilliams, "Organization and Performance of US Health Systems," Special Communication, *JAMA* 329, no. 4 (2023): 325–335, https://jamanetwork.com/journals/jama/article -abstract/2800656?resultClick=1.

54.   Karyn Schwartz, Eric Lopez, Matthew Rae, and Tricia Neuman, "What We Know About Provider Consolidation," KFF [Kaiser Family Foundation], September 2, 2020, https://www.kff.org/health-costs/issue-brief/what-we-know-about-provider -consolidation/.

55.   Schwartz et al., "What We Know."

56.   Schwartz et al., "What We Know."

57. Congressional Budget Office, *Policy Approaches to Reduce What Commercial Insurers Pay for Hospitals' and Physicians' Services* (Washington, DC: Congressional Budget Office, September 2022), https://www.cbo.gov/publication/58222.

Chapter 5. The Strange World of Pharmacy Commerce

1. Brian Palmer, "Jonas Salk: Good at Virology, Bad at Economics," Slate, April 13, 2014, https://slate.com/technology/2014/04/the-real-reasons-jonas-salk -didnt-patent-the-polio-vaccine.html.

2. Uwe E. Reinhardt, "Perspectives on the Pharmaceutical Industry," *Health Affairs* 20, no. 5 (2001): 136–149, https://www.healthaffairs.org/doi/full/10.1377 /hlthaff.20.5.136.

3. For example, see Fred D. Ledley, Sarah Shonka McCoy, and Gregory Vaughan, "Profitability of Large Pharmaceutical Companies Compared with Other Large Companies," *JAMA* 323, no. 9 (2020): 834–843, https://jamanetwork.com/journals /jama/fullarticle/2762308; David M. Cutler, "Are Pharmaceutical Companies Earning Too Much?," *JAMA* 323, no. 9 (2020): 829–830, https://jamanetwork.com/journals /jama/article-abstract/2762289.

4. "History of Federal Regulation: 1902–Present," FDAReview.org, https://www .fdareview.org/issues/history-of-federal-regulation-1902-present/ [accessed September 21, 2023].

5. Michael Rosenblatt, "The Large Pharmaceutical Company Perspective," *New England Journal of Medicine* 376, no. 1 (2017): 52–60, https://www.nejm.org/doi/full /10.1056/NEJMra1510069.

6. See, for example, Thomas Sullivan, "A Tough Road: Cost to Develop One New Drug Is $2.6 Billion," *Policy & Medicine*, March 21, 2019, https://www.policymed.com /2014/12/a-tough-road-cost-to-develop-one-new-drug-is-26-billion-approval-rate-for -drugs-entering-clinical-de.html; Jerry Avorn, "The $2.6 Billion Pill—Methodological and Policy Considerations," *New England Journal Medicine* 372, no. 20 (2015): 1877–1879, https://www.nejm.org/doi/full/10.1056/NEJMp1500848.

7. Richard G. Frank and Kathleen Hannick, "5 Things to Understand About Pharmaceutical R&D," *USC-Brookings Schaeffer Initiative for Health Policy* (blog), *Brookings*, June 2, 2022, https://www.brookings.edu/blog/usc-brookings-schaeffer -on-health-policy/2022/06/02/five-things-to-understand-about-pharmaceutical-rd/.

8. Mike McCaughan, "Patent Settlements," Health Policy Brief: Prescription Drug Pricing #4, *Health Affairs*, July 21, 2017, https://www.healthaffairs.org/do/10 .1377/hpb20170721.583967/full/; Jonathan J. Darrow, Jerry Avorn, and Aaron S. Kesselheim, "FDA Approval and Regulation of Pharmaceuticals, 1983–2018," *JAMA* 323, no. 2 (2020): 164–176, https://jamanetwork.com/journals/jama/article-abstract /2758605?appId=scweb.

9. In re Restasis (Cyclosporine Ophthalmic Emulsion) Antitrust Litigation, 333 F. Supp.3d 135 (E.D.N.Y. 2020).

10. Kerstin Noëlle Vokinger, Aaron S. Kesselheim, Jerry Avorn, and Ameet Sarpatwari, "Strategies That Delay Market Entry of Generic Drugs," Special

Communication, *JAMA Internal Medicine* 177, no. 11 (2017): 1665–1669, https://jamanetwork.com/journals/jamainternalmedicine/article-abstract/2653452.

11. Gerald Posner, *Pharma: Greed, Lies, and the Poisoning of America* (New York: Simon & Schuster, 2020).

12. Many of the empirical papers published by George Loewenstein are cited in Troyen A. Brennan, David J. Rothman, Linda Blank, David Blumenthal, Susan C. Chimonas, Jordan J. Cohen, Janlori Goldman, et al., "Health Industry Practices That Create Conflicts of Interest: A Policy Proposal for Academic Medical Centers," *JAMA* 295, no. 4 (2006): 429–433, https://jamanetwork.com/journals/jama/fullarticle/202261.

13. C. Lee Ventola, "Direct-to-Consumer Pharmaceutical Advertising: Toxic or Therapeutic?," *P&T* [*Pharmacy and Therapeutics*] 36, no. 10 (2011): 669–674, 681–684, https://www.ncbi.nlm.nih.gov/pmc/articles/PMC3278148.

14. "Do Not Get Sold On Drug Advertising," Medications, Harvard Health Publishing, February 14, 2017, https://www.health.harvard.edu/drugs-and-medications/do-not-get-sold-on-drug-advertising/.

15. Lisa M. Schwartz and Steven Woloshin, "Medical Marketing in the United States, 1997–2016," Special Communications, *JAMA* 321, no. 1 (2016): 80–96, https://jamanetwork.com/journals/jama/fullarticle/2720029.

16. "Advanced Search," Open Payments Search Tool, Open Payments Data, CMS [Centers for Medicare & Medicaid Services], last updated January 2023, https://openpaymentsdata.cms.gov/search/physicians/by-name-and-location/.

17. "Drug Price Increases Have Slowed, but New Analysis Shows Launch Prices Pushing Costs into Orbit," 46Brooklyn, October 15, 2019, https://www.46brooklyn.com/research/2019/10/11/three-two-one-launch-rfmyr/.

18. "Genzyme," Wikipedia, https://en.wikipedia.org/wiki/Genzyme [accessed April 2, 2022].

19. Tony Kish, Andrew Aziz, and Monica Sorio, "Hepatitis C in a New Era: A Review of Current Therapies," *P&T* [*Pharmacy and Therapeutics*] 42, no. 5 (2017): 316–329, https://www.ncbi.nlm.nih.gov/pmc/articles/PMC5398625.

20. Christine Y. Lu, Dennis Ross-Degnan, Fang Zhang, Robert LeCates, Caitlin Lupton, Michael Sherman, and Anita Wagner, "Cost Burden of Hepatitis C Virus Treatment in Commercially Insured Patients," *AJMC* [*American Journal of Managed Care*] 25, no. 12 (2019): e379–e386, https://www.ajmc.com/view/cost-burden-of-hepatitis-c-virus-treatment-in-commercially-insured-patients/.

21. James Surowiecki, "Biotech's Hard Bargain," Financial Page, *New Yorker*, April 21, 2014, https://www.newyorker.com/magazine/2014/04/28/biotechs-hard-bargain/.

22. Mehdi Najafzadeh, Karin Andersson, William H. Shrank, Alexis A. Krumme, Olga S. Matlin, Troyen Brennan, Jerry Avorn, et al., "Cost Effectiveness of Novel Regimes for the Treatment of Hepatitis C," *Annals of Internal Medicine* 162, no. 6 (2015): 407–419, https://www.acpjournals.org/doi/full/10.7326/M14-1152.

23. U.S. Bureau of Labor Statistics, "Employee Tenure in 2020," news release no. USDL-22-1894, September 22, 2020, https://www.bls.gov/news.release/pdf/tenure.pdf.

24. "America's Biggest Charitable Giving: $5.7 Billion in Patient Assistance Programs," Patients Rising Now, November 13, 2019, https://patientsrisingnow.org/patient-assistance-programs-biggest-charity/.

25. David H. Howard, "Drug Companies' Patient Assistance Programs—Helping Patients or Profits?," Perspective, *New England Journal of Medicine* 371, no. 2 (2014): 97–99, https://www.nejm.org/doi/full/10.1056/NEJMp1401658.

26. Ashley Kirzinger, Audrey Kearney, Mellisha Stokes, and Mollyann Brodie, "KFF Health Tracking Poll—May 2021: Prescription Drug Prices Top Public's Health Care Priorities," KFF [Kaiser Family Foundation], June 3, 2021, https://www.kff.org/health-costs/poll-finding/kff-health-tracking-poll-may-2021/.

27. Lev Facher, "Pharma Is Showering Congress with Cash, Even as Drug Makers Race to Fight the Coronavirus," Prescription Politics, *Stat*, August 10, 2020, https://www.statnews.com/feature/prescription-politics/prescription-politics/.

28. Victoria Knight, Rachana Pradhan, and Elizabeth Lucas, "Pharma Campaign Cash Delivered to Key Lawmakers with Surgical Precision," KFF [Kaiser Family Foundation] Health News, October 27, 2021, https://khn.org/news/article/pharma-campaign-cash-delivered-to-key-lawmakers-with-surgical-precision/.

29. One good recent review is by Andrew W. Mulcahy and Vishnupriya Kareddy, *Prescription Drug Supply Chains: An Overview of Stakeholders and Relationships* (Santa Monica, CA: RAND Corporation, October 2021), https://www.rand.org/pubs/research_reports/RRA328-1.html.

30. Lawton R. Burns, *The Healthcare Value Chain: Demystifying the Roles of GPOs and PBMs* (New York: Palgrave Macmillan, 2022).

31. Adam J. Fein, "The Top Pharmacy Benefit Managers of 2020: Vertical Integration Drives Consolidation," Drug Channels, April 6, 2021, https://www.drugchannels.net/2021/04/the-top-pharmacy-benefit-managers-pbms.html.

32. Allison Dabbs Garrett and Robert Garis, "Leveling the Playing Field in the Pharmacy Benefit Management Industry," Valpo Scholar, *Valparaiso University Law Review* 42, no. 1 (2007): 33–80, https://scholar.valpo.edu/cgi/viewcontent.cgi?referer=https://en.wikipedia.org/&httpsredir=1&article=1131&context=vulr.

33. Elizabeth Seeley and Aaron S. Kesselheim, "Pharmacy Benefit Managers: Practices, Controversies, and What Lies Ahead," Issue Briefs, Commonwealth Fund, March 26, 2019, https://www.commonwealthfund.org/publications/issue-briefs/2019/mar/pharmacy-benefit-managers-practices-controversies-what-lies-ahead/.

34. Olivier J. Wouters, Panos G. Kanavos, and Martin McKee, "Comparing Generic Drug Markets in Europe and the United States: Prices, Volumes, and Spending," *Milbank Quarterly* 95, no. 3 (2017): 554–601, https://www.ncbi.nlm.nih.gov/pmc/articles/PMC5594322.

35. KFF [Kaiser Family Foundation], "Poll: Nearly 1 in 4 Americans Taking Prescription Drugs Say It's Difficult to Afford Their Medicines, Including Larger Shares among Those with Health Issues, with Low Incomes and Nearing Medicare Age," news release, March 1, 2019, https://www.kff.org/health-costs/press-release

/poll-nearly-1-in-4-americans-taking-prescription-drugs-say-its-difficult-to-afford
-medicines-including-larger-shares-with-low-incomes/.

36. Katherine Eban, *Bottle of Lies: The Inside Story of the Generic Drug Boom* (New York: Ecco, 2019).

37. Adam J. Fein, "The Big Three Generic Drug Mega-Buyers Drove Double Digit Deflation in 2018: Stability Ahead?," Drug Channels, January 8, 2019, https://www
.drugchannels.net/2019/01/the-big-three-generic-drug-mega-buyers.html.

38. Adam J. Fein, "Generic Deflation Roils the Channel—and Will Get Worse," Drug Channels, August 10, 2017, https://www.drugchannels.net/2017/08/generic
-deflation-roils-channeland-will.html.

39. Bruce Japsen, "Walgreen's New Battle: Winning Back Express Scripts Customers," *Forbes*, September 28, 2012, https://www.forbes.com/sites/brucejapsen
/2012/09/28/walgreen-admits-challenge-ahead-in-return-of-customers-lost-in
-express-scripts-battle/?sh=734f99146ddf.

40. Evan Sweeney, "CVS, Express Scripts Provide a Rare Moment of Transparency on Rebate Profits," Fierce Healthcare, August 10, 2018, https://www.fiercehealthcare
.com/payer/cvs-caremark-express-scripts-pbm-pass-through-cigna-merger/.

41. Susan Morse, "Pharmacy Benefit Managers Keep Less Than 1 Percent of Rebates for Medicare Part D Drugs, GAO Says," More on Pharmacy, *Healthcare Finance*, August 14, 2019, https://www.healthcarefinancenews.com/news/pharmacy-benefit
-managers-keep-less-1-percent-rebates-medicare-part-d-drugs-says-gao-report/.

42. Charles Roehrig, "Rebates, Coupons, PBMs, and the Cost of the Prescription Drug Benefit," *Health Affairs Forefront* (blog), *Health Affairs*, April 26, 2018, https://
www.healthaffairs.org/content/forefront/rebates-coupons-pbms-and-cost
-prescription-drug-benefit/.

43. See "Section 5. Epclusa and Harvoni," in Eric Sagonowsky, "Top 10 Drugs Losing Exclusivity in 2019," Special Report, Fierce Pharma, February 26, 2019, https://www.fiercepharma.com/special-report/5-epclusa-and-harvoni/.

44. Ashley Kirzinger, Alex Mongtero, Grace Sparks, Isabelle Valdes, and Liz Hamel, "Public Opinion on Prescription Drugs and Their Prices," Polling, KFF [Kaiser Family Foundation], August 4, 2023, https://www.kff.org/health-costs/poll-finding
/public-opinion-on-prescription-drugs-and-their-prices/.

45. Kirzinger et al., "Public Opinion."

46. Dena Bunis, "High Prescription Drug Prices Lead Many Consumers to Ignore Doctors' Orders," Politics & Society, AARP [American Association of Retired Persons)], August 21, 2019, https://www.aarp.org/politics-society/advocacy/info
-2019/drug-prices-consumer-impact.html.

47. "2019 Drug Trend Report," Express Scripts, https://www.express-scripts
.com/corporate/node/2089.

48. Centers for Medicare & Medicaid Services, "National Health Expenditures by Type of Service and Source of Funds, CY1960–2021 (ZIP)," National Health Expenditure Data: Historical, CMS.gov, https://www.cms.gov/data-research
/statistics-trends-and-reports/national-health-expenditure-data/historical/
[accessed September 21, 2023].

49. "Where Does Your Health Care Dollar Go?," AHIP [America's Health Insurance Plan], September 6, 2022, https://www.ahip.org/resources/where-does -your-health-care-dollar-go/.

50. Ezekiel J. Emanuel, Cathy Zhang, Aaron Glickman, Emily Gudbranson, Sarah S. P. DiMagno, and John W. Unwin, "Drug Reimbursement in 6 Peer Countries," Special Communication, *JAMA Internal Medicine* 180, no. 11 (2020): 1510–1517, https://jamanetwork.com/journals/jamainternalmedicine/article-abstract /2771097.

51. Ways and Means Committee Staff, U.S. House of Representatives, *A Painful Pill to Swallow: U.S. vs. International Prescription Drug Prices* (Washington, DC: [House] Committee on Ways and Means, September 2019, Readkong, https://www .readkong.com/page/a-painful-pill-to-swallow-u-s-vs-international-1427505.

52. Neeraj Sood, Han de Vries, Italo Gutierrez, Darius N. Lakdawalla, and Dana P. Goldman, "The Effect of Regulation on Pharmaceutical Revenues: Experience in Nineteen Countries," Web Exclusives, *Health Affairs* 27, Suppl. 1 (2008): 125–137, https://www.healthaffairs.org/doi/full/10.1377/hlthaff.28.1.w125.

53. GAO [U.S. Government Accountability Office], *Prescription Drugs: Department of Veterans Affairs Paid About Half as Much as Medicare Part D for Selected Drugs in 2017*, Report GAO-21-111 (Washington, DC: U.S. Government Accountability Office, December 2020), https://www.gao.gov/assets/gao-21-111.pdf.

54. Kirzinger et al., "Public Opinion."

55. Juliette Cubanski, Tricia Neuman, Meredith Freed, and Anthony Damico, "How Will the Prescription Drug Provisions in the Inflation Reduction Act Affect Medicare Beneficiaries?," KFF [Kaiser Family Foundation], January 24, 2023, https://www.kff.org/medicare/issue-brief/how-will-the-prescription-drug -provisions-in-the-inflation-reduction-act-affect-medicare-beneficiaries/.

56. Nitzan Arad and Mark B. McClellan, "Drug Pricing Reform in the Inflation Reduction Act: What Are the Implications?," *Health Affairs Forefront* (blog), *Health Affairs*, December 14, 2022, https://www.healthaffairs.org/content/forefront/drug -pricing-reform-inflation-reduction-act-implications-part-1/.

Chapter 6. The Commercial Parts of Medicare

1. Jonathan Oberlander and Theodore Marmor, "The Road Not Taken: What Happened to Medicare for All?," in *Medicare and Medicaid at 50: America's Entitlement Programs in the Age of Affordable Care*, ed. Alan B. Cohen, David C. Colby, Keith Walloo, and Julian E. Zelizer (New York: Oxford University Press, 2015), chapter 4.

2. Uwe E. Reinhardt, "Medicare Innovations in the War over the Key to the US Treasury," in *Medicare and Medicaid at 50*, chapter 9.

3. "What's a MAC," CMS [Centers for Medicare & Medicaid Services], last modified March 16, 2023, https://www.cms.gov/Medicare/Medicare-Contracting /Medicare-Administrative-Contractors/What-is-a-MAC/.

4. "Local Versus National Medicare Coverage," Business of the Business: Washington Consult, *Journal of Oncology Practice* 3, no. 5 (2007): 256, https://www .ncbi.nlm.nih.gov/pmc/articles/PMC2793851.

5. James D. Chambers, Matthew Chenoweth, Michael J. Cangelosi, Junhee Pyo, Joshua T. Cohen, and Peter J. Neumann, "Medicare Is Scrutinizing Evidence More Tightly for National Coverage Decisions," *Health Affairs* 34, no. 2 (2015): 253–260, https://www.healthaffairs.org/doi/10.1377/hlthaff.2014.1123.

6. Aaron L. Schwartz, Troyen A. Brennan, Dorothea J. Verbrugge, and Joseph P. Newhouse, "Measuring the Scope of Prior Authorization Policies: Applying Private Insurer Rules to Medicare Part B," *JAMA Health Forum* 2, no. 5 (2021): e210859, https://jamanetwork.com/journals/jama-health-forum/fullarticle/2780396.

7. "2023 Medicare Parts A & B Premiums and Deductibles 2023 Medicare Part D Income-Related Monthly Adjustment Amounts," Centers for Medicare & Medicaid Services, September 27, 2022, https://www.cms.gov/newsroom/fact-sheets/2023 -medicare-parts-b-premiums-and-deductibles-2023-medicare-part-d-income-related -monthly/.

8. Kathryn M. Langwell and James P. Hadley, "Capitation and the Medicare Program: History, Issues, and Evidence," *Health Care Financing Review* 1986 Suppl. (1986): 9–20, https://www.ncbi.nlm.nih.gov/pmc/articles/PMC4195086; Ellen M. Morrison and Harold S. Luft, "Health Maintenance Organization Environments in the 1980s and Beyond," *Health Care Financing Review* 12, no. 1 (1990): 81–90, https://www.ncbi.nlm.nih.gov/pmc/articles/PMC4193099; Thomas G. McGuire, Joseph P. Newhouse, and Anna D. Sinaiko, "An Economic History of Medicare Part C," *Milbank Quarterly* 89, no. 2 (2011): 289–332, https://www.ncbi.nlm.nih.gov/pmc /articles/PMC3117270.

9. Yash M. Patel and Stuart Guterman, "The Evolution of Private Plans in Medicare," Issue Briefs, Commonwealth Fund, December 8, 2017, https://www .commonwealthfund.org/publications/issue-briefs/2017/dec/evolution-private-plans -medicare/.

10. McGuire et al., "Economic History of Medicare," 306.

11. McGuire et al., "Economic History of Medicare," figure 4.

12. Robert E. Moffit and Marie Fishpaw, eds. *Modernizing Medicare: Harnessing the Power of Consumer Choice and Market Competition* (Baltimore: Johns Hopkins University Press, 2023).

13. Patel and Guterman, "The Evolution of Private Plans."

14. Patel and Guterman, "The Evolution of Private Plans."

15. "Improving Medicare Advantage Quality Measurement," White Paper, Better Medicare Alliance, October 2018, https://bettermedicarealliance.org/wp-content /uploads/2020/03/BMA_StarRatings_WhitePaper_2018_10_24.pdf.

16. Jeannie Fuglesten Biniek, Meredith Freed, Anthony Damico, and Tricia Neuman, "Medicare Advantage in 2021: Star Ratings and Bonuses," KFF [Kaiser Family Foundation], June 21, 2021 [no longer available online].

17. Nancy Ochieng, Jeannie Fuglesten Biniek, Meredith Freed, Anthony Damico, and Tricia Neuman, "Medicare Advantage in 2023: Premiums, Out-of-Pocket Limits, Cost Sharing, Supplemental Benefits, Prior Authorization, and Star Ratings," KFF [Kaiser Family Foundation], August 9, 2023, https://www.kff.org/medicare

/issue-brief/medicare-advantage-in-2021-premiums-cost-sharing-out-of-pocket
-limits-and-supplemental-benefits/.

18.   Meredith Freed, Anthony Damico, and Tricia Neuman, "A Dozen Facts about Medicare Advantage in 2020," KFF [Kaiser Family Foundation], January 13, 2021, https://healthsprockets.com/content/kff-dozen-facts-about-medicare -advantage-2020/.

19.   Nick Herro and Julianna Wokurka, "As Medicare Advantage Enrollment Booms, Healthcare Entities Need to Plan Around Key Trends," Chartis, March 29, 2021, https://www.chartis.com/as-medicare-advantage-enrollment-booms -healthcare-entities-need-to-plan-around-key-trends/.

20.   MedPAC [Medicare Payment Advisory Committee], *Report to the Congress; Medicare Payment Policy* (Washington, DC: MedPAC, March 2023), 13–15, https:// www.medpac.gov/wp-content/uploads/2023/03/Mar23_MedPAC_Report_To _Congress_v2_SEC.pdf.

21.   MedPAC, *Medicare Payment Policy*, figure 11-6.

22.   Lynn Nonnemaker and Mark Hamelburg, "Correcting the Record: Medicare Advantage Costs Far Less Than Fee-for-Service Medicare," AHIP [America's Health Insurance Plan], February 24, 2021, https://www.ahip.org/news/articles/correcting -the-record-medicare-advantage-costs-far-less-than-fee-for-service-medicare/.

23.   Richard Gilfillan and Donald M. Berwick, "The Emperor Still Has No Clothes: A Response to Halvorson and Crane," *Health Affairs Forefront* (blog), *Health Affairs*, June 6, 2022, https://www.healthaffairs.org/do/10.1377/forefront.20220602 .413644.

24.   Better Medicare Alliance, *Sustaining and Strengthening Medicare Advantage: Policy Recommendations to Maintain Accountability and Support Beneficiaries* (Washington, DC: Better Medicare Alliance, December 2022), https://bettermedicarealliance .org/wp-content/uploads/2022/12/BMA-Sustaining-and-Strengthening-Medicare -Advantage-2022.pdf.

25.   Richard Gilfillan, Donald M. Berwick, and Richard Kronick, "How Medicare Advantage Plans Can Support the United States' Reinvestment in Health," *Health Affairs Forefront* (blog), *Health Affairs*, January 10, 2022, https://www.healthaffairs .org/content/forefront/medicare-advantage-plans-can-support-united-states -reinvestment-health/; Richard Kronick and F. Michael Chua, "Industry-Wide and Sponsor-Specific Estimates of Medicare Advantage Coding Intensity," SSRN [Social Sciences Research Network], November 11, 2021, https://ssrn.com/abstract =3959446.

26.   MedPAC, *Medicare Payment Policy*, 442.

27.   J. Michael McWilliams, "Don't Look Up? Medicare Advantage's Trajectory and the Future of Medicare," *Health Affairs Forefront* (blog), *Health Affairs*, March 24, 2022, https://www.healthaffairs.org/do/10.1377/forefront.20220323.773602.

28.   Bob Herman and Tara Bannow, "Medicare Advantage Insurers to Repay Billions Under Final Federal Audit," Insurance, *Stat*, January 30, 2023, https://www .statnews.com/2023/01/30/medicare-advantage-insurers-to-repay-billions/.

29.   United Healthcare Insurance v. Becerra, No. 18-5326, United States Court of Appeal for the DC Circuit, decided August 13, 2021, https://www.govinfo.gov/content /pkg/USCOURTS-caDC-18-05326/pdf/USCOURTS-caDC-18-05326-0.pdf.

30.   Letter from Michael Chernew, chair, MedPAC, to Chiquita Brooks-LaSure, administrator, Centers for Medicare & Medicaid Services, March 1, 2023, https:// www.medpac.gov/wp-content/uploads/2023/03/Mar2023_MA_C_AND_D_CY-2024 _MedPAC_COMMENT_v2_SEC.pdf.

31.   Anesh Chopra, Adam Boehler, and Gary Bacher, "Risk Adjustment: It's Time for Reform," *Health Affairs Forefront* (blog), *Health Affairs*, January 9, 2023, https:// www.healthaffairs.org/content/forefront/risk-adjustment-s-time-reform/.

32.   Richard Gilfillan and Donald Berwick, "Born on Third Base: Medicare Advantage Thrives on Subsidies, Not Better Care," *Health Affairs Forefront* (blog), *Health Affairs*, March 27, 2023, https://www.healthaffairs.org/content/forefront/born -third-base-medicare-advantage-thrives-subsidies-not-better-care/.

33.   Letter from MedPAC to Xavier Becerra, secretary, Health and Human Services, and Chiquita Brooks-LaSure, administrator, Centers for Medicare & Medicaid Services, March 6, 2023, https://thecapitolforum.com/wp-content/uploads /2023/03/MA-Advance-Notice-gp19-Comment-final-9-030923.pdf.

34.   Lauren Skopec, Bowen Garrett, and Anuj Gangopadhyaya, "Reimagining the Medicare Advantage Risk Adjustment Program," Urban Institute, May 19, 2023, https://www.urban.org/research/publication/reimagining-medicare-advantage-risk -adjustment-program/.

35.   Richard G. Frank and Conrad Milhaupt, "Profits, Medical Loss Ratios, and the Ownership Structure of Medicare Advantage Plans," *USC-Brookings Schaeffer Initiative for Health Policy* (blog), *Brookings*, July 13, 2022, https://www.brookings.edu /blog/usc-brookings-schaeffer-on-health-policy/2022/07/13/profits-medical-loss -ratios-and-the-ownership-structure-of-medicare-advantage-plans/.

36.   Nathan Eddy, "Medicare Advantage Profit Structure Under Scrutiny in New Report," More on Medicare & Medicaid, *Healthcare Finance News*, July 15, 2022, https://www.healthcarefinancenews.com/news/medicare-advantage-profit-structure -under-scrutiny-new-report/.

37.   Robert A. Berenson, Jonathan H. Sunshine, David Helms, and Emily Lawton, "Why Medicare Advantage Plans Pay Hospitals Traditional Medicare Prices," *Health Affairs*, 34, no. 8 (2015): 1289–1295, https://www.healthaffairs.org/doi/10.1377 /hlthaff.2014.1427.

38.   Nona Tepper, "Mayo, United Healthcare Dispute Could Set Tone for All Medicare Advantage Negotiations," Modern Healthcare, February 14, 2022, https:// www.modernhealthcare.com/payment/mayo-unitedhealthcare-dispute-could-set -tone-all-medicare-advantage-negotiations/.

39.   Erin Trish, Paul Ginsburg, Laura Gascue, and Geoffrey Joyce, "Physician Reimbursement in Medicare Advantage Compared with Traditional Medicare and Commercial Health Insurance," *JAMA Internal Medicine* 177, no. 9 (2017): 1287–1295, https://jamanetwork.com/journals/jamainternalmedicine/fullarticle/2643349.

40. Karyn Schwartz, Jeannie Fuglesten Biniek, Matthew Rae, Tricia Neuman, and Larry Levitt, "Limiting Private Insurance Reimbursement to Medicare Rates Would Reduce Health Spending by About $350 Billion in 2021," KFF [Kaiser Family Foundation], March 1, 2021, https://www.kff.org/medicare/issue-brief/limiting -private-insurance-reimbursement-to-medicare-rates-would-reduce-health-spending -by-about-350-billion-in-2021/.

41. Canile Jamieson, Monisha Machado-Pereira, Stephanie Carlton, and Cara Repasky, "Assessing the Medicare Star Advantage Ratings," McKinsey & Company on Health Care, July 2018 [no longer available online].

42. Soleil Shah and Eric Sun, "Rating the Medicare Advantage Star Ratings— Improving the Status Quo," *Health Affairs Forefront* (blog), *Health Affairs*, February 4, 2021, https://www.healthaffairs.org/content/forefront/rating-medicare-advantage -star-ratings-improving-status-quo/.

43. Biniek et al., "Medicare Advantage in 2021" [no longer available online].

44. Jeannie Fuglesten Biniek, Anthony Damico, and Tricia Neuman. "Spending on Medicare Advantage Quality Bonus Payments Will Reach at Least $12.8 Billion in 2023," KFF [Kaiser Family Foundation], August 9, 2023, https://www.kff.org /medicare/issue-brief/spending-on-medicare-advantage-quality-bonus-payments -will-reach-at-least-12-8-billion-in-2023/.

45. "Medicare Advantage Outperforms FFS Medicare in Caring for Beneficiaries with Chronic Conditions Fact Sheet," Better Medicare Alliance, July 12, 2018, https://bettermedicarealliance.org/publication/medicare-advantage-outperforms-ffs -medicare-in-caring-for-beneficiaries-with-chronic-conditions-fact-sheet/.

46. Kenneth E. Thorpe, "Beneficiaries with Chronic Conditions More Likely to Actively Choose Medicare Advantage," Better Medicare Alliance, September 2018, https://bettermedicarealliance.org/wp-content/uploads/2020/03/BMA _ThorpeReport_2018_09_13.pdf.

47. Kenton Johnson, Gmerice Hammond, David J. Meyers, and Karen E. Joynt Maddox, "Association of Race and Ethnicity and Medicare Program Type with Ambulatory Care Access and Quality Measures," *JAMA* 326, no. 7 (2021): 628–636, https://jamanetwork.com/journals/jama/fullarticle/2783067.

48. Avalere, "Medicare Advantage Achieves Better Health Outcomes and Lower Utilization of High-Cost Services Compared to Fee-For-Service Medicare," press release, July 11, 2018, https://avalere.com/press-releases/medicare-advantage -achieves-better-health-outcomes-and-lower-utilization-of-high-cost-services -compared-to-fee-for-service-medicare/.

49. Adam A. Markovitz, John Z. Ayanian, Devraj Sukul, and Andrew M. Ryan, "The Medicare Advantage Quality Bonus Program Has Not Improved Plan Quality," *Health Affairs* 40, no. 12 (2021): 1918–1925, https://www.healthaffairs.org/doi/pdf/10 .1377/hlthaff.2021.00606.

50. Rajender Agarwal, John Connolly, Shweta Gupta, and Amol S. Navthe, "Comparing Medicare Advantage and Traditional Medicare: A Systematic Review," *Health Affairs* 40, no. 6 (2021): 937–944, https://www.healthaffairs.org/doi/abs/10 .1377/hlthaff.2020.02149.

51.   Nancy Ochieng and Jeannie Fuglesten Biniek, "Beneficiary Experience, Affordability, Utilization, and Quality in Medicare Advantage and Traditional Medicare: A Review of the Literature," KFF [Kaiser Family Foundation], September 16, 2022, https://www.kff.org/medicare/report/beneficiary-experience -affordability-utilization-and-quality-in-medicare-advantage-and-traditional -medicare-a-review-of-the-literature/.

52.   "Medicare Advantage Outperforms Fee-for-Service Medicare on Cost Protections for Low Income and Diverse Populations," Data Brief, Better Medicare Alliance, April 2022, https://bettermedicarealliance.org/wp-content/uploads/2022 /04/BMA-Medicare-Advantage-Cost-Protections-Data-Brief_FIN.pdf.

53.   Rahul Agarwal, Suhas Gondi, and Rishi K. Wadhera, "Comparison of Medicare Advantage vs Traditional Medicare for Health Care Access, Affordability, and Use of Preventive Services among Adults with Low Income," *JAMA Network Open* 5, no. 6 (2022): e22152227, https://jamanetwork.com/journals/jamanetwork open/fullarticle/2793106.

54.   Bruce E. Landon, Timothy S. Anderson, Vilsa E. Curto, Peter Cram, Christina Fu, Gabe Weinreb, Alan M. Zaslavsky, and John Z. Ayanian, "Association of Medicare Advantage vs. Traditional Medicare with 30 Day Mortality among Patients with Acute Myocardial Infarction," *JAMA* 328, no. 21 (2022): 2126–2135, https:// jamanetwork.com/journals/jama/fullarticle/2799152.

55.   Adam L. Beckman, Austin B. Frakt, Ciara Duggan, Jie Zheng, John Orav, Thomas C. Tsai, and Jose F. Figueroa, "Evaluation of Potentially Avoidable Acute Care Utilization among Patients Insured by Medicare Advantage vs Traditional Medicare," *JAMA Health Forum* 4, no. 2 (2023): e225530, https://jamanetwork.com /journals/jama-health-forum/fullarticle/2801779.

56.   Bruce E. Landon, Alan M. Zaslavsky, Timothy S. Anderson, Jeffrey Souza, Vilsa Curto, and John Z. Ayanian, "Difference in Use of Services and Quality of Care in Medicare Advantage and Traditional Medicare, 2010 and 2017," *Health Affairs* 42, no. 4 (2023): 459–468, https://www.healthaffairs.org/doi/full/10.1377/hlthaff.2022 .00891.

57.   Kenneth Cohen, Omid Ameli, Christine E. Chaisson, Kierstin Catlett, Jonathan Chiang, Amy Kwong, Samira Kamrudin, and Boris Vabson, "Comparison of Care Quality Metrics in 2-Sided Risk Medicare Advantage vs Fee-for-Services Medicare Programs," Health Policy, *JAMA Network Open* 5, no. 12 (2022): e2246064, https://jamanetwork.com/journals/jamanetworkopen/fullarticle/2799376.

58.   Brook Getachew, Matt Kazan, and Christine Liow, "MedPAC Proposes Replacement for MA Star Ratings Program," Avalere, August 24, 2020, https:// avalere.com/insights/medpac-proposes-replacement-for-ma-star-ratings-program/.

59.   MedPAC, *Medicare Payment Policy*, 447.

60.   Douglas B. Jacobs, Michelle Schreiber, Meena Seshamani, Daniel Tsai, Elizabeth Fowler, and Lee A. Fleischer, "Aligning Quality Measures Across CMS—the Universal Foundation," Perspective, *New England Journal of Medicine* 388, no. 9 (2023): 776–776, https://www.nejm.org/doi/full/10.1056/NEJMp2215539.

61. Riaz Ali, Aimee Cicchiello, Morgan Hanger, Lesley Hellow, Ken Williams, and Gretchen Jacobson, *How Agents Influence Medicare Beneficiaries' Plan Choices* (New York: Commonwealth Fund, April 2021), https://www.commonwealthfund.org /publications/fund-reports/2021/apr/how-agents-influence-medicare-beneficiaries -plan-choices/.

62. Ali et al., *How Agents Influence*.

63. Margot Sanger-Katz, "It's Not Just You: Picking a Health Insurance Plan Is Really Hard," The Upshot, *New York Times*, December 11, 2020, https://www.nytimes .com/2020/12/11/upshot/choosing-health-insurance-is-hard.html.

64. KFF [Kaiser Family Foundation], "7 in 10 Medicare Beneficiaries Report That They Did Not Compare Their Coverage Options during a Recent Open Enrollment Period," news release, October 13, 2021, https://www.kff.org/medicare /press-release/7-in-10-medicare-beneficiaries-report-that-they-did-not-compare -their-coverage-options-during-a-recent-open-enrollment-period/.

65. Letter from NAIC [National Association of Insurance Commissioners] to Nancy Pelosi, Speaker, U.S. House of Representatives, and Kevin McCarthy, Republican leader, U.S. House of Representatives, May 5, 2022, https://content.naic.org/sites /default/files/State%20MA%20Marketing%20Authority%20House%20Letter.pdf.

66. Tara Bannow, "Biden Administration Takes Aim at Medicare Advantage Care Denials, Misleading Ads," *Stat*, December 15, 2022, https://www.statnews.com/2022 /12/15/medicare-advantage-care-denials-misleading-ads/.

67. Nancy Ochieng, Jeannie Fuglesten Biniek, Meredith Freed, Anthony Damico, and Tricia Neuman, "Medicare Advantage in 2023: Enrollment Update and Key Trends," KFF [Kaiser Family Foundation], August 8, 2023, https://www.kff.org/medicare/issue -brief/medicare-advantage-in-2023-enrollment-update-and-key-trends/.

68. "Employer-Group Medicare Advantage Enrollment Increased 26% over 4-Year Period," Mark Farrah Associates, November 17, 2020, https://www.markfarrah .com/mfa-briefs/employer-group-medicare-advantage-enrollment-increased-26-over -4-year-period/.

69. Meredith Freed, Tricia Neuman, Matthew Rae, and Jeannie Fuglesten Biniek, "Medicare Advantage Coverage Is Rising for the Declining Share of Medicare Beneficiaries with Retiree Health Benefits," KFF [Kaiser Family Foundation], December 1, 2022, https://www.kff.org/medicare/issue-brief/medicare-advantage-coverage-is-rising-for -the-declining-share-of-medicare-beneficiaries-with-retiree-health-benefits/.

70. Aaron L. Schwartz, Yujun Chen, Chris L. Jagmin, Dorothea J. Verbrugge, Troyen A. Brennan, Peter W. Groeneveld, and Joseph P. Newhouse, "Coverage Denials: Government and Private Insurer Policies for Medical Necessity in Medicare," *Health Affairs* 42, no. 1 (2022): 120–130, https://www.healthaffairs.org/doi/full/10 .1377/hlthaff.2021.01054.

71. Office of the Inspector General, "Some Medicare Advantage Organization Denials of Prior Authorization Requests Raise Concerns about Beneficiary Access to Medically Necessary Care," U.S. Department of Health and Human Services, April 27, 2022, https://oig.hhs.gov/oei/reports/OEI-09-18-00260.asp.

72. Kelly E. Anderson, Michael Darden, and Amit Jain, "Improving Prior Authorization in Medicare Advantage," *JAMA* 328, no. 15 (2022): 1497–1498, https://jamanetwork.com/journals/jama/fullarticle/2797197.

73. CMS [Centers for Medicare & Medicaid Services], "CMS Proposes Rule to Expand Access to Health Information and Improve the Prior Authorization Process," press release, December 6, 2022, https://www.cms.gov/newsroom/press-releases /cms-proposes-rule-expand-access-health-information-and-improve-prior -authorization-process/.

74. Ken Terry and David Muhlestein, "Medicare Advantage for All? Not So Fast," *Health Affairs Forefront* (blog), *Health Affairs*, March 11, 2021, https://www .healthaffairs.org/content/forefront/medicare-advantage-all-not-so-fast/.

75. John S. Toussaint, George Halvorson, Laurence Kotlikoff, Richard Scheffler, Stephen M. Shortell, Peter Wadsworth, and Gail Wilensky, "How the Biden Administration Can Make a Public Option Work," Harvard Business Review, November 25, 2020, https://hbr.org/2020/11/how-the-biden-administration-can-make-a-public -option-work/.

76. Thomas R. Oliver, Phillip R. Lee, and Helene L. Lipton, "A Political History of Medicare and Prescription Drug Coverage," *Milbank Quarterly* 82, no. 2 (2004): 283–354, https://www.ncbi.nlm.nih.gov/pmc/articles/PMC2690175.

77. Public Law No. 108-173 (2003).

78. John F. Hoadley, Juliette Cubanski, and Patricia Neuman, "Medicare's Part D Benefit at 10 Years: Firmly Established but Still Evolving," Datawatch, *Health Affairs* 34, no. 10 (2015): 1682–1687, https://www.healthaffairs.org/doi/10.1377/hlthaff.2015.0927.

79. Hoadley, Cubanski, and Neuman, "Medicare's Part D Benefit."

80. "An Overview of the Medicare Part D Prescription Drug Benefit," KFF [Kaiser Family Foundation], October 19, 2022, https://www.kff.org/medicare/fact -sheet/an-overview-of-the-medicare-part-d-prescription-drug-benefit/.

81. "Overview of Medicare Part D."

82. Hoadley, Cubanski, and Neuman, "Medicare's Part D Benefit."

83. "Overview of Medicare Part D," figure 5.

84. MedPAC, *Report to the Congress: Medicare and the Health Care Delivery System* (Washington, DC: MedPAC, June 2020), 125, https://www.medpac.gov/wp-content /uploads/import_data/scrape_files/docs/default-source/reports/jun20_ch5 _reporttocongress_sec.pdf.

85. Nitzan Arad and Mark B. McClellan, "Drug Pricing Reform in the Inflation Reduction Act: What Are the Implications?," *Health Affairs Forefront* (blog), *Health Affairs*, December 15, 2022, https://www.healthaffairs.org/content/forefront/drug -pricing-reform-inflation-reduction-act-implications-part-2/.

86. MedPAC, *Report to the Congress: Medicare Payment Policy* (Washington, DC: MedPAC, March 2021), 430, https://www.medpac.gov/wp-content/uploads/2021/10 /mar21_medpac_report_ch13_sec.pdf.

87. Stacie B. Dusetzina, Shelley Jazowski, Ashley Cole, and Joehl Nguyen, "Sending the Wrong Price Signal: Why Do Some Brand Name Drugs Cost Medicare

Beneficiaries Less Than Generics?," *Health Affairs* 38, no. 7 (2019): 1188–1194, https://www.healthaffairs.org/doi/full/10.1377/hlthaff.2018.05476.

88.   Suzanne M. Kirchhoff, "Selected Health Provisions of the Inflation Reduction Act," In Focus, Congressional Research Service, September 1, 2022, https://crsreports.congress.gov/product/pdf/IF/IF12203.

89.   Juliette Cubanski, Tricia Neuman, and Anthony Damico, "How Many Medicare Part D Enrollees Had High Out-of-Pocket Drug Costs in 2017?," KFF [Kaiser Family Foundation], June 21, 2019, https://www.kff.org/medicare/issue-brief/how-many-medicare-part-d-enrollees-had-high-out-of-pocket-drug-costs-in-2017/.

90.   Juliette Cubanski, Tricia Neuman, and Anthony Damico, "Millions of Medicare Part D Enrollees Have Had Out-Of-Pocket Drug Spending Above the Catastrophic Threshold over Time," KFF [Kaiser Family Foundation], July 23, 2021, https://www.kff.org/medicare/issue-brief/millions-of-medicare-part-d-enrollees-have-had-out-of-pocket-drug-spending-above-the-catastrophic-threshold-over-time/.

91.   Harris Meyer and Kaiser Health News, "Seniors Face Steep Drug Costs as Congress Stalls on Capping Medicare Out-of-Pockets," *Fortune*, December 28, 2020, https://fortune.com/2020/12/28/senior-drug-costs-congress-medicare-annual-out-of-pocket-maximum/.

92.   J. Michael McWilliams, Alan M. Zaslavsky, and Haiden A. Huskamp, "Implementation of Medicare Part D and Nondrug Medical Spending for Elderly Adults with Limited Prior Drug Coverage," *JAMA* 306, no. 4 (2011): 402–409, https://jamanetwork.com/journals/jama/fullarticle/1104150.

93.   Daniel A. Ollendorf, Patricia G. Synnott, and Peter J. Neumann, "External Reference Pricing: The Drug-Pricing Reform America Needs?," Issue Briefs, Commonwealth Fund, May 27, 2021, https://www.commonwealthfund.org/publications/issue-briefs/2021/may/external-reference-pricing-drug-pricing-reform-america-needs/; Erin Slifer and Alyssa Llamas, "Bipartisan Congressional Support for PBM Reform Grows," *Controlling Health Care Costs* (blog), *Commonwealth Fund*, June 21, 2023, https://www.commonwealthfund.org/blog/2023/bipartisan-congressional-support-pbm-reform-grows/.

94.   Joseph Newhouse, "Patients at Risk: Health Reform and Risk Adjustment," *Health Affairs* 13, no. 1 (1994): 132–146, https://www.healthaffairs.org/doi/full/10.1377/hlthaff.13.1.132.

95.   Aaron L. Schwartz, Seyoun Kim, Amol S. Navathe, and Atul Gupta, "Growth of Medicare Advantage after Plan Payment Reductions," *JAMA Health Forum* 4, no. 6 (2023): e231744, https://jamanetwork.com/journals/jama-health-forum/fullarticle/2806616.

Chapter 7. The Affordable Care Act

1.   John McDonough, *Inside National Health Reform* (Berkeley: University of California Press, 2011).

2.   Stuart Altman and David Schactman, *Power, Politics, and Universal Health Care: The Inside Story of a Century-Long Battle* (New York: Prometheus, 2011).

3. Jonathan Cohn, *The Ten Year War: Obamacare and the Unfinished Crusade for Universal Coverage* (New York: St. Martin's, 2021).

4. Julia Paradise, Barbara Lyon, and Diane Rowland, *Medicaid at 50* (Menlo Park, CA: KFF [Kaiser Family Foundation], May 2015), https://files.kff.org /attachment/report-medicaid-at-50/.

5. 42 U.S.C. Section 1369 (May 29, 2003).

6. Paradise, Lyon, and Rowland, *Medicaid at 50*, 10.

7. Kathleen Gifford, Eileen Ellis, Barbara Coulter Edwards, Aimee Lashbrook, Elizabeth Hinton, Larisa Antonisse, Allison Valentine, and Robin Rudowitz, "Medicaid Moving Ahead in Uncertain Times: Results from a 50-State Medicaid Budget Survey for State Fiscal Years 2017 and 2018," KFF [Kaiser Family Foundation], October 19, 2017, https://www.kff.org/medicaid/report/medicaid-moving-ahead-in -uncertain-times-results-from-a-50-state-medicaid-budget-survey-for-state-fiscal -years-2017-and-2018/.

8. Alison Mitchell, *Medicaid's Federal Medical Assistance Percentage (FMAP)* (Washington, DC: Congressional Research Service, updated July 29, 2020), https:// fas.org/sgp/crs/misc/R43847.pdf.

9. Title XXI of the Social Security Act, 42 U.S.C. Section 1397aa.

10. Barry R. Furrow, Thomas L. Greaney, Sandra H. Johnson, Timothy S. Jost, Robert L. Schwartz, Bretta R. Clark, Erin C. Fuse Brown, et al., *The Law of Health Care Organization and Finance*, 8th edition (St. Paul, MN: West Academic, 2018), 452.

11. Cindy Mann and Deborah Bachrach, "Medicaid as Health Insurer: Evolution and Implications," *To The Point* (blog), *Commonwealth Fund*, July 23, 2015, https:// www.commonwealthfund.org/blog/2015/medicaid-health-insurer-evolution-and -implications/.

12. Anthony Albanese, "The Past, Present, and Future of Section 1115: Learning from History to Improve the Medicaid-Waiver Regime Today," Forum, *Yale Law Journal* 128 (2018–2019): 128, https://www.yalelawjournal.org/forum/the-past -present-and-future-of-section-1115.

13. Benjamin D. Sommers, Lucy Chen, Robert J. Blendon, John Orav, and Arnold M. Epstein, "Medicaid Work Requirements in Arkansas: Two-Year Impacts on Coverage, Employment, and Affordability of Care," *Health Affairs* 39, no. 9 (2020): 1522–1530, https://www.healthaffairs.org/doi/abs/10.1377/hlthaff.2020.00538.

14. Andy Schneider, "Overview of Medicaid Managed Care Provisions in the Balanced Budget Act of 1997—Report," KFF [Kaiser Family Foundation], November 29, 1997, https://www.kff.org/medicaid/report/overview-of-medicaid-managed -care-provisions-in-2/.

15. Elizabeth Hinton and Jada Raphael, "10 Things to Know about Medicaid Managed Care," KFF [Kaiser Family Foundation], updated March 1, 2023, https://www .kff.org/medicaid/issue-brief/10-things-to-know-about-medicaid-managed-care/.

16. Hinton and Raphael, "10 Things to Know."

17. Robert H. Miller and Harold S. Luft, "Does Managed Care Lead to Better or Worse Quality of Care?," *Health Affairs* 16, no. 5 (1997): 7–25, https://www

.healthaffairs.org/doi/10.1377/hlthaff.16.5.7; Chima D. Ndumele, William L. Schpero, Mark J. Schlesinger, and Amal N. Trivedi, "Association between Health Plan Exit from Medicaid Managed Care and Quality of Care, 2006–2014," *JAMA* 317, no. 24 (2017): 2524–2531, https://jamanetwork.com/journals/jama/fullarticle/2633914.

18. "Quality Requirements under Medicaid Managed Care," MACPAC [Medicaid and CHIP Payment and Access Commission], https://www.macpac.gov/subtopic /quality-requirements-under-medicaid-managed-care/ [accessed July 21, 2021].

19. AHIP [America's Health Insurance Plan], "New Study: Quality Performance Is Up Across the Board for Medicaid Managed Care Plans," press release, March 3, 2020, https://www.ahip.org/news/press-releases/new-study-quality-performance-is -up-across-the-board-for-medicaid-managed-care-plans/; Hinton and Raphael, "10 Things to Know."

20. Courtney R. Zott and Andrew M. Ryan, "Medicaid Managed Care: Further Reform Needed to Deliver on Promise," *AJMC* [*American Journal of Managed Care*] 27, no. 2 (2021): 53–56, https://www.ajmc.com/view/medicaid-managed-care-further -reform-needed-to-deliver-on-promise/.

21. Stephen Zuckerman, Laura Skopec, and Joshua Aarons, "Medicaid Physician Fees Remained Substantially below Fees Paid by Medicare in 2019," *Health Affairs* 40, no. 2 (2021): 343–348, https://www.healthaffairs.org/doi/abs/10.1377/hlthaff.2020 .00611.

22. GAO [U.S. Government Accountability Office], *Medicaid Payment: Comparisons of Selected Services under Fee-for-Service, Managed Care, and Private Insurance* (Washington, DC: U.S. Government Accountability Office, July 2014), https://www .gao.gov/assets/670/664782.pdf.

23. Kayla Holgash and Martha Heberlein, "Physician Acceptance of New Medicaid Patients: What Matters and What Does Not," *Health Affairs Forefront* (blog), *Health Affairs*, April 10, 2019, https://www.healthaffairs.org/content /forefront/physician-acceptance-new-medicaid-patients-matters-and-doesn-t/.

24. Steven B. Spivack, Genevra F. Murray, Hector P. Rodriguez, and Valerie A. Lewis, "Avoiding Medicaid: Characteristics of Primary Care Practices with No Medicaid Revenue," *Health Affairs* 40, no. 1 (2021): 98–104, https://www.healthaffairs .org/doi/abs/10.1377/hlthaff.2020.00100.

25. Pamela Herd and Donald Moynihan, *Administrative Burden: Policy Making by Other Means* (New York: Russel Sage Foundation, 2018).

26. Paradise, Lyon, and Rowland, *Medicaid at 50*, 7.

27. Centers for Disease Control and Prevention, "Nearly 44 Million in United States without Health Insurance in 2008," press release, July 1, 2009, https://www .cdc.gov/media/pressrel/2009/r090701.htm.

28. Barack Obama, *A Promised Land* (New York: Crown, 2020), 378.

29. Obama, *A Promised Land*, 379.

30. Ashley Kirzinger, Alex Montero, Liz Hamel, and Mollyann Brodie, "5 Charts about Public Opinion on the Affordable Care Act and the Supreme Court," KFF [Kaiser Family Foundation], April 14, 2022, https://www.kff.org/health-reform/poll

-finding/5-charts-about-public-opinion-on-the-affordable-care-act-and-the-supreme
-court/.

31. Paul Starr, *Remedy and Reaction: The Peculiar American Struggle over Health Care Reform* (New Haven, CT: Yale University Press, 2013), 23.

32. McDonough, *Inside National Health Reform*, 135; Karen Davis, "Expanding Medicare and Employer Plans to Achieve Universal Health Insurance," *JAMA* 265, no. 19 (1991): 2525–2528, https://jamanetwork.com/journals/jama/article-abstract /385940; Jacob S. Hacker, "Between the Waves: Building Power for a Public Option," *Journal of Health Politics, Policy and Law* 46, no. 4 (2021): 535–547, https://isps.yale .edu/research/publications/isps21-22.

33. McDonough, *Inside National Health Reform*, 67

34. Katherine Swartz and Deborah W. Garnick, "Lessons from New Jersey's Creation of a Market for Individual Health Insurance," *Journal of Health Politics, Policy and Law* 25, no.1 (2000): 45–70.

35. Katie Keith, "What It Means to Cover Preexisting Conditions," *Health Affairs Forefront* (blog), *Health Affairs*, September 11, 2020, https://www.healthaffairs.org /content/forefront/means-cover-preexisting-conditions/.

36. McDonough, *Inside National Health Reform*, 69.

37. McDonough, *Inside National Health Reform*, 117.

38. McDonough, *Inside National Health Reform*, 128.

39. Matthew Fiedler, "The Case for Replacing 'Silver Loading,'" Brookings, May 20, 2021, https://www.brookings.edu/essay/the-case-for-replacing-silver-loading/.

40. Stan Dorn and Timothy Jost, "ACA Metal-Tier Mispricing: Improving Affordability by Solving an Actuarial Mystery," *Health Affairs Forefront* (blog), *Health Affairs*, January 27, 2023, https://www.healthaffairs.org/content/forefront/aca-metal -tier-mispricing-improving-affordability-solving-actuarial-mystery/.

41. Molly Frean, Jonathan Gruber, and Benjamin Sommers, "Disentangling the ACA's Coverage Effects—Lessons for Policymakers," Perspective, *New England Journal of Medicine* 375, no. 17 (2016): 1605–1608, https://www.nejm.org/doi/full/10 .1056/NEJMp1609016.

42. Sarah Kliff, "Republicans Killed the Obamacare Mandate: New Data Shows It Didn't Really Matter," *New York Times*, September 18, 2020, updated September 21, 2021, https://www.nytimes.com/2020/09/18/upshot/obamacare-mandate-republi cans.html.

43. Julia Pak, "5 States Are Restoring the Individual Mandate to Buy Health Insurance," HealthCare Insider, March 19, 2021, https://healthcareinsider.com/states -with-individual-mandate-177178.

44. Vanessa C. Forsberg, *Overview of Health Insurance Exchanges* (Washington, DC: Congressional Research Service, updated March 2023), figure 1, https://fas.org /sgp/crs/misc/R44065.pdf.

45. Cynthia Cox, Karen Politz, Krutika Amin, and Jared Ortaliza, "Nine Changes to Watch in ACO Open Enrollment," KFF [Kaiser Family Foundation], October 27, 2022, https://www.kff.org/policy-watch/nine-changes-to-watch-in-open -enrollment-2023/.

46. Forsberg, *Overview*.

47. Forsberg, *Overview*.

48. Daniel McDermott, Nisha Kurani, Giorlando Ramirez, Nicolas Shanosky, and Cynthia Cox, "2021 Premium Changes on ACA Exchanges and the Impact of COVID-19 on Rates," KFF [Kaiser Family Foundation], October 19, 2020, https:// www.kff.org/private-insurance/issue-brief/2021-premium-changes-on-aca-exchanges -and-the-impact-of-covid-19-on-rates/.

49. ASPE [Office of the Assistant Secretary for Planning and Evaluation], "2021 Poverty Guidelines," February 1, 2021, https://aspe.hhs.gov/2021-poverty-guidelines/.

50. Helen Levy, Andrew Ying, and Nicholas Bagley, "What's Left of the Affordable Care Act? A Progress Report," *RSF: Russell Sage Foundation Journal of the Social Sciences* 6, no. 2 (2020): 42–66, https://www.rsfjournal.org/content/rsfjss/6/2 /42.full.pdf.

51. McDonough, *Inside National Health Reform*, 146.

52. Alison Mitchell, Angela Napili, Evelyne P. Baumrucker, Cliff Binder, Kirsten J. Colello, and Julia A. Keyser, *Medicaid: An Overview* (Washington, DC: Congressional Research Service, updated February 2021), https://crsreports.congress .gov/product/pdf/R/R43357/16.

53. Mitchell et al., *Medicaid*.

54. Sara Rosenbaum and Timothy M. Westmoreland, "The Supreme Court's Surprising Decision on the Medicaid Expansion: How Will the Federal Government and States Proceed?," Analysis & Commentary, *Health Affairs* 31, no. 8 (2021): 1663–1672, https://www.healthaffairs.org/doi/full/10.1377/hlthaff.2012.0766.

55. 567 U.S. 519 (2012).

56. Sara Rosenbaum, "Confronting the Consequences of *National Federation of Independent Business v. Sebelius* to Insure the Poor," *Quarterly Opinion* (blog), *Milbank Quarterly*, April 13, 2021, https://www.milbank.org/quarterly/opinions/confronting -the-consequences-of-national-federation-of-independent-business-v-sebelius-to -insure-the-poor/.

57. "Status of State Medicaid Expansion Decisions: Interactive Map," KFF [Kaiser Family Foundation], July 27, 2023, https://www.kff.org/medicaid/issue-brief /status-of-state-medicaid-expansion-decisions-interactive-map/.

58. "Exhibit 10. Medicaid Enrollment and Total Spending Levels and Annual Growth," MACPAC [Medicaid and CHIP Payment and Access Commission], December 2022, https://www.macpac.gov/publication/medicaid-enrollment-and-total -spending-levels-and-annual-growth/.

59. Bradley Coralio and Sophia Moreno, "Analysis of Recent National Trends in Medicaid and CHIP Enrollment during the COVID-19 Pandemic," KFF [Kaiser Family Foundation], April 4, 2023, https://www.kff.org/coronavirus-covid-19/issue-brief /analysis-of-recent-national-trends-in-medicaid-and-chip-enrollment/.

60. Madeline Guth, Rachel Garfield, and Robin Rudowitz, *The Effects of Medicaid Expansion under the ACA: Updated Findings from a Literature Review* (San Francisco: KFF [Kaiser Family Foundation], March 2020), https://files.kff.org/attachment

/Report-The-Effects-of-Medicaid-Expansion-under-the-ACA-Updated-Findings-from
-a-Literature-Review.pdf.

61.　Manatt, Phelps & Phillips, LLP, "Medicaid's Impact on Health Care Access,
Outcomes and State Economies," Robert Wood Johnson Foundation, February 1,
2019, https://www.rwjf.org/en/library/research/2019/02/medicaid-s-impact-on
-health-care-access-outcomes-and-state-economies.html.

62.　Elizabeth Rosenthal, "The End of the Covid Emergency Could Mean a Huge
Loss of Health Insurance," KFF [Kaiser Family Foundation] Health News, April 6,
2022, https://khn.org/news/article/the-end-of-the-covid-emergency-could-mean-a
-huge-loss-of-health-insurance/.

63.　Jennifer Tolbert, Patrick Drake, and Anthony Damico, "Key Facts about the
Uninsured Population," KFF [Kaiser Family Foundation], December 19, 2022,
https://www.kff.org/uninsured/issue-brief/key-facts-about-the-uninsured
-population/.

64.　U.S. Department of Health and Human Services, "New HHS Report Shows
National Uninsured Rate Reached All-Time Low in 2022," press release, August 2,
2022, https://www.hhs.gov/about/news/2022/08/02/new-hhs-report-shows-national
-uninsured-rate-reached-all-time-low-in-2022.html.

65.　Benjamin D. Sommers, "Health Insurance Coverage: What Comes after the
ACA?," *Health Affairs* 39, no. 3 (2020): 502–508, https://www.healthaffairs.org/doi
/abs/10.1377/hlthaff.2019.01416.

66.　John Holahan, Matthew Buettgens, Jessica S. Banthin, and Michael
Simpson, *Filling the Gap in States That Have Not Expanded Medicaid Eligibility* (New
York: Commonwealth Fund, June 2021, corrected October 2021), https://www
.commonwealthfund.org/publications/issue-briefs/2021/jun/filling-gap-states-not
-expanded-medicaid/.

67.　Patricia Mae G. Santos, Kanan Shah, Francesca M. Gany, and Fumiko Chino,
"Health Reform and Equity for Undocumented Immigrants—When Crisis Meets
Opportunity," *New England Journal of Medicine* 388, no. 9 (2023): 771–773, https://
www.nejm.org/doi/full/10.1056/NEJMp2213751.

68.　"Baseline Projections: Medicaid," Congressional Budget Office, May 2022,
https://www.cbo.gov/system/files/2022-05/51301-2022-05-medicaid.pdf.

69.　Rabah Kamal and Julie Hudman, "What Do We Know about Spending
Related to Public Health in the U.S. and Comparable Countries?," Peterson-KFF
[Kaiser Family Foundation] Health System Tracker, September 30, 2020, https://
www.healthsystemtracker.org/chart-collection/what-do-we-know-about-spending
-related-to-public-health-in-the-u-s-and-comparable-countries/#item-start/.

70.　Y. Natalia Alfonso, Jonathon P. Leider, Beth Resnick, J. Mac McCullough,
and David Bishal, "US Public Health Neglected: Flat or Declining Spending Left
States Ill Equipped to Respond to COVID-19," *Health Affairs* 40, no. 4 (2021): 664–671,
https://www.healthaffairs.org/doi/full/10.1377/hlthaff.2020.01084.

71.　Levy, Ying, and Bagley, "What's Left," 56.

72.　McDonough, *Inside National Health Reform*, 180.

73. Phil Galewitz, "Obamacare Co-Ops down from 23 to Final '3 Little Miracles,'" KFF [Kaiser Family Foundation] Health News, September 9, 2020, https://khn.org/news/obamacare-co-ops-down-from-23-to-final-3-little-miracles/.

74. Sabrina Corlette, Sean Miskell, Julia Lerche, and Justin Giovannelli, *Why Are Many CO-OPS Failing? How New Nonprofit Health Plans Have Responded to Market Competition* (New York: Commonwealth Fund, December 2015), https://www.commonwealthfund.org/sites/default/files/documents/___media_files_publications_fund_report_2015_dec_1847_corlette_why_are_many_coops_failing.pdf.

75. Brad Smith, "CMS Innovation Center at 10 Years—Progress and Lessons Learned," Sounding Board, *New England Journal of Medicine* 384, no. 8 (2021): 759–764, https://www.nejm.org/doi/full/10.1056/NEJMsb2031138.

76. Philip Rocco and Andrew S. Kelly, "An Engine of Change? The Affordable Care Act and the Shifting Politics of Demonstration Projects," *RSF: Russell Sage Foundation Journal of Social Science* 6, no. 2 (2020): 67–84, https://www.rsfjournal.org/content/rsfjss/6/2/67.full.pdf.

77. Smith, "CMS Innovation Center."

78. Melinda Beeuwkes Buntin and John A. Graves, "How the ACA Dented the Cost Curve," *Health Affairs* 39, no. 3 (2020): 403–412, https://www.healthaffairs.org/doi/abs/10.1377/hlthaff.2019.01478.

79. David Blumenthal and Melinda Abrams, "The Affordable Care Act at 10 Years—Payment and Delivery System Reforms," *New England Journal of Medicine* 382, no. 11 (2020): 1057–1063, https://www.nejm.org/doi/full/10.1056/NEJMhpr1916092.

Chapter 8. Entering the 2020s

1. Expert Panel® Forbes Councils Member, "15 Human Resources Goals Every Company Should Set for Q1 2021," *Forbes*, December 30, 2020, https://www.forbes.com/sites/forbeshumanresourcescouncil/2021/12/30/15-human-resources-goals-every-company-should-set-for-q1-2021/?sh=76dc9aab66aa.

2. Gary Claxton, Matthew Rae, Emma Wagner, Gregory Young, Heidi Whitmore, Jason Kearns, Greg Shmavonia, and Anthony Damico, "Section 5: Market Share of Health Plans," *Employer Health Benefits: 2022 Annual Survey* (San Francisco: Kaiser Family Foundation, 2022), 73, https://files.kff.org/attachment/Report-Employer-Health-Benefits-2022-Annual-Survey.pdf.

3. Claxton et al., "Section 1: Cost of Health Insurance," *2022 Annual Survey*, 40, https://files.kff.org/attachment/Report-Employer-Health-Benefits-2022-Annual-Survey.pdf.

4. Paul Lendner, "With Direct Contracting Boeing Cuts Out the Middleman," Managed Care, https://www.managedcaremag.com/archives/2017/11/direct-contracting-boeing-cuts-out-middleman/.

5. Michael F. Furukawa, Laura Kimmey, David J. Jones, Rachel M. Machta, Jing Guo, and Eugene C. Rich, "Consolidation of Providers into Health Systems Increased Substantially, 2016–18," *Health Affairs* 39, no. 8 (2020): 1321–1325, https://www.healthaffairs.org/doi/10.1377/hlthaff.2020.00017.

6. Michael Cohen, Jared Maeda, and Daria Pelech, *The Prices That Commercial Health Insurers and Medicare Pay for Hospital and Physician Services* (Washington, DC: Congressional Budget Office, January 2022), https://www.cbo.gov/publication /57778.

7. Nancy Beaulieu, Leemore S. Dafny, Bruce E. Landon, Jesse B. Dalton, Ifedayo Kuye, and J. Michael McWilliams, "Changes in Quality of Care after Hospital Mergers and Acquisitions," Special Article, *New England Journal of Medicine* 382, no.1 (2020): 51–59, https://www.nejm.org/doi/full/10.1056/NEJMsa1901383.

8. Leemore Dafny, Mark Duggan, and Subramaniam Ramanarayanan, "Paying a Premium on Your Premium? Consolidation in the US Health Insurance Industry," *American Economic Review* 102, no. 2 (2012): 1161–1185, https://pubs.aeaweb.org/doi /pdfplus/10.1257/aer.102.2.1161.

9. Leemore S. Dafny, "Good Riddance to Big Insurance Mergers," *New England Journal of Medicine* 376, no. 19 (2017): 1804–1806, https://www.nejm.org/doi/full/10 .1056/NEJMp1616553.

10. Leemore S. Dafny, "Does CVS-Aetna Spell the End of Business as Usual?," Perspective, *New England Journal of Medicine* 378, no. 7 (2018): 593–595, https://www .nejm.org/doi/full/10.1056/NEJMp1717137.

11. Leemore Dafny, "Address Consolidation in Health Care Markets," Viewpoint, *JAMA* 325, no. 10 (2021): 927–928, https://jamanetwork.com/journals/jama /fullarticle/2776037.

12. Traci Prevost, Ion Skillrun, Windy Gerhardt, and Debanshu Mukherjee, "The Potential for Rapid Consolidation of Health Systems: How Can Hospitals Use M&A to Innovate for the Future?," *Deloitte Insights* (blog), *Deloitte*, December 10, 2020, https://www2.deloitte.com/us/en/insights/industry/health-care/hospital -mergers-acquisition-trends.html.

13. U.S. Bureau of Labor Statistics, "Employee Tenure in 2022," news release no. USDL-22-1894, September 22, 2022, https://www.bls.gov/news.release/pdf/tenure.pdf.

14. Ryan J. Russo, Bernadette Fernandez, Vanessa Forsberg, and Katherine M. Kehres, *Federal Requirements on Private Health Insurance Plans* (Washington, DC: Congressional Research Service, updated March 2023), https://fas.org/sgp/crs/misc /R45146.pdf.

15. Katie Keith, "Fifth Circuit Upholds Ruling Greenlighting Non-ACA Arrange-ments," *Health Affairs Forefront* (blog), *Health Affairs*, August 23, 2022, https://www .healthaffairs.org/content/forefront/fifth-circuit-upholds-ruling-greenlighting-non -aca-arrangements/.

16. "Average Wage Index," Social Security Administration, https://www.ssa.gov /oact/cola/awidevelop.html [accessed September 24, 2023].

17. Claxton et al., "Section 6: Worker and Employer Contributions for Premi-ums," *2022 Annual Survey*, 79–80.

18. Stephen Miller, "IRS Raises 2021 Employer Health Plan Affordability Threshold to 9.83% of Pay," SHRM [Society for Human Resources Management], updated September 4, 2020, https://www.shrm.org/resourcesandtools/hr-topics

/benefits/pages/irs-raises-2021-affordability-threshold-for-employer-health-plans
.aspx.

19.   Troyen A, Brennan, *Just Doctoring: Medical Ethics in the Liberal State*
(Berkeley: University of California Press, 1991).

20.   Sherry A. Glied and Benjamin Zhu, *Catastrophic Out-of-Pocket Health Care
Costs: A Problem Mainly for Middle Income Americans with Employer Coverage* (New
York: Commonwealth Fund, April 2020), https://www.commonwealthfund.org
/publications/issue-briefs/2020/apr/catastrophic-out-of-pocket-costs-problem
-middle-income/.

21.   Sara R. Collins, Munira Z. Gunja, and Gabriella N. Aboulafia, "U.S. Health
Insurance Coverage in 2020: A Looming Crisis in Affordability," Issue Briefs,
Commonwealth Fund, August 19, 2020, https://www.commonwealthfund.org
/publications/issue-briefs/2020/aug/looming-crisis-health-coverage-2020-biennial/.

22.   Raymond Kluender, Neale Mahoney, Francis Wong, and Wesley Yin,
"Medical Debt in the US: 2009–2020," *JAMA* 326, no. 3 (2021): 250–256, https://
jamanetwork.com/journals/jama/article-abstract/2782187.

23.   David U. Himmelstein, Samuel L. Dickman, Danny McCormick, David H.
Bor, Adam Gaffney, and Steffie Woolhandler, "Prevalence and Risk Factors for
Medical Debt and Subsequent Changes in Social Determinants of Health in the US,"
JAMA Network Open 5, no. 9 (2022): e2231898, https://jamanetwork.com/journals
/jamanetworkopen/fullarticle/2796358.

24.   Caroline Hudson, "Insured Patients Become Top Reason for Bad Debt at
Providers," Modern Healthcare, August 23, 2022, https://www.modernhealthcare
.com/finance/insured-patients-become-top-reason-bad-debt-providers/.

25.   John A. Poisal, Andrea M. Sisko, Gigi A. Cuckler, Sheila D. Smith, Sean P.
Keehan, Jacqueline A. Fiore, Andrew J. Madison, and Kathryn E. Rennie, "National
Health Expenditure Projections, 2021–30: Growth to Moderate as COVID-19 Wanes,"
Health Affairs 41, no. 4 (2022): 474–486, https://www.healthaffairs.org/doi/10.1377
/hlthaff.2022.00113.

26.   Michael E. Chernew, "National Health Expenditure Projections and a Few
Ways We Might Avoid Our Fate," *Health Affairs Forefront* (blog), *Health Affairs*,
March 28, 2022, https://www.healthaffairs.org/do/10.1377/forefront.20220324.48476.

27.   Anne B. Martin, Micah Hartman, Joseph Benson, and Aaron Catlin,
"National Health Care Spending in 2021: Decline in Federal Spending Outweighs
Greater Use of Health Care," *Health Affairs* 42, no. 1 (2023): 6–17, https://www
.healthaffairs.org/doi/10.1377/hlthaff.2022.01397.

28.   Michael E. Chernew, Maximilian J. Pany, and Leemore S. Dafny, "Two
Approaches to Capping Health Care Costs," *Health Affairs Forefront* (blog), *Health
Affairs*, March 31, 2022, https://www.healthaffairs.org/do/10.1377/forefront
.20220329.385487/full/.

29.   Robert A. Berenson and Robert B. Murray, "How Price Regulation Is Needed
to Advance Market Competition," *Health Affairs* 41, no. 1 (2022): 26–34, https://www
.healthaffairs.org/doi/full/10.1377/hlthaff.2021.01235.

30.   Troyen A. Brennan, "Maryland Hospital All-Payer Model: Can It Be Emulated?," *Health Affairs Forefront* (blog), *Health Affairs*, May 31, 2022, https://www.healthaffairs.org/do/10.1377/forefront.20220526.939479.

31.   Aaron Baum, Zirui Song, Bruce E. Landon, Russell S. Phillips, Asaf Bitton, and Sanjay Basu, "Health Care Spending Slowed after Rhode Island Applied Affordability Standards to Commercial Insurers," *Health Affairs* 38, no. 2 (2019): 237–245, https://www.healthaffairs.org/doi/10.1377/hlthaff.2018.05164.

32.   Jake Spiegel and Paul Fronstin, "What Employers Say about the Future of Employer-Sponsored Insurance," Issue Briefs, Commonwealth Fund, January 26, 2023, https://www.commonwealthfund.org/publications/issue-briefs/2023/jan/what-employers-say-future-employer-health-insurance/.

33.   William C. Hsiao, Peter Braun, Daniel Dunn, and Edmund R. Becker, "Resource-Based Relative Values: An Overview," *JAMA* 260, no. 16 (1988): 2347–2353, https://jamanetwork.com/journals/jama/article-abstract/374653.

34.   "RVS Update Committee (RUC)," AMA [American Medical Association], updated August 1, 2023, https://www.ama-assn.org/about/rvs-update-committee-ruc/rvs-update-committee-ruc/.

35.   W. D. Donovan, "What Is the RUC?," *AJNR: American Journal of Neuroradiology* 32, no. 9 (2011): 1583–1584, https://www.ncbi.nlm.nih.gov/pmc/articles/PMC7965394.

36.   Uwe E. Reinhardt, "The Little-Known Decision-Makers for Medicare Physician Fees," *Economix* (blog), *New York Times*, December 10, 2011, http://economix.blogs.nytimes.com/2010/12/10/the-little-known-decision-makers-for-medicare-physicans-fees/.

37.   David C. Chan, Johnny Huynh, and David M. Studdert, "Accuracy of Valuations of Surgical Procedures in the Medicare Fee Schedule," *New England Journal of Medicine* 380, no. 16 (2019): 1546–1554, https://www.nejm.org/doi/full/10.1056/NEJMsa1807379; John W. Urwin, Emily Gudbranson, Danielle Graham, Dawei Xie, Eric Hume, and Ezekiel J. Emanuel, "Accuracy of the Relative Value Scale Update Committee's Time Estimates and Physician Fee Schedule for Joint Replacement," *Health Affairs* 38, no. 7 (2019): 1079–1086, https://www.healthaffairs.org/doi/abs/10.1377/hlthaff.2018.05456?mi=78999w&af=R&AllField=test&target=default/.

38.   John W. Urwin and Ezekiel J. Emanuel, "The Relative Value Scale Update Committee: Time for an Update," Viewpoint, *JAMA* 322, no. 12 (2019): 1137–1138, https://jamanetwork.com/journals/jama/fullarticle/2751242.

39.   Brian Klepper, "The RUC, Health Care Finance's Star Chamber, Remains Untouchable," *Health Affairs Forefront* (blog), *Health Affairs*, February 1, 2013, https://www.healthaffairs.org/content/forefront/ruc-health-care-finance-s-star-chamber-remains-untouchable/.

40.   Robert Berenson and John Goodson, "Finding Value in Unexpected Places—Fixing Medicare Physician Fee Schedule," *New England Journal of Medicine* 374, no. 14 (2016): 1306–1308, https://www.nejm.org/doi/full/10.1056/NEJMp1600999.

41.   Clifford Marks, "America's Looming Primary-Care Crisis," *New Yorker*, July 25, 2020, https://www.newyorker.com/science/medical-dispatch/americas-looming-primary-care-crisis/.

42. Laurence F. McMahon, Kim Rize, NiJuanna Irby-Johnson, and Vineet Chopra, "Designed to Fail? The Future of Primary Care," *Journal of General Internal Medicine* 36, no. 2 (2021): 515–517, https://www.ncbi.nlm.nih.gov/pmc/articles/PMC7390445.

43. Linda McCauley, Robert L. Phillips, Marc Meisnere, and Sarah K. Robinson, eds., *Implementing High-Quality Primary Care: Rebuilding the Foundation of Health Care* (Washington, DC: National Academies Press, May 2021), https://nap.nationalacademies.org/read/25983/chapter/4.

44. Deborah Peikes, Erin Fries Taylor, Ann S. O'Malley, and Eugene C. Rich, "The Changing Landscape of Primary Care: Effects of the ACA and Other Efforts over the Past Decade," *Health Affairs* 39, no. 3 (2020): 421–428, https://www.healthaffairs.org/doi/abs/10.1377/hlthaff.2019.01430.

45. Celli Horstman, Corinne Lewis, and Melinda K. Abrams, "Strengthening Primary Health Care: The Importance of Payment Reform," *To the Point* (blog), *Commonwealth Fund*, December 10, 2021, https://www.commonwealthfund.org/blog/2021/strengthening-primary-health-care-importance-payment-reform/.

46. Rachel O. Reid, Ashlyn K. Tom, Rachel M. Ross, Erin L. Duffy, and Cheryl L. Damberg, "Physician Compensation Arrangements and Financial Performance Incentives in US Health Systems," *JAMA Health Forum* 3, no. 1 (2022): e214634, https://jamanetwork.com/journals/jama-health-forum/fullarticle/2788514.

47. Kelly L. Lenahan, Donald E. Nichols, Rebecca M. Gertler, and James D. Chambers, "Variation in Use and Content of Prescription Drug Step Therapy Protocols, within and across Health Plans," *Health Affairs* 40, no. 11 (2021): 1749–1757, https://www.healthaffairs.org/doi/pdf/10.1377/hlthaff.2021.00822.

48. Steven D. Pearson, Molly Bewinfeld, Noemi Fluetsch, Maggie O'Grady, Kanya Shah, and Sarah K. Emond, *Assessment of Barriers to Fair Access* (Boston: Institute for Clinical and Economic Review, December 2021), https://icer.org/wp-content/uploads/2021/05/Barriers-to-Fair-Access-Assessment-Final-Report-120121.pdf.

49. Zarek C. Brot-Goldberg, Samantha Burn, Timothy Layton, and Boris Vabson, "Rationing Medicine Through Bureaucracy: Authorization Restrictions in Medicare," Working Paper no. 30878, National Bureau of Economic Research, Cambridge, MA, January 2023, https://www.nber.org/papers/w30878.

50. AMA [American Medical Association], "2022 Update: Measuring Progress in Improving Prior Authorization," https://www.ama-assn.org/system/files/prior-authorization-reform-progress-update.pdf [accessed September 24, 2023].

51. Tiernan Meyer, Rebecca Yip, Yonaton Mengesha, Daymelis Santiesteban, and Richard Hamilton, *Utilization Management Trends in the Commercial Market, 2014–2020* (Washington, DC: Avalere Health, November 2021), https://avalere.com/wp-content/uploads/2021/11/UM-Trends-in-the-Commercial-Market.pdf.

52. Wendy Warring and Lauren E. M. Bedel, *Streamlining Prior Authorization: Final Report & Recommendations* (Boston: NEHI [Network for Excellence in Health Innovation], September 2021), https://www.nehi-us.org/reports/streamlining-prior-authorization/.

53. "2022 AMA Prior Authorization (PA) Physician Survey," AMA [American Medical Association], https://www.ama-assn.org/system/files/prior-authorization -survey.pdf [accessed September 24, 2023].

54. Warring and Bedel, *Streamlining Prior Authorization*.

55. CAQH [Council for Affordable Quality Healthcare] Explorations, *2020 CAQH Index; Closing the Gap; The Industry Continues to Improve, but Opportunities for Automation Remain* (Washington, DC: CAQH [Council for Affordable Quality Healthcare], 2020), https://www.caqh.org/sites/default/files/explorations/index /2020-caqh-index.pdf.

56. Rayyan Abid, "Evaluating Physician Burnout and the Need for Organizational Support," *Missouri Medicine* 118, no. 3 (2021): 185–190, https://www .ncbi.nlm.nih.gov/pmc/articles/PMC8211002.

57. Joey Berlin, "TMA Gets a Win on Anti-Medication-Switching Bill," Texas Medical Association, May 6, 2021, https://www.texmed.org/TexasMedicineDetail .aspx?id=56795&utm_source=Informz&utm_medium.

58. CMS [Centers for Medicare & Medicaid Services], "CMS Proposes Rule to Expand Access to Health Information and Improve the Prior Authorization Process," press release, December 6, 2022, https://www.cms.gov/newsroom/press-releases /cms-proposes-rule-expand-access-health-information-and-improve-prior -authorization-process/.

59. Uwe E. Reinhardt, "The Disruptive Innovation of Price Transparency in Health Care," *JAMA* 310, no. 18 (2013): 1927–1928, https://jamanetwork.com /journals/jama/article-abstract/1769895.

60. "Hospital Price Transparency," CMS [Centers for Medicare & Medicaid Services], last modified June 20, 2023, https://www.cms.gov/hospital-price -transparency/; "Consumer Information and Insurance Oversight," CMS [Centers for Medicare & Medicaid Services], last modified March 23, 2022, https://www.cms .gov/cciio/.

61. Dan Diamond, "Nearly All Hospitals Flout Federal Requirement to Post Prices, Report Finds," *Washington Post*, July 16, 2021, https://www.washingtonpost .com/health/2021/07/16/hospital-cost-transparency/.

62. Harris Meyer and Kaiser Health News, "New Trump Administration Rule Directs Insurers to Reveal What They Pay for Prescriptions," *Fortune*, November 19, 2020, https://fortune.com/2020/11/19/health-insurance-prescription-drug-out-of -pocket-costs-trump-administration/.

63. Paige Minemyer, "PCMA, Chamber of Commerce Sue to Block Trump Admin's Insurer Transparency Rule," Fierce Healthcare, August 12, 2021, https://www .fiercehealthcare.com/payer/pcma-chamber-commerce-sue-to-block-trump-admin-s -insurer-transparency-rule/.

64. Troyen A. Brennan and William H. Shrank, "New Regulation for Pharmacy Benefit Managers," Health Affairs Forefront, August 25, 2023, https://www .healthaffairs.org/content/forefront/new-regulation-pharmacy-benefit-managers/.

65. Jack Hoadley, Kevin Lucia, and Maanasa Kona, "States Efforts to Protect Consumers from Balance Billing," *To the Point* (blog), *Commonwealth Fund*, January 18, 2019, https://www.commonwealthfund.org/blog/2019/state-efforts-protect -consumers-balance-billing/.

66. Jane M. Zhu, "Private Equity Investment in Physician Practices: New Study Describes Recent Acquisitions," Leonard Davis Institute of Health Economics, February 15, 2020, https://ldi.upenn.edu/our-work/research-updates/private-equity -investment-in-physician-practices/.

67. Issac Arnsdorf, "How Rich Investors, Not Doctors, Profit from Marking Up ER Bills," ProPublica, June 12, 2020, https://www.propublica.org/article/how-rich -investors-not-doctors-profit-from-marking-up-er-bills/.

68. "Surprise Medical Bills: New Protections for Consumers Take Effect in 2022," KFF [Kaiser Family Foundation], February 4, 2021, https://www.kff.org /private-insurance/fact-sheet/surprise-medical-bills-new-protections-for-consumers -take-effect-in-2022/.

69. Jack Hoadley, Madeline O'Brien, and Kevin Lucia, *No Surprises Act: A Federal-State Partnership to Protect Consumers from Surprise Medical Bills* (New York: Commonwealth Fund, October 2022), https://www.commonwealthfund.org /publications/fund-reports/2022/oct/no-surprises-act-federal-state-partnership -protect-consumers/.

70. Rachel Cohrs, "Federal Court Strikes Down Part of HHS Surprise Billing Rule," Stat, February 23, 2022, https://www.statnews.com/2022/02/23/federal-court -strikes-down-hhs-surprise-billing-rules/.

71. Benjamin L. Chartock, Loren Adler, Bich Ly, Erin Duffy, and Erin Trish, "Arbitration over Out-of-Network Medical Bills: Evidence from New Jersey Payment Disputes," *Health Affairs* 40, no. 1 (2021): 130–137, https://www.healthaffairs.org/doi /abs/10.1377/hlthaff.2020.00217.

72. "More Than 2 Million Surprise Bills Avoided During January–February 2022," AHIP [America's Health Insurance Plan] and BlueCross BlueShield Association, May 2022, https://www.ahip.org/documents/202205-AHIP-BCBSA_NSA -Survey-v02.pdf.

73. Tianna Tu, David Muhlstein, S. Lawrence Kocot, and Ross White, *Origins and Future of Accountable Care Organizations* (Washington, DC: Brookings Institution, May 2015), https://www.brookings.edu/wp-content/uploads/2016/06/impact-of -accountable-careorigins-052015.pdf.

74. D. Muhlstein, A. Croshaw, T. Merrill, C. Pena, and B. James, "The Accountable Care Paradigm: More Than Just Managed Care 2.0," May 22, 2013 [no longer available online].

75. Michael Zhu, Robert S. Saunders, David Muhlstein, William Bleser, and Mark B. McClellan, "The Medicare Shared Saving Program in 2020: Positive Movement (and Uncertainty) during a Pandemic," *Health Affairs Forefront* (blog), *Health Affairs*, October 14, 2021, https://www.healthaffairs.org/do/10.1377/forefront.20211008.785640.

76.   J. Michael McWilliams, Laura A. Hatfield, Bruce E. Landon, Pasha Hamed, and Michael E. Chernew, "Medicare Spending after 3 Years of the Medicare Shared Savings Program," *New England Journal of Medicine* 379, no. 12 (2018): 1139–1149, https://www.nejm.org/doi/full/10.1056/nejmsa1803388.

77.   Sherrie Wang, Frank McStay, Robert S. Saunders, David Muhlstein, William K. Bleser, and Mark B. McClellan, "Performance Results of the Medicare Shared Savings Program in 2021: Continued Uncertainty with Positive Movement," *Health Affairs Forefront* (blog), *Health Affairs*, October 30, 2022, https://www .healthaffairs.org/content/forefront/performance-results-medicare-shared-savings -program-2021-continued-uncertainty-positive/.

78.   Matthew J. Trombley, J. Michael McWilliams, Betty Fout, and Brant Morefield, "ACO Investment Model Produced Savings, but the Majority of Partici- pants Exited When Faced with Downside Risk," *Health Affairs* 41, no. 1 (2022): 138–146, https://www.healthaffairs.org/doi/full/10.1377/hlthaff.2020.01819.

79.   "Largest Medicare Risk Program Failing to Ignite Volume-to-Value Transi- tion," Gist Health Care, October 21, 2022, https://gisthealthcare.com/wp-content /uploads/2022/10/MSSP-Value-Image.png.

80.   William K. Bleser, Frank McStay, David Muhlestein, and Mark B. McClellan, "Accountable Care in 2023: Evolving Terminology, Current State, and Priorities," *Health Affairs Forefront* (blog), *Health Affairs*, February 24, 2023, https://www .healthaffairs.org/content/forefront/accountable-care-2023-evolving-terminology -current-state-and-priorities/.

81.   David Muhlestein, William K. Bleser, Robert S. Saunders, and Mark B. McClellan, "All-Payer Spread of ACOs and Value-Based Payment Models in 2021: The Crossroads and Future of Value-Based Care," *Health Affairs Forefront* (blog), *Health Affairs*, June 17, 2021, https://www.healthaffairs.org/do/10.1377/forefront.20210609 .824799.

82.   Charmaine Girdish, Alina Rossina, Bryce S. Sutton, Alexis K. Parents, and Benjamin L. Howell, "The Longitudinal Impact of a Multistate Commercial Account- able Care Program on Cost, Use, and Quality," *Health Affairs* 41, no. 12 (2022): 1795–1803, https://www.healthaffairs.org/doi/epdf/10.1377/hlthaff.2022.00279.

83.   Rachael Matulis and Jim Lloyd, *The History, Evolution, and Future of Medicaid Accountable Care Organizations* (Hamilton, NJ: Center for Health Care Strategies, February 2018), https://www.chcs.org/media/ACO-Policy-Paper_022718.pdf.

84.   Douglas Jacobs, Porva Rawal, Liz Fowler, and Meena Seshamani, "Expand- ing Accountable Care's Reach among Medicare Beneficiaries," Perspective, *New England Journal of Medicine* 387, no.2 (2022): 99–102, https://www.nejm.org/doi/full /10.1056/NEJMp2202991.

85.   Center for Medicare & Medicaid Innovation, *2022 Report to Congress* (Baltimore: Centers for Medicare & Medicaid Services, 2022), https://innovation.cms .gov/data-and-reports/2022/rtc-2022.

86.   Rachel E. Yount, "CMS Announces Changes to the MSSP Designed to Increase Participation and Promote Equity within the MSSP," Mintz Consulting,

November 17, 2022, https://www.mintz.com/insights-center/viewpoints/2146/2022
-11-17-cms-announces-changes-mssp-designed-increase-mssp/.

87. "ACO REACH," CMS [Centers for Medicare & Medicaid Services], last
updated August 14, 2023, https://innovation.cms.gov/innovation-models/aco-reach/.

88. Ravi B. Parikh, Ezekiel J. Emanuel, Colleen M. Brensinger, Connor W. Boyle,
Eboni G. Price-Haywood, Jeffrey H. Burton, Sabrina B. Heltz, and Amol S. Navathe,
"Evaluation of Spending Differences between Beneficiaries in Medicare Advantage
and the Medicare Shared Savings Program," *JAMA Open Network* 5, no. 8 (2022):
e2228529, https://jamanetwork.com/journals/jamanetworkopen/fullarticle/2795554.

89. Jonah Comstock, "HIMSS Launches New Definition of Digital Health,"
Mobi Health News, March 10, 2020, https://www.mobihealthnews.com/news/himss
-launches-new-definition-digital-health/.

90. "Beyond Telehealth: Hybrid Care Enabled by One Platform, One Partner,"
Amwell [AmericanWell], https://business.amwell.com/converge-hybrid-care
-platform#:~:text=Our%20hybrid%20care%20enablement%20platform,improving%20
outcomes%20and%20reducing%20costs/ [accessed September 24, 2023].

91. Sadiq Y. Patel, Ateev Mehrotra, Haiden A. Huskamp, Lori Uscher-Pines,
Ishani Ganguli, and Michael Lawrence Barnett, "Variation in Telemedicine Use and
Outpatient Care during the COVID-19 Pandemic in the United States," *Health Affairs*
40, no. 2 (2021): 349–358, https://www.healthaffairs.org/doi/abs/10.1377/hlthaff
.2020.01786.

92. David C. Whitehead and Ateev Mehrotra, "The Growing Phenomenon of
'Virtual-First' Primary Care," *JAMA* 326, no. 23 (2021): 2365–2366, https://
jamanetwork.com/journals/jama/fullarticle/2786666.

93. "Take Charge of Your Health," Livongo, https://hello.livongo.com/GEN
/TLD/ [accessed September 24, 2023].

94. "How Sleepio Works," Sleepio, https://www.sleepio.com
/#howSleepioWorks/ [accessed September 24, 2023].

95. Hui Ling Soh, Roger C. Ho, Cyrus S. Ho, and Wilson W. Tam, "Efficacy of
Digital Cognitive Behavioral Therapy for Insomnia: A Meta-Analysis of Randomised
Controlled Trials," *Sleep Medicine* 75 (2020): 315–325, https://doi.org/10.1016/j.sleep
.2020.08.020.

96. Julia Adler-Milstein and Ateev Mehrotra, "Paying for Digital Health
Care—Problems with the Fee-for-Service System," Perspective, *New England Journal
of Medicine* 385, no. 10 (2021): 871–873, https://www.nejm.org/doi/full/10.1056
/NEJMp2107879.

97. Adriana Krasniansky, Megan Zweig, and Bill Evans, "H1 2021 Digital Health
Funding: Another Blockbuster Year . . . in Six Months," Rock Health, https://rock
health.com/reports/h1-2021-digital-health-funding-another-blockbuster-year-in-six
-months/.

98. Norman Levine, "Venture Capital and the Future of Dermatology: A Reassess-
ment," Dermatology Times, November 1, 2017, https://www.dermatologytimes.com
/view/venture-capital-and-future-dermatology-reassessment/.

99. "StartUps and Newcomers Disrupting Primary Care," MaC Venture Capital, https://macventurecapital.com/startups-and-newcomers-disrupting-primary-care/ [accessed September 24, 2023].

100. Heather Landi, "Crossover Health Scores $168M to Grow Primary Care Services for Employers, Health Plans," Fierce Health Care, March 31, 2021, https://www.fiercehealthcare.com/tech/heels-amazon-employee-clinic-expansion-crossover-health-scores-168m-series-d-round/.

101. Amy Farley, "This Startup Has Raised $600 Million to Give Lower-Income Americans Better Healthcare," Fast Company, March 2, 2023, https://www.fastcompany.com/90850515/cityblock-health-lower-income-better-healthcare#:~:text=This%20startup%20has%20raised%20%24600,lower%2Dincome%20Americans%20better%20healthcare/.

102. Paige Minemyer, "One Medical to Acquire Iora Health in $2.1B All-Stock Deal," Fierce Healthcare, June 7, 2021, https://www.fiercehealthcare.com/practices/one-medical-to-acquire-iora-health-2-1b-all-stock-deal/.

103. Jordan Anderson, Brian Powers, and Sachin H. Jain, "The Innovative Potential of Venture-Backed Primary Care," *Health Affairs Forefront* (blog), *Health Affairs*, May 16, 2016, https://www.healthaffairs.org/content/forefront/innovative-potential-venture-backed-primary-care/.

104. Indeed Editorial Team, "How Long Should You Stay at a Job? 6 Questions to Ask," Indeed, February 22, 2021, updated March 10, 2023, citing a 2020 Bureau of Labor Statistics study, https://www.indeed.com/career-advice/career-development/how-long-should-you-stay-at-a-job/.

105. Gretchen Jacobson, Tricia Neuman, and Anthony Damico, "Medicare Plan Switching: Exception or Norm?," KFF [Kaiser Family Foundation], September 20, 2016, https://www.kff.org/report-section/medicare-advantage-plan-switching-exception-or-norm-issue-brief/.

106. John Tozzi, "UnitedHealth Chases 10,000 More Doctors for Biggest U.S. Network," Bloomberg, March 5, 2021, https://www.bloomberg.com/news/articles/2021-03-05/unitedhealth-s-deal-machine-scoops-up-covid-hit-doctor-groups/.

107. Bruce Japsen, "Humana Buys $100 Million Stake in Doctor House Call Company, Heal," *Forbes*, July 29, 2020, https://www.forbes.com/sites/brucejapsen/2020/07/29/humana-buys-100-million-stake-in-primary-care-house-call-company-heal/?sh=50c4c80452b0.

108. Xenia Shih Bion, "Is Vertical Integration Bad for Health Care Consumers?," *CHCF Blog, California Health Care Foundation*, June 21, 2018, https://www.chcf.org/blog/is-vertical-integration-bad-consumers/.

109. Rick Goddard, "Healthcare Vertical Integration: Back to the Future," Insights, Lumeris, September 14, 2022, https://www.lumeris.com/healthcare-vertical-integration-back-to-the-future/.

110. Yashaswini Singh, Zirui Song, Daniel Polsky, Joseph D. Bruch, and Jane M. Zhu, "Association of Private Equity Acquisition of Physician Practices with Changes in Health Care Spending and Utilization," *JAMA Health Forum* 3, no. 9 (2022):

e222886, https://pubmed.ncbi.nlm.nih.gov/36218927; Amber La Forgia, Ameila M. Bond, Robert Tyler Braun, Leah Z. Yao, Klaus Kjaer, Manyao Zhang, and Lawrence P. Casalino, "Association of Physician Management Companies and Private Equity Investments with Commercial Health Care Prices Paid to Anesthesia Practitioners," *JAMA Internal Medicine* 182, no. 4 (2022): 396–404, https://pubmed.ncbi.nlm.nih.gov /35226052.

111.   Sherry Glied and Thomas D'Aunno, "Efficiency and Arbitrage in Health Services Innovation," *JAMA Health Forum* 3, no. 3 (2022): e220619, https:// jamanetwork.com/journals/jama-health-forum/fullarticle/2789838.

112.   Jeff Lagasse, "Moody's Downgrades Envision Healthcare, Says Bankruptcy Possible," Healthcare Finance, September 26, 2022, https://www.healthcarefinance news.com/news/moodys-downgrades-envision-healthcare-says-bankruptcy -possible/.

113.   Benjamin Goodair and Aaron Reeves, "Outsourcing Health-Care Services to the Private Sector and Treatable Mortality Rates in England, 2013–20: An Observational Study of NHS Privatisation," *Lancet Public Health* 7. no. 7 (2022): e638–e646, https://www.thelancet.com/pdfs/journals/lanpub/PIIS2468-2667(22)00133-5.pdf.

114.   Susan Rupe, "Most Workers Say They Are Satisfied with Their Employer's Health Benefits," Health/Employee Benefit News, July 25, 2022, https://insurance newsnet.com/innarticle/most-workers-say-they-are-satisfied-with-their-employer -health-benefits/.

115.   Avalere Health, *Return on Investment for Offering Employer-Sponsored Insurance* (Washington, DC: Avalere Health, June 2022), https://www.uschamber.com /assets/documents/20220622_Chamber-of-Commerce_ESI-White-Paper_Final.pdf.

116.   "Morgan Health: Improving Employer-Sponsored Health Care Requires Federal Policymakers to Prioritize Value-Based Reforms," JPMorgan Chase & Co., June 8, 2023, https://www.jpmorganchase.com/news-stories/morgan-health -improving-employer-sponsored-health-care/.

Chapter 9. The Evolution of American Health Insurance

1.   Liran Einav and Amy Finkelstein, *We've Got You Covered: Rebooting American Health Care* (New York: Portfolio/Penguin, 2023).

2.   "NHE [National Health Expenditures] Fact Sheet: Historical NHE, 2021," Centers for Medicare & Medicaid Services, September 6, 2023, https://www.cms.gov /data-research/statistics-trends-and-reports/national-health-expenditure-data/nhe -fact-sheet/.

3.   John Z. Ayanian, Bruce E. Landon, Alan M. Zaslavsky, Robert C. Saunders, L. Gregory Pawlson, and Joseph P. Newhouse, "Medicare Beneficiaries More Likely to Receive Appropriate Ambulatory Services in HMOs Than in Traditional Medicare," Better Medicare Alliance, June 1, 2017, https://bettermedicarealliance.org /publication/medicare-beneficiaries-more-likely-to-receive-appropriate-ambulatory -services-in-hmos-than-in-traditional-medicare/.

4.   Anna Wilde Matthews, "Physicians, Hospitals Meet Their New Competitor: Insurer-Owned Clinics," *Wall Street Journal*, February 23, 2020, https://www.wsj.com

/articles/physicians-hospitals-meet-their-new-competitor-insurer-owned-clinics
-11582473600; Chad Mulvany, "Analysis: Optum to Empower Its Physicians via
Advanced Analytics to Improve Care and Coordinate Referrals," *Innovation and
Disruption* (blog), *HFMA* [Healthcare Financial Management Association], September 9, 2019, https://www.hfma.org/topics/finance-and-business-strategy/article
/analysis-optum-empower-physicians-via-access-advanced-analytics.html.

5.   Humana, "Humana Announces New Primary Care Value-Based Model," press
release, December 10, 2020, https://press.humana.com/news/news-details/2020
/Humana-Announces-New-Primary-Care-Value-Based-Model/#gsc.tab=0.

6.   Walgreens, "Walgreens and VillageMD to Open 500 to 700 Full Service
Doctor Offices within Next Five Years in a Major Industry First," news release,
July 8, 2020, https://news.walgreens.com/press-center/news/walgreens-and
-villagemd-to-open-500-to-700-full-service-doctor-offices-within-next-five-years-in
-a-major-industry-first.htm.

7.   George C. Halvorsen, Stephen M. Shortell, Laurence Kotlikoff, Elizabeth
Mitchell, Richard M. Scheffler, John S. Toussaint, Peter A. Wadsworth, and Gail R.
Wilensky, "'Better Care Plan': A Public Option Choice," *Health Affairs Forefront* (blog),
Health Affairs, November 16, 2020, https://www.healthaffairs.org/content/forefront
/better-care-plan-public-option-choice/.

8.   Regina Herzlinger and Barak Richman, "Give Employees Cash to Purchase
Their Own Insurance," Harvard Business Review, December 9, 2020, https://hbr.org
/2020/12/give-employees-cash-to-purchase-their-own-insurance/.

9.   Regina E. Herzlinger, Richard J. Boxer, and James Wallace, "Bipartisan
Tax-Free Solution to Health Care Financing: Coupling HRAs with a Public Option,"
Health Affairs Forefront (blog), *Health Affairs*, June 30, 2020, https://www
.healthaffairs.org/content/forefront/bipartisan-tax-free-solution-health-care
-financing-coupling-hras-public-option/.

10.   Nikhil R. Sahni, Brandon Carrus, and David M. Cutler, "Administrative
Simplification and the Potential for Saving a Quarter-Trillion Dollars in Health Care,"
Viewpoint, *JAMA* 326, no. 17 (2021): 1677–1678, https://jamanetwork.com/journals
/jama/fullarticle/2785480.

11.   Nikhil R. Sahni, Prakriti Mishra, Brandon Carrus, and David M. Cutler,
*Administrative Simplification: How to Save a Quarter-Trillion Dollars in US Health Care;
Perspectives on the Productivity Imperative in US Healthcare Delivery* (Detroit: McKinsey Center for US Health System Reform, October 2021), https://www.mckinsey.com
/industries/healthcare/our-insights/administrative-simplification-how-to-save-a
-quarter-trillion-dollars-in-us-healthcare/.

12.   Sachin H. Jain, "Medicare for All? The Better Route to Universal Coverage
Would Be Medicare Advantage for All," Modern Healthcare, January 9, 2021,
https://www.modernhealthcare.com/opinion-editorial/medicare-all-better-route
-universal-coverage-would-be-medicare-advantage-all/.

13.   Paul B. Ginsburg and Steven M. Lieberman, "The Debate on Overpayment in
Medicare Advantage: Pulling It Together," *Health Affairs Forefront* (blog), *Health*

Affairs, February 24, 2022, https://www.healthaffairs.org/do/10.1377/forefront
.20220223.736815; Richard Gilfillan and Donald Berwick, "Born on Third Base:
Medicare Advantage Thrives on Subsidies, Not Better Care," *Health Affairs Forefront*
(blog), *Health Affairs*, March 27, 2023, https://www.healthaffairs.org/content
/forefront/born-third-base-medicare-advantage-thrives-subsidies-not-better-care/.

14.　Gretchen Jacobsen, Aimee Cicchiello, Janet P. Sutton, and Arnav Shah,
*Medicare Advantage vs. Traditional Medicare: How Do Beneficiaries' Characteristics and
Experiences Differ?* (New York: Commonwealth Fund, October 2021), https://www
.commonwealthfund.org/publications/issue-briefs/2021/oct/medicare-advantage-vs
-traditional-medicare-beneficiaries-differ/.

15.　MedPAC [Medicare Payment Advisory Committee], *Report to the Congress:
Medicare Payment Policy* (Washington, DC: MedPAC, March 2021), 356, https://www
.medpac.gov/wp-content/uploads/2021/10/mar21_medpac_report_ch12_sec.pdf.

16.　Douglas B. Jacobs, Michelle Schreiber, Meena Seshamani, Daniel Tsai,
Elizabeth Fowler, and Lee A. Fleisher, "Aligning Quality Measures across CMS—the
Universal Foundation," *New England Journal of Medicine* 388, no. 9 (2023): 776–779,
https://www.nejm.org/doi/full/10.1056/NEJMp2215539.

17.　Sherry Glied and Thomas D'Aunno, "Efficiency and Arbitrage in Health
Services Innovation," *JAMA Health Forum* 3, no. 3 (2022): e220619, https://
jamanetwork.com/journals/jama-health-forum/fullarticle/2789838.

18.　Ryan Crowley, Omar Atiq, and David Hilden, "Financial Profit in Medicine: A
Position Paper from the American College of Physicians," *Annals of Internal Medicine*
174, no. 10 (2021): 1447–1449, https://www.acpjournals.org/doi/full/10.7326/M21-1178.

19.　Robert Doherty, Thomas G. Cooney, Ryan D. Mire, Lee S. Engel, and
Jason M. Goldman, "Envisioning a Better U.S. Health Care System for All: A Call to
Action by the American College of Physicians," *Annals of Internal Medicine* 172, no. 2,
Suppl. (2020): S3–S6, https://www.acpjournals.org/doi/10.7326/M19-2411.

20.　Gary Claxton, Larry Levitt, Shawn Gremminger, Bill Kramer, and Matthew
Rae, "How Corporate Executives View Rising Health Care Cost and the Role of
Government," KFF [Kaiser Family Foundation] Health Reform, April 29, 2021,
https://www.kff.org/report-section/how-corporate-executives-view-rising-health
-care-cost-and-the-role-of-government-findings/.

21.　Bruce Japsen, "Progressives Won't Give Up on 'Medicare at 60' in Budget
Package," *Forbes*, July 14, 2021, https://www.forbes.com/sites/brucejapsen/2021/07/14
/progressives-wont-give-up-on-medicare-at-60-in-budget-package/?sh=3741c8164770.

22.　KFF [Kaiser Family Foundation], *Employer Health Benefits; 2022 Summary of
Findings* (Washington, DC: KFF [Kaiser Family Foundation], 2022), https://files.kff.org
/attachment/Summary-of-Findings-Employer-Health-Benefits-2022-Annual-Survey.pdf.

23.　Aaron Schwartz, Khalil Zlaoui, Robin P. Foreman, Troyen A. Brennan, and
Joseph P. Newhouse, "Health Care Utilization and Spending in Medicare Advantage
vs Traditional Medicare: A Difference-in-Differences Analysis," *JAMA Health Forum* 2,
no. 12 (2021): e214001, https://jamanetwork.com/journals/jama-health-forum
/fullarticle/2787081.

24. Eric Lopez, Tricia Neuman, Gretchen Jacobsen, and Larry Levitt, "How Much More Than Medicare Do Private Insurers Pay? A Review of the Literature," KFF [Kaiser Family Foundation], April 15, 2020, https://www.kff.org/medicare/issue -brief/how-much-more-than-medicare-do-private-insurers-pay-a-review-of-the -literature/.

25. Linda J. Blumberg, John Holahan, Stacey McMorrow, and Michael Simpson, *Estimating the Impact of a Public Option or Capping Provider Payment Rates* (Washington, DC: Urban Institute, March 2020), https://www.urban.org/sites/default/files /2020/03/23/estimating-the-impact-of-a-public-option-or-capping-provider-payment -rates.pdf.

26. John Holahan, Matthew Buettgens, Andrew Green, Michael Simpson, and Jessica Banthin, *Lowering the Age of Medicare Eligibility to 60: Effects on Coverage and Spending* (Washington, DC: Urban Institute, June 2022), https://www.urban.org /sites/default/files/2022-06/Lowering%20the%20Age%20of%20Medicare%20 Eligibility%20to%2060.pdf.

27. Kate Zernike, "The Hidden Subsidy That Helps Pay for Health Insurance," *New York Times*, July 7, 2017, https://www.nytimes.com/2017/07/07/health/health -insurance-tax-deduction.html.

28. Sherrod Brown, "Brown Reintroduces Legislation Allowing Retired First Responders to Buy Into Medicare at 50," news release, June 25, 2021, https://www .brown.senate.gov/newsroom/press/release/retired-first-responders-buy-medicare-50/.

29. John S. Toussaint, George Halvorson, Laurence Kotikoff, Richard Scheffler, Stephen M. Shortell, Peter Wadsworth, and Gail Wilensky, "How the Biden Administration Can Make a Public Option Work," Harvard Business Review, November 25, 2020, https://hbr.org/2020/11/how-the-biden-administration-can-make-a-public -option-work/.

30. Brad Smith, "CMS Innovation Center at 10 Years—Progress and Lessons Learned," *New England Journal of Medicine* 384, no. 8 (2021): 759–764, https://www .nejm.org/doi/full/10.1056/NEJMsb2031138.

31. Michael Zhu, Robert S. Saunders, David Muhlestein, William K. Bleser, and Mark B. McClellan, "The Medicare Shared Savings Program in 2020: Positive Movement (and Uncertainty) during a Pandemic," *Health Affairs Frontline* (blog), *Health Affairs*, October 14, 2021, https://www.healthaffairs.org/do/10.1377 /hblog20211008.785640/full/.

32. Imani Telesford, Shameek Rakshit, Matthew McGough, Emma Wagner, and Krutika Amin, "How Has US Spending on Healthcare Changed over Time?," Peterson-KFF [Kaiser Family Foundation] Health System Tracker, February 7, 2023, https://www.healthsystemtracker.org/chart-collection/u-s-spending-healthcare -changed-time/#item-start/.

33. Jeannie Fuglesten Biniek, Meredith Freed, Anthony Damico, and Tricia Neuman, "Medicare Advantage 2021 Spotlight: First Look," KFF [Kaiser Family Foundation], October 29, 2020, https://www.kff.org/medicare/issue-brief/medicare -advantage-2021-spotlight-first-look/.

34. J.D. Power, "Customers Perceive Shortfall in Medicare Advantage Plan Coverage of Mental Health and Substance Abuse Services, J.D. Power Finds," press release, August 18, 2022, https://www.jdpower.com/business/press-releases/2022-us-medicare-advantage-study/.

35. J.D. Power, "Normalizing Utilization and Pivot to Value-Based Care Delivery Models Present Opportunities for Employer-Sponsored Health Plans, J.D. Power Finds," press release, May 26, 2022, https://www.jdpower.com/business/press-releases/2022-us-commercial-member-health-plan-study/.

36. Justin W. Timble, Andy Bogart, Cheryl L. Damberg, Marc N. Elliott, Ann Haas, Sarah J. Gaillot, Elizabeth H. Goldstein, and Susan M. Paddock, "Medicare Advantage and Fee-for-Service Performance on Clinical Quality and Patient Experience Measures: Comparison from Three Large States," *Health Services Research* 52, no. 6 (2017): 2038–2060, https://www.ncbi.nlm.nih.gov/pmc/articles/PMC5682140.

37. Better Medicare Alliance, "Poll: Medicare Advantage Satisfaction Hits New High amid COVID-19 Crisis," press release, January 21, 2021, https://bettermedicarealliance.org/news/poll-medicare-advantage-satisfaction-hits-new-high-amid-covid-19-crisis/.

38. Momotazur Rahman, Laura Keohane, Amal N. Trivedi, and Vincent Mor, "High-Cost Patients Had Substantial Rates of Leaving Medicare Advantage and Joining Traditional Medicare," *Health Affairs* 34, no. 10 (2015): 117–189, https://pubmed.ncbi.nlm.nih.gov/26438743/.

39. Qijuan Li, Laura M. Keohane, Kali Thomas, Yoojin Lee, and Amal N. Trivedi, "Association of Cost-Sharing with Use of Home Health Services among Medicare Advantage Enrollees," *JAMA Internal Medicine* 177, no. 7 (2017): 1012–1018, https://jamanetwork.com/journals/jamainternalmedicine/fullarticle/2626195.

40. Sungchul Park, Lindsay White, Paul Fishman, Eric B. Larson, and Norma B. Coe, "Health Care Utilization, Care Satisfaction, and Health Status for Medicare Advantage and Traditional Medicare Beneficiaries with and without Alzheimer Disease and Related Dementia," *JAMA Network Open* 3, no. 3 (2020): e201809, https://jamanetwork.com/journals/jamanetworkopen/fullarticle/2763477.

41. David M. Dosa, Amal N. Trivedi, and Vincent Mor, "Implications of Medicare Advantage for Patients with Alzheimer Disease and Related Dementias," *JAMA Open Network* 3, no. 3 (2020): e201853, https://jamanetwork.com/journals/jamanetworkopen/fullarticle/2763472.

42. David J. Meyers, Amal N. Trivedi, Ira B. Wilson, Vincent Mor, and Momotazur Rahman, "Higher Medicare Advantage Ratings Are Associated with Improvements in Patient Outcomes," *Health Affairs* 40, no. 2 (2021): 243–250, https://www.healthaffairs.org/doi/pdf/10.1377/hlthaff.2020.00845.

43. David J. Meyers, Vincent Mor, Momotazur Rahman, and Amal N. Trivedi, "Growth in Medicare Advantage Greatest among Black and Hispanic Enrollees," *Health Affairs* 40, no. 6 (2021): 945–950, https://www.healthaffairs.org/doi/epdf/10.1377/hlthaff.2021.00118.

44. David J. Meyers, Momotazur Rahman, Vincent Mor, Ira B. Wilson, and Amal N. Trivedi, "Association of Medicare Advantage Star Ratings with Racial, Ethnic, and Socioeconomic Disparities in Quality of Care," *JAMA Health Forum* 2, no. 6 (2021): e210793, https://jamanetwork.com/journals/jama-health-forum /fullarticle/2781100.

45. Rachel R. Hardeman, Patricia A. Homan, Tongtan Chantarat, Brigette A. Davis, and Tyson H. Brown, "Improving the Measurement of Structural Racism to Achieve Antiracist Health Policy," *Health Affairs* 41, no. 2 (2022): 179–186, https:// www.healthaffairs.org/doi/full/10.1377/hlthaff.2021.01489.

46. Chiquita Brooks-LaSure, "My First 100 Days and Where to Go from Here: A Strategic Vision for CMS," *CMS.gov* (blog), *Centers for Medicare & Medicaid Services*, September 9, 2021, https://www.cms.gov/blog/my-first-100-days-and-where-we-go -here-strategic-vision-cms/.

47. Miriam Blümel and Reinhart Busse, "The German Health Care System," in 2020 *International Profiles of Health Care Systems*, ed. Roosa Tikkanen, Robin Osborn, Elias Mossialos, Ana Djordjevic, and George Wharton (New York: Commonwealth Fund, December 2020), https://www.commonwealthfund.org/sites/default/files /2020-12/International_Profiles_of_Health_Care_Systems_Dec2020.pdf.

48. Michael K. Gusmano, Miriam Laugesen, Victor G. Rodwin, and Lawrence D. Brown, "Getting the Price Right: How Some Countries Control Spending in a Fee-for-Service System," *Health Affairs* 39, no. 11 (2020): 1867–1874, https://www .healthaffairs.org/doi/10.1377/hlthaff.2019.01804.

49. Ezekiel Emanuel, *Which Country Has the Best Health Care?* (New York: Public Affairs, 2020), 170.

50. Richard Gilfillan and Donald Berwick, "Born on Third Base: Medicare Advantage Thrives on Subsidies, Not Better Care," *Health Affairs Forefront* (blog), *Health Affairs*, March 27, 2023, https://www.healthaffairs.org/content/forefront/born -third-base-medicare-advantage-thrives-subsidies-not-better-care/.

Chapter 10. Medicare for All

1. John Z. Ayanian, "Crucial Questions for the US Health Policy in the Next Decade," Editorial, *JAMA* 325, no. 14 (2021): 1397–1399, https://jamanetwork.com /journals/jama/fullarticle/2778510.

2. Ezekiel J. Emanuel, "The Near Term Future of Health Care Reforms," Editorial, *JAMA* 325, no. 14 (2021): 1394–1397, https://jamanetwork.com/journals /jama/fullarticle/2778508.

3. Bob Kocher and Rahul Rajkumar, "Setting the Stage for the Next Ten Years of Health Care Payment Innovation," Viewpoint, *JAMA* 326, no. 10 (2021): 905–906, https://jamanetwork.com/journals/jama/fullarticle/2783356.

4. Cynthia Cox, Robin Rudowitz, Juliette Cubanski, Karen Pollitz, MaryBeth Musumeci, Usah Ranji, Michelle Long, Meredith Freed, and Tricia Neuman, "Potential Costs and Impact of Health Provisions in the Build Back Better Act," KFF [Kaiser Family Foundation], November 23, 2021, https://www.kff.org/health-costs/issue-brief /potential-costs-and-impact-of-health-provisions-in-the-build-back-better-act/.

5. CMS [Centers for Medicare & Medicaid Services], "The Inflation Reduction Act Lowers Health Care Costs for Millions of Americans," press release, October 5, 2022, https://www.cms.gov/newsroom/fact-sheets/inflation-reduction-act-lowers -health-care-costs-millions-americans/.

6. Colin Baker, Scott Laughery, and Asha Saavoss, "How CBO Estimated the Budgetary Impact of Key Prescription Drug Provisions in the 2022 Reconciliation Act," Congressional Budget Office, February 2023, https://www.cbo.gov/system/files /2023-02/58850-IRA-Drug-Provs.pdf.

7. "Health and Benefits Coverage: What Marketplace Health Insurance Plans Cover," HealthCare.gov, https://www.healthcare.gov/coverage/what-marketplace -plans-cover/ [accessed January 3, 2023].

8. Elizabeth Hinton and Jada Raphael, "10 Things to Know about Medicaid Managed Care," KFF [Kaiser Family Foundation], updated March 1, 2023, https://www .kff.org/medicaid/issue-brief/10-things-to-know-about-medicaid-managed-care/.

9. Nikhil R. Sahni, Prakriti Mishra, Brandon Carrus, and David M. Cutler, *Administrative Simplification: How to Save a Quarter-Trillion Dollars in US Health Care; Perspectives on the Productivity Imperative in US Healthcare Delivery* (Detroit: McKinsey Center for US Health System Reform, October 2021), https://www.mckinsey.com /industries/healthcare/our-insights/administrative-simplification-how-to-save-a -quarter-trillion-dollars-in-us-healthcare/.

10. Sherry Glied and Katherine Swartz, "Stopping the 'Medicaid Churn'— Addressing Medicaid Coverage after the COVID-19 Public Health Emergency Ends," *JAMA Health Forum* 3, no. 11 (2022): e224814, https://pubmed.ncbi.nlm.nih.gov /36326753.

11. Troyen A. Brennan, *Just Doctoring: Medical Ethics in the Liberal State* (Berkeley: University of California Press, 1991).

12. Thomas Piketty, *Capital in the Twenty-First Century*, trans. Arthur Goldham- mer (Cambridge, MA: Harvard University Press, 2013).

13. Branko Milanovic, *Capitalism Alone: The Future of the System That Rules the World* (Cambridge, MA: Harvard University Press, 2019).

14. David U. Himmelstein, Terry Campbell, and Steffie Woolhandler, "Health Care Administrative Costs in the United States and Canada, 2017," *Annals of Internal Medicine* 172, no. 2 (2020): 134–142.

15. Andrew Longhurst, "How (and How Much) Doctors Are Paid: Why It Matters," Policynote, January 15, 2019, https://www.policynote.ca/how-and-how -much-doctors-are-paid-why-it-matters/.

16. Sara Allin, Greg Marchildon, and Allie Peckhamin, "International Health Care System Profiles: Canada," in *2020 International Profiles of Health Care Systems*, ed. Roosa Tikkanen, Robin Osborn, Elias Mossialos, Ana Djordjevic, and George Wharton (New York: Commonwealth Fund, December 2020), https://www .commonwealthfund.org/international-health-policy-center/countries/canada/.

17. Jonathan Oberlander, "Navigating the Shifting Terrain of US Health Care Reform—Medicare for All, Single Payer, and the Public Option," *Milbank Quarterly* 97, no. 4 (2019): 939–953, https://pubmed.ncbi.nlm.nih.gov/31523855.

18.   Himmelstein, Campbell, and Woolhandler, "Health Care Administrative Costs."

19.   Sahni et al., *Administrative Simplification*.

20.   Christopher Cai, Jackson Runte, Isabel Ostrer, Kacey Berry, Ninez Ponce, Michael Rodriguez, Stefano Bertozzi, Justin S. White, and James G. Kahn, "Projected Costs of Single-Payer Healthcare Financing in the United States: A Systematic Review of Economic Analyses," *PLoS Medicine* 17, no. 1 (2020): e1003013, https://journals.plos.org/plosmedicine/article?id=10.1371/journal.pmed.1003013.

21.   Adam Gaffney, David U. Himmelstein, Steffie Woolhandler, and James G. Kahn, "Pricing Universal Health Care: How Much Would the Use of Medical Care Rise?," *Health Affairs* 40, no. 1 (2021): 105–112, https://www.healthaffairs.org/doi/abs/10.1377/hlthaff.2020.01715.

22.   Cai et al., "Projected Costs."

23.   Cai et al., "Projected Costs."

24.   Phil Swagel, "How CBO Analyzes the Costs of Proposals for a Single-Payer Health Care System," *CBO Blog, Congressional Budget Office*, https://www.cbo.gov/publication/56898; Jaeger Nelson, "Economic Effects of Five Illustrative Single-Payer Health Care Systems," Working Paper no. 2022-02, Congressional Budget Office, Washington, DC, February 2022, https://www.cbo.gov/system/files/2022-02/57637-Single-Payer-Systems.pdf.

25.   Abdul El-Sayed and Micah Johnson, *Medicare for All: A Citizen's Guide* (New York: Oxford University Press, 2021). I rely on their fine book for much of the discussion in the present volume. The authors are advocates for a single-payer system, but their arguments are clear and transparent.

26.   El-Sayed and Johnson, *Medicare for All*, 145–148.

27.   "Hospital Rate Setting: Successful in Maryland but Challenging to Replicate," Research Brief no. 1, Healthcare Value Hub, updated May 2020, https://www.healthcarevaluehub.org/advocate-resources/publications/hospital-rate-setting-promising-challenging-replicate/.

28.   El-Sayed and Johnson, *Medicare for All*, 163.

29.   Sara Heath, "Prescription Drug Spending Varies by Private, Public Payers," Private Payers News, HealthPayer Intelligence, May 30, 2019, https://healthpayerintelligence.com/news/prescription-drug-spending-varies-by-private-public-payers/.

30.   Nelson, "Economic Effects," 43.

31.   John Holahan and Linda Blumberg, *Estimating the Cost of a Single-Payer Plan* (Washington, DC: Urban Institute. October 2018), https://www.urban.org/sites/default/files/publication/99151/estimating_the_cost_of_a_single-payer_plan_0.pdf.

32.   Chad Reese, "Medicare for All: $32 Trillion in New Costs or $2 Trillion in Savings?," Mercatus Center, August 9, 2018, https://www.mercatus.org/economic-insights/expert-commentary/medicare-all-32-trillion-new-costs-or-2-trillion-savings/.

33.   "Choices for Financing Medicare for All," Committee for a Responsible Federal Budget, March 17, 2020, https://www.crfb.org/papers/choices-financing-medicare-all/.

34. Oberlander, "Navigating the Shifting Terrain."

35. Suhas Gondi and Zirui Song, "Expanding Health Insurance through a Public Choice—Choices and Trade-Offs," *JAMA Health Forum* 2, no. 3 (2021): e210305, https://jamanetwork.com/journals/jama-health-forum/fullarticle/2778162.

36. Gondi and Song, "Expanding Health Insurance."

37. Karen Davis, "Expanding Medicare and Employer Plans to Achieve Universal Health Insurance," *JAMA* 265, no. 19 (1991): 2525–2528, https://jamanetwork.com/journals/jama/article-abstract/385940; Cathy Schoen, Karen Davis, and Sara R. Collins, "Building Blocks for Reform: Achieving Universal Coverage with Private and Public Group Health Insurance," *Health Affairs* 27, no. 3 (2008): 646–657, https://www.healthaffairs.org/doi/10.1377/hlthaff.27.3.646.

38. Helen A. Halpin and Peter Harbage, "The Origins and Demise of the Public Option," *Health Affairs* 29, no. 6 (2010): 1117–1124, https://www.healthaffairs.org/doi/pdf/10.1377/hlthaff.2010.0363.

39. Jacob S. Hacker, "Between the Waves: Building Power for a Public Option," *Journal of Health Politics, Policy and Law* 46, no. 4 (2021): 535–547, https://isps.yale.edu/research/publications/isps21-22.

40. Hacker, "Between the Waves," 538.

41. Hacker, "Between the Waves," 538.

42. Michael Sparer, "Redefining the 'Public Option': Lessons from Washington State and New Mexico," *Milbank Quarterly* 98, no, 2 (2020): 260–278, https://www.ncbi.nlm.nih.gov/pmc/articles/PMC7296433.

43. Stephanie Carlton, Jessica Kahn, and Mike Lee, "Cascade Select: Insights from Washington's Public Option," *Health Affairs Forefront* (blog), *Health Affairs*, August 30, 2021, https://www.healthaffairs.org/content/forefront/cascade-select-insights-washington-s-public-option/.

44. Markian Hawryluk, "Colorado Option's Big Test: Open Enrollment," KFF [Kaiser Family Foundation] Health News, December 7, 2022, https://khn.org/news/article/colorado-public-option-test-open-enrollment/.

45. Christine Monahan and Kevin Lucia, "Congressional Proposals for a Federal Public Health Insurance Option," *To the Point* (blog), *Commonwealth Foundation*, November 3, 2022, https://www.commonwealthfund.org/blog/2022/congressional-proposals-federal-public-health-insurance-option/.

46. "Adopting a Single-Payer Health System," APHA [American Public Health Association], October 26, 2021, https://www.apha.org/Policies-and-Advocacy/Public-Health-Policy-Statements/Policy-Database/2022/01/07/Adopting-a-Single-Payer-Health-System/.

47. El-Sayed and Johnson, *Medicare for All*, chapter 5.

48. "ACO REACH," CMS [Centers for Medicare & Medicaid Services], last updated August 14, 2023, https://innovation.cms.gov/innovation-models/aco-reach/.

49. Oberlander, "Navigating the Shifting Terrain," 7.

INDEX

claims submission process, 13, 64, 98, 118–19, 135–36, 201, 212, 227, 262

Clinton, Hillary, 66

Clinton administration, health care reform initiative, 13, 14–16, 24, 55, 64–74, 166, 183, 258

Clover Health, 246

CMMI. *See* Center for Medicare & Medicaid Innovation

CMS. *See* Centers for Medicare & Medicaid

codes and coding, 22, 43, 48, 144–47, 201, 218–19, 255, 259, 263, 269, 274, 291, 294, 311

Cohen, Joel, 73–74

co-insurance, 11, 13, 31, 32–33, 34, 56, 93, 126, 137, 231; drug coverage and, 34, 119, 122, 126–27, 161, 162, 163

commercial health insurance. *See* private (commercial) health insurance

Committee for a Responsible Federal Budget, 301

Committee on the Costs of Medical Care, 4

Commonwealth Foundation, 213–14

Commonwealth Fund, viii, 156, 214, 221

Community Living and Assistance Services and Supports Act (CLASS), 198

community ratings, 10, 11, 185

conflicts of interest, xix, xvii, 109–10, 146, 218–19

Congressional Budget Office (CBO), 67, 83, 98, 187, 195, 210, 286, 293–94, 295, 302, 306; *2023 Long-Term Budget Outlook*, 84–88

Congressional Research Service, 188

connector exchanges, 185

consolidation, of providers, 70, 71, 73, 77, 97–99, 100–101, 209, 210, 211, 227–28, 235, 244, 248, 253–54, 255, 266. *See also* integrated health care systems

consumer choice and decision making, 32–35, 44–45, 56, 62, 220, 229

Conway, Patrick, 200, 201

co-op program, for new insurance plans, 198–99, 204–5

co-payments, 11, 31, 32–33, 34, 56, 59, 93, 100, 231; drug coverage and, 115, 119, 122, 126–27, 162, 163

corporate practice of medicine laws, 7, 14–15, 91, 92

corporation model, of physician practices, 90, 100

cost accounting, 38–39

cost containment, in health care: ACA reforms for, 196–201, 204; in ACOs, 238; CMMI's role, 199–201; digital health–based, 240, 242; in employer-sponsored health insurance, 94, 207–8, 209, 211–13, 216, 248, 254, 258–59, 268, 269; in fee-for-service environment, 61; in government-sponsored health insurance programs, 35–40, 46, 52, 100, 101; in HMOs, 69–70; as insurers' function, 26–27; in Medicaid and Medicare, 34, 35–42, 43, 46, 52, 101, 197, 204, 310; Medicare Advantage and, 268; moral hazard and, 10–11, 27, 31–35; as motivation for government-sponsored health insurance, 77; premium contributions as, 57; in staff model HMOs, 69–70; with wellness and disease management programs, 48–51. *See also* codes and coding; cost sharing; managed care; reimbursement/reimbursement rates, for providers (general, hospitals, in Medicare and Medicaid, physicians); utilization management

costs, of health care, viii; as bankruptcy cause, 96; benefits actuarial value, 56; COVID-19 pandemic and, 214–15; defensive medicine–related, 46; as driver of health insurance, 26–27; in elderly population, 80; employers' concerns about, 266; governmental, 65; government-negotiated downward pressure on, 284; increases, 44, 61, 85; low-value, health care–related, 44; in managed care, 6–7; overtreatment-related, 44–45; as percentage of GDP, 85; per person, 85; price negotiations, 20–23; SGR initiative, 43. *See also* administrative costs

cost sharing, 10–11, 13; under ACA, 93, 202; distinguished from premium contributions, 93–94; in employer-sponsored health insurance, 34–35, 93, 305; in health exchanges, 187; moral hazard and, 10–11, 31–35; in pharmacy benefit management, 119, 126; restrictions on, 185; thicker vs. thinner, 32. *See also* co-insurance; co-payments; deductibles

COVID-19 mRNA vaccines, 113

COVID-19 pandemic, 80, 84, 91, 105, 189, 192–93, 196, 214–15, 237, 240–41, 247, 285; Families First Coronavirus Act, 288 cross-subsidization: under ACA, 100, 173, 202; in consolidated and integrated systems, 100, 253–54, 274; effect on employer-sponsored insurance, 81, 96, 97, 100, 132, 173, 208, 209–10, 216, 256–57; effect on provider reimbursement rates, 39, 72, 97, 100, 208–10, 209–10, 248, 253, 274; in fee-for-service environment, 208–9, 211; of Medicaid and uninsured patients, 72, 300; of Medicare, 39, 72, 81, 96; Medicare Advantage–type plans and, 270, 274; pharmaceutical industry's response to, 132, 167; premiums and, 257; of reimbursement / reimbursement rates, for providers (hospitals), 4, 39, 81, 96, 97, 100, 132, 167, 208–10, 211, 216, 255, 291; single-payer systems and, 291, 300; unsustainability, 40, 254, 255

Current Procedural Terminology (CPT) code, 40–42, 43

Cutler, David, 90

CVS, 118, 119, 144, 147–48, 164; CVS Health / Aetna, 247, 260

D'Aunno, Thomas, 247–48, 264

Davis, Gray, 303

Davis, Karen, 184, 303

deductibles, 31, 32–33, 56, 93, 95, 214, 229, 231; cross-subsidization and, 100; for drugs, 115–16, 122, 124, 126–27, 162, 163; high deductible health plans, 94–95, 207–8, 317n4; in Medicare Advantage plans, 155, 156; in Medicare Part D plans, 162, 163; patient assistance programs and, 126–27; public option and, 304

deficit spending, 77, 82–90, 100, 160, 251–52, 254, 255, 263, 301–2

Deloitte, 211

Democratic Party, ix, 36, 65, 66–67, 75–76, 87, 88, 89, 147, 204, 283, 284, 286, 287; ACA and, 171–72, 186, 188–89, 193, 196, 198, 204, 303; drug price regulation policy, 116, 131; IPAB and, 196–97; Medicaid, 176, 193, 287; public option advocacy, 304; single-payer-system advocacy, 283, 289–90, 301–2, 304. *See also specific Democratic presidential administrations*

demographic changes, 74, 76, 77–83, 265

demonstration/pilot programs, 50, 137–38, 199–201, 221, 235

denial of coverage, 19, 222, 257; appeals process and objective reviews, 46, 47, 223–24; lifetime/annual payout limits, 30–31, 56, 181, 184–85, 186, 212

diabetes, 80, 104, 130, 241–42

diagnosis-related groups (DRGs), 36–38, 40, 41, 43, 47

digital health / telemedicine / virtual medicine, 49, 51, 121; integration with primary care, 221, 225–26, 239–43, 245, 247–48, 249, 264, 279; "transparency" tools, 229

direct payment, 4–5, 7–8

disabled populations, vii, 81, 173–74, 178, 192, 198

disease management programs, 48–50, 51, 269

Drug Price Competition and Patent Restoration Act (Hatch-Waxman Act), 107–8, 112, 199

Drug Pricing Program, 129

electronic medical records, 219, 220, 225–26

Eli Lilly, 104

Ellwood, Paul, 14

Elzinga-Hogarty market test, 98

EmCare, 233

emergency and urgent care, 36, 152, 231, 232–34, 241, 244

Emmanuel, Ezekiel, xii, 129–30, 284

Employee Retirement Income Security Act (ERISA), 14, 16–20, 23, 47, 56, 76, 186, 234, 258, 267, 268; ACA-based modifications, 93–94, 186, 212–13, 254, 258–59; denials-of-coverage oversight, 46, 47, 223; preemption doctrine, 16; premium and out-of-pocket costs regulations, 93, 94, 254, 255; self-insurance under, 17, 60, 66, 207, 223

employer mandate, 13, 15, 65–66, 171, 185, 203, 256

employer-sponsored health insurance, 10, 26, 206–34; ACA's impact on, 172–73, 183, 202; ACO programs, 237, 238; choice of insurance plans, 207–8; cost-containment strategies, 94, 207–8, 209, 211–13, 216, 248, 258–59, 268, 269; cost pressures, 103, 230, 252–53, 255, 256–57, 259, 312; current market dynamics, 206–17; decrease, 94; design of plans, 93; drug costs and rebates, 114–15, 123–24, 128, 132, 300–301;

France, 129–30, 289
fraud and abuse, 43, 44, 156

Garfield, Sidney, 6
Gates, Bill, 80
Genentech, 224
generic medications, 107–8, 113, 120; Medicare Part D coverage, 159–60, 161, 162, 163–64, 286; prices, 32, 107–8, 121, 129, 131, 159, 286; purchasing collaboratives, 120–21; tiered use, 119, 159, 162
Genzyme, 112–13
Germany, 1, 9, 129–30, 278–79
Gilead, 114, 125
Gilfillan, Richard, 145–46, 147, 200, 201, 263, 280–81
Ginsburg, Paul, 263
Gist Health Care consulting group, 236–37
Glied, Sherry, 247–48, 264
global budgets, 6–7, 84, 261, 291, 297, 298–300, 306–7, 311
Gondi, Suhas, 303
Google, 270
government-sponsored health insurance programs, 101, 310; cost-containment approaches (for medications), 117; cost-effectiveness decisions, 46, 52, 198; cost sharing in, 34–35; equity in provider payments, 180; fairness and justice, 31; impact on employer-sponsored and private insurance, xi, xii, 1–2, 205, 206, 211, 230, 252, 310; as percentage of total health care expenditures, 2–3; private insurer–administered, 26, 27; quality-of-care metrics, 142–43; superiority over private health insurance, xiii, 2, 31. *See also* Medicaid; Medicare; Medicare Advantage; public option; US Department of Veterans Affairs (VA) health system
Gross Domestic Product (GDP), 84, 88–89, 215, 301–2
Gruber, Jon, 271
guaranteed issue, 185

Hackbarth, Andrew, 44
Hacker, Jacob, 184, 303, 304, 305
Halpin, Helen, 303
Harbage, Peter, 303
Harris, Kamala, 302
Harvoni, 125

Haven program, 216
health care, citizens' entitlement to, 182–83, 204, 288, 310
Healthcare Common Procedure Coding System, 41
Healthcare Effectiveness Data and Information Set, 26, 277
health care expenditures, 215; in 1980 and 1990, 22–23; 2020s–2030s, 252; under ACA, 195, 204; comparison of governmental and employer payers, 252–53; as percentage of GDP, 83, 84–85, 215; primary care as percentage of, 221; in single-payer systems, 293–94
Health Care Financing Administration, 37, 40, 41, 141, 175
Healthcare Information and Management Systems Society, 239
Health Care Payment Learning and Action Network, 237
health care reform/policies: 1990s, 55–74; 2020s–2030s, 248–49, 283–88; government's role, 230; incrementalism, xiv–xv, 96, 131–32, 182, 192, 204, 267–68, 307, 309; Kennedy-Mills plan, 13–14; political influences, 75–76; trends affecting (2020s–2050), 75–101. *See also* Affordable Care Act; single-payer systems; *and individual presidential administrations*
Health Care Value Chain, The (Burns), 118
health exchanges (ACA Title I), xi, xii, 2, 64, 101, 171, 172, 193–94, 195, 198, 204, 250, 252, 309, 310; co-op plans, 198–99; cost-sharing revenues, 187–88; Healthcare.gov website, 300; impact on employer-sponsored insurance, 211, 256, 261; impact on private insurance, 183–90, 202; Massachusetts program and, 184–86; Medicaid integration, 188, 189–91, 193, 194; under Medicare for All, xi, 286–87, 297; public option, 304, 311; reimbursement fees, 184, 190, 205; utilization management, 226
health insurance: 1913–1970s, 3–12; 1970s–1990s, 12–23; beneficiaries' dissatisfaction with, 19, 20, 27, 77, 207, 208; citizens' entitlement to, 202, 309; coverage limits, 30–31, 56, 181, 184–85, 186, 212; development of new formats, 198–99, 216; government's responsibility to provide, 170–71, 172; lack of transparency, 29; origin and

Inslee, Jay, 305–6
Institute for Clinical and Economic Review, 167, 224
integrated health care systems, xvii–xviii, 70, 71–72, 97, 236, 239, 241, 255, 299
interest rates, 86, 87, 88–89
Internal Revenue Service, 9, 213
International Classification of Disease (ICD-10) codes, 146–47, 263
interstate medical practice, 240–41
Iora Health, 245–46, 261

Jain, Sachin, 262
Japan, 77–78, 79, 89, 130
Jayapal, Pramila, 295, 296
J.D. Power, 276
Johnson, Lyndon B., 134
JPMorgan Chase, 216, 249, 308

Kaiser: Family Foundation, 22–23, 73, 93, 95, 99, 116, 120, 127, 131, 150, 165, 177, 178–79, 189, 220, 266, 275; Foundation Health Plan, 276; group health coverage, 6, 7; Permanente, 7, 57, 70, 73–74, 144, 147–48, 300
Kennedy, Edward, 13–14
Klitzka, Laura, 181–82, 204
Knox-Keene Health Care Service Plan Act, 7
Kronick, Richard, 145–46

labor unions, 3, 4, 8, 13, 118, 271, 272
Leavitt Partners, 235–36
Lederle Labs, 104
Lieberman, Joe, 303
Lieberman, Steven, 263
Livongo, 241–42
Loewenstein, George, 33–34, 109–10
Long, Russell, 13
long-term care, 35, 159, 173–74, 178
low-income populations: health exchange coverage, 191. See also Medicaid; underinsured population

Magaziner, Ira, 66
malpractice litigation/liability, 45–46, 55, 217, 235
managed care, 6–7, 53–74, 93, 201, 221, 252, 284; ACOs and, 235–36, 307–8; Clinton administration reform initiative, 64–74, 258; consolidation of providers and, 253; cost-containment function, 6–7, 252; in

employer-sponsored insurance, 55–57, 203; fee-for-service care and, 6–7, 15, 23, 58; impact of HMO Act on, 14–16, 57; indemnity plans, 59, 60–61; integration into single-payer system, 306–9; as managed competition, 61–64, 67–68, 258; in Medicaid, 176–77, 178; in Medicare Advantage for All, 306–7, 311; in Medicare Advantage-type plans, 272, 274; organized medicine's opposition to, 15, 91, 177; PCP cockpit formula, 245–46; public option approach, 307, 308; selection bias in, 137–38; upside and downside risk aspects, 236; value-based care and, 15–16, 58–59. See also health maintenance organizations; Medicare Advantage; preferred provider organizations
managed competition, 61–64, 66–67, 68–69, 73, 303
Manchin, Joe, 131, 283
Mankiw, N. Gregory, 88–89
Mann, Cindy, 176
market basket prices/revenue, 39, 48, 167
Mattke, Soeren, 51
McClellan, Mark, 235
McDonough, John, 184–86, 197
McKinsey & Company, 262, 287, 292
McWilliams, Michael, 146
Medicaid, vii, xii, 2, 13, 114, 171, 182, 206, 227, 284, 285; ACO plans, 237–38; alternative benefit plans, 191, 286–87; budget deficit issue, 89; capitation payment system, 177–78, 200–201; CMS oversight, 175, 226, 237–38; cost control in, 101; denial of coverage appeals, 47; dual Medicare eligibility, 140; elderly population coverage, 173–74, 178; eligibility criteria, 173–76, 183, 188, 190, 191, 193–94, 287; enrollment process, 176, 180, 193; expansion (ACA Title II), xiii, 171, 173, 183, 185, 190–94, 203, 252, 285, 309; expenditures, 192, 252–53, 274–75; funding, 174–75, 176, 195; gap population, 193–94, 195; HCPCS use, 41; health exchange integration, 188, 189–91, 193, 194; managed care aspect, 176–77, 178–79, 180, 201, 204, 238, 256; mandatory and optional benefits, 173–76; under Medicare Advantage–based socialized insurance, xi, 286–87; modified adjusted gross income (MAGI) approach, 191; moral

Medicare for All, ix, 74, 137, 157, 238, 250, 263, 282–312; administrative costs and, 262; CMS oversight, 297, 299, 311; comparison with Medicare Advantage, 305, 309; efficiency-based argument for, 290–91; employer-sponsored insurance participation, 283, 288, 302, 311–12; equity in, 288–90; financial analysis, 290–302; global budgets, 297, 298–300, 306–7, 311; as health exchanges replacement, 283; as Medicaid replacement, 283; political advocacy for, 295–302; private insurance and, 291, 301; public option format, 302–4, 306–7, 308–9; public support for, 302–3; pure and hybrid versions, 302; transition time, 297, 299, 302; utilization management, 298

Medicare for All (El-Sayed and Johnson), 297–300, 307

Medicare Modernization Act, 135, 140–41, 142, 156, 158, 159

Medicare Part A, 81, 82–83, 134, 139, 141, 149, 166; Hospital Insurance (HI) Trust Fund financing, 82–83, 84

Medicare Part B, 166; bankruptcy and, 81–82; drug prices, 149, 286; funding, 134–35; Inflation Reduction Act and, 132; under Medicare Advantage plans, 149, 286; payments to insurers, 141; Supplementary Medical Insurance Trust Fund financing, 81–82

Medicare Part C. *See* Medicare Advantage

Medicare Part D, 81, 103, 123, 127, 130, 134, 158–69, 198, 252, 255–56, 265–66; annealed with Medicare Advantage, 160–61, 163, 168; catastrophic phase, 160, 161–62, 163–65; CMS oversight, 162–63; co-payments, 34; cost sharing, 161–62; coverage phase, 161; "donut hole" (coverage gap), 160, 161, 163; drug costs, 117, 159–60, 163, 164–65; drug plans, 159, 160–61; expanded availability, 266; expenditures, 161, 163; federal reimbursement structure, 161–65; federal re-insurance payments, 161–62, 163–64; Inflation Reduction Act and, 132, 163, 164–65, 166–67; low-income subsidy program, 160, 162; managed care aspect, 168–69; under Medicare Advantage plans, 286; negotiated drug prices, 131–32, 149, 159, 163, 165, 168, 230, 269, 285, 286; policy recommendations, 165–68; risk adjust-

ment/management, 159–60, 162, 163–64, 168; Star quality ratings, 160; utilization management, 159, 162

Medicare Payment Advisory Committee, 78, 83, 98, 144–45, 146, 154, 163–64, 165, 196–97, 203–4, 215, 259, 263–64, 277

Medicare Shared Savings Program, 236–37, 239, 273, 274

MedPac. *See* Medicare Payment Advisory Committee

mental health, 152, 240

Merck, 103, 104

Mills, Wilbur, 13–14

modern monetary theory, 88–90

Molina, 189–90, 275

monopolies, 97, 105, 107–8, 111–12, 116, 131, 303

moral hazard, 10–11, 27, 31–35, 185

Muller, Ralph, 70

National Academies of Science, Engineering, and Medicine, *Rebuilding the Foundation of Health Care*, 221–22

National Association of Insurance Commissioners, 156

National Bureau of Economic Research, 88–89

National Business Group on Health, 255

National Committee for Quality Assurance, 26

National Health Board, 66, 67

National Research Council, 79

Newhouse, Joseph, 168

Nixon administration, 13–14, 57, 65

noncitizens, 193–94, 196, 202, 283, 294, 305

nonprofit corporations (foundations), 21–23

nonprofit health insurance plans, 10, 198–99, 204–5

Norway, 130

Oak Street Health, 261

Obama, Barack, 181–82, 193, 200, 312. *See also* Affordable Care Act

Oberlander, Jonathan, 302–3, 310–11

old age dependency ratio (OADR), 79

Omnibus Budget Reconciliation Act, 42

open enrollment, 32, 188–89, 260, 268, 306

Organization for Economic Co-Operation and Development (OECD), viii, 167

out-of-network providers, 39–40, 148–49, 258

physician-staffing firms, 233, 248

Piketty, Thomas, 289

play or pay reform. *See* employer mandate

PPOs. *See* preferred provider organizations

preemption doctrine, 16

preexisting conditions, 30, 182, 184–85, 186, 202, 295

preferred payment, 4

preferred provider organizations, 57, 59, 60, 73, 93, 95, 139, 140, 207–8, 210, 217, 228, 248, 268

pregnant women, Medicaid coverage for, 174, 177–78

premiums, 18, 19, 30, 32, 57, 61, 94, 208; under ACA, 57, 93, 187, 188, 189; average monthly, 95–96; under CLASS Act, 198; employee contributions, 19, 57, 61, 93–94, 95–96, 208, 213; federal oversight, 57; guaranteed issue reform and, 185; in health exchanges, 187, 188, 189; hospital/physician integration and, 99; increases, 94, 96, 208, 213; inflationary pressure on, 94–95; in managed care, 61; in Medicare, 81–82; in Medicare Advantage, 141, 144, 150, 155, 156, 157, 247, 270, 286, 310; in Medicare Part D, 160–61; medication costs and, 126; as percentage of income, 214; preexisting conditions and, 184–85; provider payment rate–based, 12; relation to wages, 95–96, 213; risk-based, 5, 10; silver-loading phenomenon, 188; in single-payer systems, 296; subsidized, 185, 285; tax credits for, 194

prepaid health care, 6–7, 15, 70, 177

prescription medications, coverage and prices, 101–33; ACA Title VII coverage, 196; adjudicated prices, 122, 126, 130; biosimilar drugs, 199, 286; brand-name, 119, 122–27, 130, 159, 162, 164–65, 190–91, 199, 242; cross-subsidies, 167; digital health–based cost control, 242; efficacy validation, 45; elimination of coverage, 259; FDA approval, 102–3, 106–8, 112, 120; formulary/rebate-based prices, 122–27, 128, 129, 159, 162, 164–65, 166, 167, 286; government price negotiations and regulations, 116, 130–32, 159, 165, 166–67, 229–30, 269, 286, 300–301, 304; insurance beneficiaries' dissatisfaction with, 116–17, 132; international comparisons, 129–30; labeling, 106, 110; launch prices, 112, 113–16, 125, 129–30, 166–67;

Medicaid coverage, 175, 178, 190–91, 300–301; Medicare coverage, 300–301, 304; over-the-counter, 106; patents, 105, 108, 111–12, 113, 114, 115, 116, 122–23; price controls, 42, 103, 105, 117–27, 242, 284, 286; price inflation, 112, 113–18, 123, 127, 128, 129, 131, 163–64, 166; price setting practices, 111–17, 121–22, 166–67, 229; price transparency, 127, 128, 131, 229–30; price uncertainty, 122; prior authorization requirement, 120, 121, 157–58, 162; rebates, 122–27, 128, 129, 159, 162, 164–65, 166, 167, 190–91; reference pricing, 167; single-payer-system coverage, 300–301; small- and large-molecule medications, 113, 286; specialty medications, 124–25, 163, 166, 259; spread pricing, 129, 159; tiered use, 119, 120, 159, 161, 162, 163. *See also* generic medications; Medicare Part D; pharmacy commerce

preventive health care, 6–7, 49, 50–51, 145, 152, 153, 186, 241–42, 243, 246. *See also* disease management programs; wellness / wellness programs

primary care: investments in, 239, 243–48, 261; practice groups, 73–74, 261, 307; public option and, 304

primary care physicians, viii, 217–21; capitated payments and risk, 68, 142, 221, 238, 307; comprehensive primary care initiatives, 221; fee-for-service environment, 54, 60, 217–18, 220, 221; in IPAs, 58–59; as managed care gatekeepers, 54, 57, 58–59, 60, 69–70, 218, 221, 259; Medicaid participation, 180; Medicare Advantage participation, 158, 246, 259, 260–61; reimbursement/reimbursement rates, 22, 23, 24, 68, 74–75, 217–21; RVU codes, 42; shortage, 220

primary care–type health insurance, 249

prior authorization, 11, 47, 120, 121, 138, 157–58, 162, 220, 222, 225–26, 238, 257

private equity firms, 91, 233, 247–48

private (commercial) health insurance, xii, 10, 26, 310; under ACA, 184–86, 202, 203; ACO programs, 237; annual expenditures, 150; cost inflation, 83, 251; cost-sharing practice, 10–11; designated subsidiaries, 11; elimination under Medicare for All, 283; expenditures, 252–53, 275; government oversight, 177, 310; government-sponsored insurance's superiority over, 2, 132; health exchanges and, 183–90, 202; hospital reimbursement rates, 37–40; impact of government-sponsored insurance on, 132, 205; inability to control health costs, 101; managed care and, 252; Medicare Advantage, 272; in Medicare Advantage for All, vii, 280, 283, 301, 310–11; Medicare Advantage payments to, 141–42, 143–50; nonparticipating physicians, 232, 233; "Partners Program" and, 13–14; as payment claims intermediaries, 13; per capita spending, 139; price transparency, 229; profit margins, 98; provider consolidation–based payments, 98–99, 210–11; public option and, 305–6; relationship with employer-sponsored insurance, 248; replacement with government-sponsored insurance, 101, 250; risk management practices, 10, 12, 29, 258; self-insurance-based, 16–20, 26; in single-payer systems, 291, 292–93, 297; in socialized health insurance, vii, x, 250–51; surprise billing practices, 233, 234; utilization management practice, 11, 12, 46. *See also* Medicare Advantage

procedure-based health care, 45, 299; costs, 11, 28, 31, 69, 222, 226, 242; digital medicine and, 243; in fee-for-service environment, 222, 226, 247; Medicare and Medicaid coverage, 136, 141, 226; profits/revenue from, 22, 53, 200–201, 222, 226, 247, 273, 274; reimbursement rates, 218–29, 228, 244; unnecessary, viii–ix, 11, 46, 69, 226, 274; utilization management, 222–23, 224–25

profit motive. *See* for-profit influences, in health care

prospective payment system, 36–37

provider networks: costs to health insurers, 22; insurers' negotiated payments to, 35–44, 48; in Medicare Advantage, 259–60; narrow, 211, 228, 275–76; reimbursement rates, 210. *See also* integrated health care systems

provider-sponsored organizations, 139

public health, viii, 196, 212

public option, 183–84, 204–5, 264, 302–9, 311; employers' participation, 216, 303, 304–5, 308; failure, 183–84, 203, 204; Medicare Advantage–like, 261, 311–12; Medicare for All and, 306–7, 308–9, 311–12; Medicare-like, 183–84, 203, 216, 302–3

Purdue Pharmaceuticals, 109

Pure Food and Drug Act, 106

quality of care, xiii, 284; in ACOs, 238, 307; beneficiaries' experiences domain, 27, 150–51; CMMI's role in, 199–201; cost containment and, 47, 52; government oversight of, 1–2, 142–43; as health insurers' function, 26; hospital consolidation and, 98; IAPB and, 196–97; in managed care, 54–55; in Medicaid, 178–80; in Medicare Advantage, 26, 142–43, 144, 150–55, 257, 262, 309; outcomes domain, 150–51; privatization-related decline, 248; processes domain, 150–51; Star quality ratings, 26, 142–44, 150–51, 154, 157, 159–60, 225, 257, 262, 278; utilization management and, 47

racial/ethnic minorities: demographic changes, 80; health care equity, viii–ix, x, 80, 153, 155, 180, 192–93, 205, 221, 276–78, 288–89; as Medicare Advantage beneficiaries, 152

randomized control trials, 45, 51

rationality, in health care decision making, xiv, 33–34, 61–64

rationed health care, 197–98

Rawls, John, 213

Reagan administration, 138, 289

regional health alliances, 66

reimbursement/reimbursement rates, for providers (general), 1–2; under ACA, 189, 190, 195, 203; CMS oversight, 98–99, 135, 166, 217–19, 221, 244; coding-based enhancement, 43–44, 201; commercial insurance/Medicare/Medicaid disparities, 210, 211; in employer-sponsored health insurance, 209, 252, 254–55; government control over, 1–2; government-sponsored insurance programs and, 208–11, 252; in health exchanges, 189, 190, 205, 256–57; health investments, 284; homogenization, 205; negotiated payments, 209–10, 254–55; payment model alignment, 284; public option concept, 183–84, 216; rate shopping, 228–29; revenue cycles, 284; in single-payer systems, 293–94; utilization management and, 248. *See also* capitation payments; cross-subsidization; fee-for-service payments

Health Policy Books from **HOPKINS PRESS**

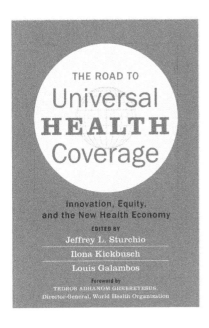

THE ROAD TO
Universal
HEALTH
Coverage

Innovation, Equity,
and the New Health Economy

EDITED BY

Jeffrey L. Sturchio

Ilona Kickbusch

Louis Galambos

Foreword by
TEDROS ADHANOM GHEBREYESUS,
Director-General, World Health Organization

modernizing
medicare

HARNESSING
THE POWER OF
CONSUMER CHOICE
AND MARKET
COMPETITION

EDITED BY

Robert Emmet Moffit
and Marie Fishpaw

THE
PRESENT
ILLNESS

AMERICAN HEALTH CARE AND ITS AFFLICTIONS

MARTIN F. SHAPIRO, MD, PhD, MPH

BUILDING A
UNIFIED
AMERICAN
HEALTH CARE
SYSTEM

A BLUEPRINT FOR COMPREHENSIVE REFORM

GILEAD I LANCASTER, MD

FOREWORD BY CONGRESSMAN JIM HIMES
FOREWORD BY DAVID L. KATZ, MD, MPH

 JOHNS HOPKINS UNIVERSITY PRESS

PRESS.JHU.EDU